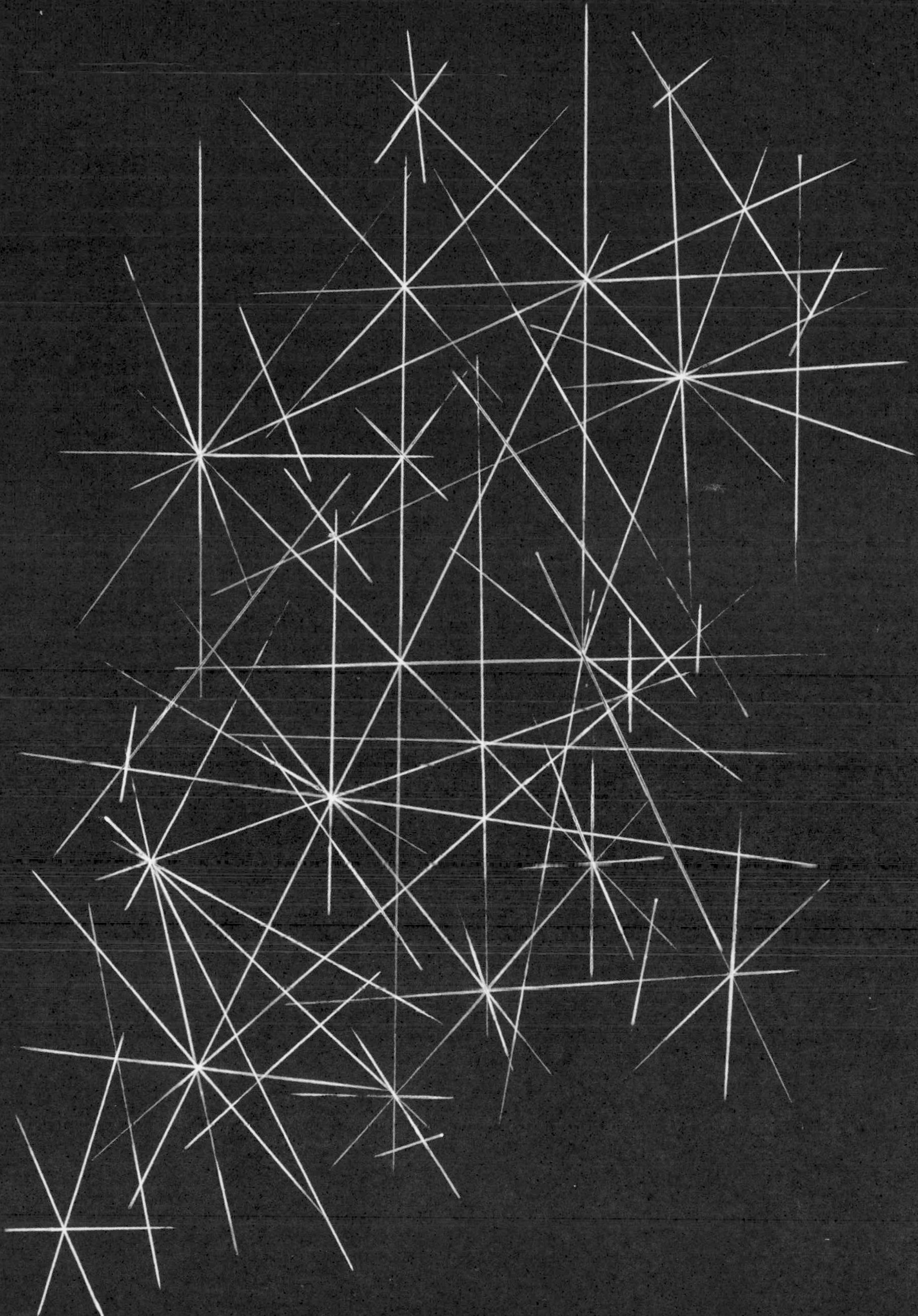

FANTAGRAPHICS BOOKS INC.
7563 Lake City Way NE
Seattle, Washington, 98115

Translated from Italian by Jamie Richards
Editor and Associate Publisher: Eric Reynolds
Book Design: Manuele Fior & Keeli McCarthy
Production: Paul Baresh
Publisher: Gary Groth

ISBN 978-1-60699-986-8
Library of Congress Control Number: 2016911483

First printing: March 2017
Printed in Hong Kong

MANUELE FIOR

THE INTERVIEW

fantagraphics books

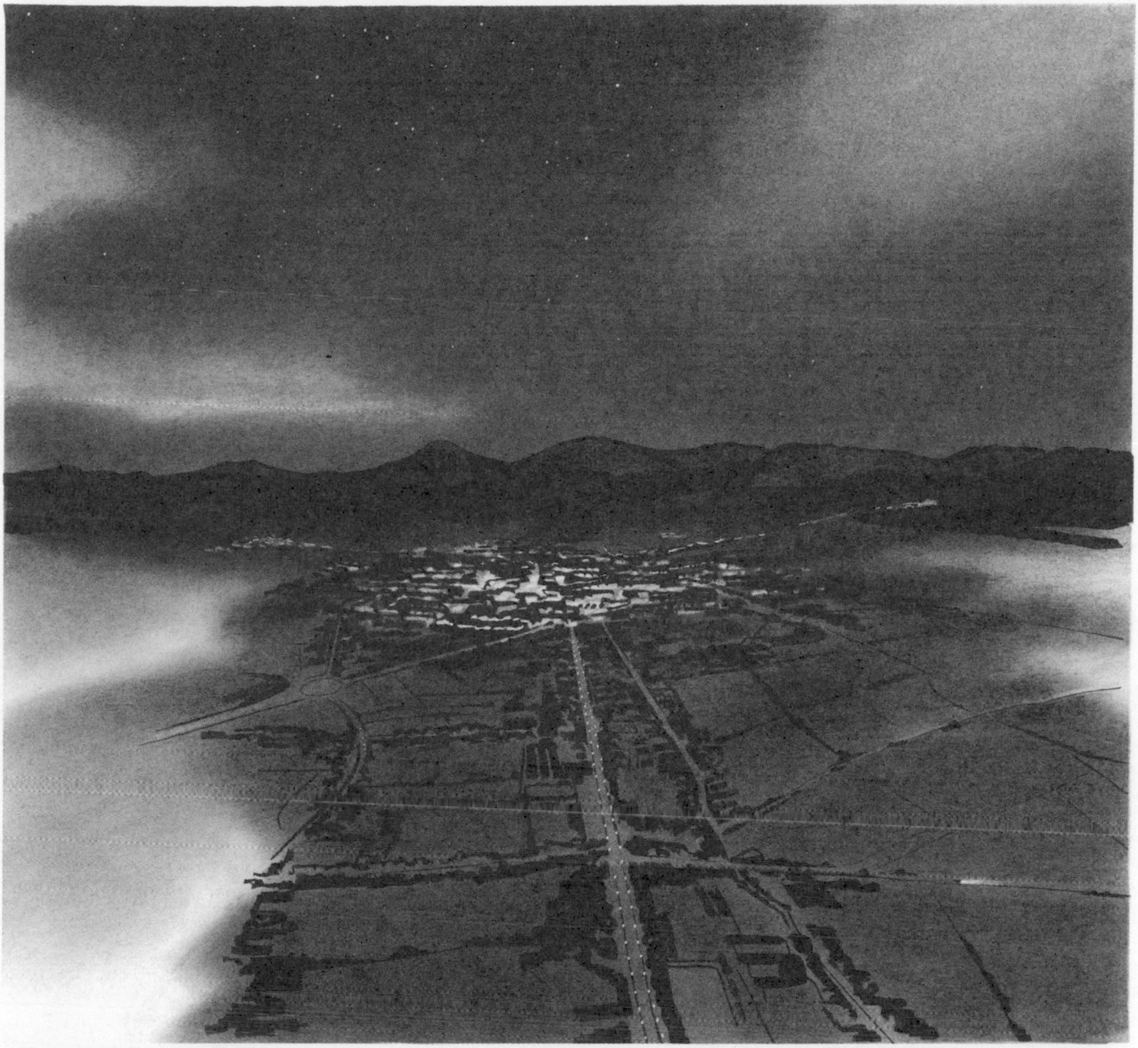

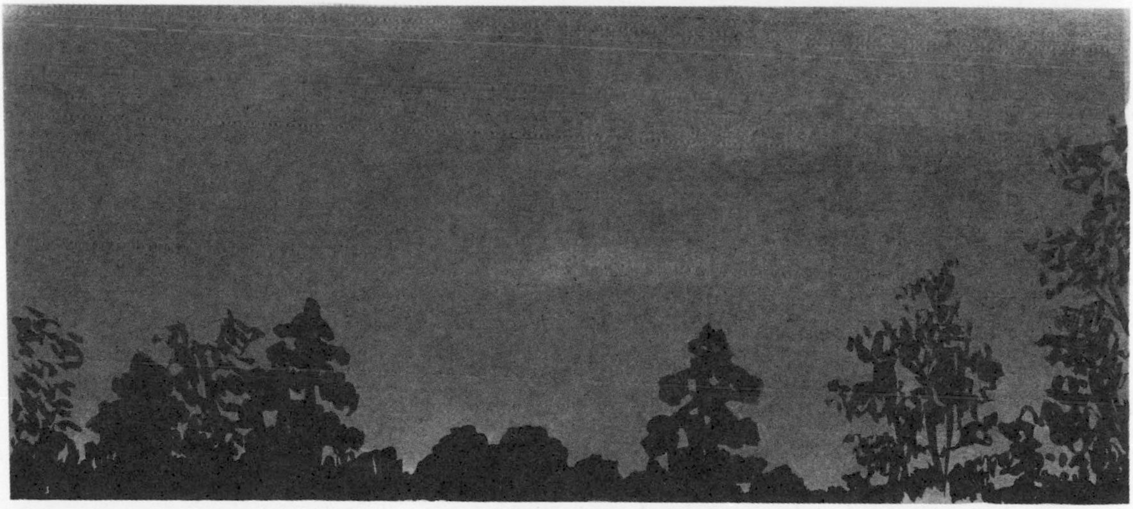

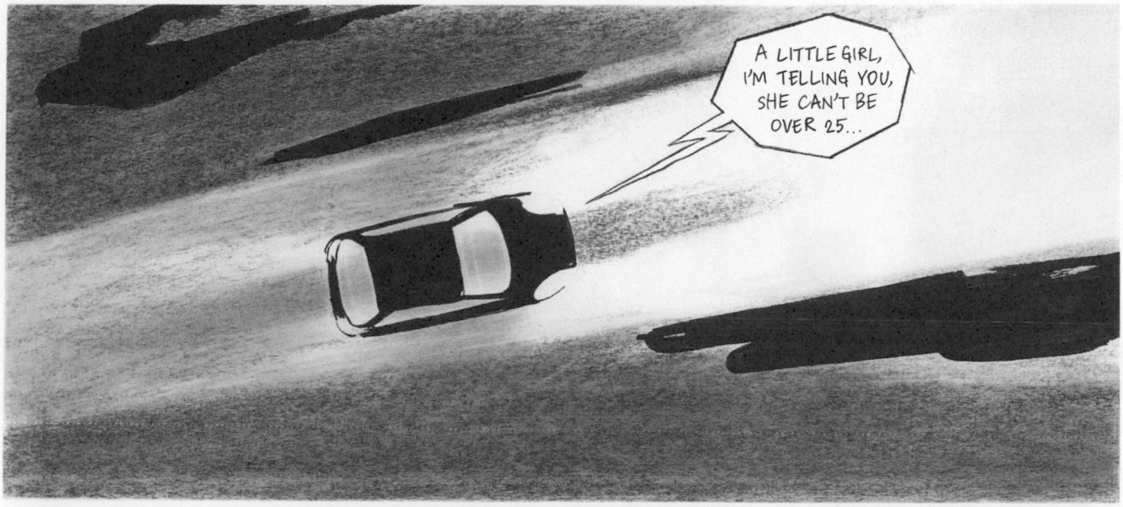
A LITTLE GIRL, I'M TELLING YOU, SHE CAN'T BE OVER 25...

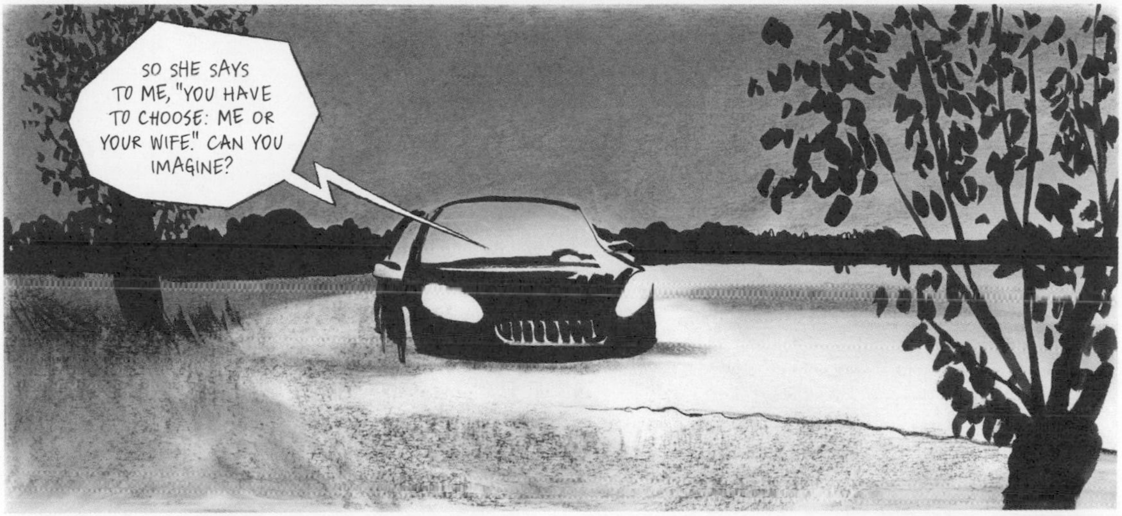
SO SHE SAYS TO ME, "YOU HAVE TO CHOOSE: ME OR YOUR WIFE." CAN YOU IMAGINE?

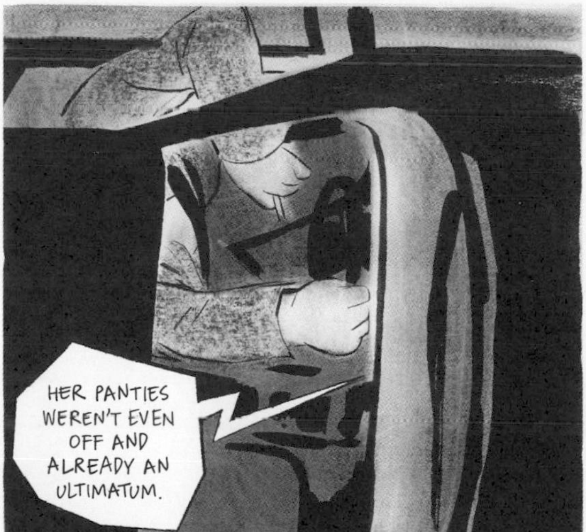
HER PANTIES WEREN'T EVEN OFF AND ALREADY AN ULTIMATUM.

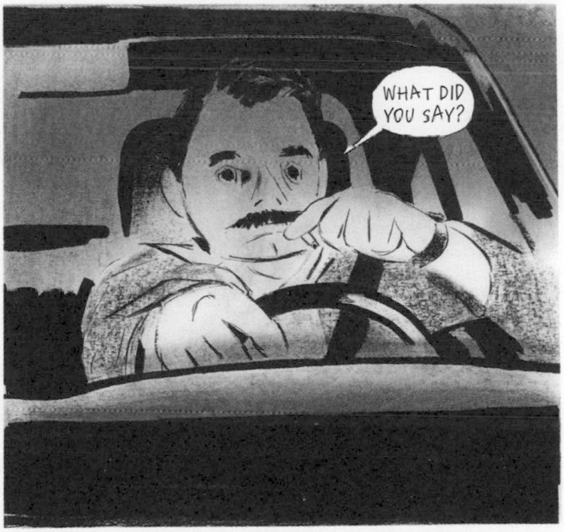
WHAT DID YOU SAY?

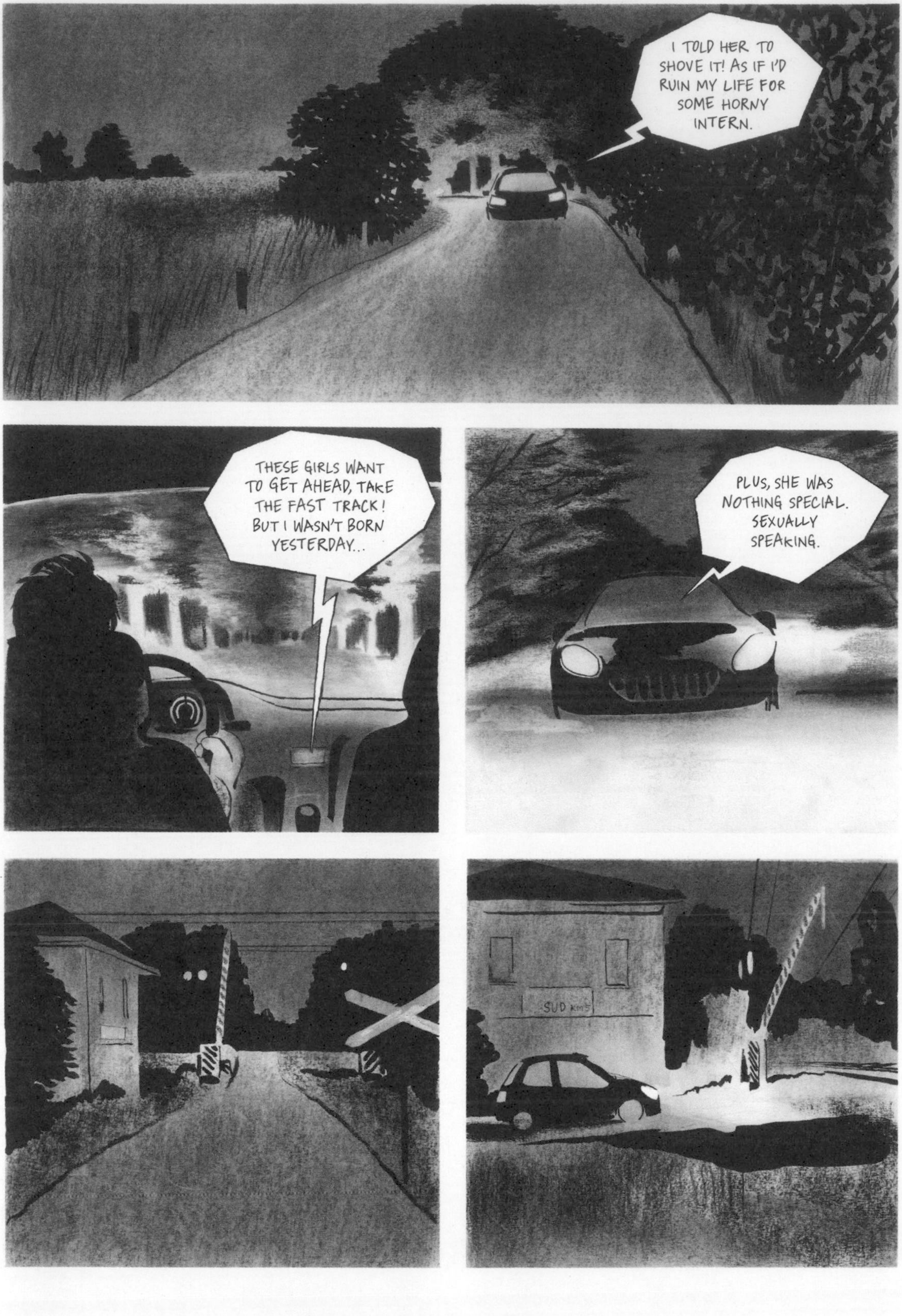
I TOLD HER TO SHOVE IT! AS IF I'D RUIN MY LIFE FOR SOME HORNY INTERN.
THESE GIRLS WANT TO GET AHEAD, TAKE THE FAST TRACK! BUT I WASN'T BORN YESTERDAY...
PLUS, SHE WAS NOTHING SPECIAL. SEXUALLY SPEAKING.
SUD

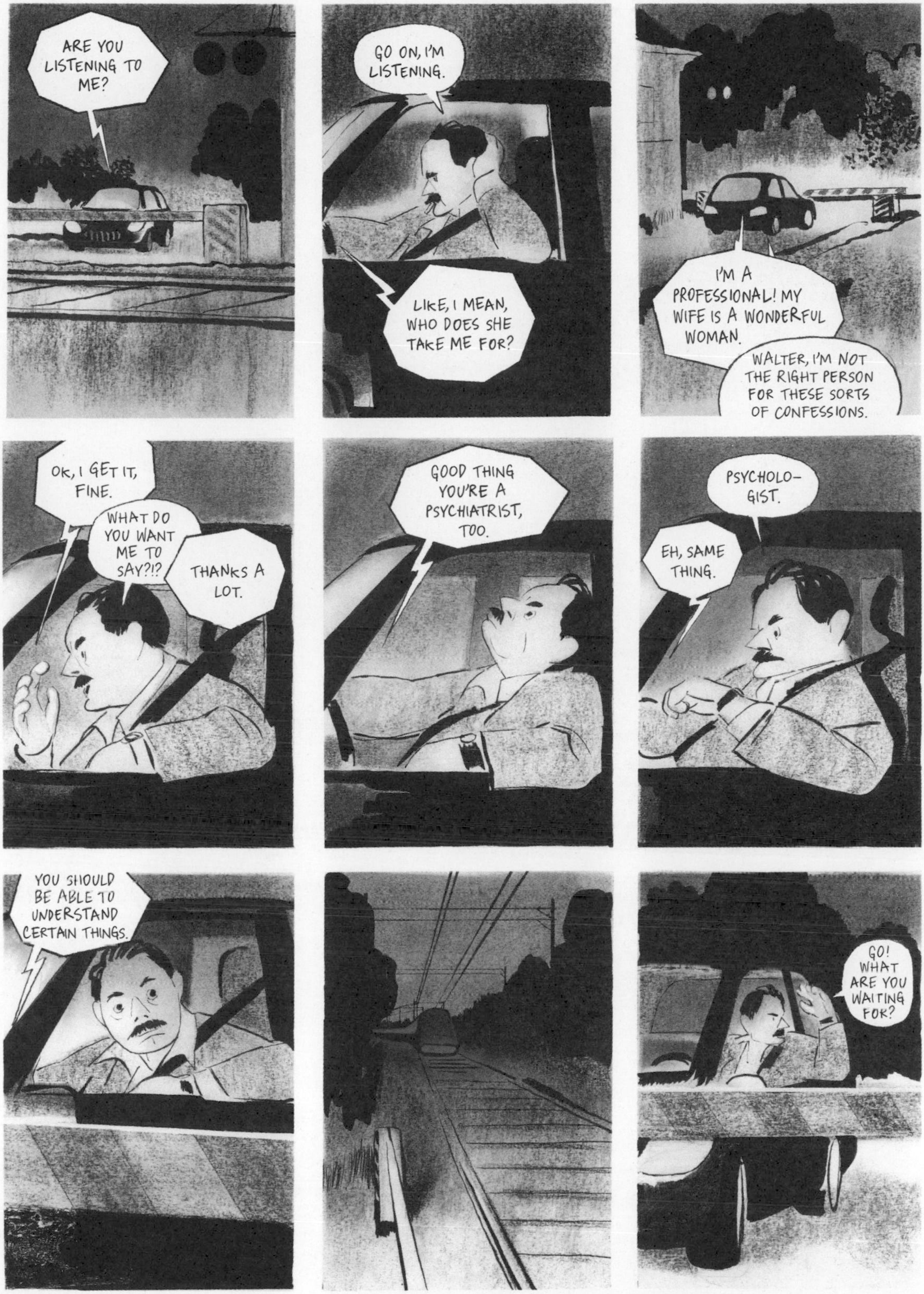
ARE YOU LISTENING TO ME?
GO ON, I'M LISTENING.
LIKE, I MEAN, WHO DOES SHE TAKE ME FOR?
I'M A PROFESSIONAL! MY WIFE IS A WONDERFUL WOMAN.
WALTER, I'M NOT THE RIGHT PERSON FOR THESE SORTS OF CONFESSIONS.
OK, I GET IT, FINE.
WHAT DO YOU WANT ME TO SAY?!?
THANKS A LOT.
GOOD THING YOU'RE A PSYCHIATRIST, TOO.
PSYCHOLO-GIST.
EH, SAME THING.
YOU SHOULD BE ABLE TO UNDERSTAND CERTAIN THINGS.
GO! WHAT ARE YOU WAITING FOR?

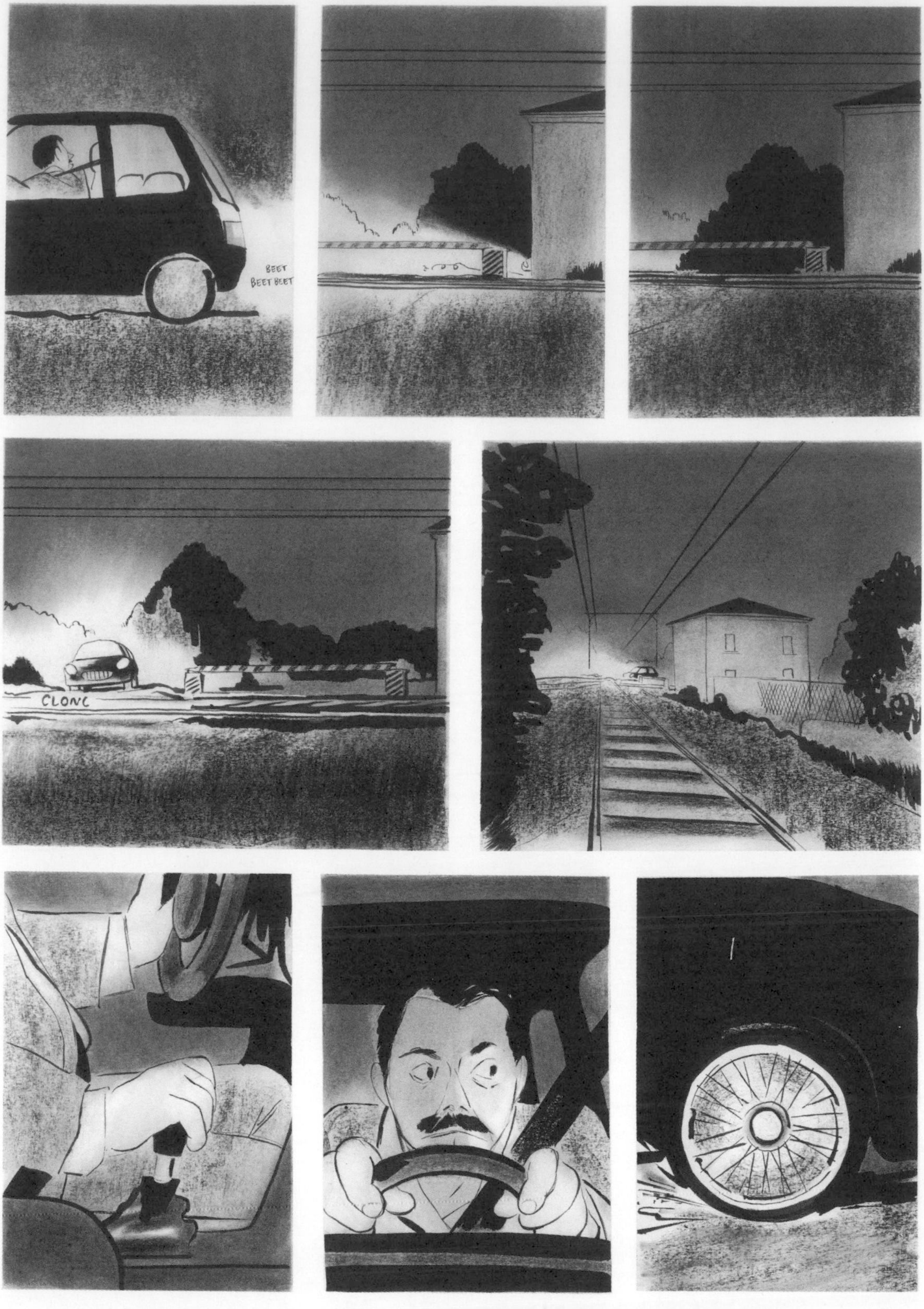
BEET
BEET BEET
CLONC

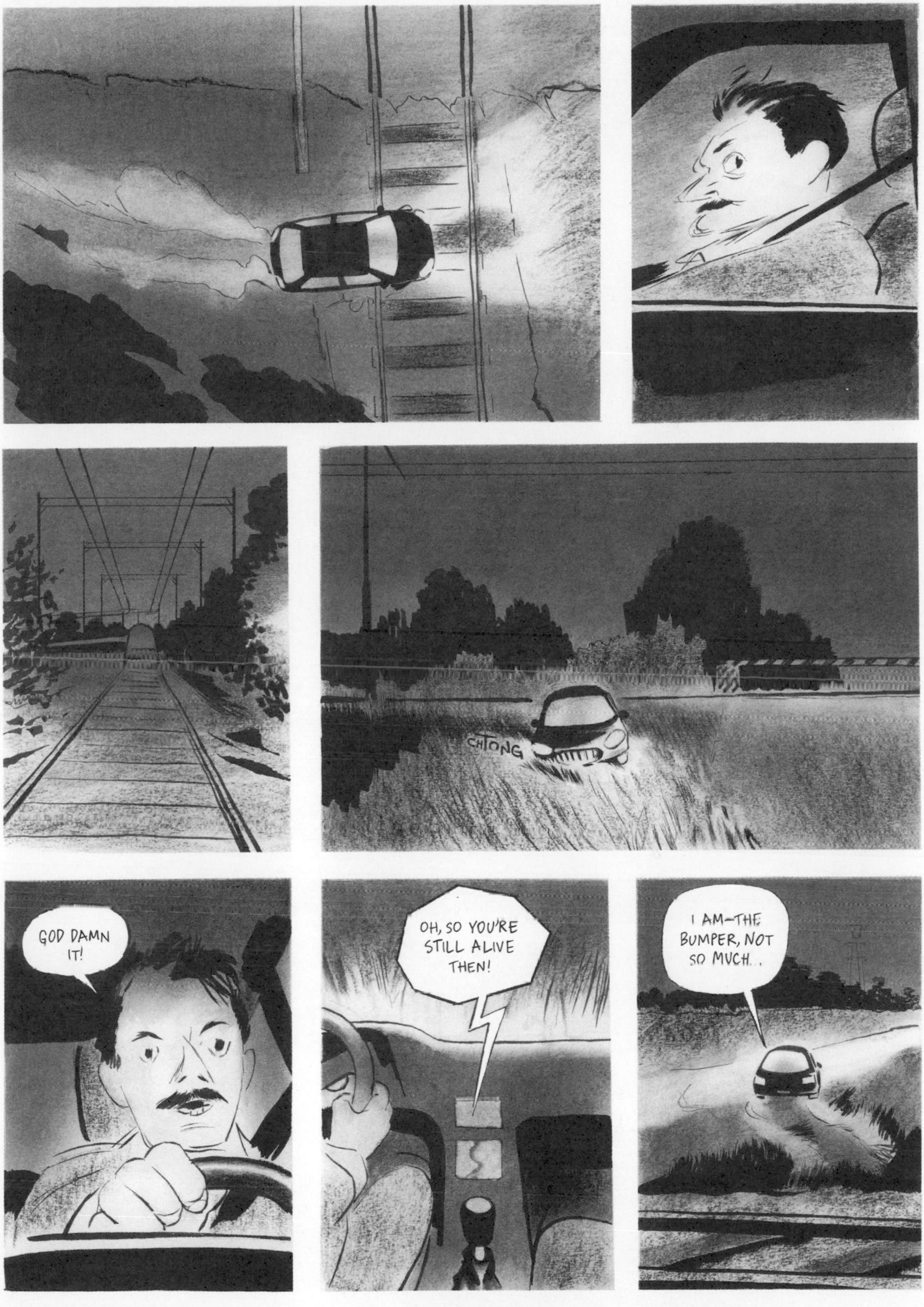
CHTONG
GOD DAMN IT!
OH, SO YOU'RE STILL ALIVE THEN!
I AM—THE BUMPER, NOT SO MUCH...

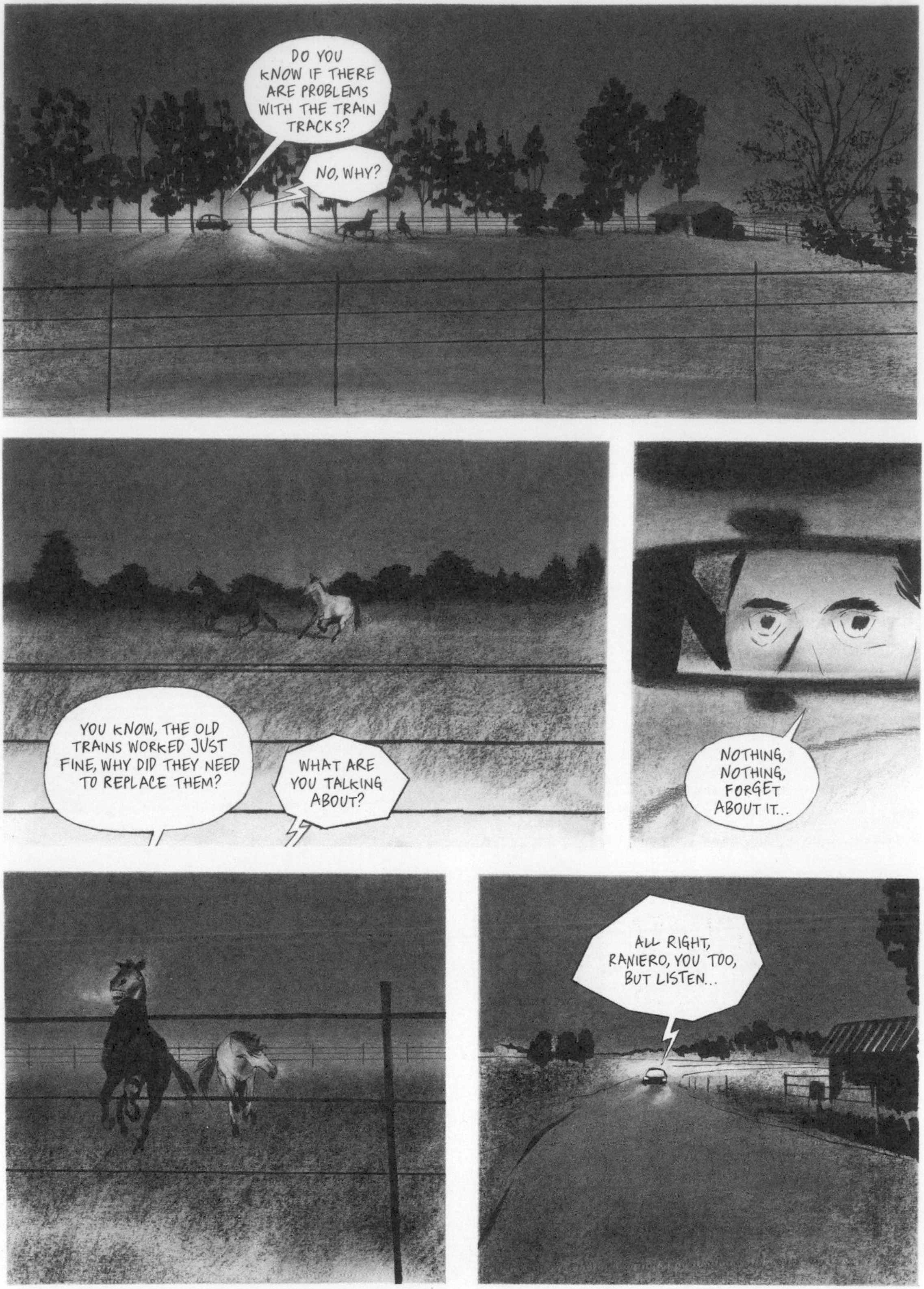

DO YOU KNOW IF THERE ARE PROBLEMS WITH THE TRAIN TRACKS?
NO, WHY?
YOU KNOW, THE OLD TRAINS WORKED JUST FINE, WHY DID THEY NEED TO REPLACE THEM?
WHAT ARE YOU TALKING ABOUT?
NOTHING, NOTHING, FORGET ABOUT IT...
ALL RIGHT, RANIERO, YOU TOO, BUT LISTEN...

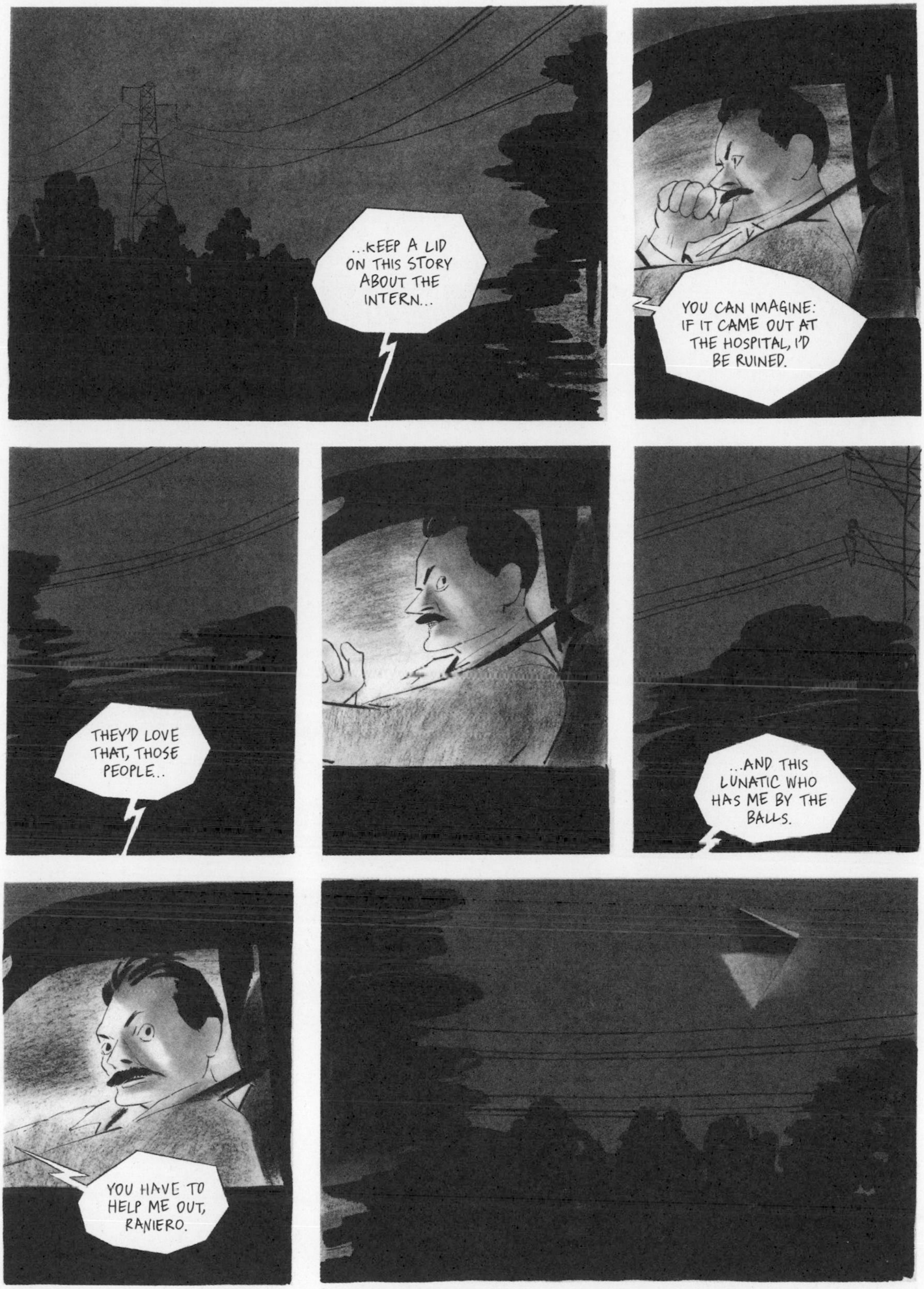
...KEEP A LID ON THIS STORY ABOUT THE INTERN...
YOU CAN IMAGINE: IF IT CAME OUT AT THE HOSPITAL, I'D BE RUINED.
THEY'D LOVE THAT, THOSE PEOPLE...
...AND THIS LUNATIC WHO HAS ME BY THE BALLS.
YOU HAVE TO HELP ME OUT, RANIERO.

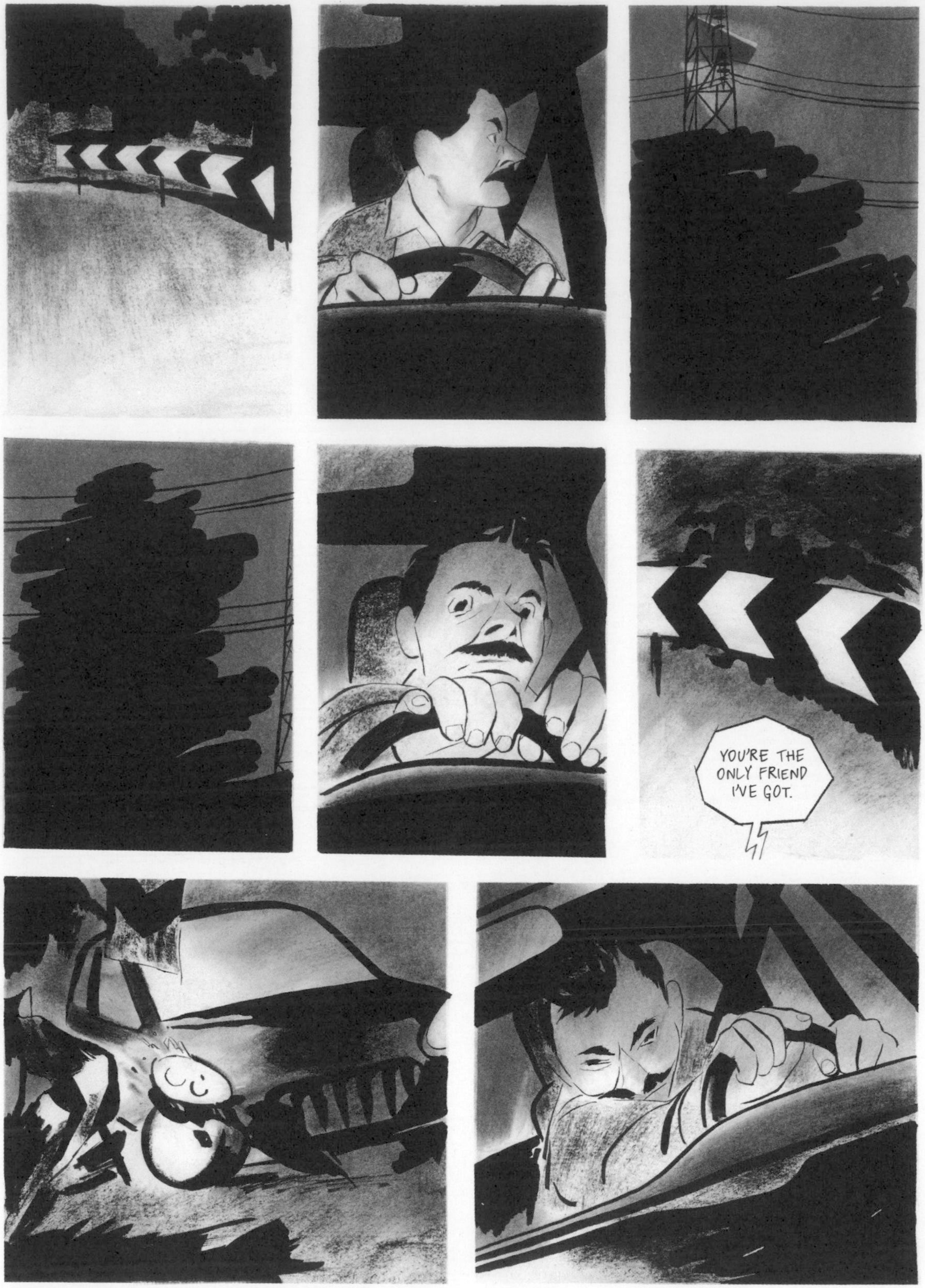
YOU'RE THE
ONLY FRIEND
I'VE GOT.

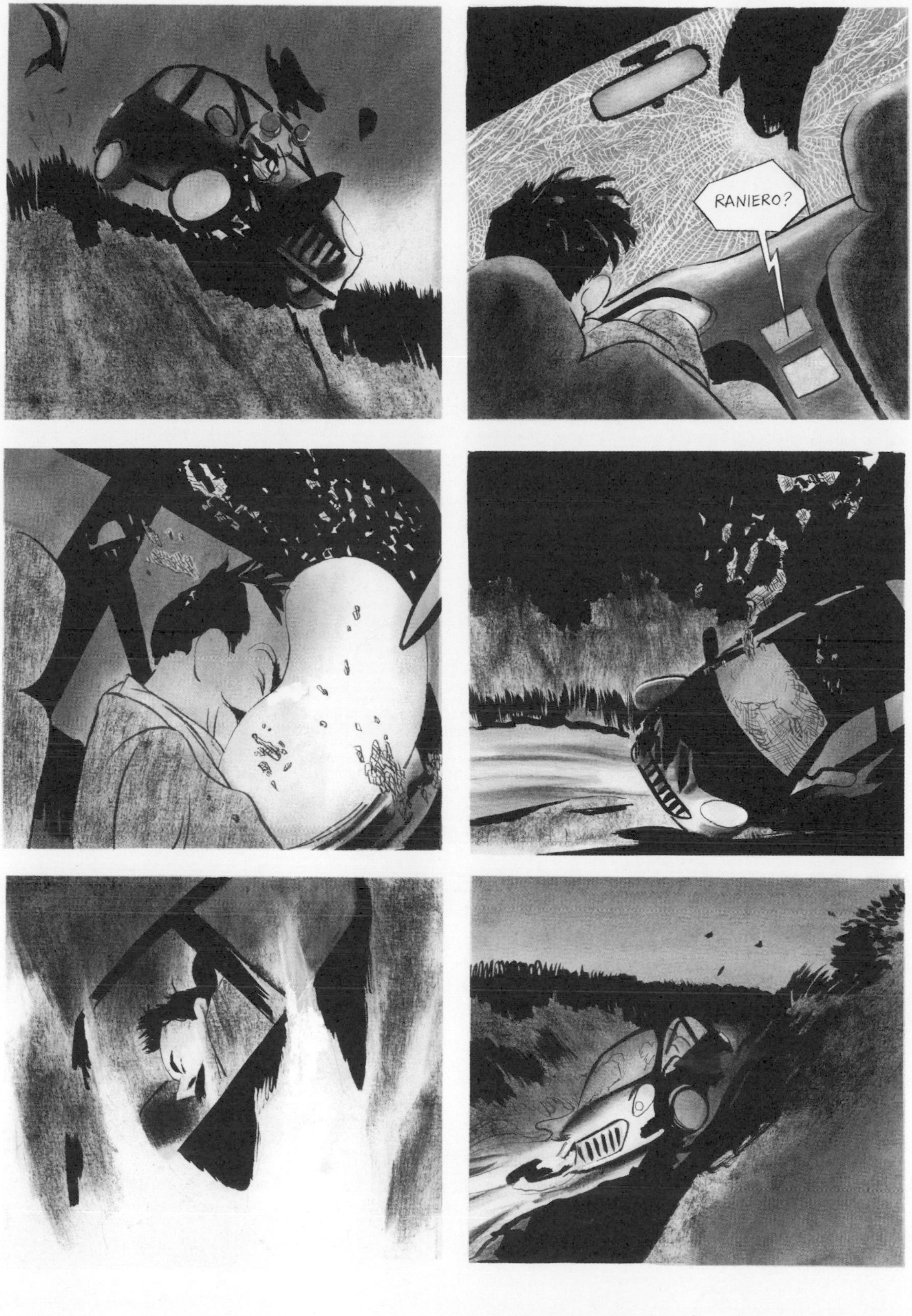
RANIERO?

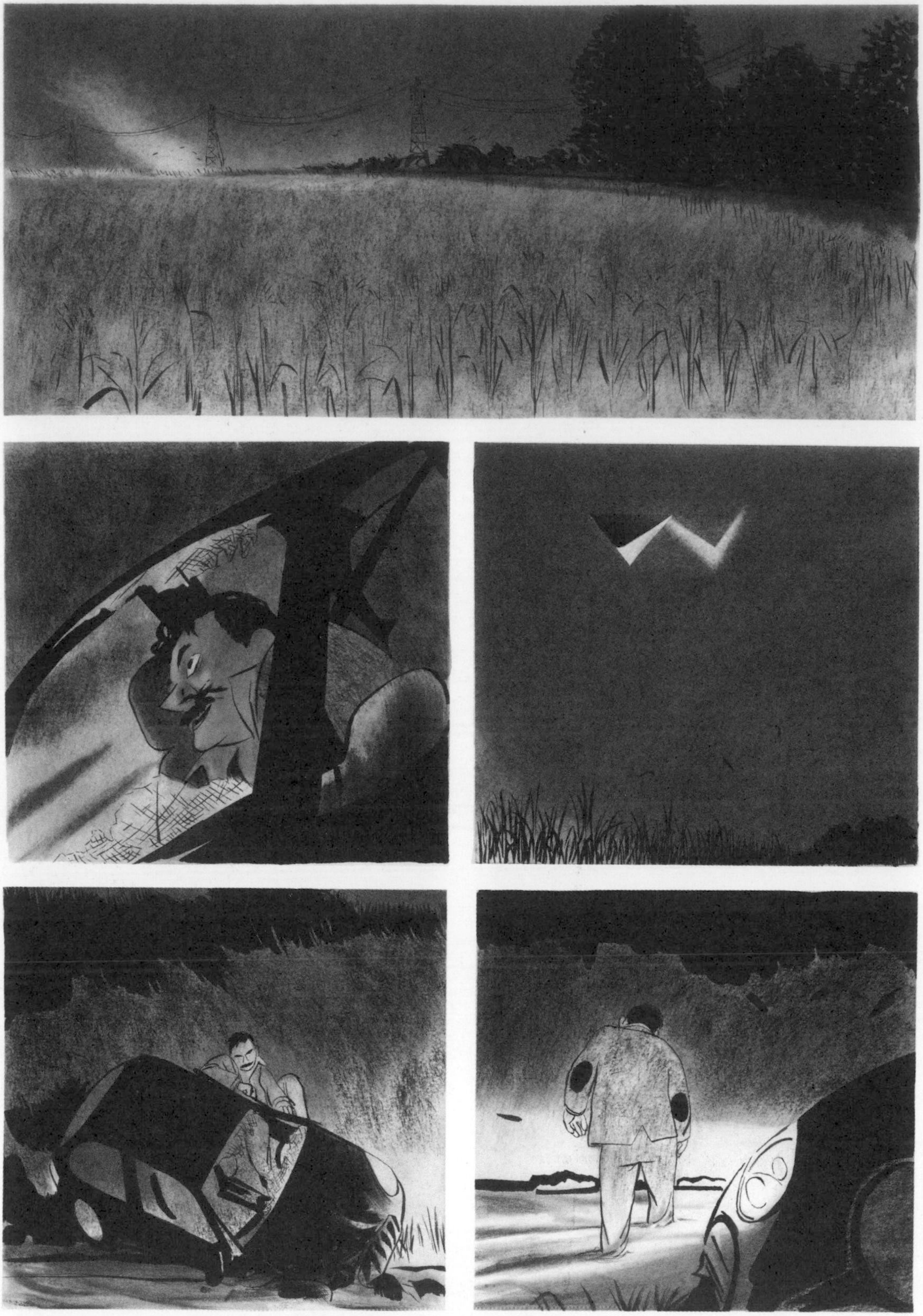

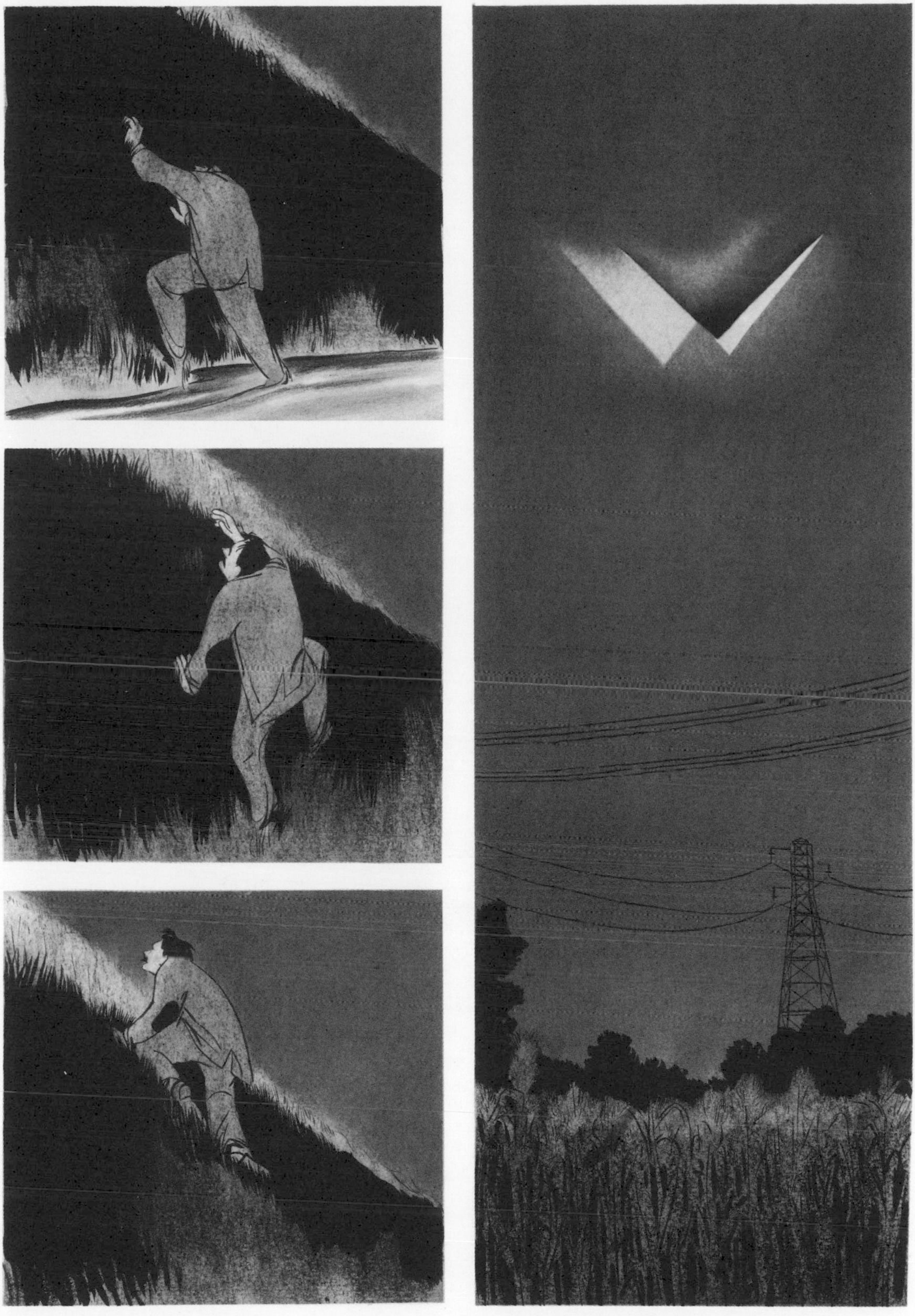

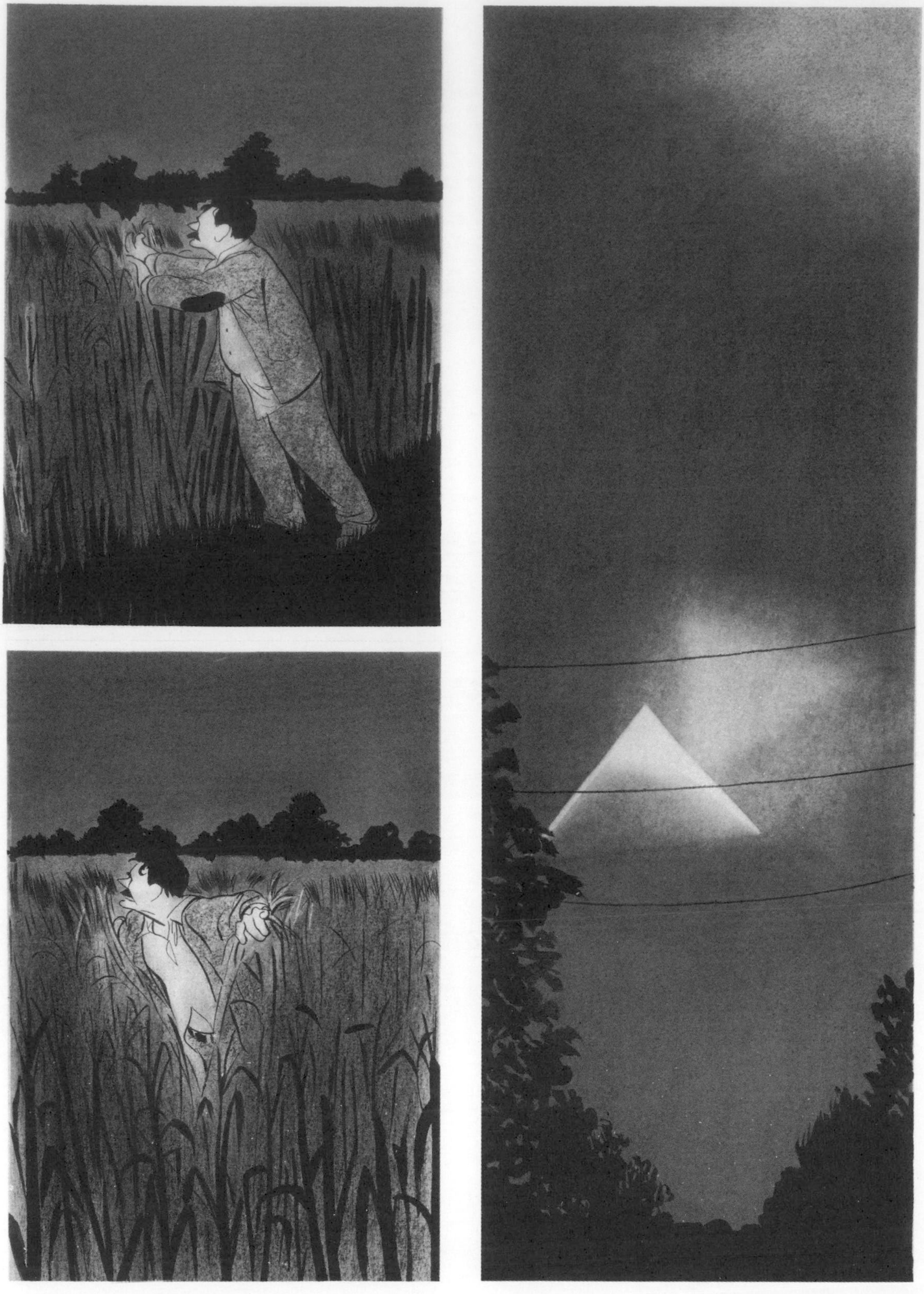

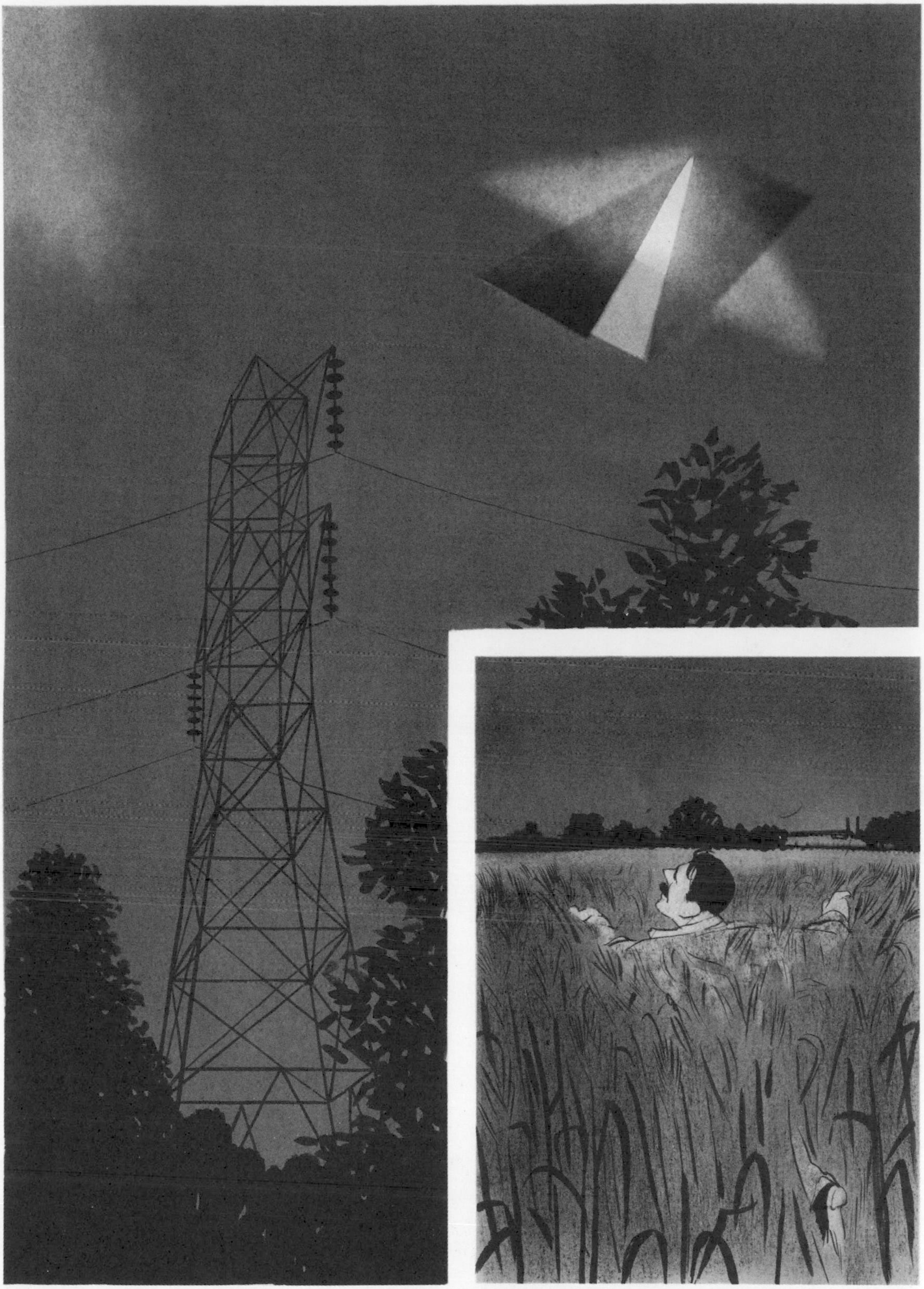

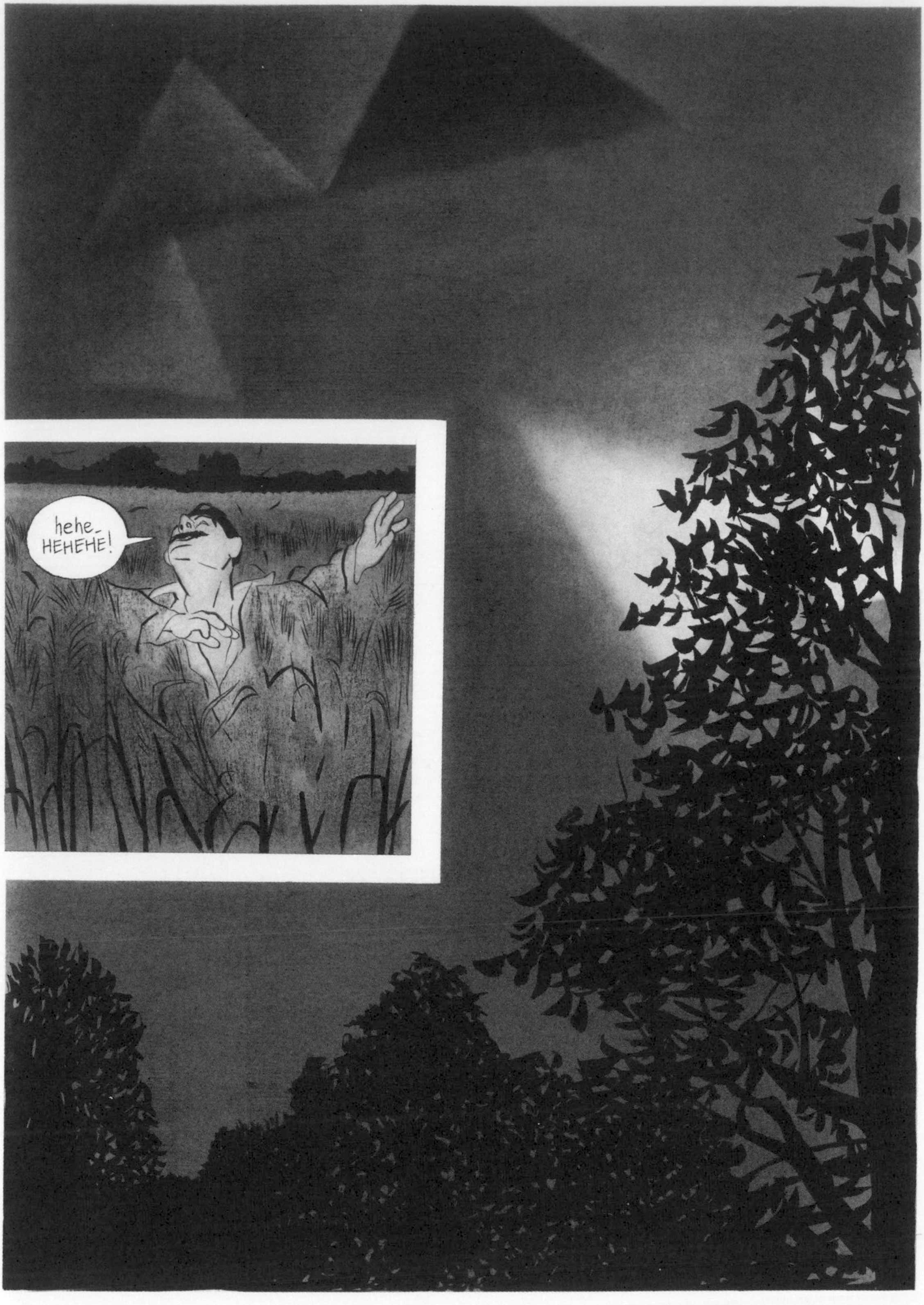
hehe_
HEHEHE!

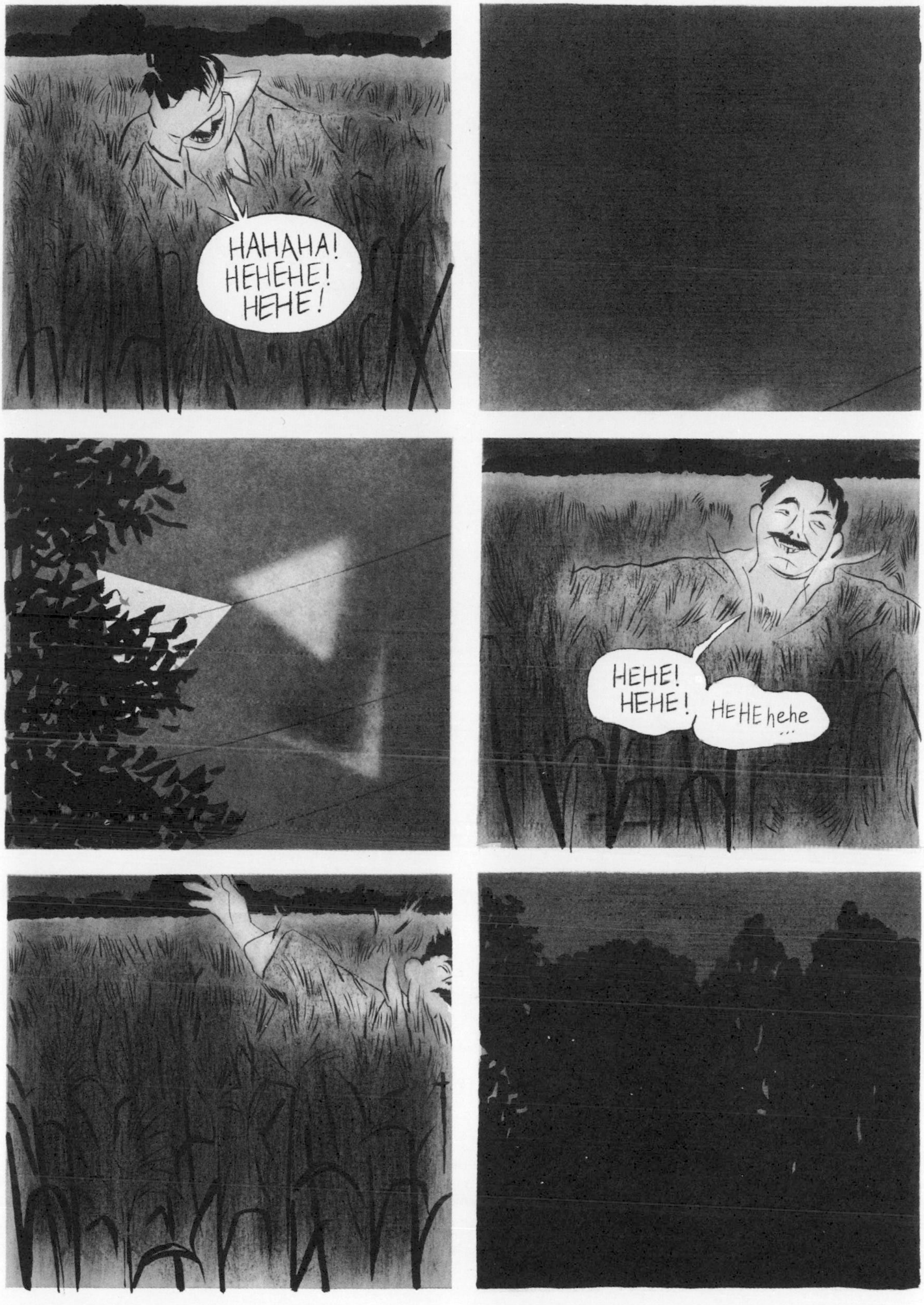
HAHAHA! HEHEHE! HEHE!
HEHE! HEHE!
HEHEhehe ...

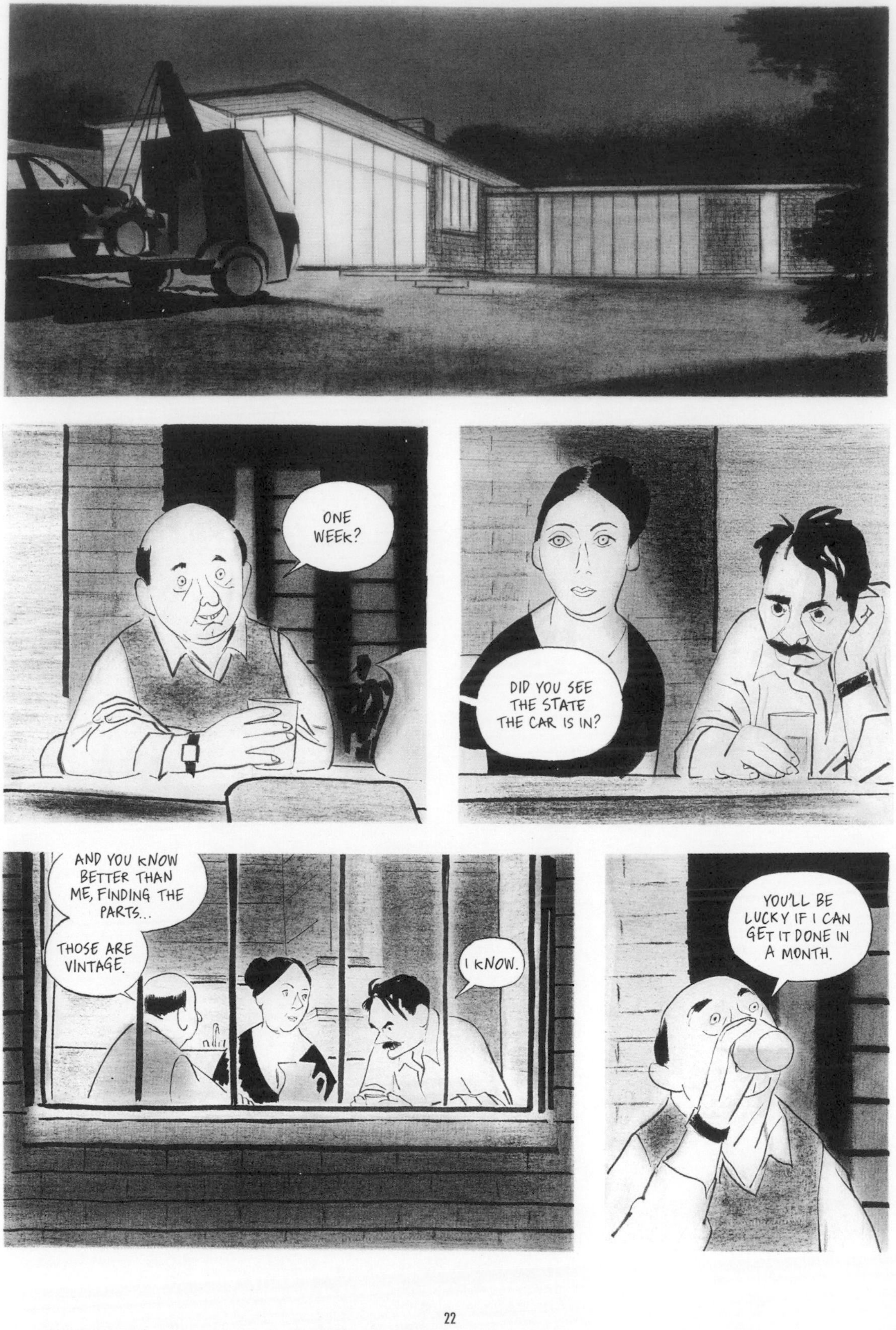
ONE WEEK?
DID YOU SEE THE STATE THE CAR IS IN?
AND YOU KNOW BETTER THAN ME, FINDING THE PARTS...
THOSE ARE VINTAGE.
I KNOW.
YOU'LL BE LUCKY IF I CAN GET IT DONE IN A MONTH.

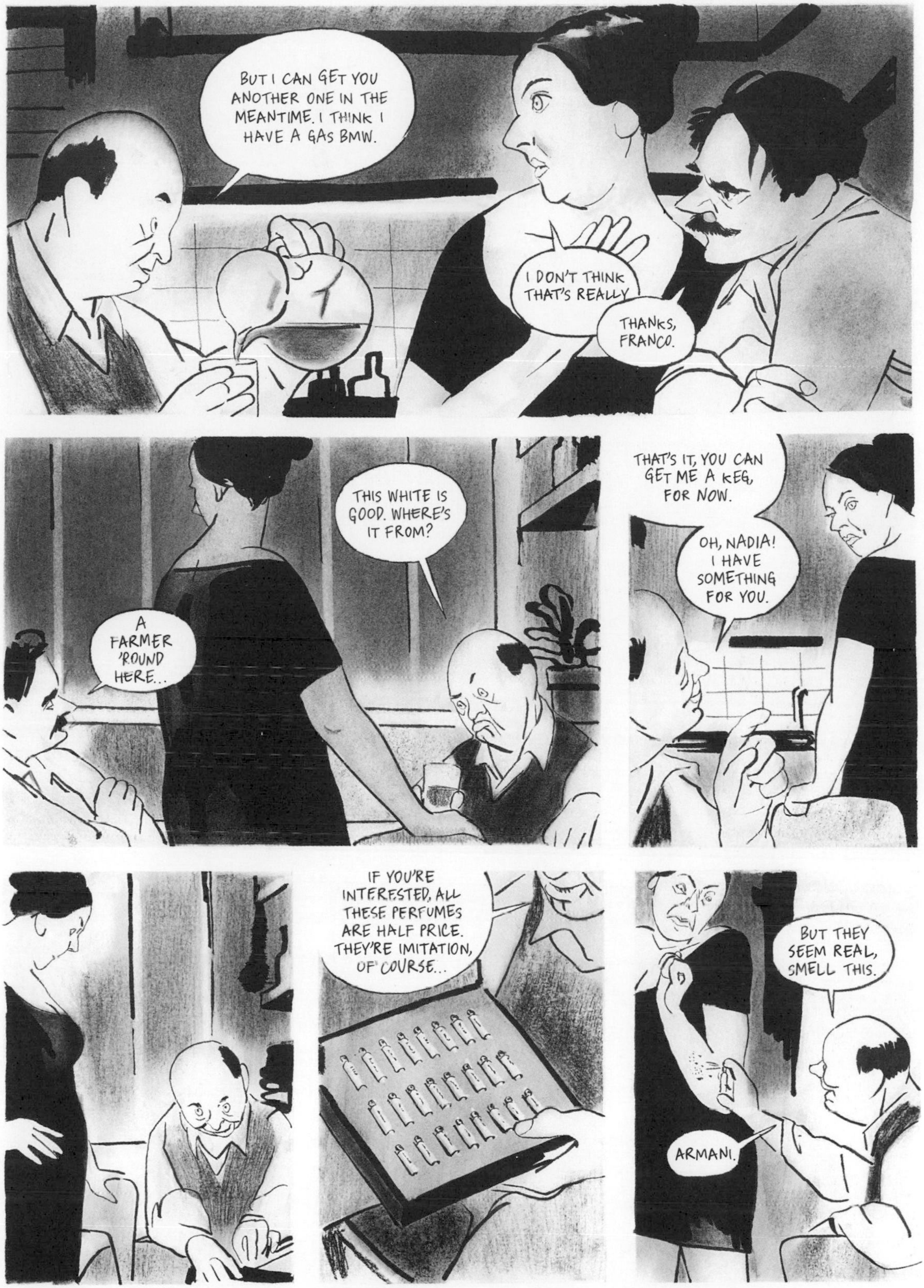
BUT I CAN GET YOU ANOTHER ONE IN THE MEANTIME. I THINK I HAVE A GAS BMW.
I DON'T THINK THAT'S REALLY
THANKS, FRANCO.
THIS WHITE IS GOOD. WHERE'S IT FROM?
A FARMER 'ROUND HERE...
THAT'S IT, YOU CAN GET ME A KEG, FOR NOW.
OH, NADIA! I HAVE SOMETHING FOR YOU.
IF YOU'RE INTERESTED, ALL THESE PERFUMES ARE HALF PRICE. THEY'RE IMITATION, OF COURSE...
BUT THEY SEEM REAL, SMELL THIS.
ARMANI.

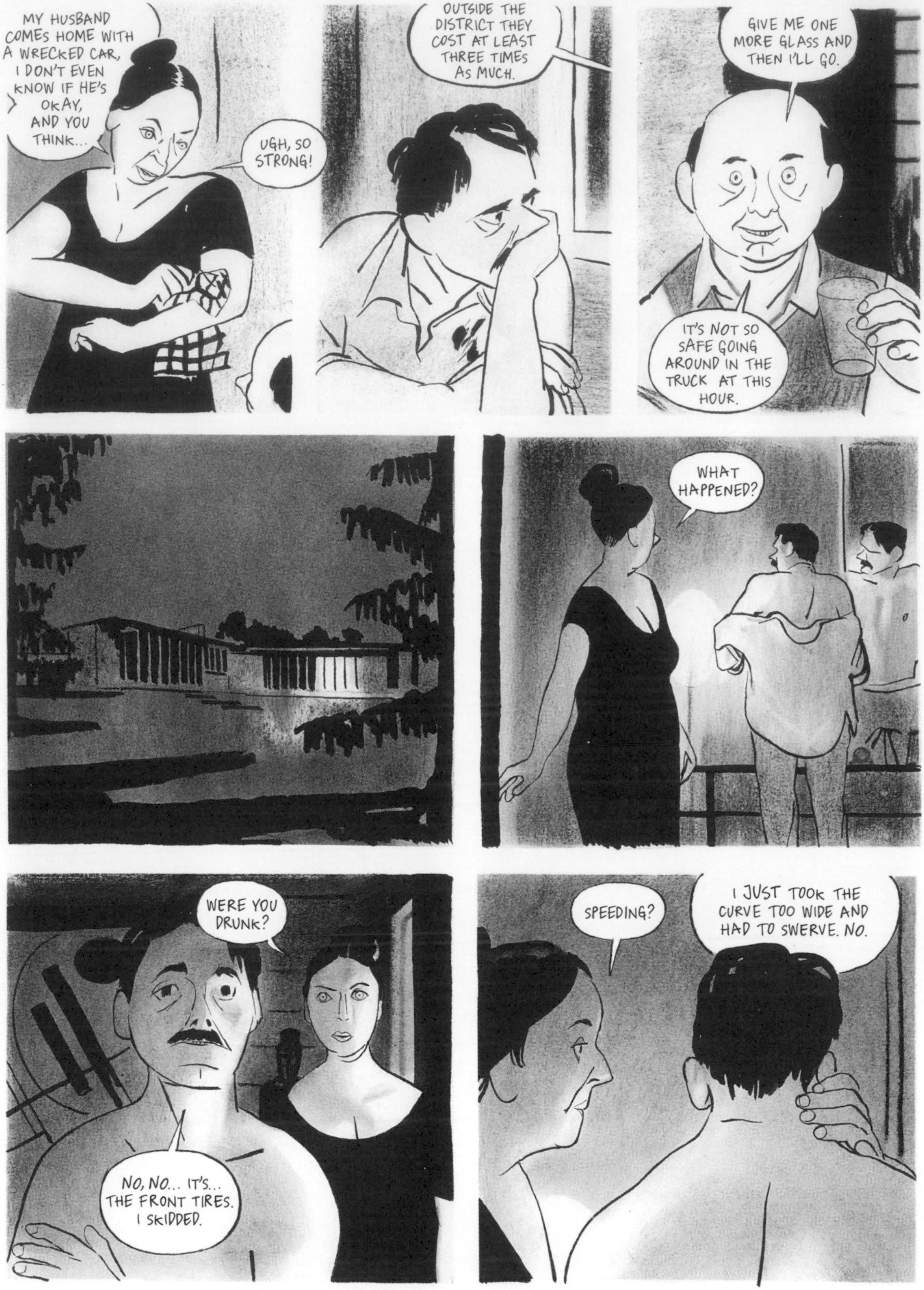
MY HUSBAND COMES HOME WITH A WRECKED CAR, I DON'T EVEN KNOW IF HE'S OKAY, AND YOU THINK...
UGH, SO STRONG!
OUTSIDE THE DISTRICT THEY COST AT LEAST THREE TIMES AS MUCH.
GIVE ME ONE MORE GLASS AND THEN I'LL GO.
IT'S NOT SO SAFE GOING AROUND IN THE TRUCK AT THIS HOUR.
WHAT HAPPENED?
WERE YOU DRUNK?
NO, NO... IT'S... THE FRONT TIRES. I SKIDDED.
SPEEDING?
I JUST TOOK THE CURVE TOO WIDE AND HAD TO SWERVE. NO.

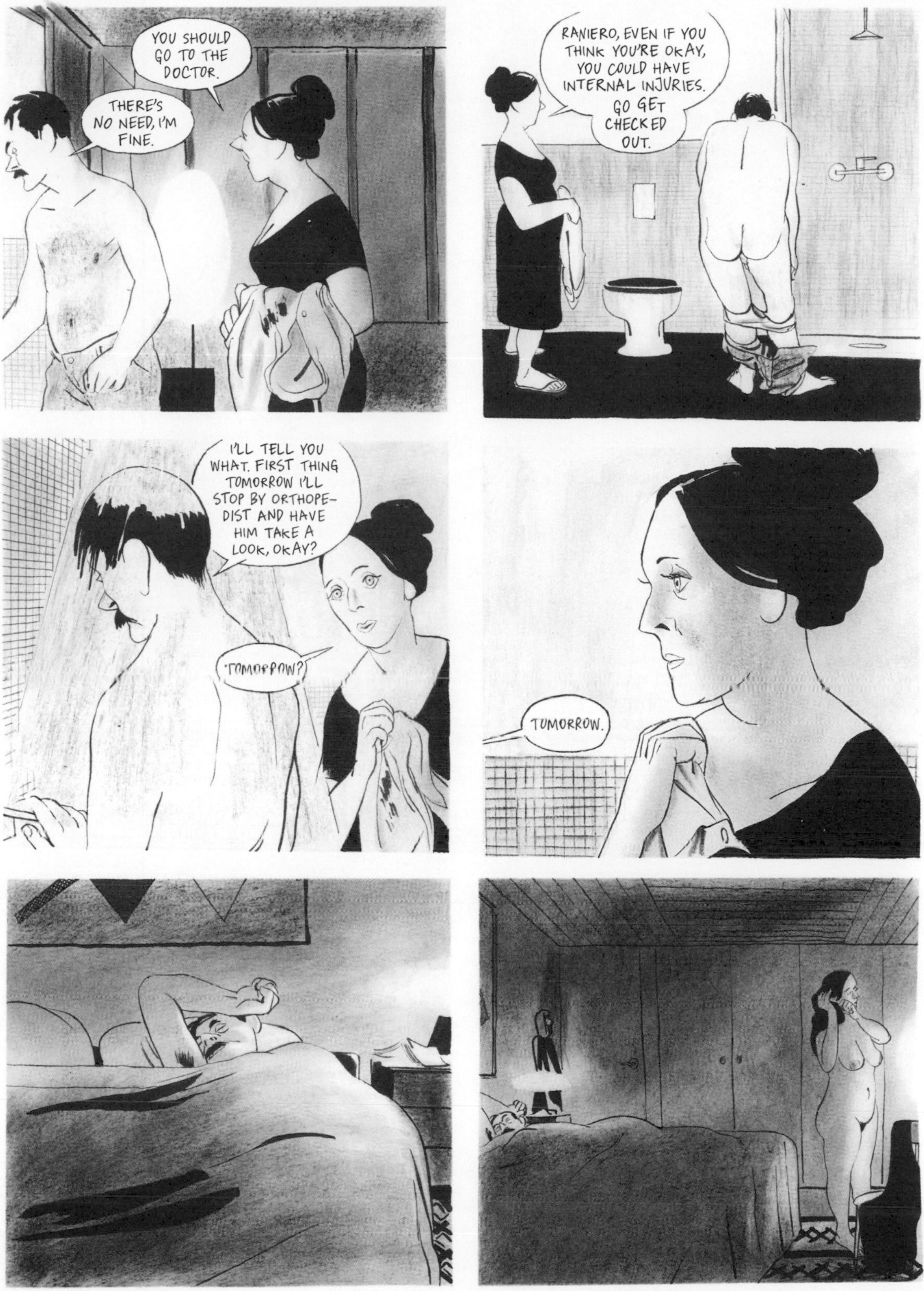
YOU SHOULD GO TO THE DOCTOR.
THERE'S NO NEED, I'M FINE.
RANIERO, EVEN IF YOU THINK YOU'RE OKAY, YOU COULD HAVE INTERNAL INJURIES. GO GET CHECKED OUT.
I'LL TELL YOU WHAT. FIRST THING TOMORROW I'LL STOP BY ORTHOPE-DIST AND HAVE HIM TAKE A LOOK, OKAY?
TOMORROW?
TOMORROW.

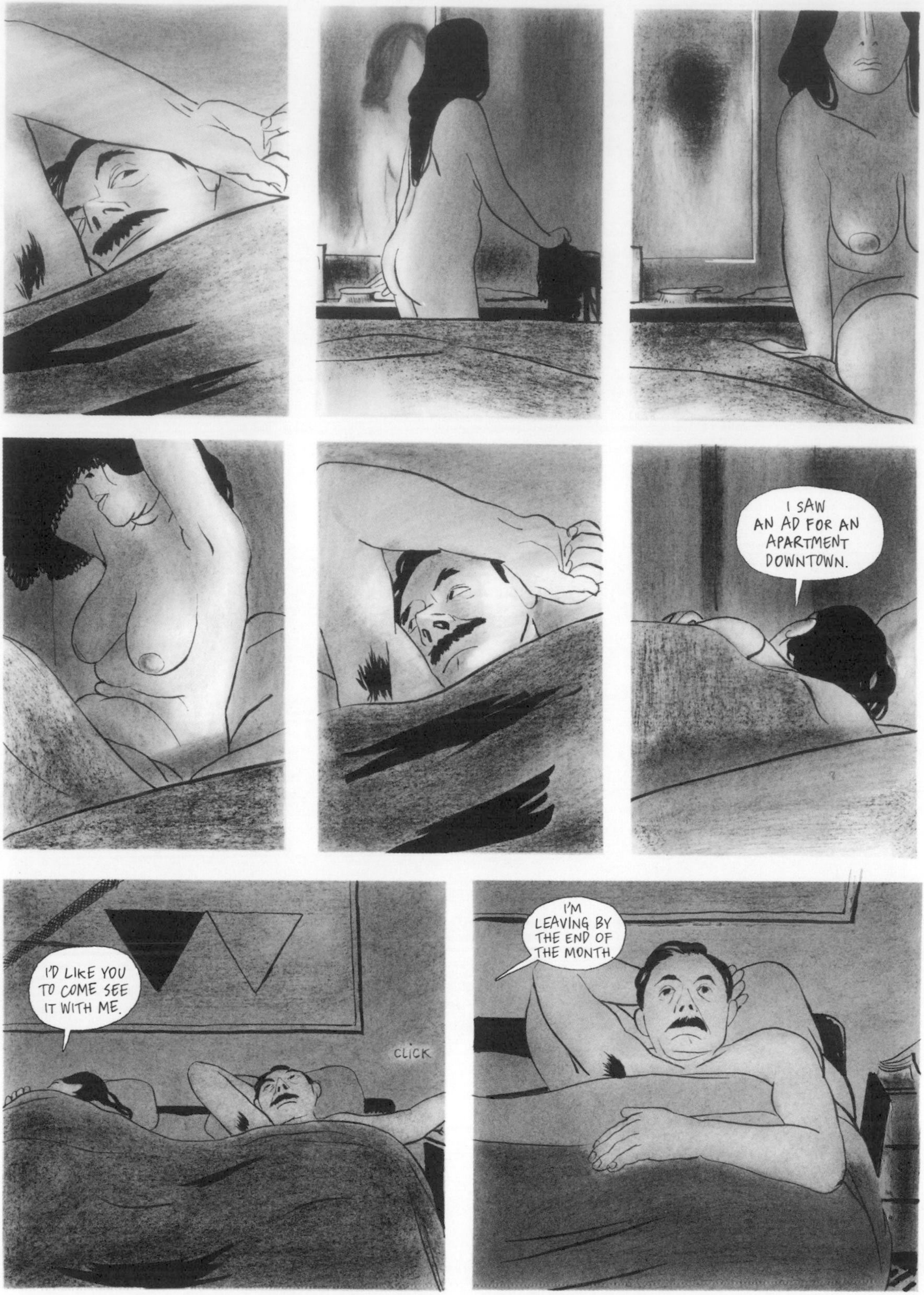
I SAW AN AD FOR AN APARTMENT DOWNTOWN.
I'D LIKE YOU TO COME SEE IT WITH ME.
CLICK
I'M LEAVING BY THE END OF THE MONTH.

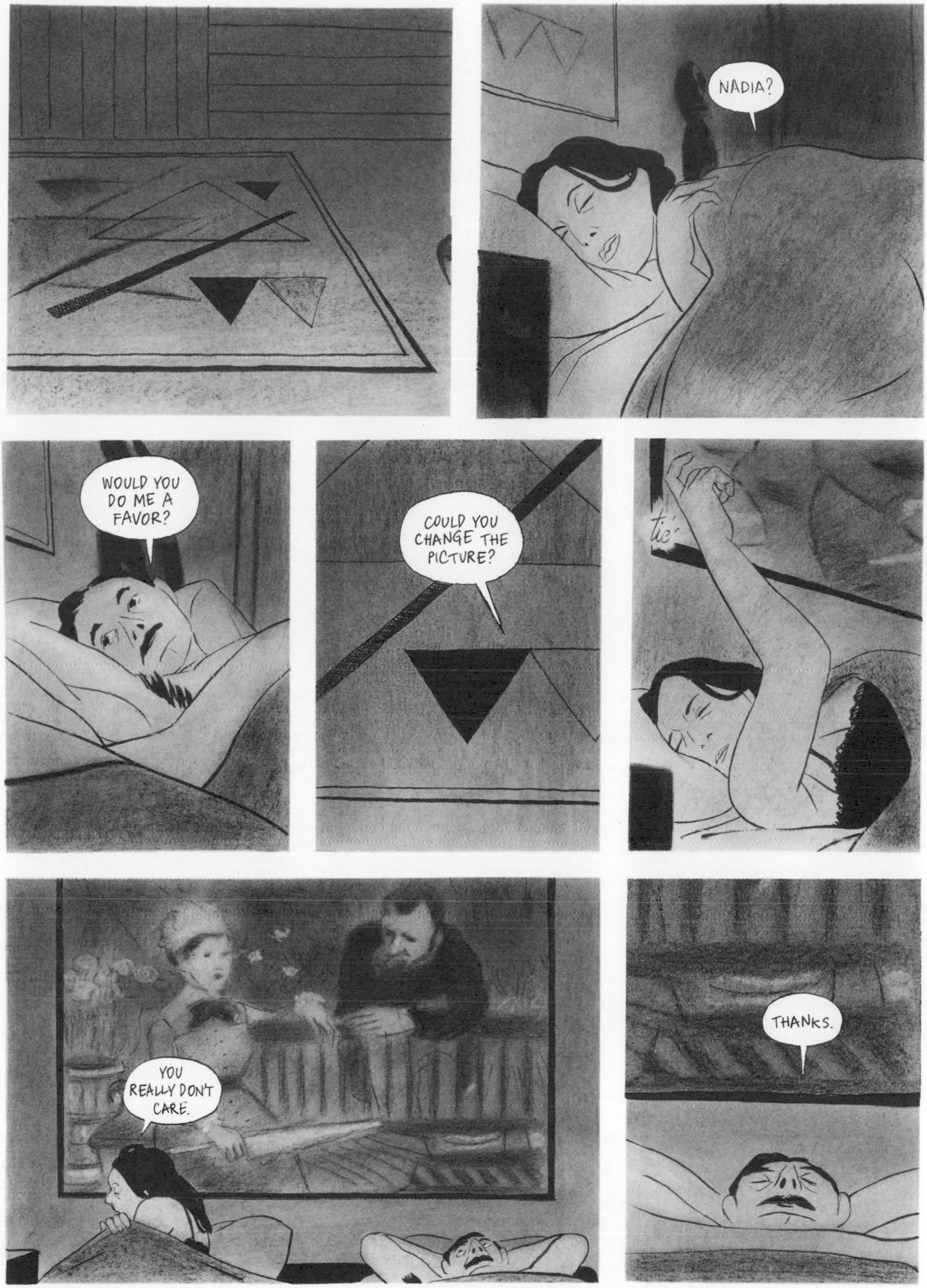
NADIA?
WOULD YOU DO ME A FAVOR?
COULD YOU CHANGE THE PICTURE?
YOU REALLY DON'T CARE.
THANKS.

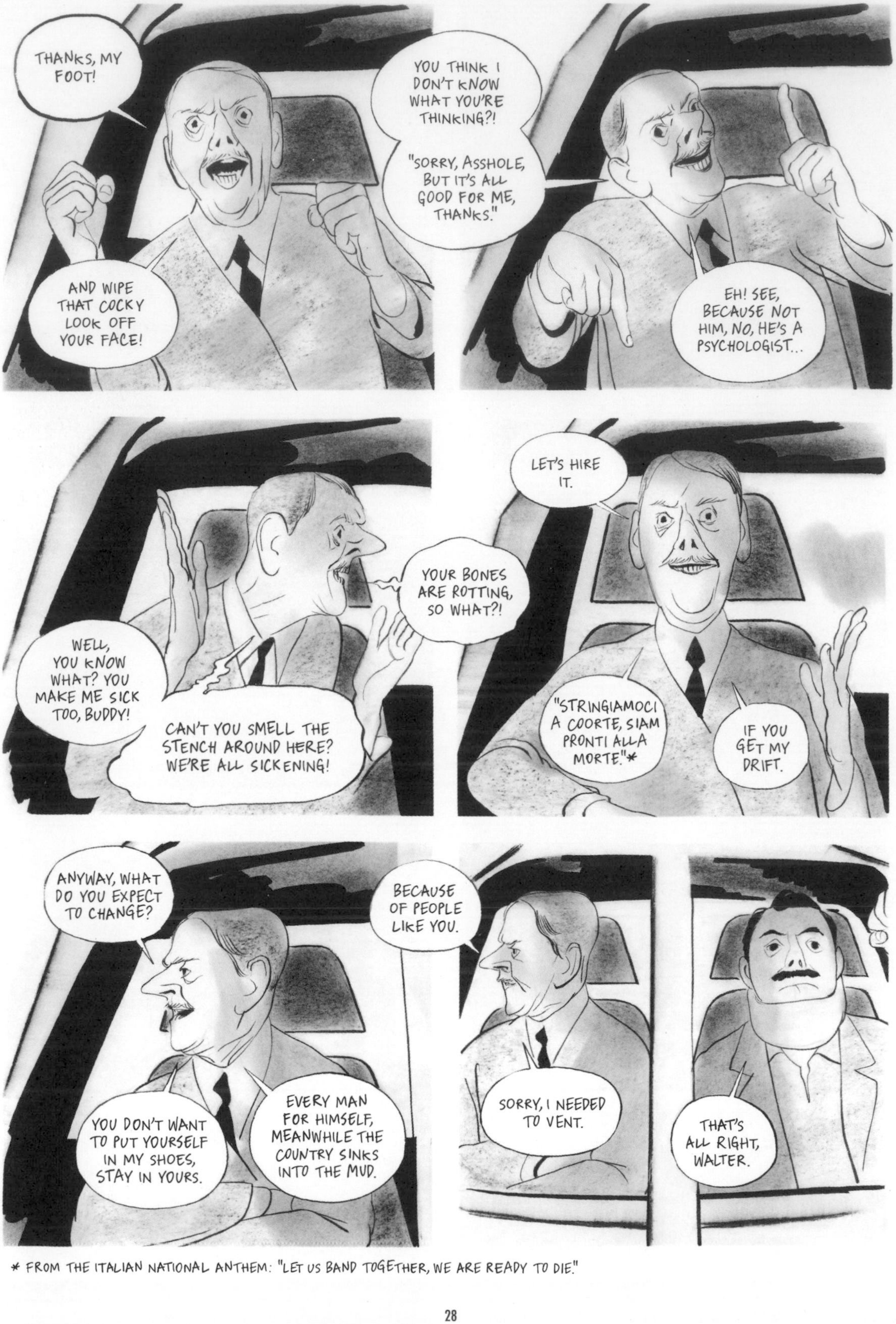
THANKS, MY FOOT!
AND WIPE THAT COCKY LOOK OFF YOUR FACE!
YOU THINK I DON'T KNOW WHAT YOU'RE THINKING?!
"SORRY, ASSHOLE, BUT IT'S ALL GOOD FOR ME, THANKS."
EH! SEE, BECAUSE NOT HIM, NO, HE'S A PSYCHOLOGIST...
YOUR BONES ARE ROTTING, SO WHAT?!
WELL, YOU KNOW WHAT? YOU MAKE ME SICK TOO, BUDDY!
CAN'T YOU SMELL THE STENCH AROUND HERE? WE'RE ALL SICKENING!
LET'S HIRE IT.
"STRINGIAMOCI A COORTE, SIAM PRONTI ALLA MORTE."*
IF YOU GET MY DRIFT.
ANYWAY, WHAT DO YOU EXPECT TO CHANGE?
YOU DON'T WANT TO PUT YOURSELF IN MY SHOES, STAY IN YOURS.
EVERY MAN FOR HIMSELF, MEANWHILE THE COUNTRY SINKS INTO THE MUD.
BECAUSE OF PEOPLE LIKE YOU.
SORRY, I NEEDED TO VENT.
THAT'S ALL RIGHT, WALTER.

* FROM THE ITALIAN NATIONAL ANTHEM: "LET US BAND TOGETHER, WE ARE READY TO DIE."

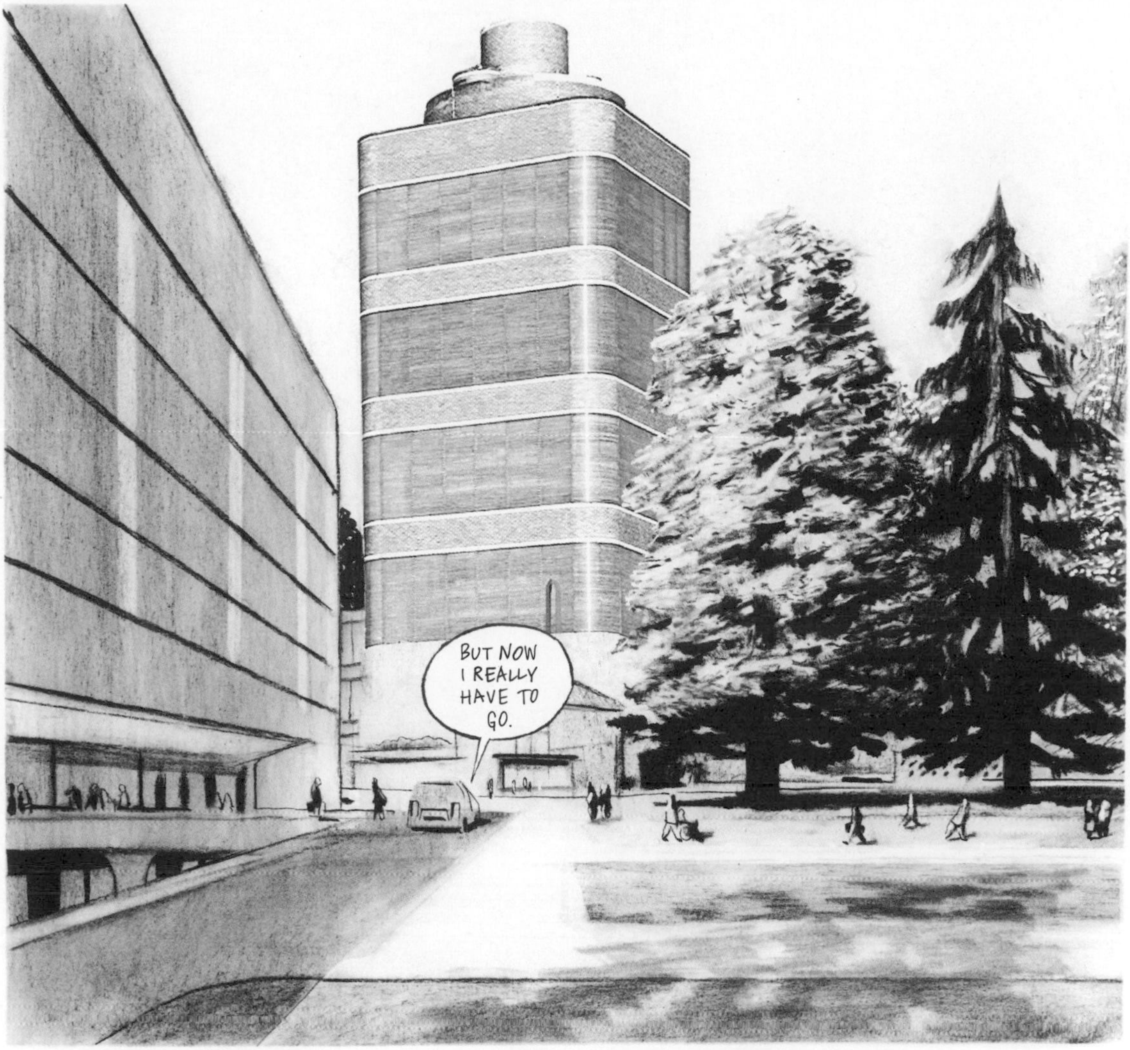
BUT NOW I REALLY HAVE TO GO.

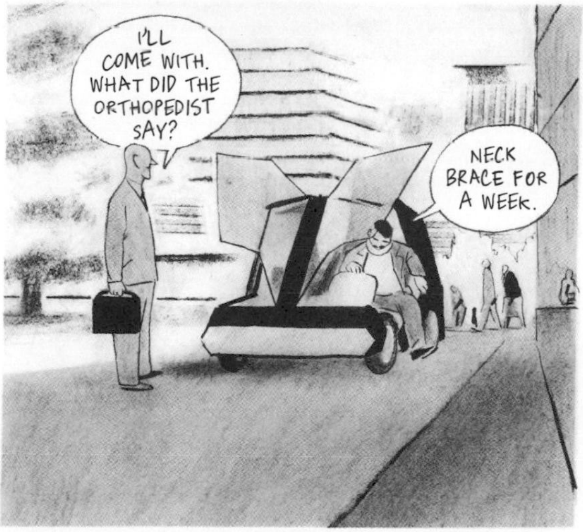
I'LL COME WITH. WHAT DID THE ORTHOPEDIST SAY?
NECK BRACE FOR A WEEK.

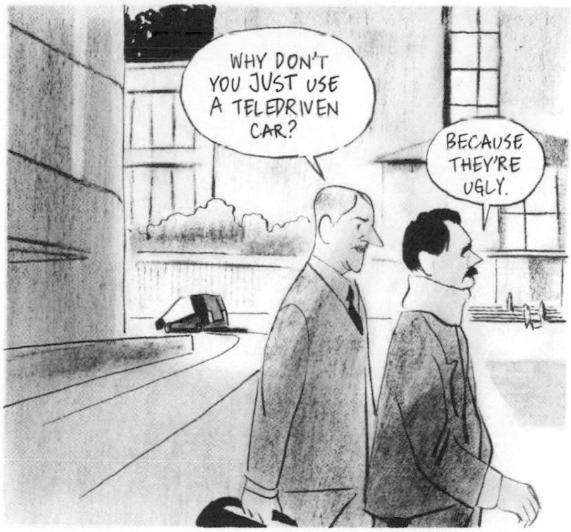
WHY DON'T YOU JUST USE A TELEDRIVEN CAR?
BECAUSE THEY'RE UGLY.

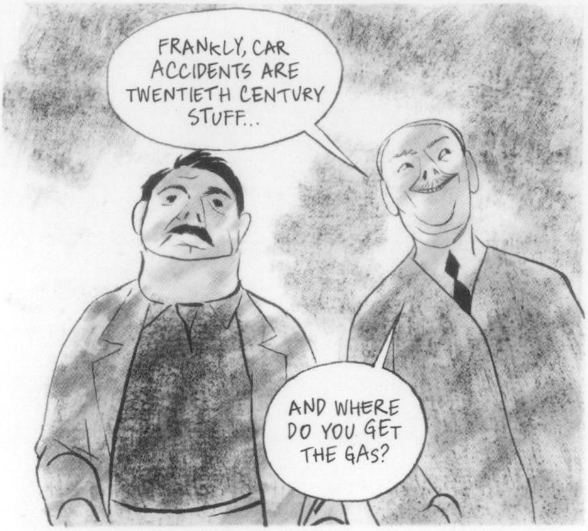
FRANKLY, CAR ACCIDENTS ARE TWENTIETH CENTURY STUFF...
AND WHERE DO YOU GET THE GAS?

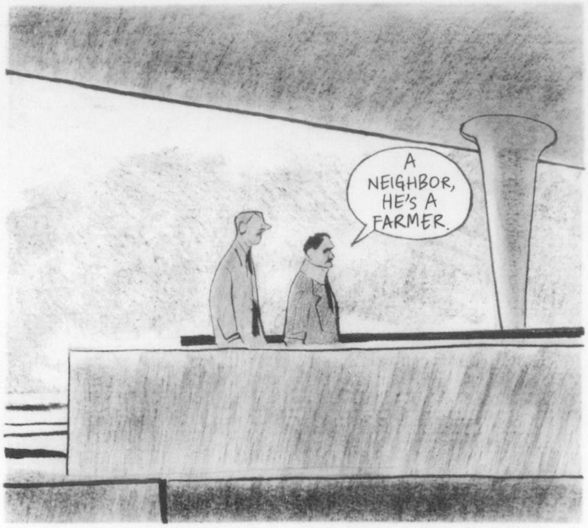
A NEIGHBOR, HE'S A FARMER.

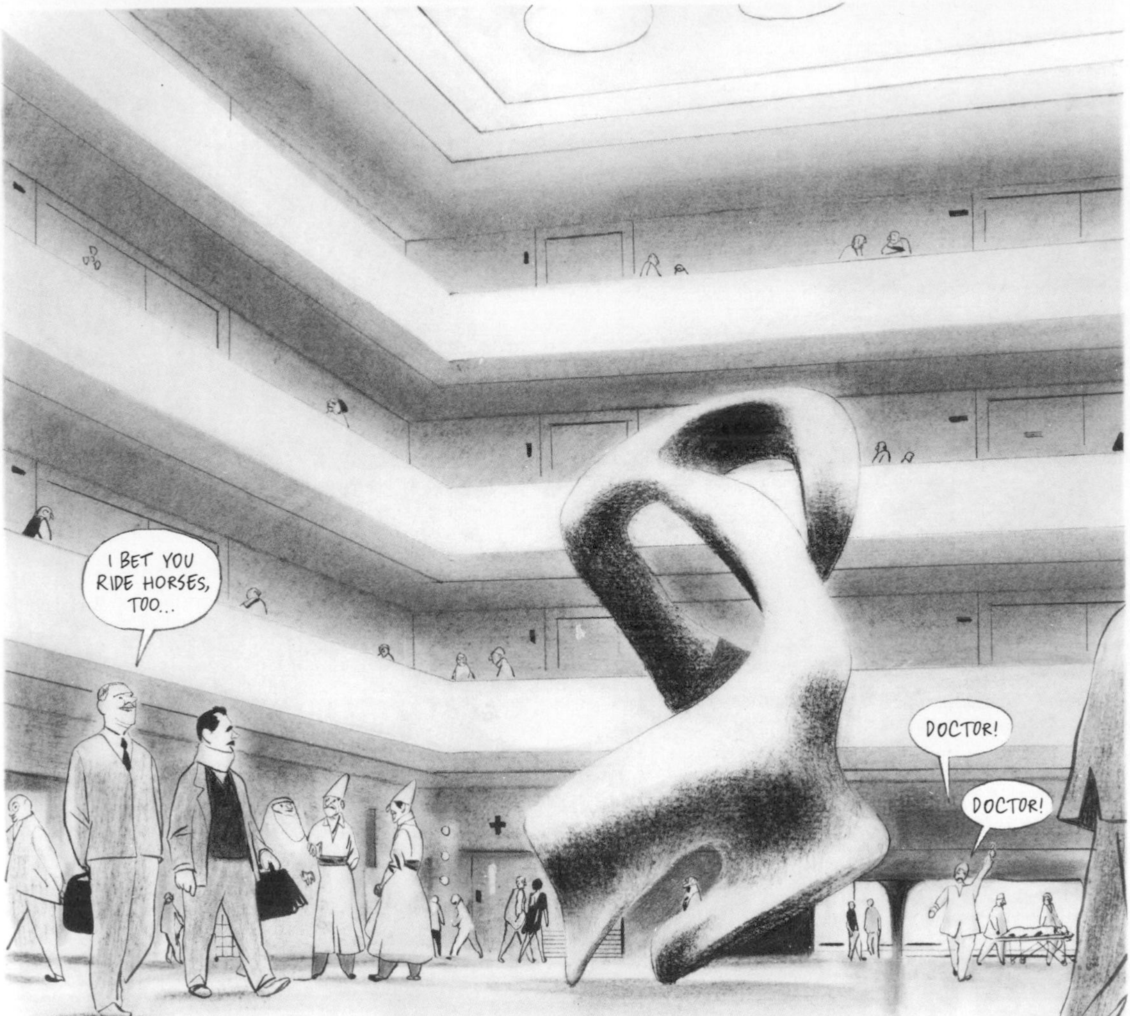
I BET YOU RIDE HORSES, TOO...
DOCTOR!
DOCTOR!

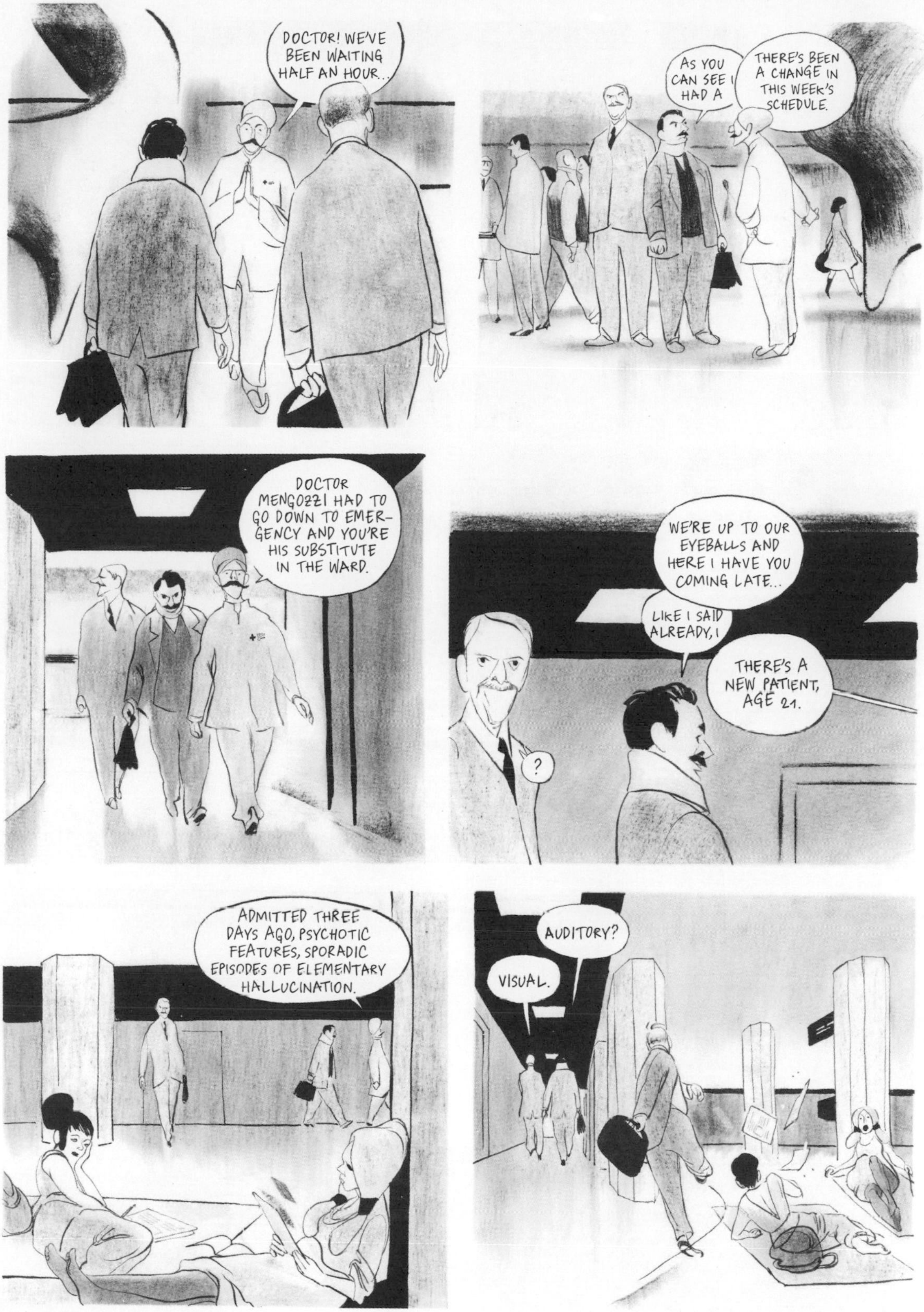
DOCTOR! WE'VE BEEN WAITING HALF AN HOUR...
AS YOU CAN SEE I HAD A
THERE'S BEEN A CHANGE IN THIS WEEK'S SCHEDULE.
DOCTOR MENGOZZI HAD TO GO DOWN TO EMERGENCY AND YOU'RE HIS SUBSTITUTE IN THE WARD.
WE'RE UP TO OUR EYEBALLS AND HERE I HAVE YOU COMING LATE...
LIKE I SAID ALREADY, I
THERE'S A NEW PATIENT, AGE 21.
?
ADMITTED THREE DAYS AGO, PSYCHOTIC FEATURES, SPORADIC EPISODES OF ELEMENTARY HALLUCINATION.
AUDITORY?
VISUAL.

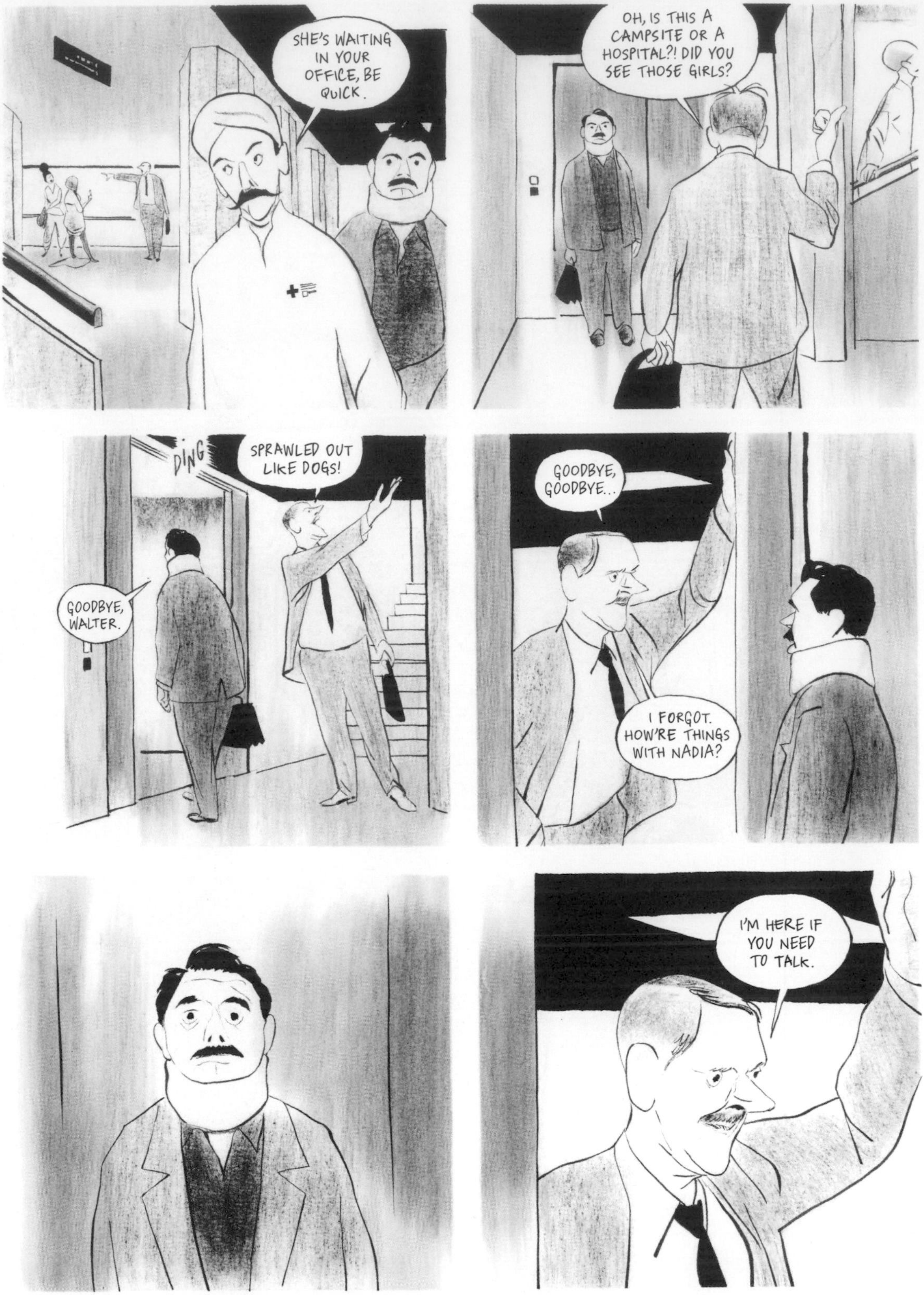
SHE'S WAITING IN YOUR OFFICE, BE QUICK.
OH, IS THIS A CAMPSITE OR A HOSPITAL?! DID YOU SEE THOSE GIRLS?
DING
SPRAWLED OUT LIKE DOGS!
GOODBYE, WALTER.
GOODBYE, GOODBYE...
I FORGOT. HOW'RE THINGS WITH NADIA?
I'M HERE IF YOU NEED TO TALK.

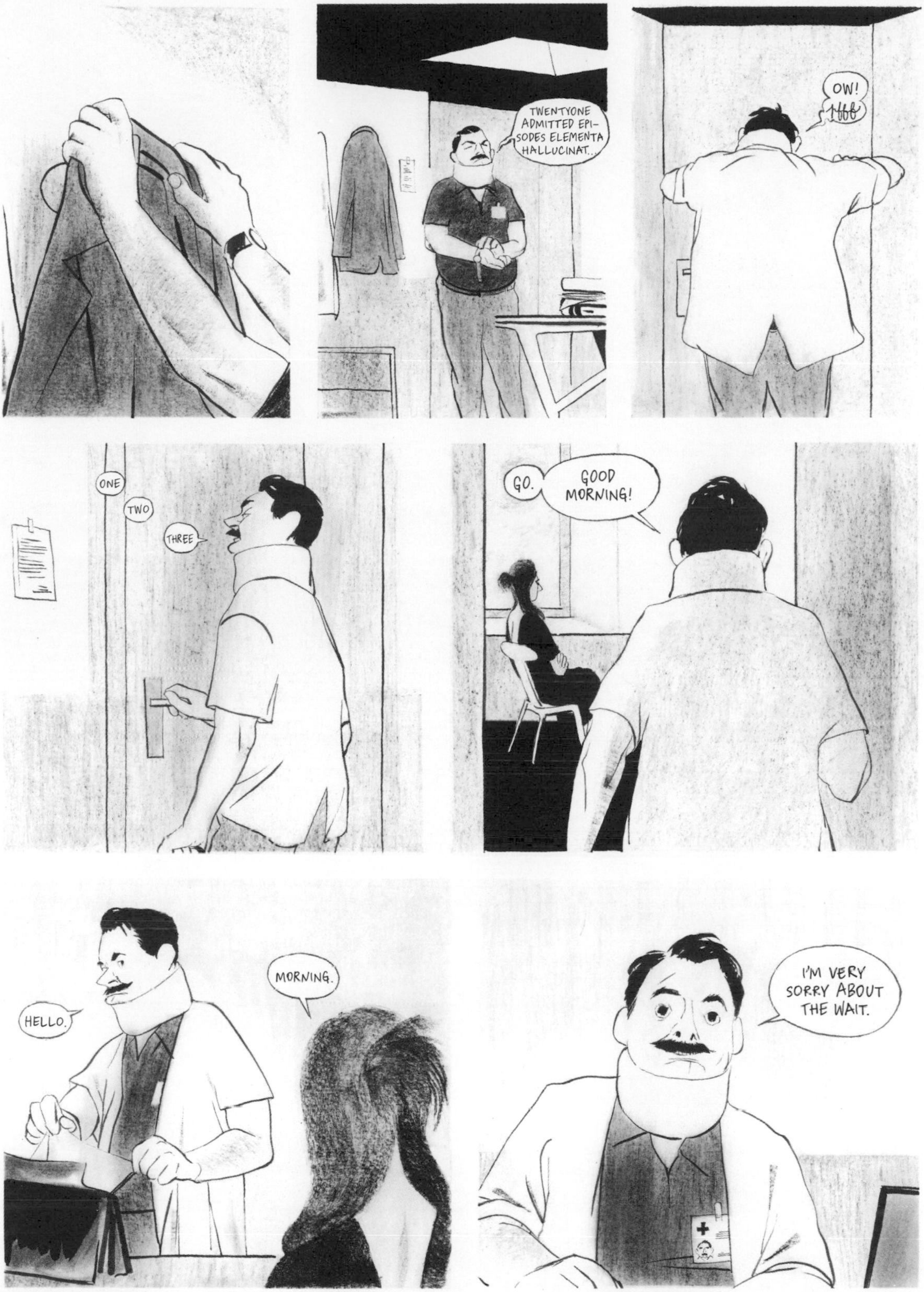
TWENTYONE ADMITTED EPI-SODES ELEMENTA HALLUCINAT...
OW!
ONE
TWO
THREE
GO.
GOOD MORNING!
HELLO.
MORNING.
I'M VERY SORRY ABOUT THE WAIT.

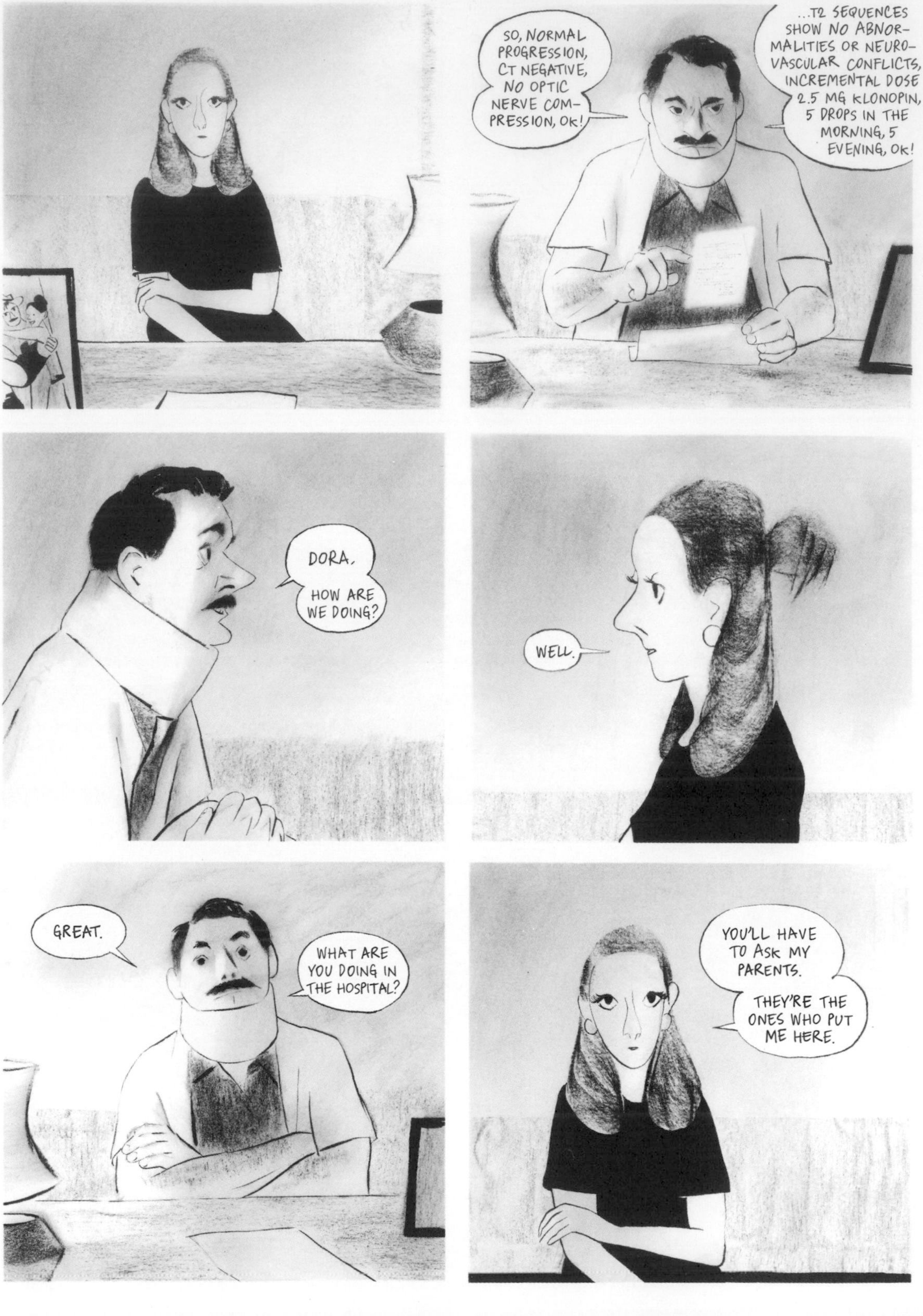
SO, NORMAL PROGRESSION, CT NEGATIVE, NO OPTIC NERVE COMPRESSION, OK!
...T2 SEQUENCES SHOW NO ABNORMALITIES OR NEUROVASCULAR CONFLICTS, INCREMENTAL DOSE 2.5 MG KLONOPIN, 5 DROPS IN THE MORNING, 5 EVENING, OK!
DORA,
HOW ARE WE DOING?
WELL.
GREAT.
WHAT ARE YOU DOING IN THE HOSPITAL?
YOU'LL HAVE TO ASK MY PARENTS.
THEY'RE THE ONES WHO PUT ME HERE.

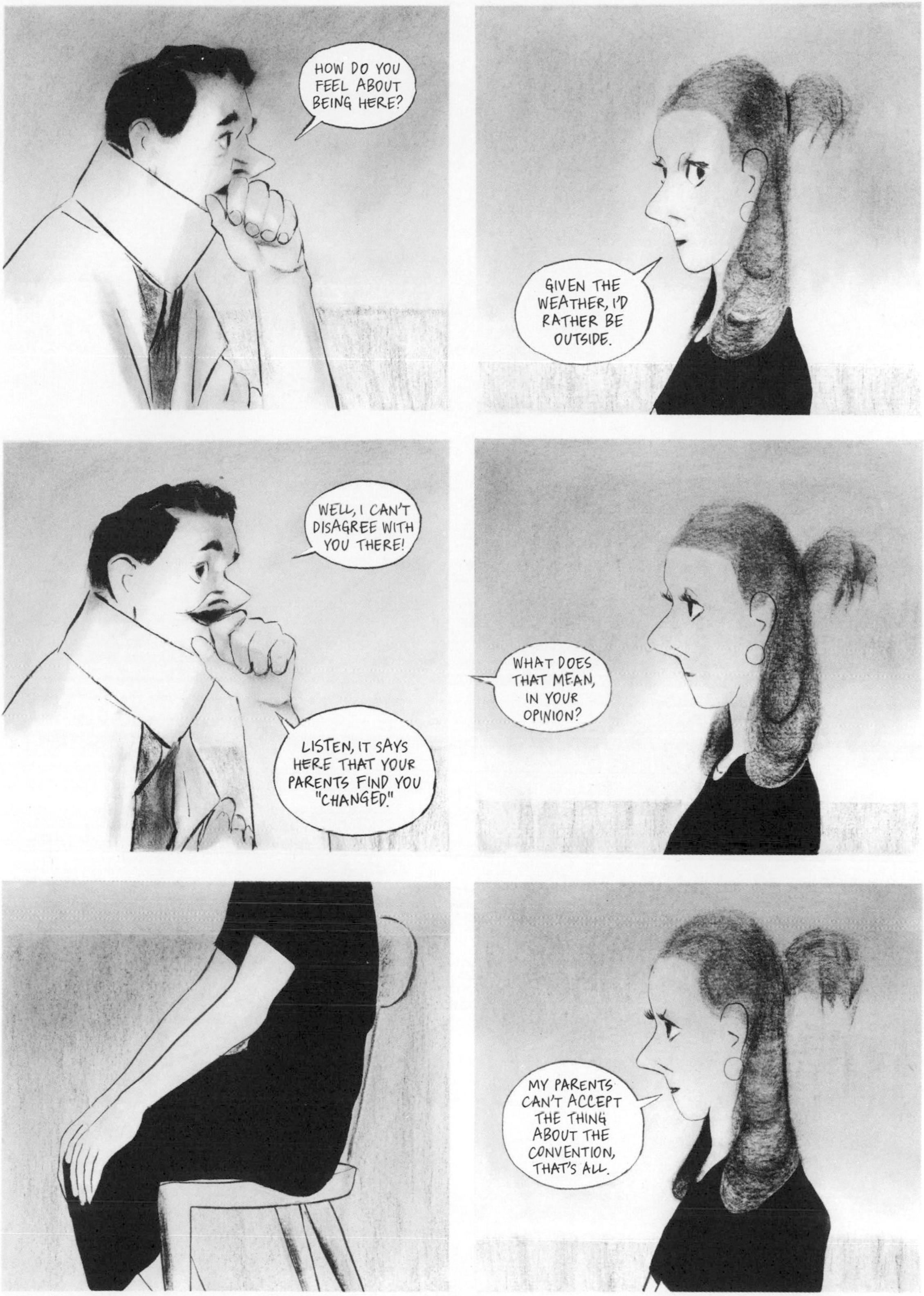
HOW DO YOU FEEL ABOUT BEING HERE?
GIVEN THE WEATHER, I'D RATHER BE OUTSIDE.
WELL, I CAN'T DISAGREE WITH YOU THERE!
LISTEN, IT SAYS HERE THAT YOUR PARENTS FIND YOU "CHANGED."
WHAT DOES THAT MEAN, IN YOUR OPINION?
MY PARENTS CAN'T ACCEPT THE THING ABOUT THE CONVENTION, THAT'S ALL.

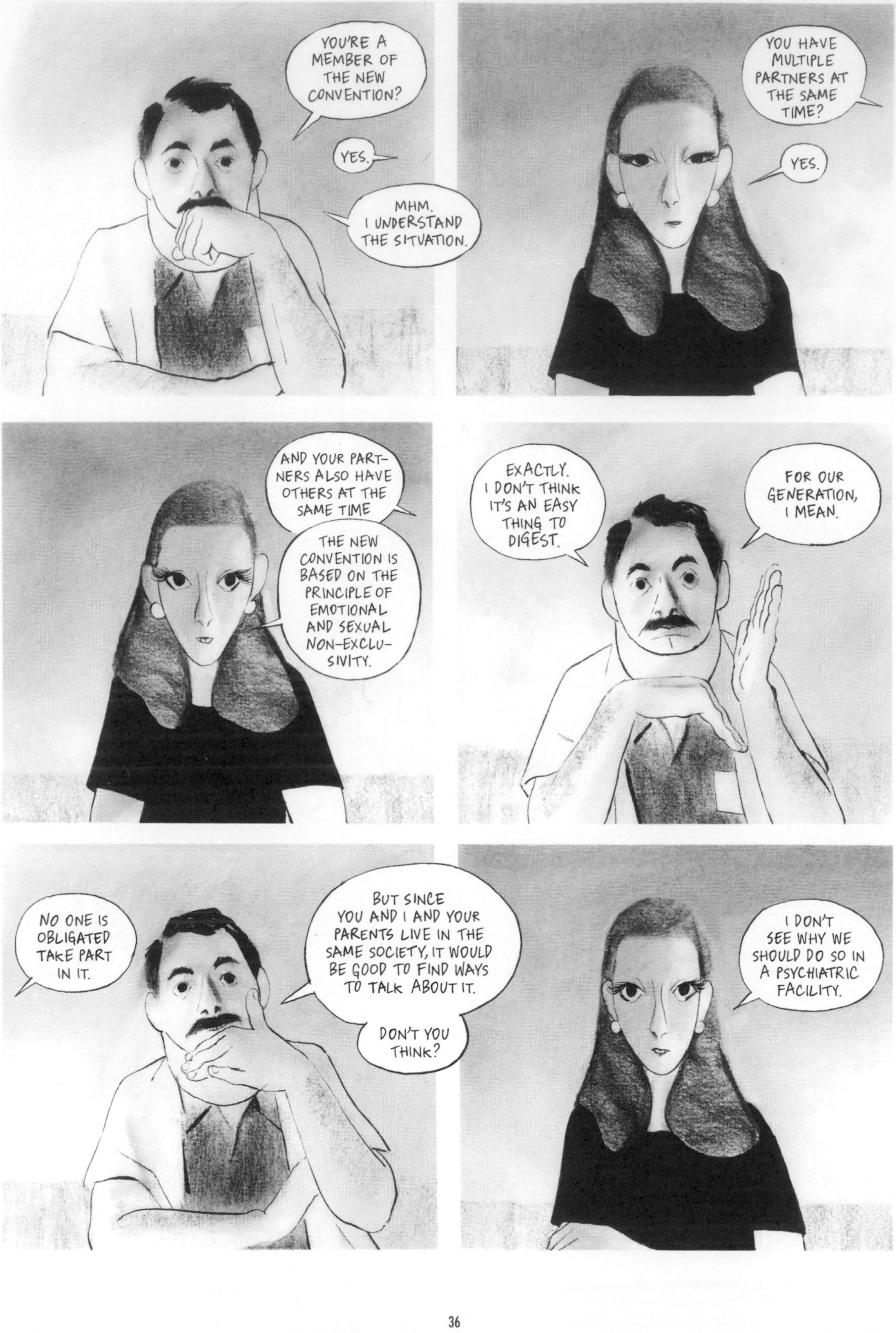
YOU'RE A MEMBER OF THE NEW CONVENTION?
YES.
MHM. I UNDERSTAND THE SITUATION.
YOU HAVE MULTIPLE PARTNERS AT THE SAME TIME?
YES.
AND YOUR PARTNERS ALSO HAVE OTHERS AT THE SAME TIME
THE NEW CONVENTION IS BASED ON THE PRINCIPLE OF EMOTIONAL AND SEXUAL NON-EXCLUSIVITY.
EXACTLY. I DON'T THINK IT'S AN EASY THING TO DIGEST.
FOR OUR GENERATION, I MEAN.
NO ONE IS OBLIGATED TAKE PART IN IT.
BUT SINCE YOU AND I AND YOUR PARENTS LIVE IN THE SAME SOCIETY, IT WOULD BE GOOD TO FIND WAYS TO TALK ABOUT IT.
DON'T YOU THINK?
I DON'T SEE WHY WE SHOULD DO SO IN A PSYCHIATRIC FACILITY.

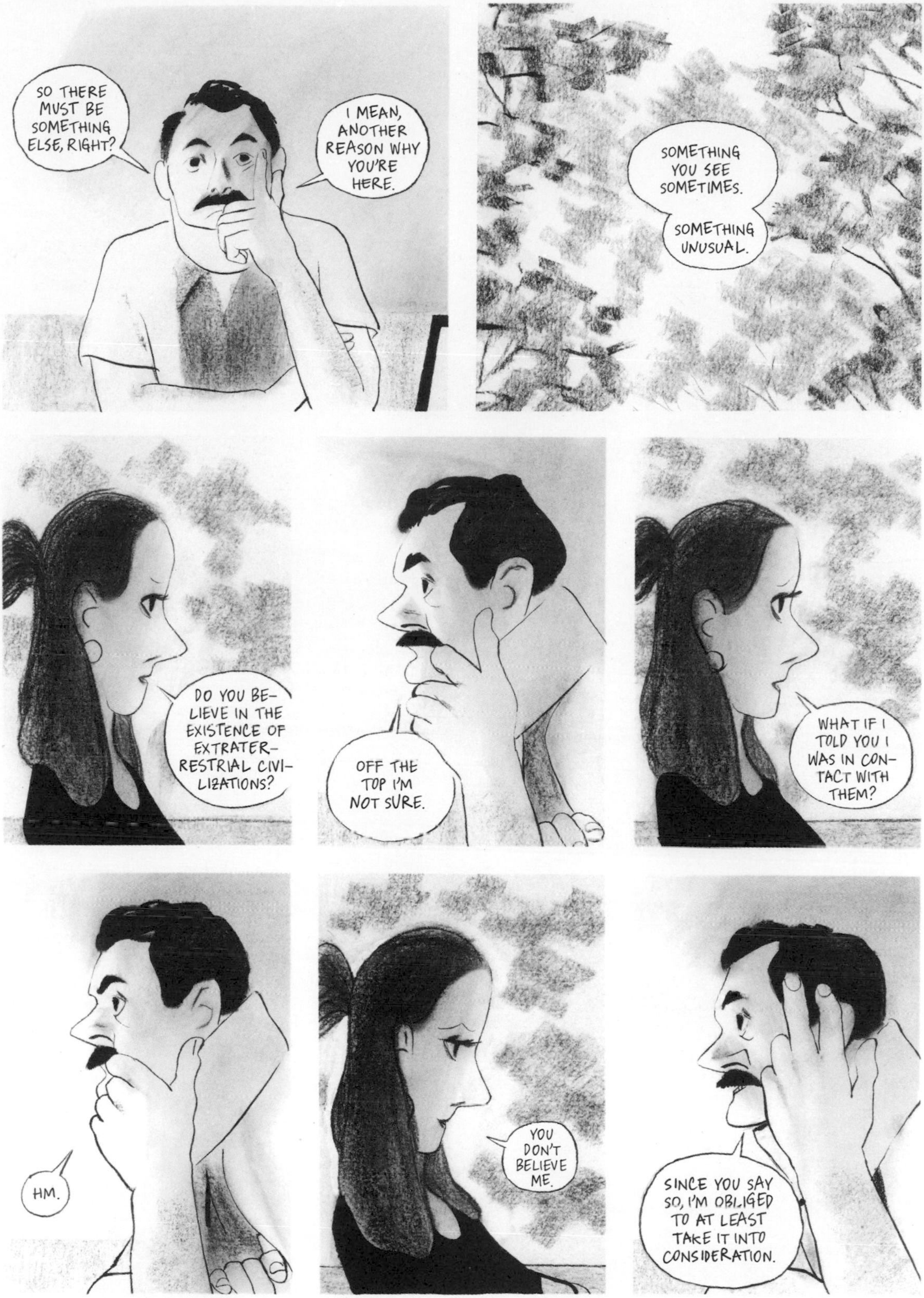
SO THERE MUST BE SOMETHING ELSE, RIGHT?
I MEAN, ANOTHER REASON WHY YOU'RE HERE.
SOMETHING YOU SEE SOMETIMES.
SOMETHING UNUSUAL.
DO YOU BE-LIEVE IN THE EXISTENCE OF EXTRATER-RESTRIAL CIVI-LIZATIONS?
OFF THE TOP I'M NOT SURE.
WHAT IF I TOLD YOU I WAS IN CON-TACT WITH THEM?
HM.
YOU DON'T BELIEVE ME.
SINCE YOU SAY SO, I'M OBLIGED TO AT LEAST TAKE IT INTO CONSIDERATION.

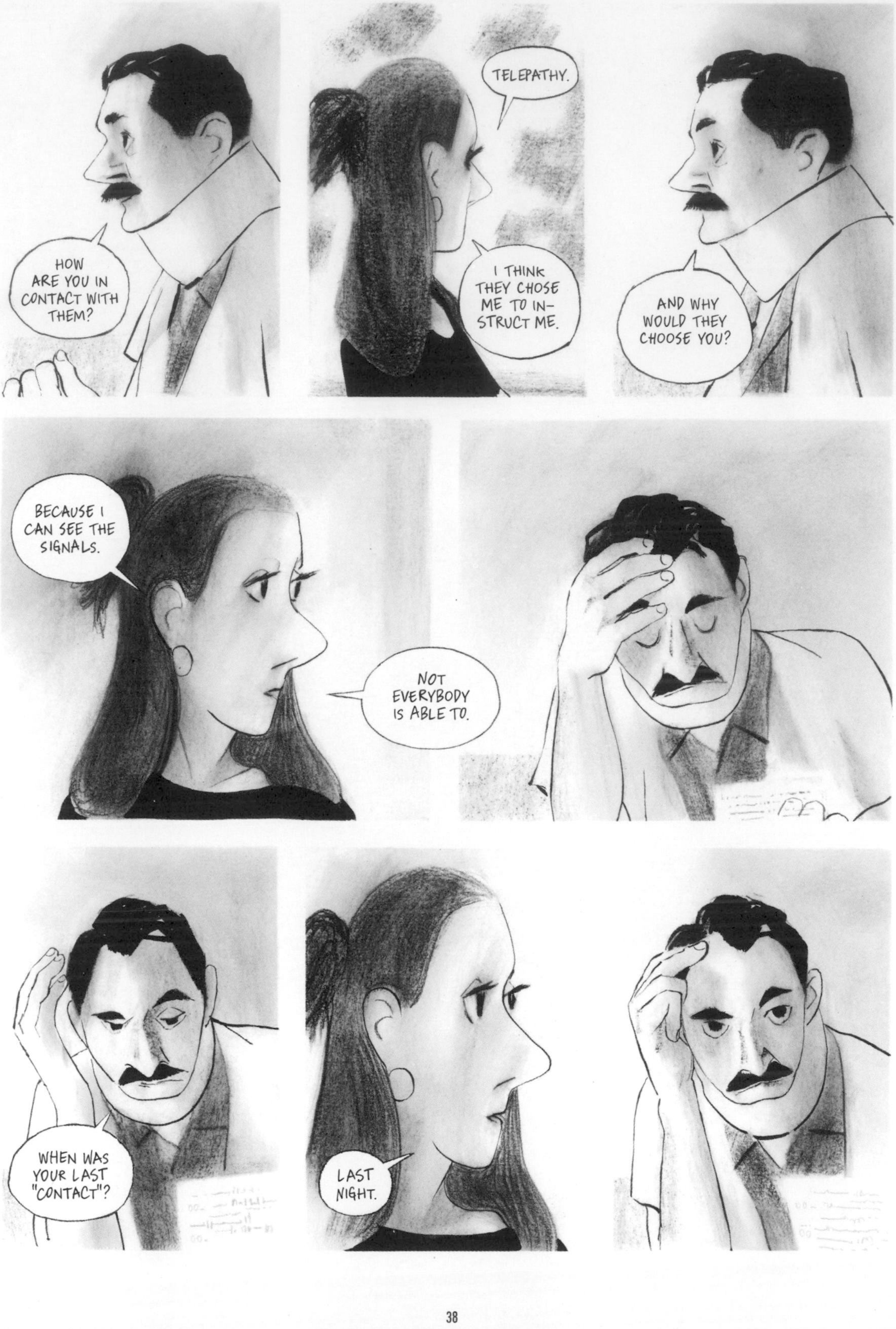
HOW ARE YOU IN CONTACT WITH THEM?
TELEPATHY.
I THINK THEY CHOSE ME TO INSTRUCT ME.
AND WHY WOULD THEY CHOOSE YOU?
BECAUSE I CAN SEE THE SIGNALS.
NOT EVERYBODY IS ABLE TO.
WHEN WAS YOUR LAST "CONTACT"?
LAST NIGHT.

IT WAS UNBELIEVABLE.
DO YOU UNDERSTAND WHAT I'M SAYING?
UNBELIEVABLE..
AS YOU CAN SEE, IT'S 30 M^2, OPTIMIZED DOWN TO THE SMALLEST DETAIL, WITH AN EXCLUSIVE VIEW. IT'S THE IDEAL CHOICE FOR AN INTIMATE GETAWAY FOR TWO.
ACTUALLY IT'S JUST FOR ME.
IT'S THE IDEAL SOLUTION FOR SATISFYING YOUR NEED FOR INDEPENDENCE, WITHOUT GIVING UP THE CONVENIENCE OF ACCESS TO THE CHARMING CITY CENTER.

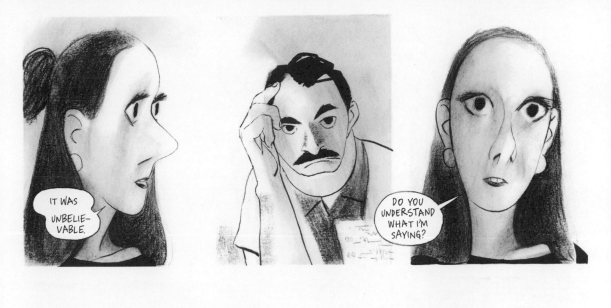

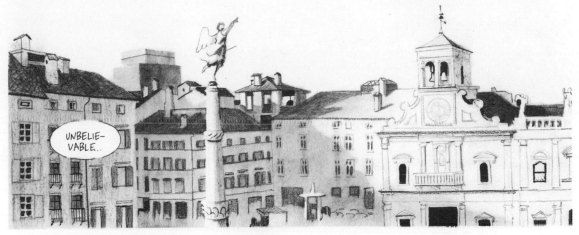

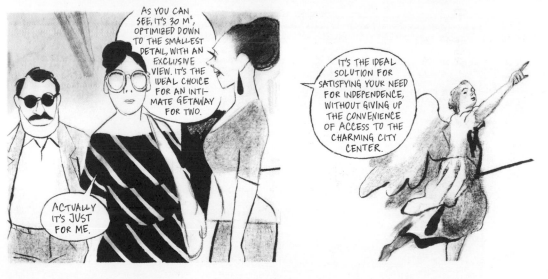

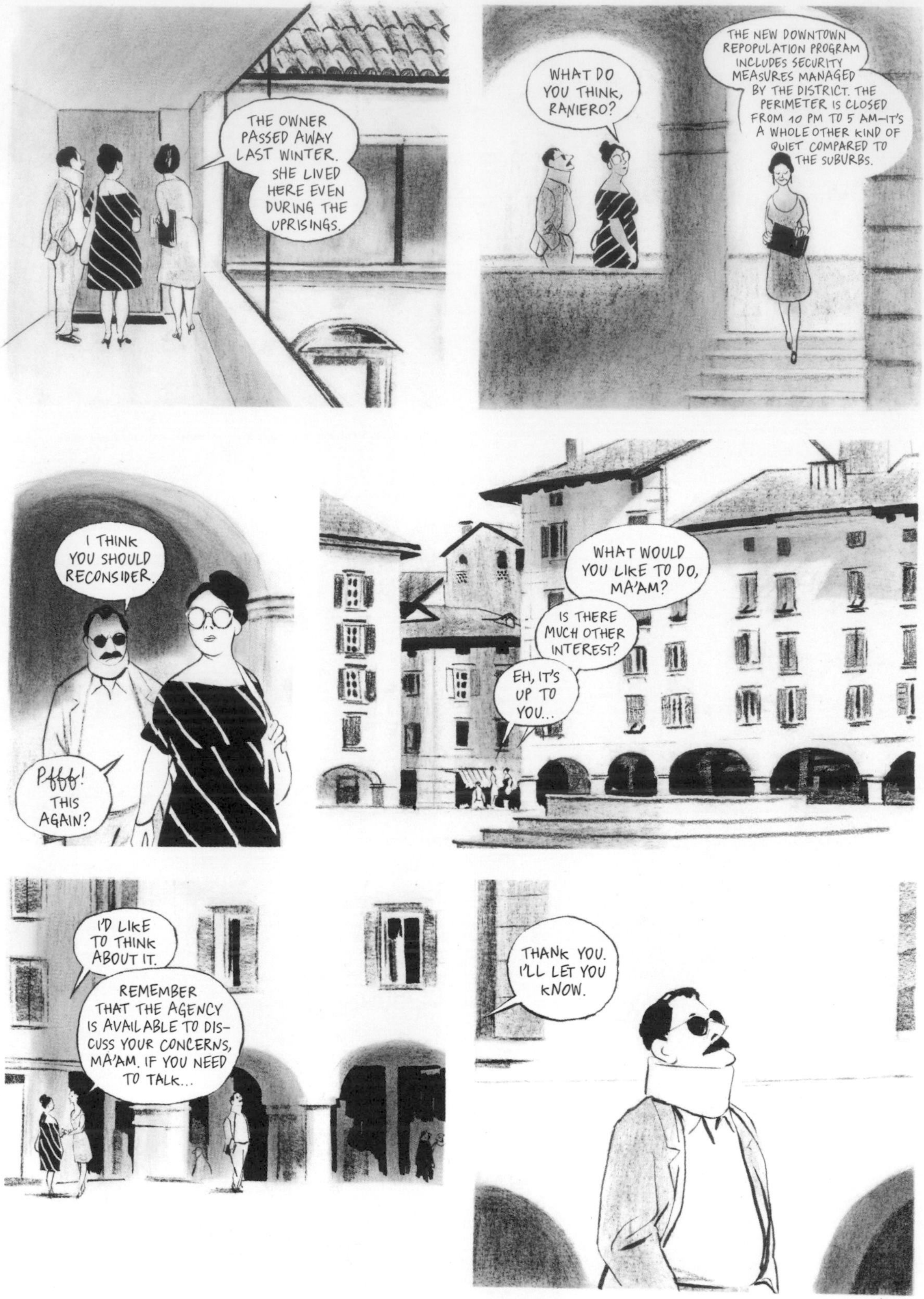
THE OWNER PASSED AWAY LAST WINTER. SHE LIVED HERE EVEN DURING THE UPRISINGS.
WHAT DO YOU THINK, RANIERO?
THE NEW DOWNTOWN REPOPULATION PROGRAM INCLUDES SECURITY MEASURES MANAGED BY THE DISTRICT. THE PERIMETER IS CLOSED FROM 10 PM TO 5 AM—IT'S A WHOLE OTHER KIND OF QUIET COMPARED TO THE SUBURBS.
I THINK YOU SHOULD RECONSIDER.
Pfff! THIS AGAIN?
WHAT WOULD YOU LIKE TO DO, MA'AM?
IS THERE MUCH OTHER INTEREST?
EH, IT'S UP TO YOU...
I'D LIKE TO THINK ABOUT IT.
REMEMBER THAT THE AGENCY IS AVAILABLE TO DISCUSS YOUR CONCERNS, MA'AM. IF YOU NEED TO TALK...
THANK YOU. I'LL LET YOU KNOW.

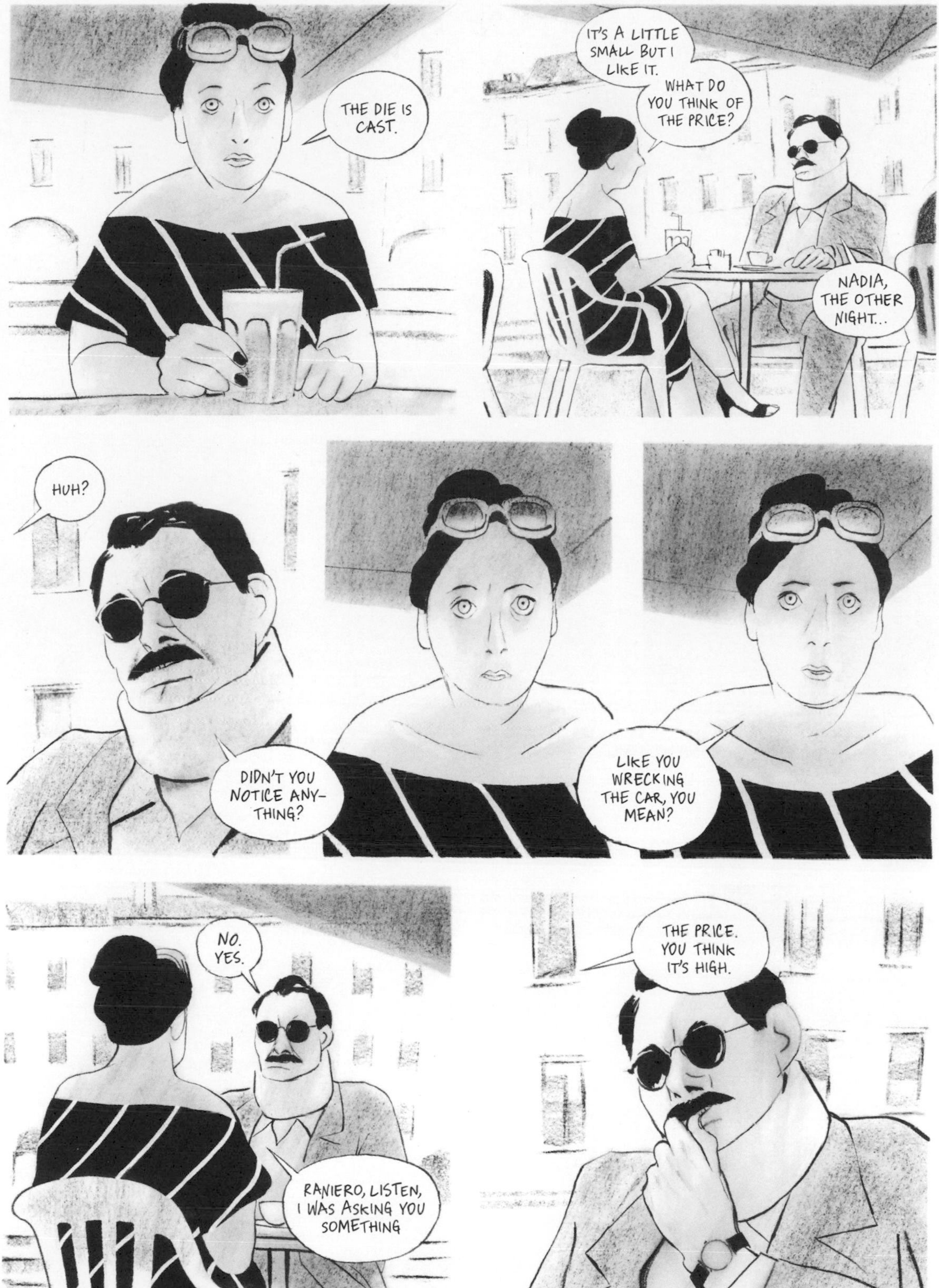
THE DIE IS CAST.
IT'S A LITTLE SMALL BUT I LIKE IT.
WHAT DO YOU THINK OF THE PRICE?
NADIA, THE OTHER NIGHT...
HUH?
DIDN'T YOU NOTICE ANY-THING?
LIKE YOU WRECKING THE CAR, YOU MEAN?
NO. YES.
RANIERO, LISTEN, I WAS ASKING YOU SOMETHING
THE PRICE. YOU THINK IT'S HIGH.

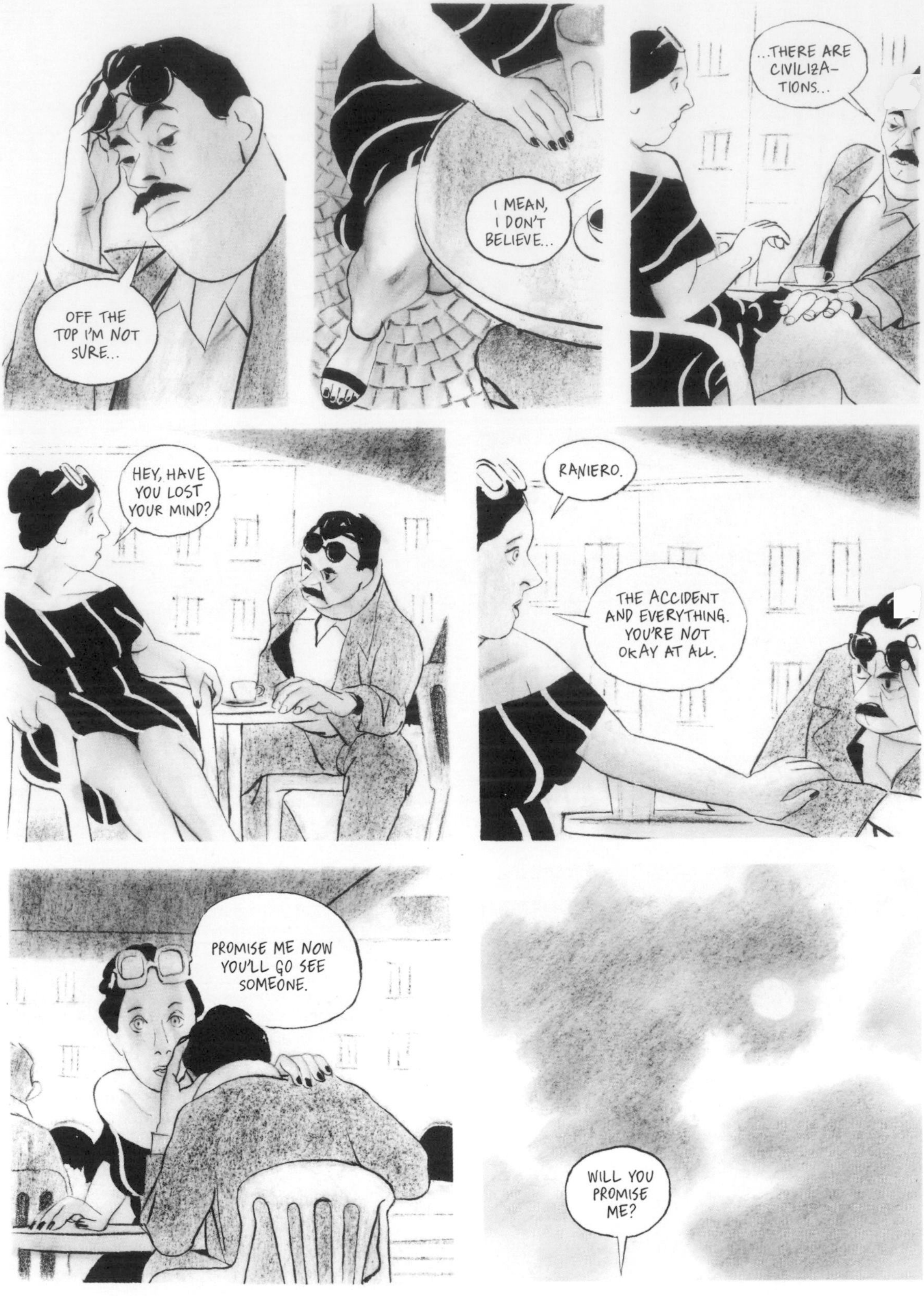
OFF THE TOP I'M NOT SURE...
I MEAN, I DON'T BELIEVE...
...THERE ARE CIVILIZA-TIONS...
HEY, HAVE YOU LOST YOUR MIND?
RANIERO.
THE ACCIDENT AND EVERYTHING. YOU'RE NOT OKAY AT ALL.
PROMISE ME NOW YOU'LL GO SEE SOMEONE.
WILL YOU PROMISE ME?

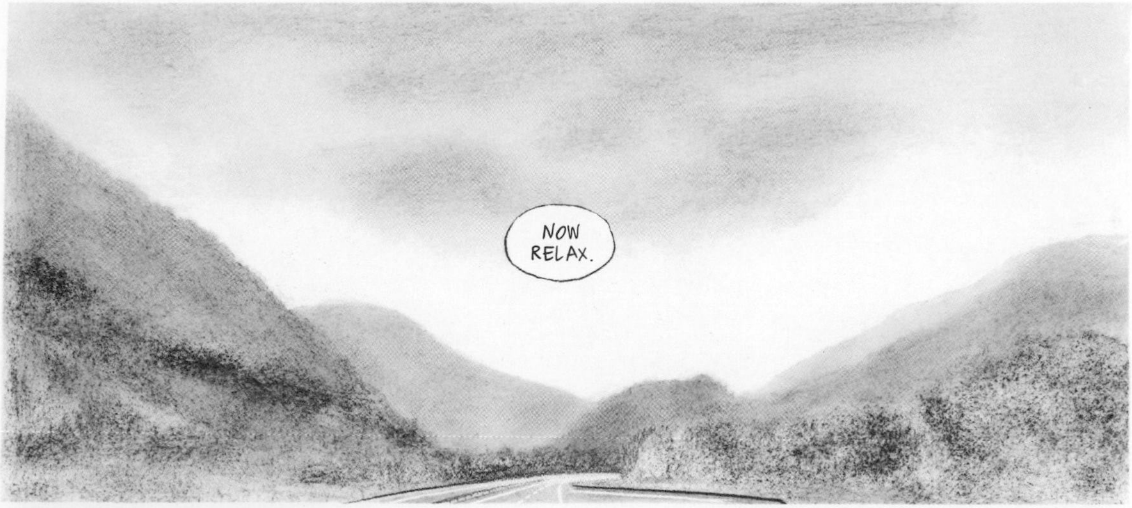
NOW RELAX.

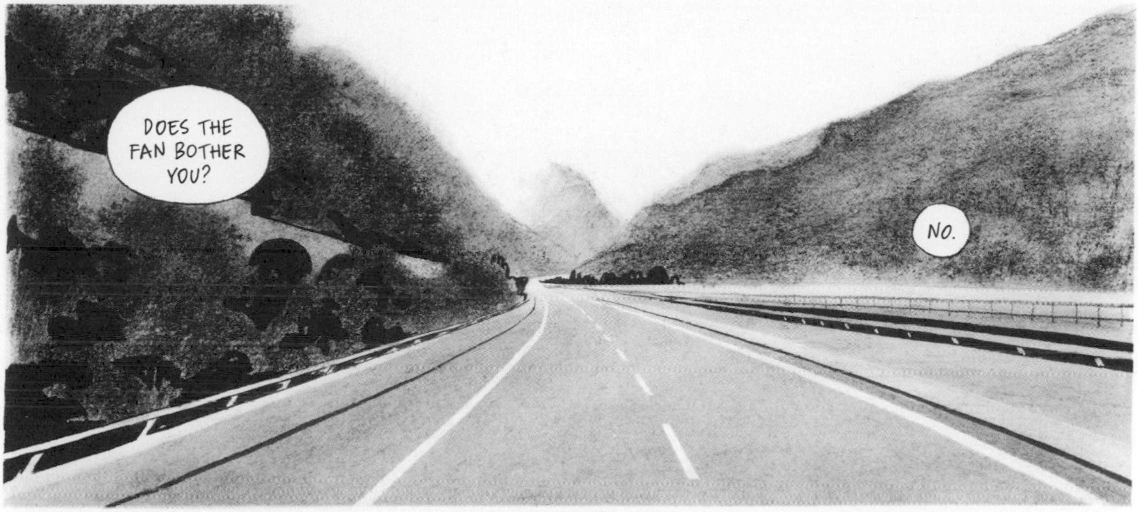
DOES THE FAN BOTHER YOU?
NO.

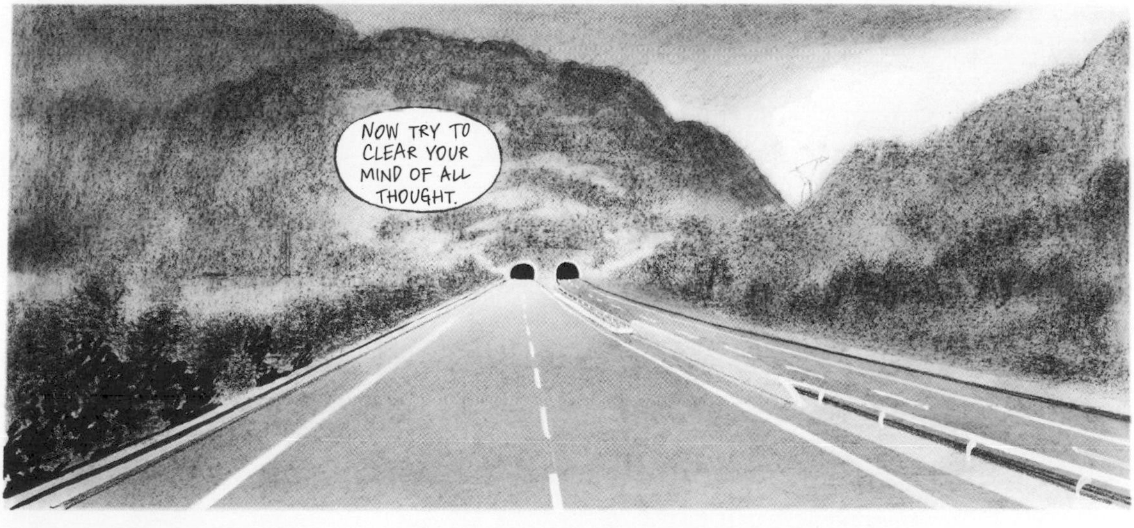
NOW TRY TO CLEAR YOUR MIND OF ALL THOUGHT.

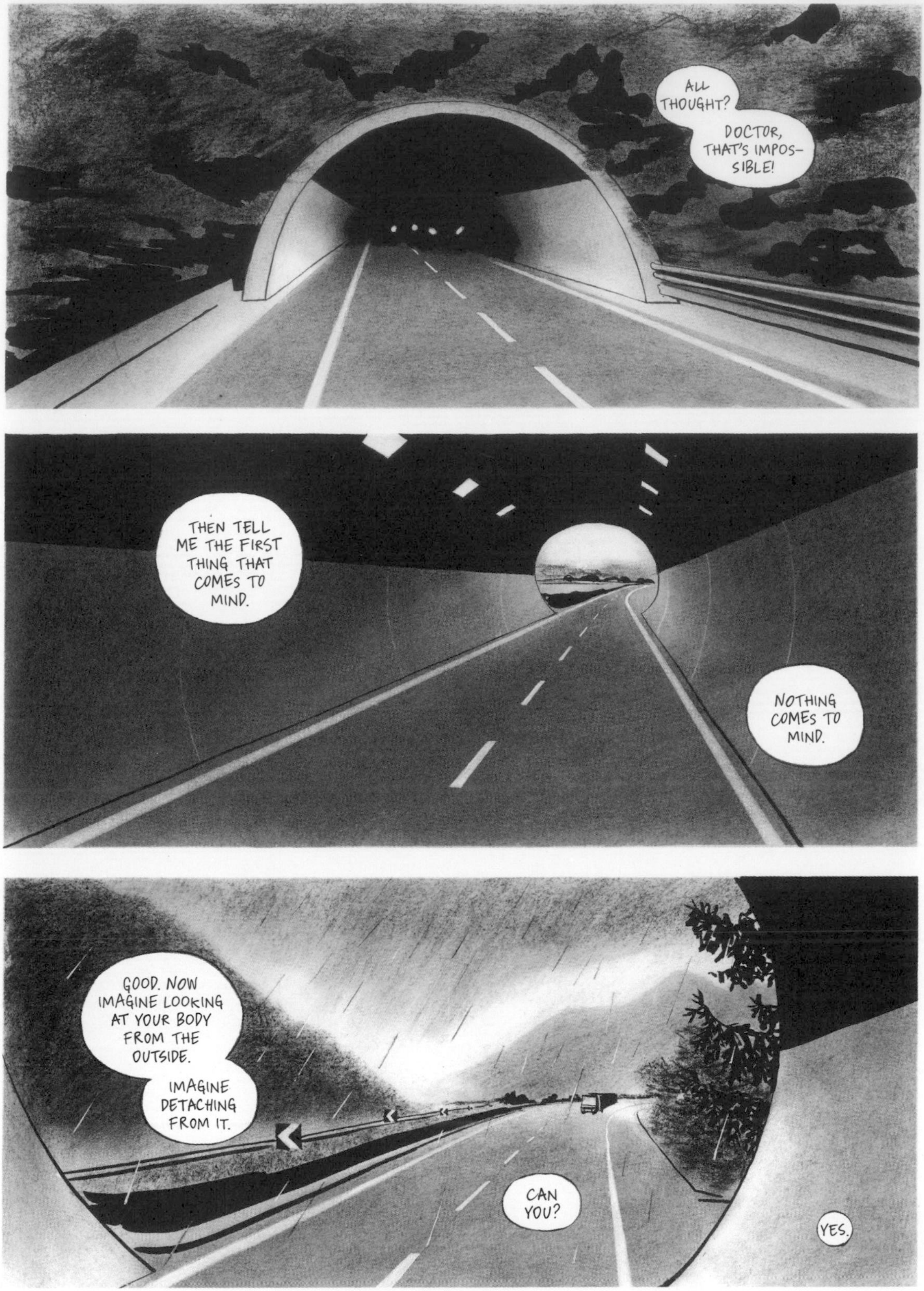
ALL THOUGHT?
DOCTOR, THAT'S IMPOSSIBLE!
THEN TELL ME THE FIRST THING THAT COMES TO MIND.
NOTHING COMES TO MIND.
GOOD. NOW IMAGINE LOOKING AT YOUR BODY FROM THE OUTSIDE.
IMAGINE DETACHING FROM IT.
CAN YOU?
YES.

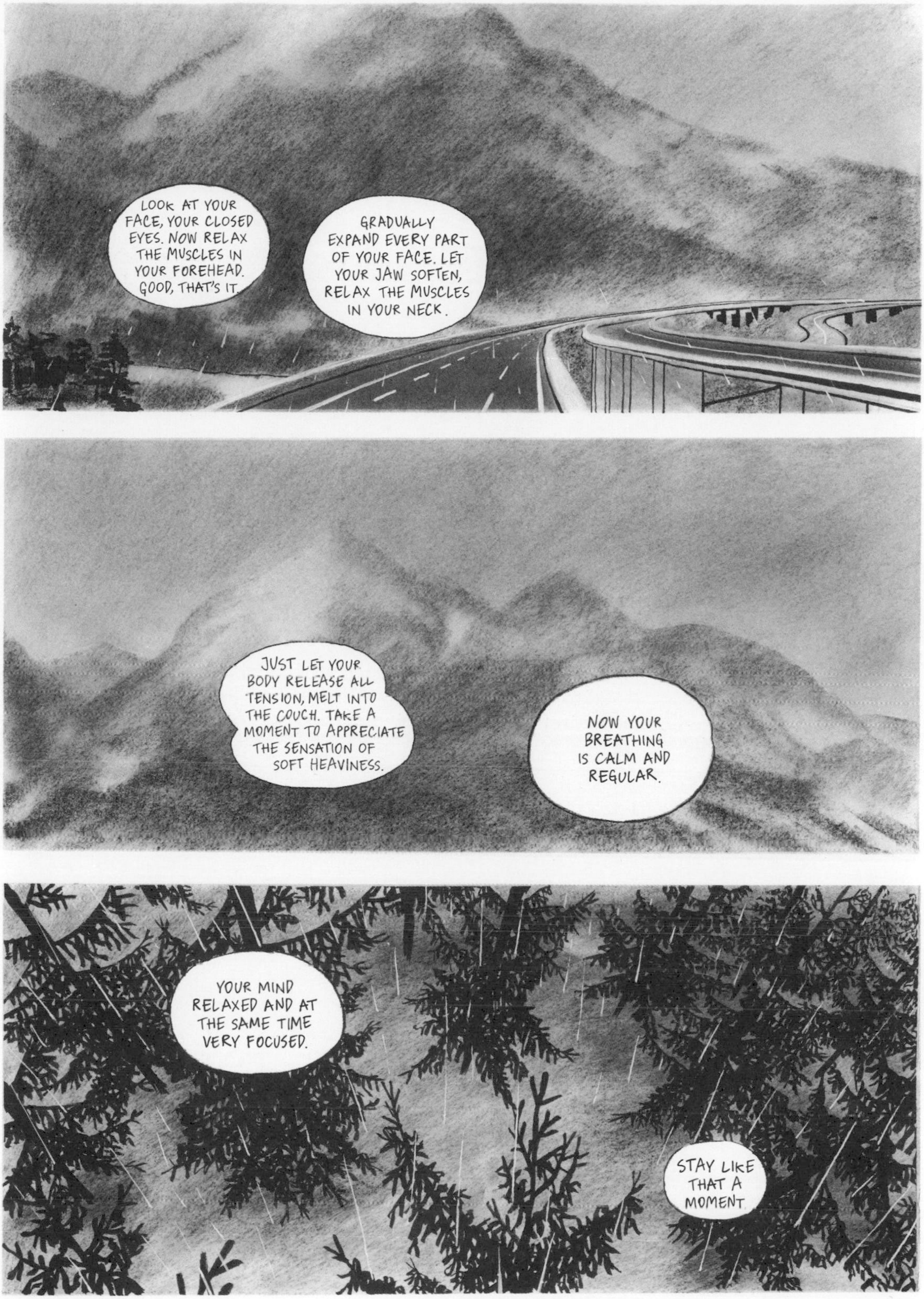
LOOK AT YOUR FACE, YOUR CLOSED EYES. NOW RELAX THE MUSCLES IN YOUR FOREHEAD. GOOD, THAT'S IT.
GRADUALLY EXPAND EVERY PART OF YOUR FACE. LET YOUR JAW SOFTEN, RELAX THE MUSCLES IN YOUR NECK.
JUST LET YOUR BODY RELEASE ALL TENSION, MELT INTO THE COUCH. TAKE A MOMENT TO APPRECIATE THE SENSATION OF SOFT HEAVINESS.
NOW YOUR BREATHING IS CALM AND REGULAR.
YOUR MIND RELAXED AND AT THE SAME TIME VERY FOCUSED.
STAY LIKE THAT A MOMENT.

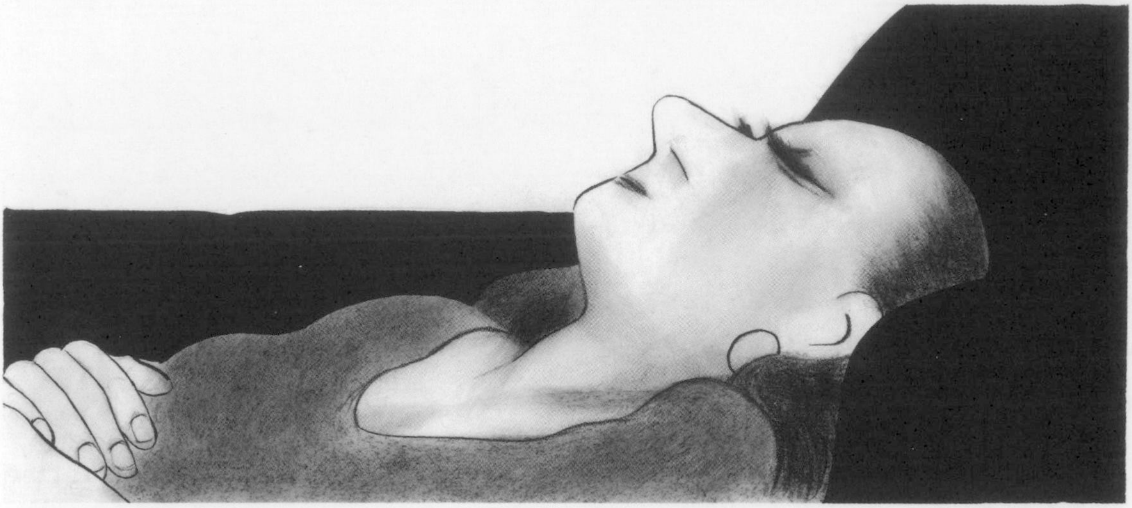

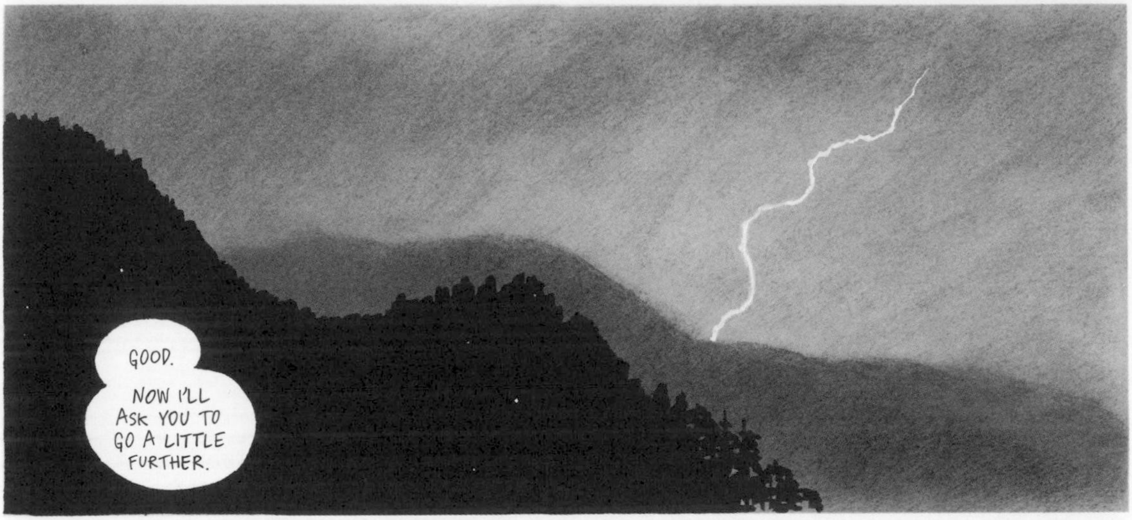
GOOD.
NOW I'LL ASK YOU TO GO A LITTLE FURTHER.

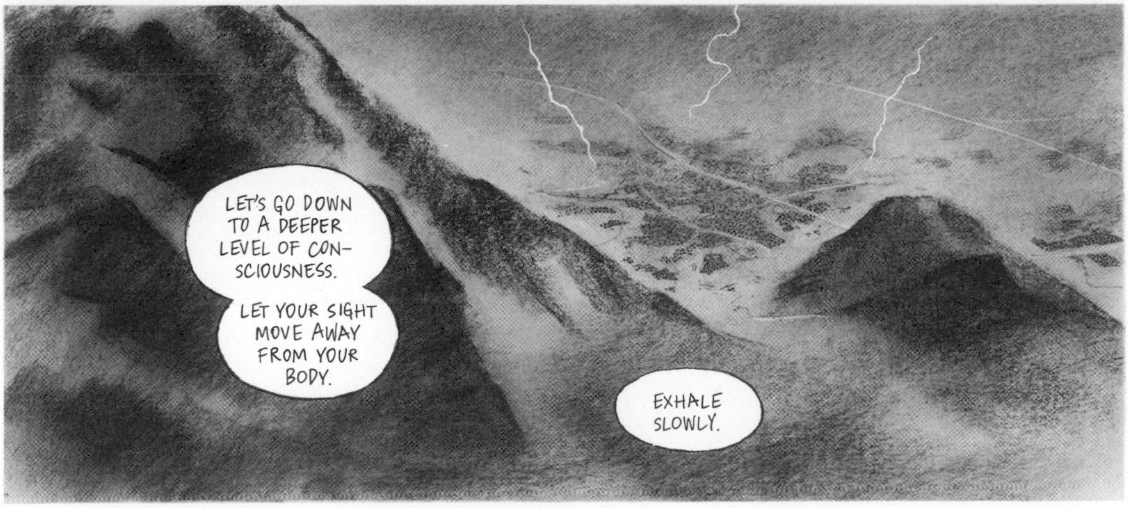
LET'S GO DOWN TO A DEEPER LEVEL OF CON- SCIOUSNESS.
LET YOUR SIGHT MOVE AWAY FROM YOUR BODY.
EXHALE SLOWLY.

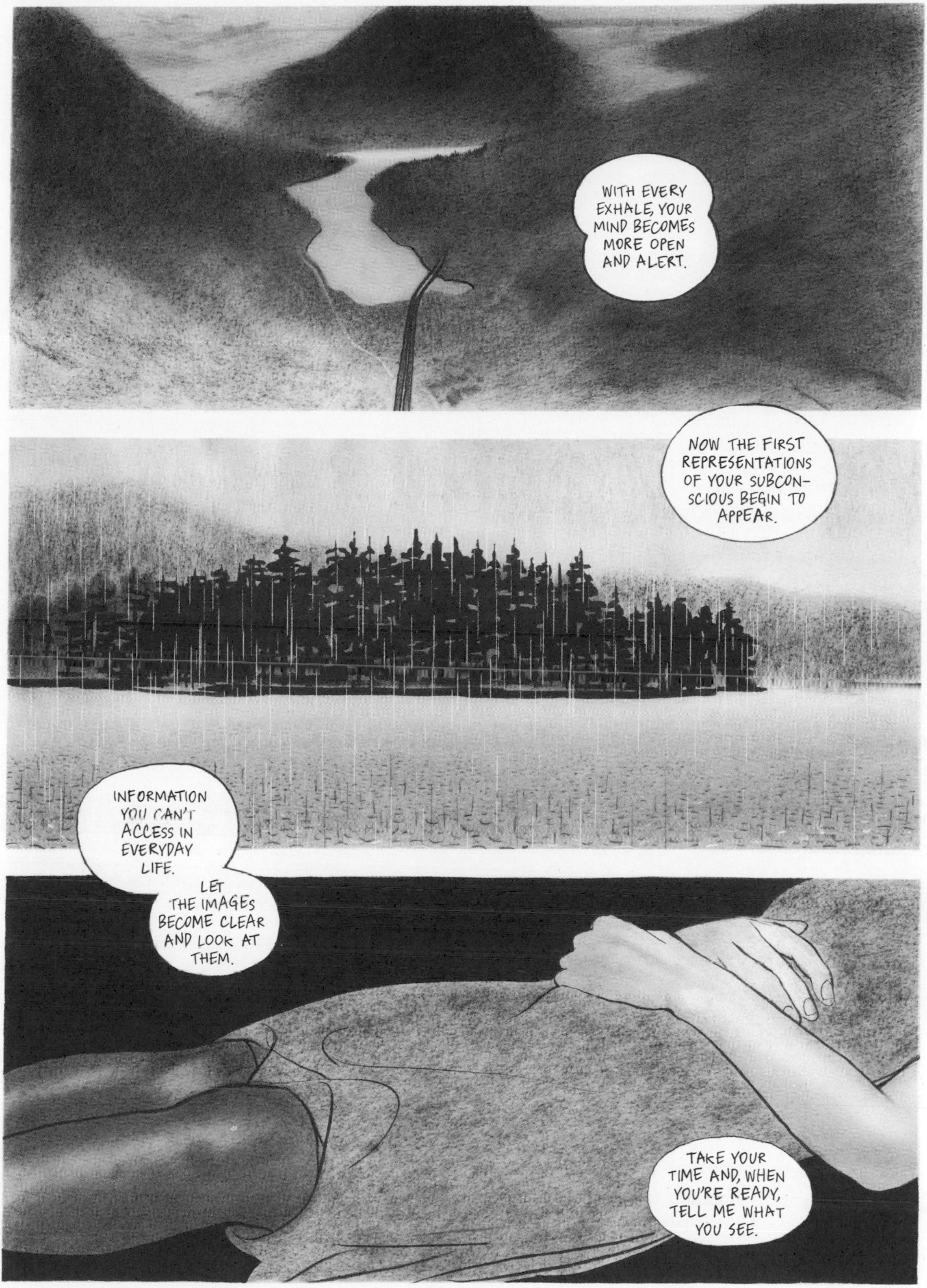
WITH EVERY EXHALE, YOUR MIND BECOMES MORE OPEN AND ALERT.
NOW THE FIRST REPRESENTATIONS OF YOUR SUBCON-SCIOUS BEGIN TO APPEAR.
INFORMATION YOU CAN'T ACCESS IN EVERYDAY LIFE.
LET THE IMAGES BECOME CLEAR AND LOOK AT THEM.
TAKE YOUR TIME AND, WHEN YOU'RE READY, TELL ME WHAT YOU SEE.

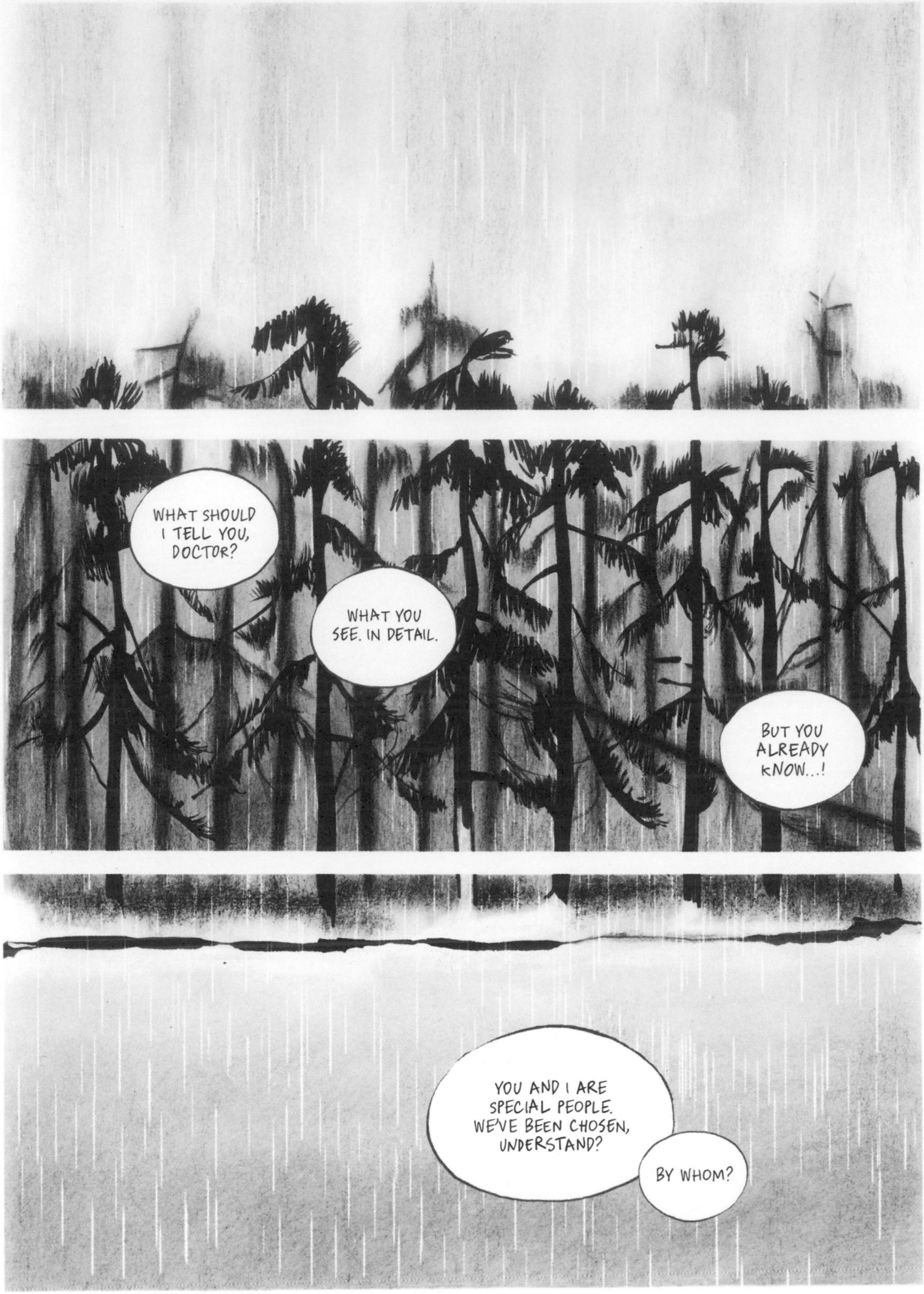
WHAT SHOULD I TELL YOU, DOCTOR?
WHAT YOU SEE. IN DETAIL.
BUT YOU ALREADY KNOW...!
YOU AND I ARE SPECIAL PEOPLE. WE'VE BEEN CHOSEN, UNDERSTAND?
BY WHOM?

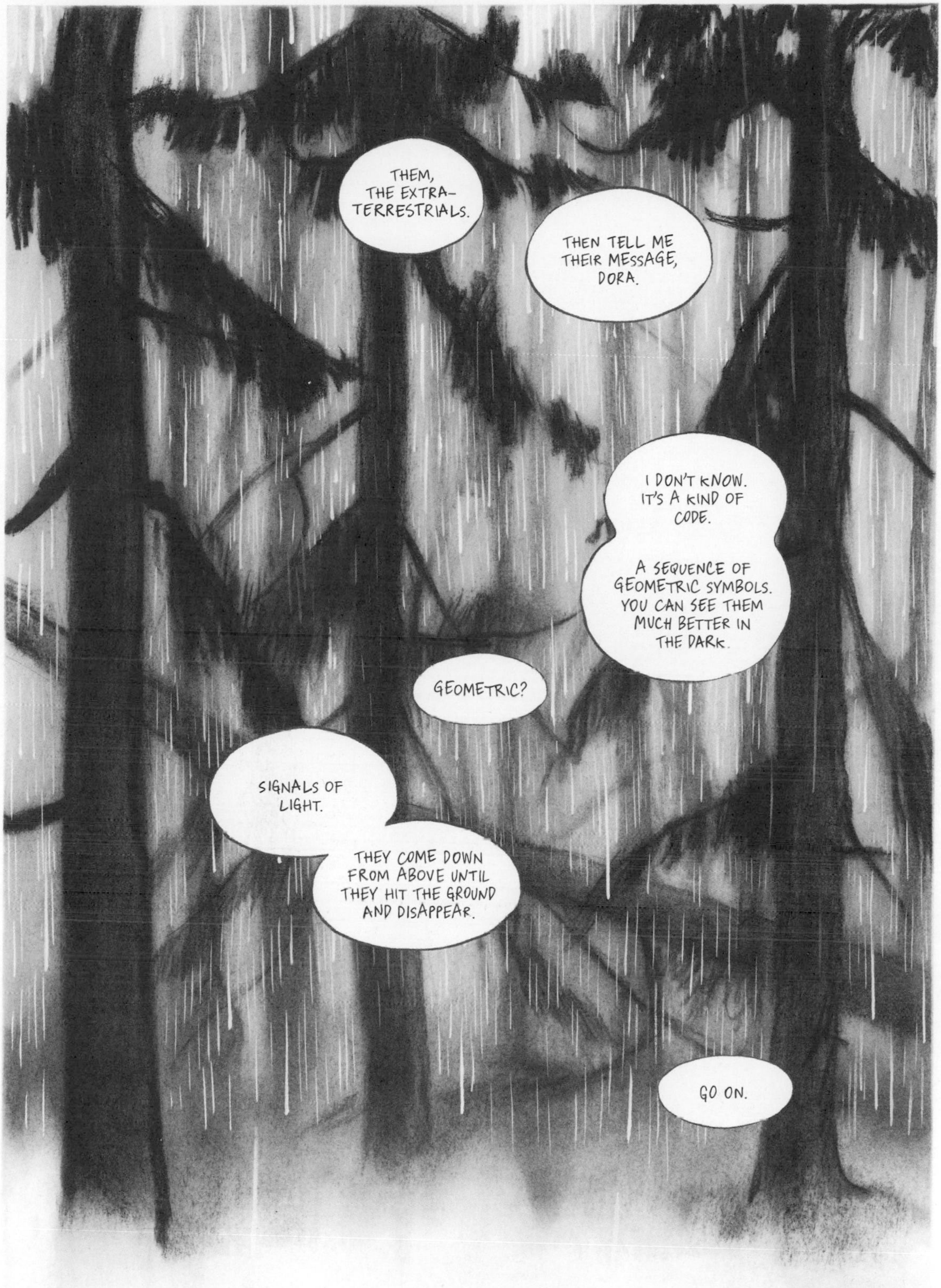
THEM, THE EXTRA-TERRESTRIALS.
THEN TELL ME THEIR MESSAGE, DORA.
I DON'T KNOW. IT'S A KIND OF CODE.
A SEQUENCE OF GEOMETRIC SYMBOLS. YOU CAN SEE THEM MUCH BETTER IN THE DARK.
GEOMETRIC?
SIGNALS OF LIGHT.
THEY COME DOWN FROM ABOVE UNTIL THEY HIT THE GROUND AND DISAPPEAR.
GO ON.

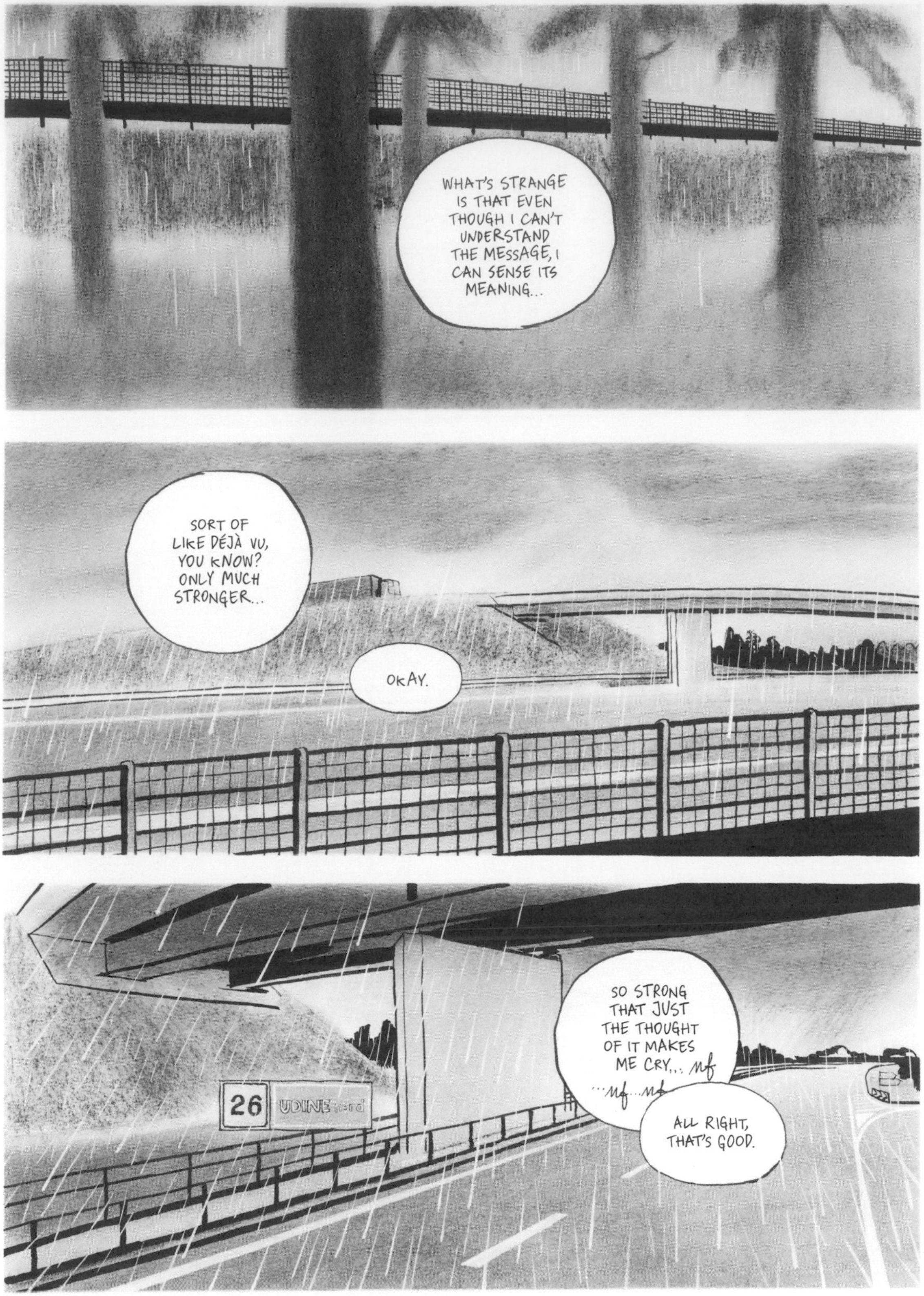
WHAT'S STRANGE IS THAT EVEN THOUGH I CAN'T UNDERSTAND THE MESSAGE, I CAN SENSE ITS MEANING...
SORT OF LIKE DÉJÀ VU, YOU KNOW? ONLY MUCH STRONGER...
OKAY.
SO STRONG THAT JUST THE THOUGHT OF IT MAKES ME CRY... MF
...MF...MF
ALL RIGHT, THAT'S GOOD.
26
UDINE nord

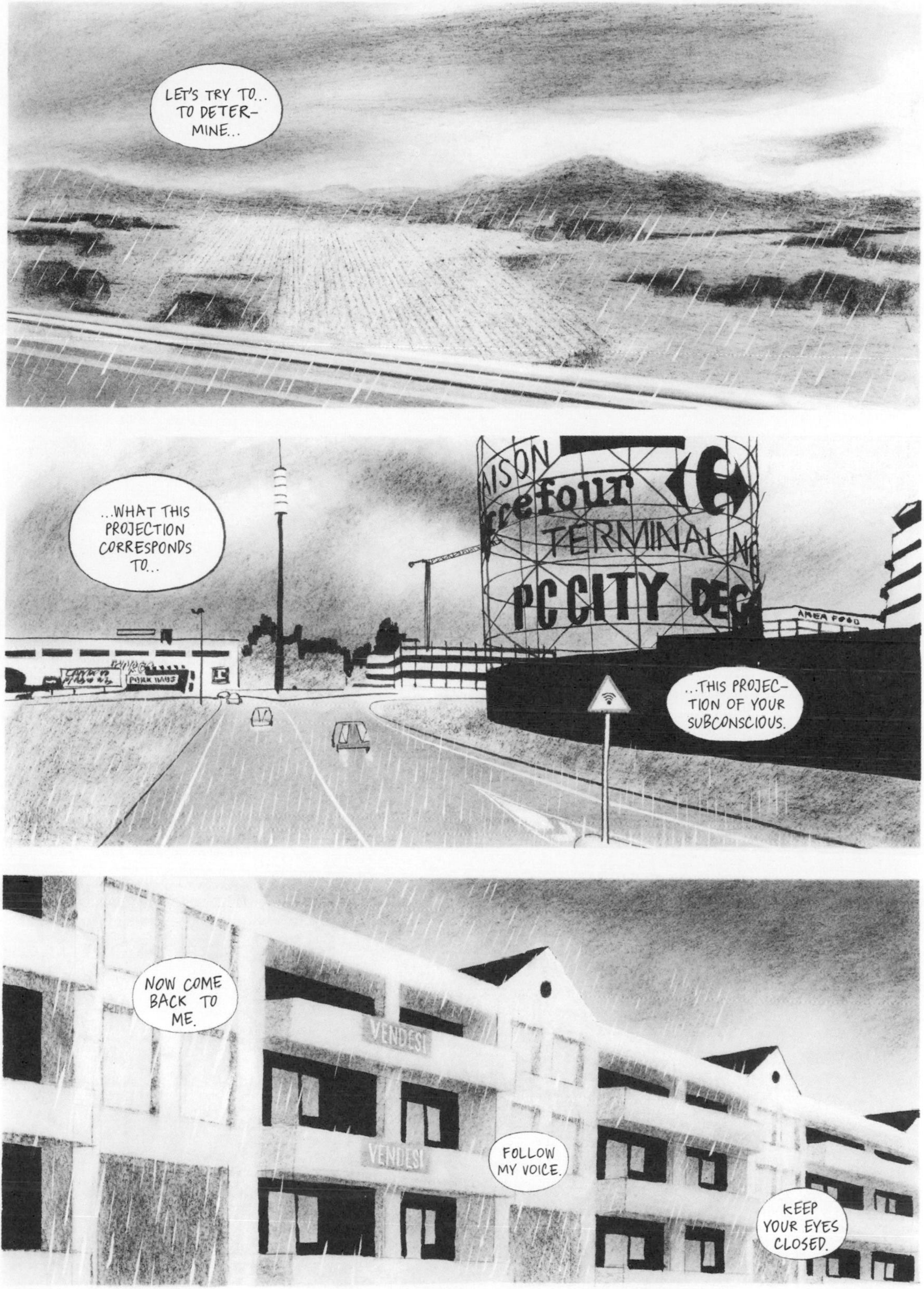
LET'S TRY TO... TO DETERMINE...
...WHAT THIS PROJECTION CORRESPONDS TO...
TERMINAL
PC CITY
...THIS PROJECTION OF YOUR SUBCONSCIOUS.
NOW COME BACK TO ME.
VENDESI
VENDESI
FOLLOW MY VOICE.
KEEP YOUR EYES CLOSED.

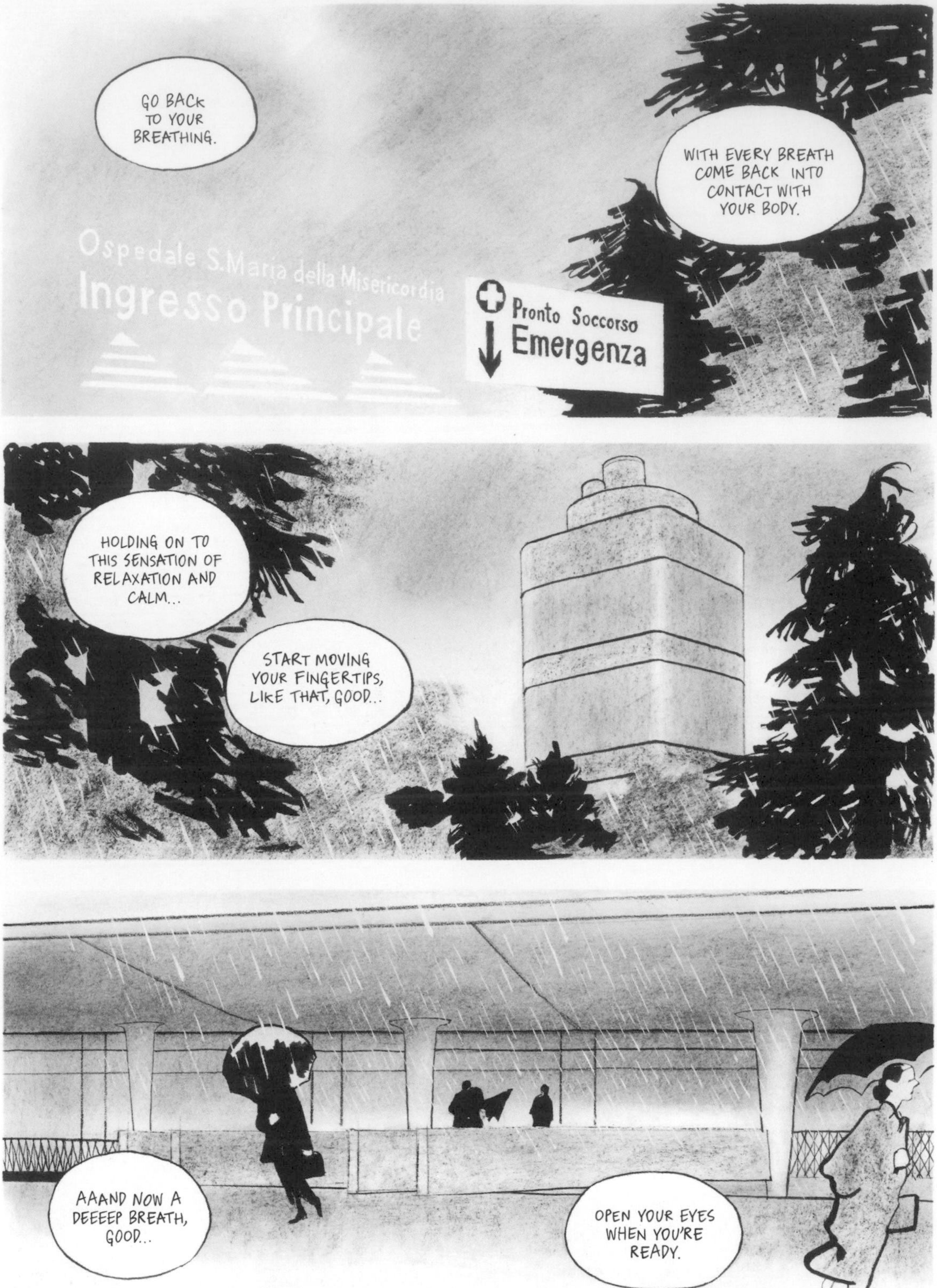
GO BACK TO YOUR BREATHING.
WITH EVERY BREATH COME BACK INTO CONTACT WITH YOUR BODY.
Ospedale S.Maria della Misericordia
Ingresso Principale
Pronto Soccorso
Emergenza
HOLDING ON TO THIS SENSATION OF RELAXATION AND CALM...
START MOVING YOUR FINGERTIPS, LIKE THAT, GOOD...
AAAND NOW A DEEEEP BREATH, GOOD...
OPEN YOUR EYES WHEN YOU'RE READY.

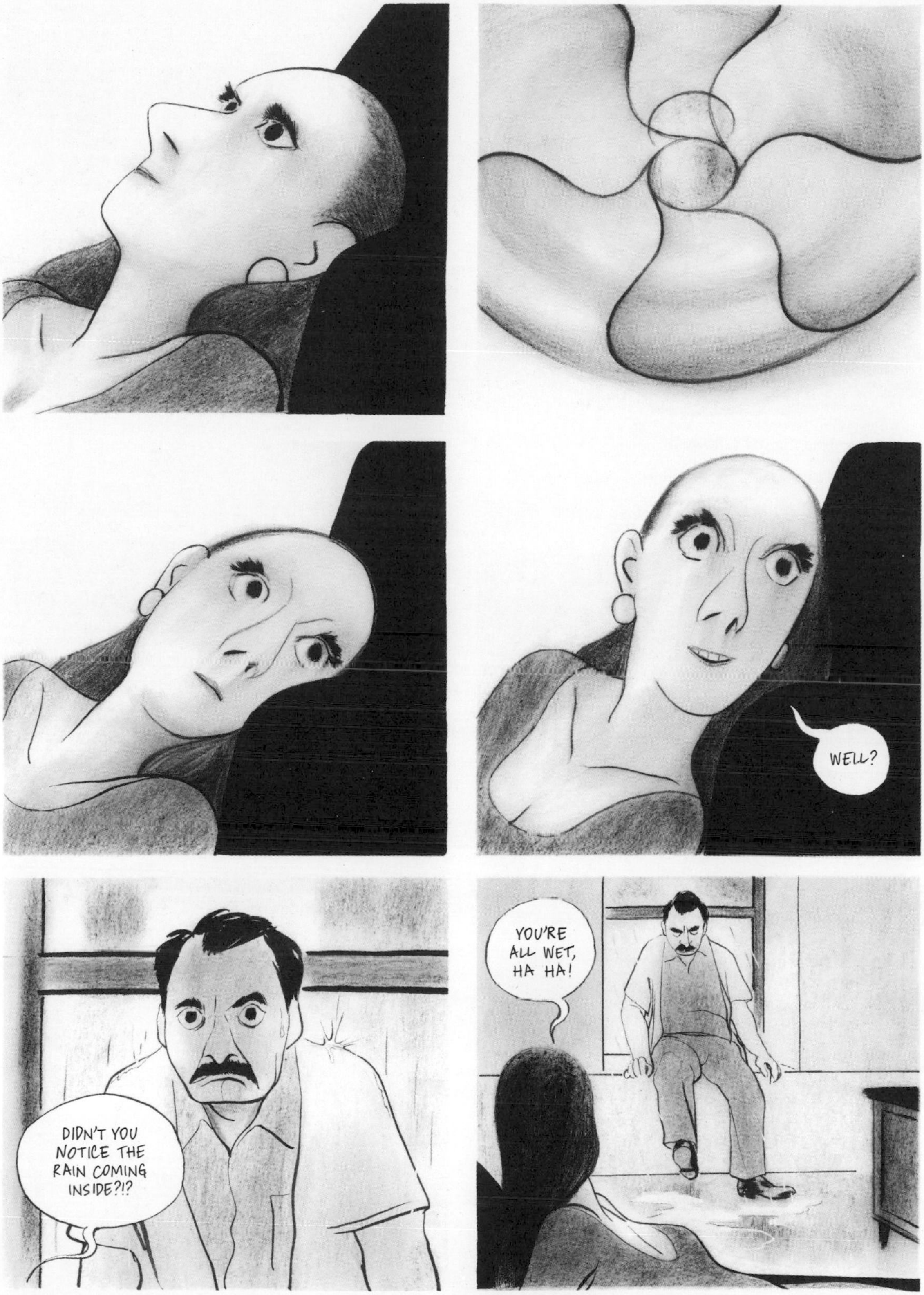
WELL?
DIDN'T YOU NOTICE THE RAIN COMING INSIDE?!?
YOU'RE ALL WET, HA HA!

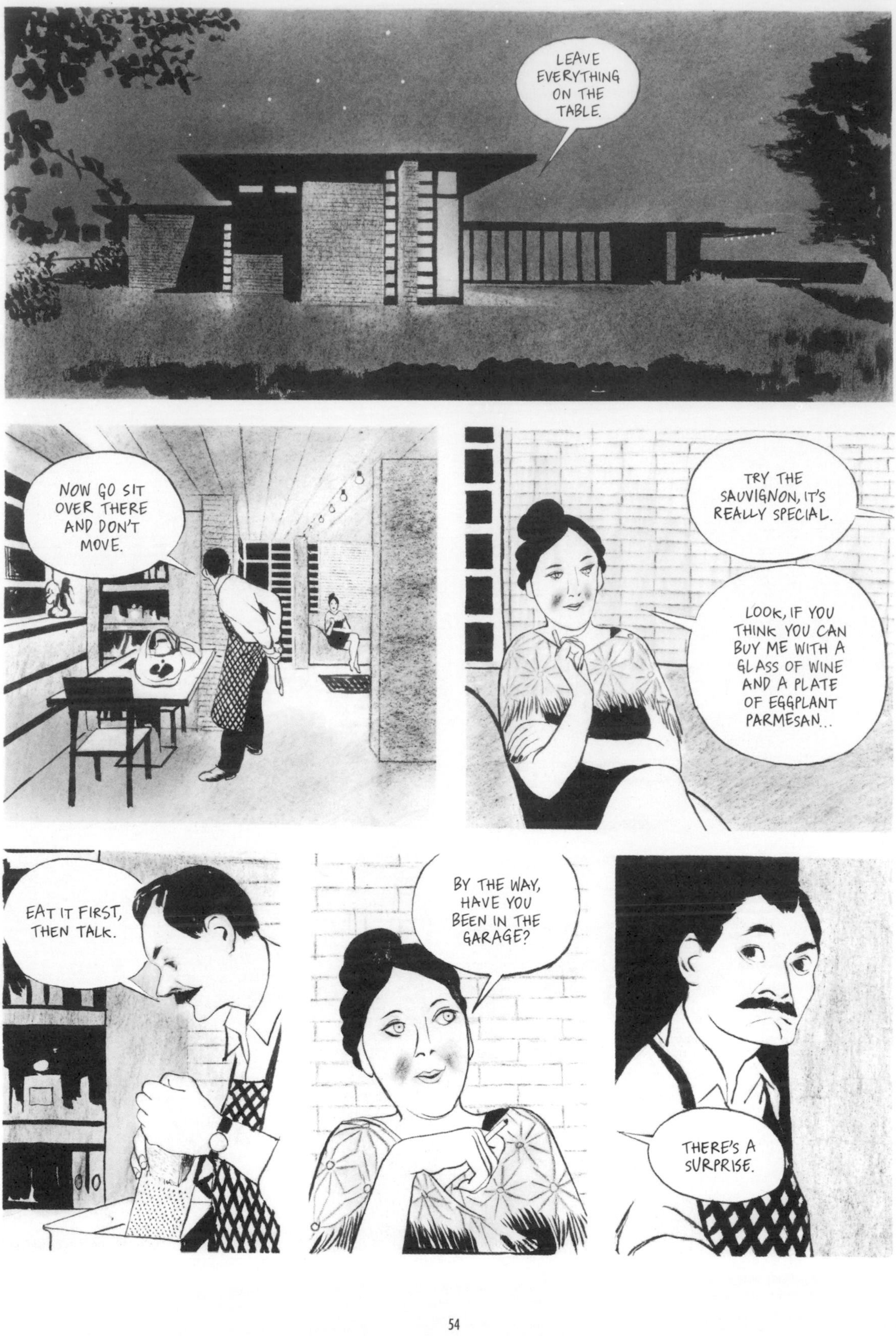

LEAVE EVERYTHING ON THE TABLE.
NOW GO SIT OVER THERE AND DON'T MOVE.
TRY THE SAUVIGNON, IT'S REALLY SPECIAL.
LOOK, IF YOU THINK YOU CAN BUY ME WITH A GLASS OF WINE AND A PLATE OF EGGPLANT PARMESAN...
EAT IT FIRST, THEN TALK.
BY THE WAY, HAVE YOU BEEN IN THE GARAGE?
THERE'S A SURPRISE.

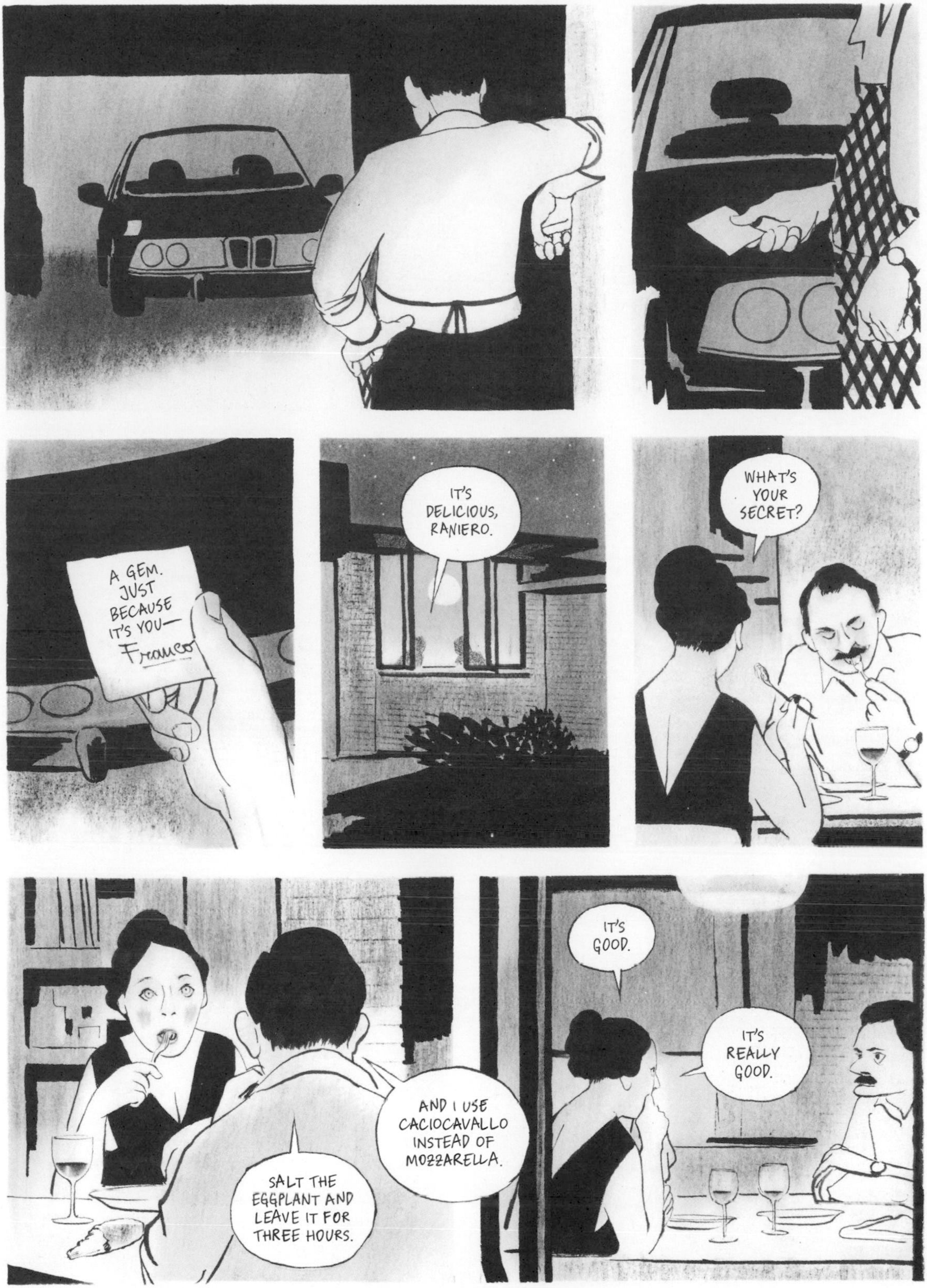
A GEM. JUST BECAUSE IT'S YOU— Franco
IT'S DELICIOUS, RANIERO.
WHAT'S YOUR SECRET?
SALT THE EGGPLANT AND LEAVE IT FOR THREE HOURS.
AND I USE CACIOCAVALLO INSTEAD OF MOZZARELLA.
IT'S GOOD.
IT'S REALLY GOOD.

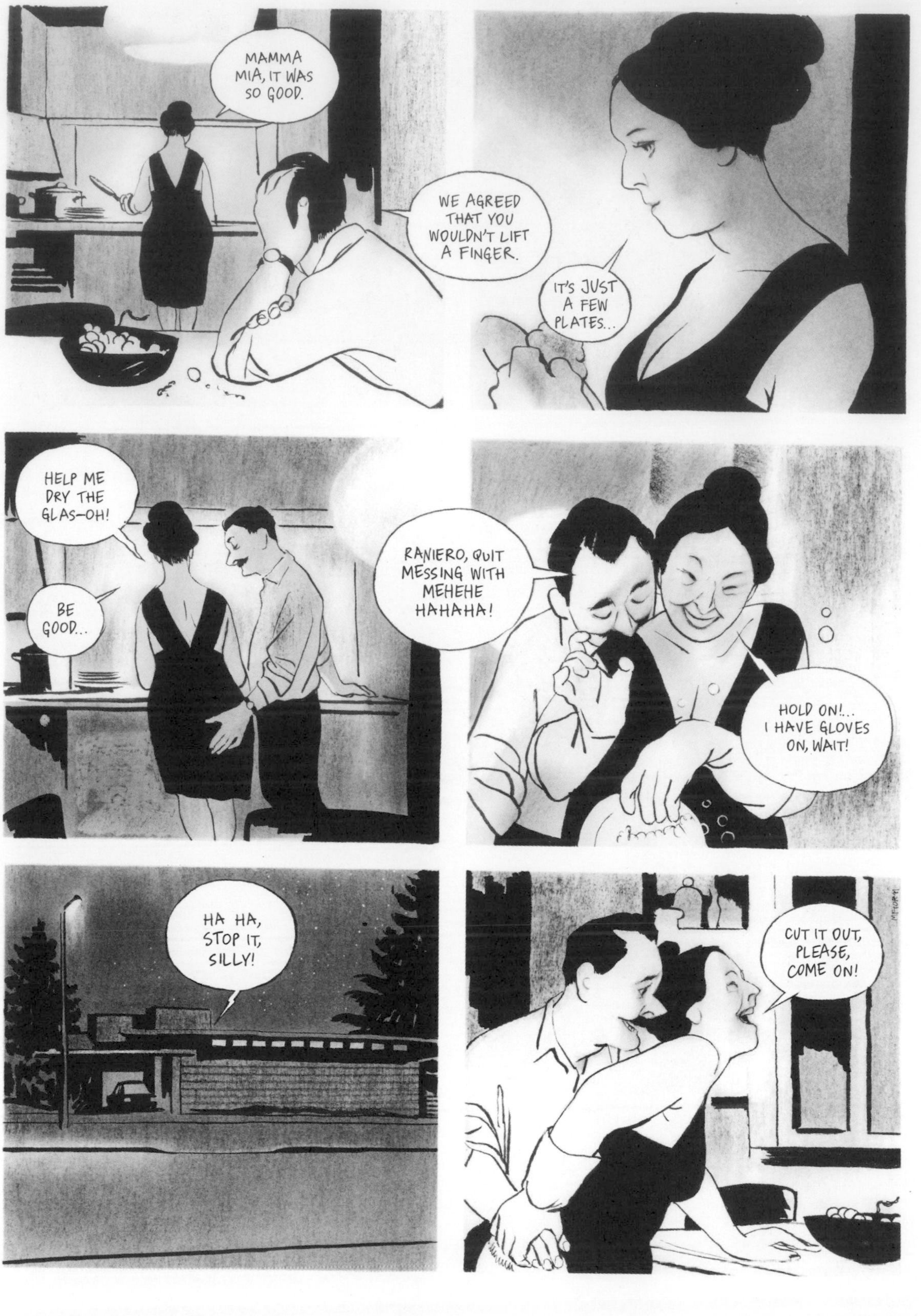
MAMMA MIA, IT WAS SO GOOD.
WE AGREED THAT YOU WOULDN'T LIFT A FINGER.
IT'S JUST A FEW PLATES...
HELP ME DRY THE GLAS-OH!
BE GOOD...
RANIERO, QUIT MESSING WITH MEHEHE HAHAHA!
HOLD ON!... I HAVE GLOVES ON, WAIT!
HA HA, STOP IT, SILLY!
CUT IT OUT, PLEASE, COME ON!

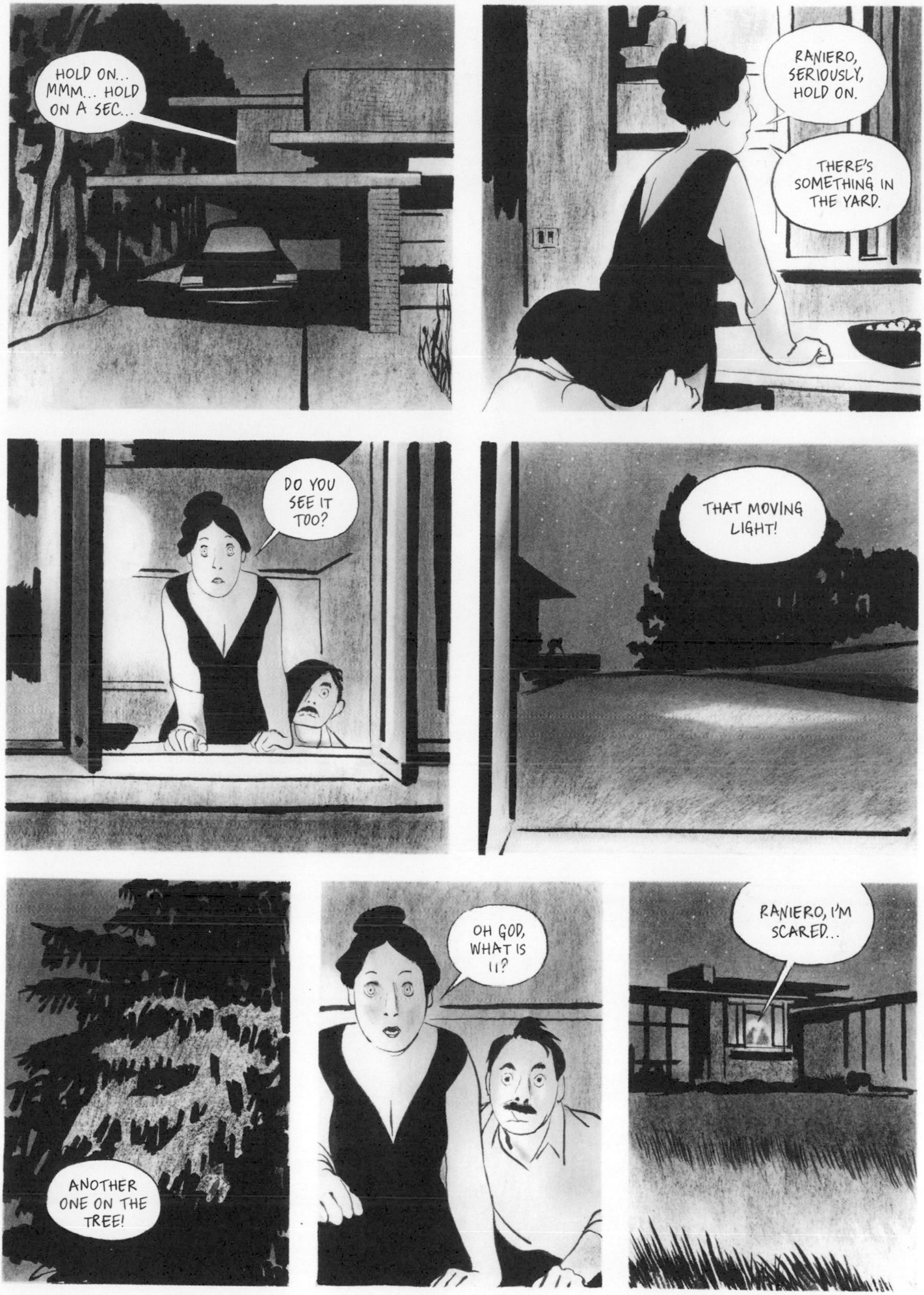
HOLD ON... MMM... HOLD ON A SEC...
RANIERO, SERIOUSLY, HOLD ON.
THERE'S SOMETHING IN THE YARD.
DO YOU SEE IT TOO?
THAT MOVING LIGHT!
ANOTHER ONE ON THE TREE!
OH GOD, WHAT IS IT?
RANIERO, I'M SCARED...

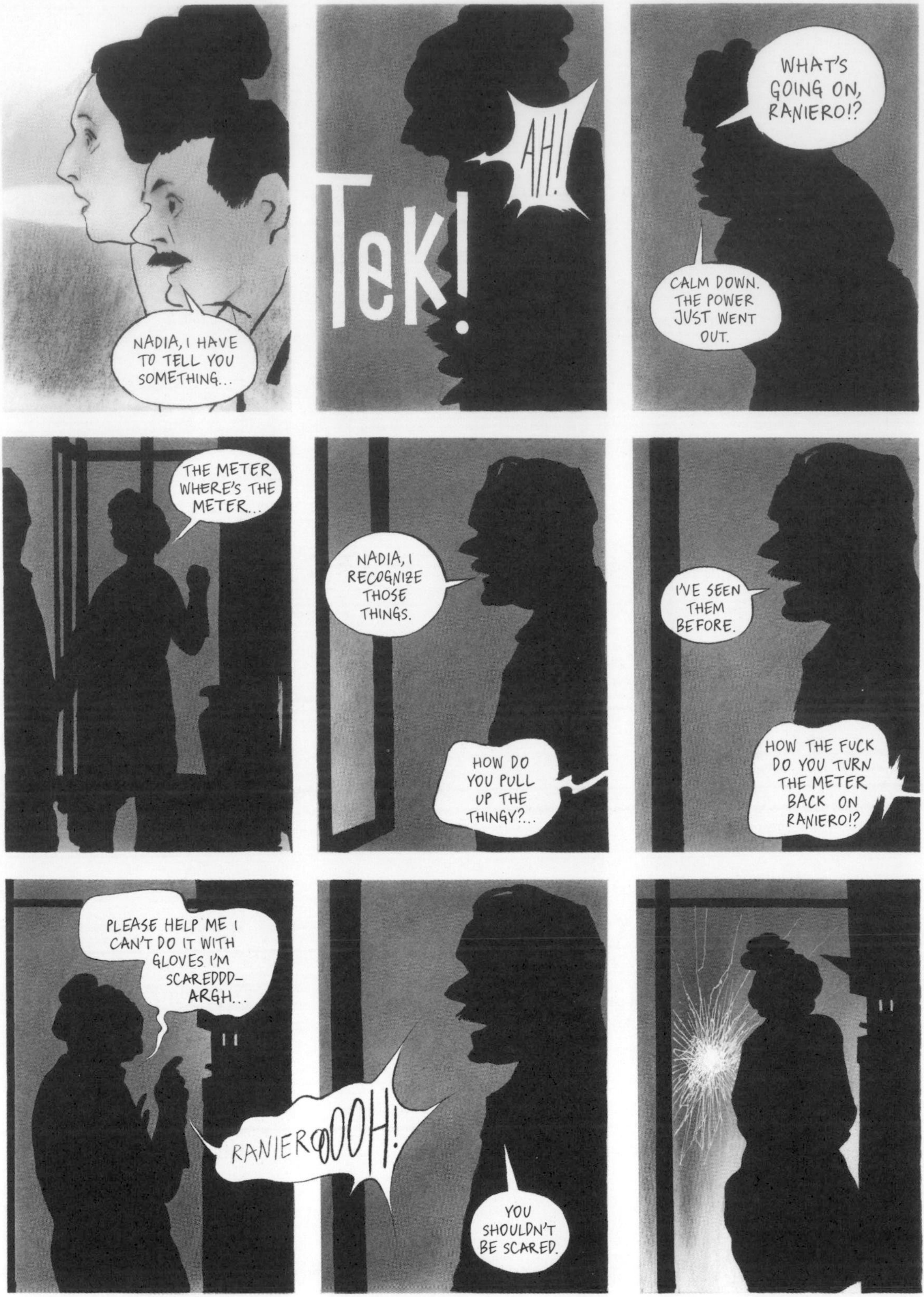
NADIA, I HAVE TO TELL YOU SOMETHING...
TEK!
AH!
WHAT'S GOING ON, RANIERO!?
CALM DOWN. THE POWER JUST WENT OUT.
THE METER WHERE'S THE METER...
NADIA, I RECOGNIZE THOSE THINGS.
HOW DO YOU PULL UP THE THINGY?...
I'VE SEEN THEM BEFORE.
HOW THE FUCK DO YOU TURN THE METER BACK ON RANIERO!?
PLEASE HELP ME I CAN'T DO IT WITH GLOVES I'M SCAREDDD-ARGH...
RANIEROOOOH!
YOU SHOULDN'T BE SCARED.

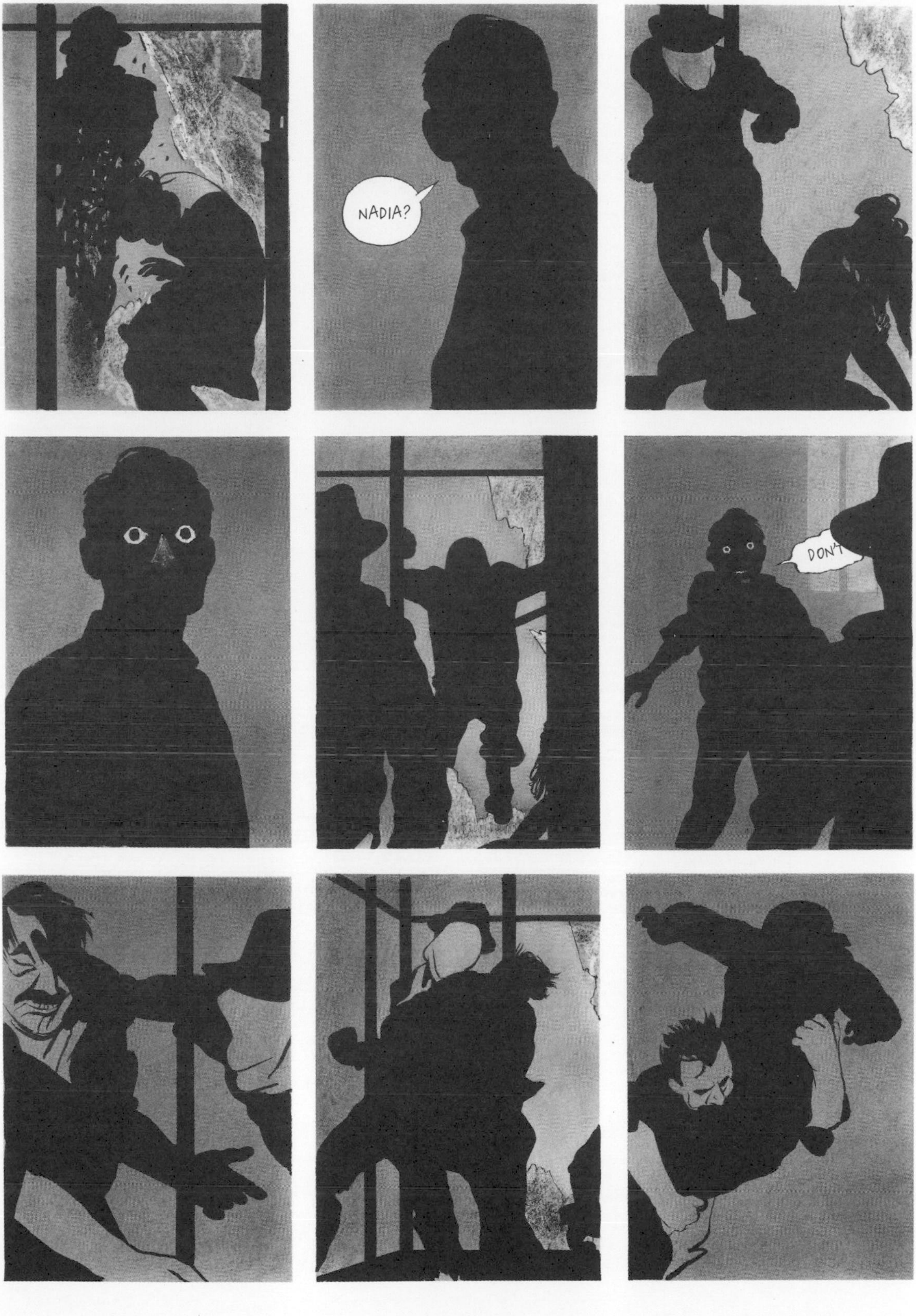
NADIA?
DON'T

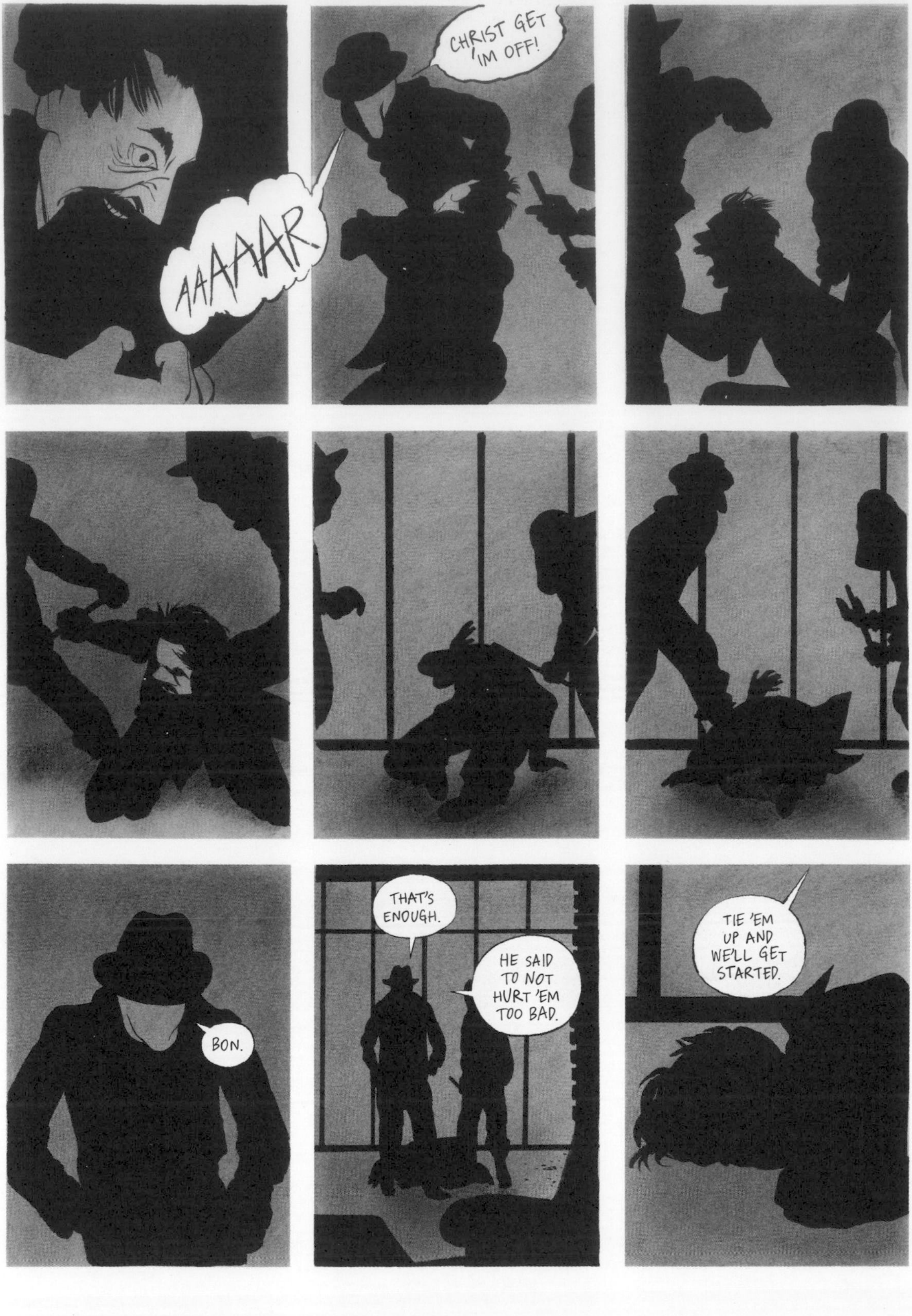
AAAAAR
CHRIST GET 'IM OFF!
BON.
THAT'S ENOUGH.
HE SAID TO NOT HURT 'EM TOO BAD.
TIE 'EM UP AND WE'LL GET STARTED.

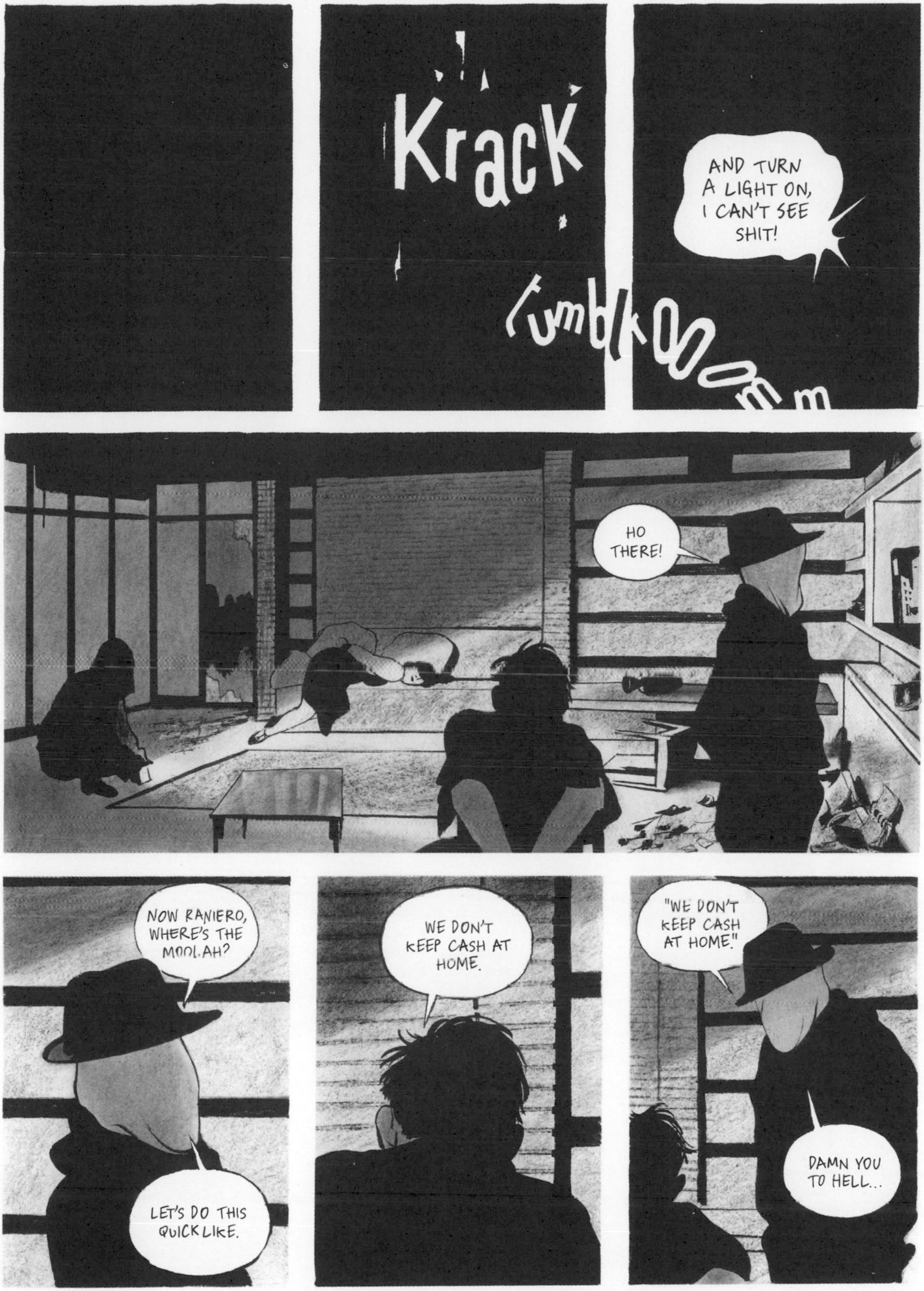
Krack
AND TURN A LIGHT ON, I CAN'T SEE SHIT!
HO THERE!
NOW RANIERO, WHERE'S THE MOOLAH?
LET'S DO THIS QUICKLIKE.
WE DON'T KEEP CASH AT HOME.
"WE DON'T KEEP CASH AT HOME."
DAMN YOU TO HELL...

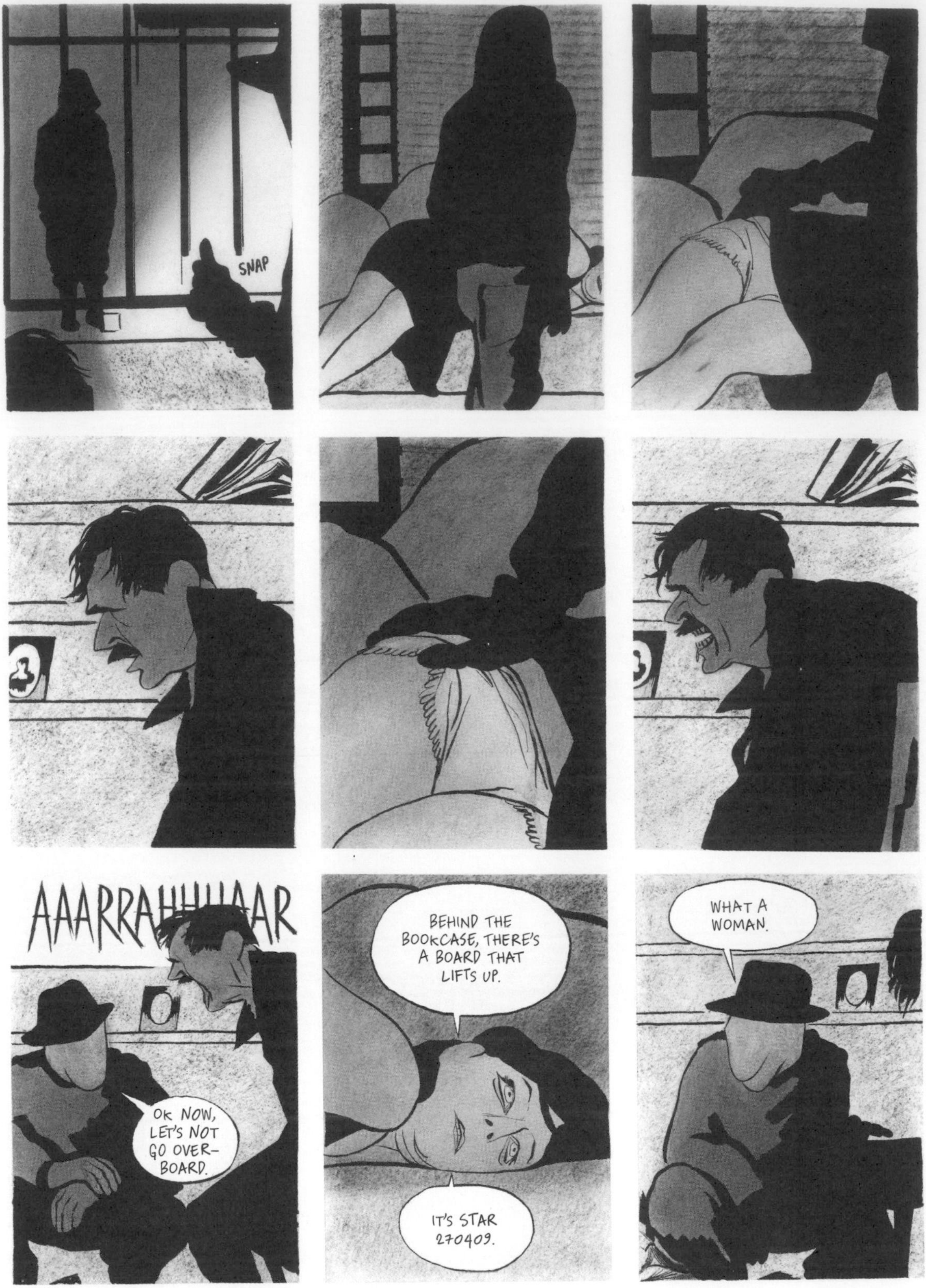
SNAP
AAARRAHHHAAR
OK NOW, LET'S NOT GO OVER-BOARD.
BEHIND THE BOOKCASE, THERE'S A BOARD THAT LIFTS UP.
IT'S STAR 270409.
WHAT A WOMAN.

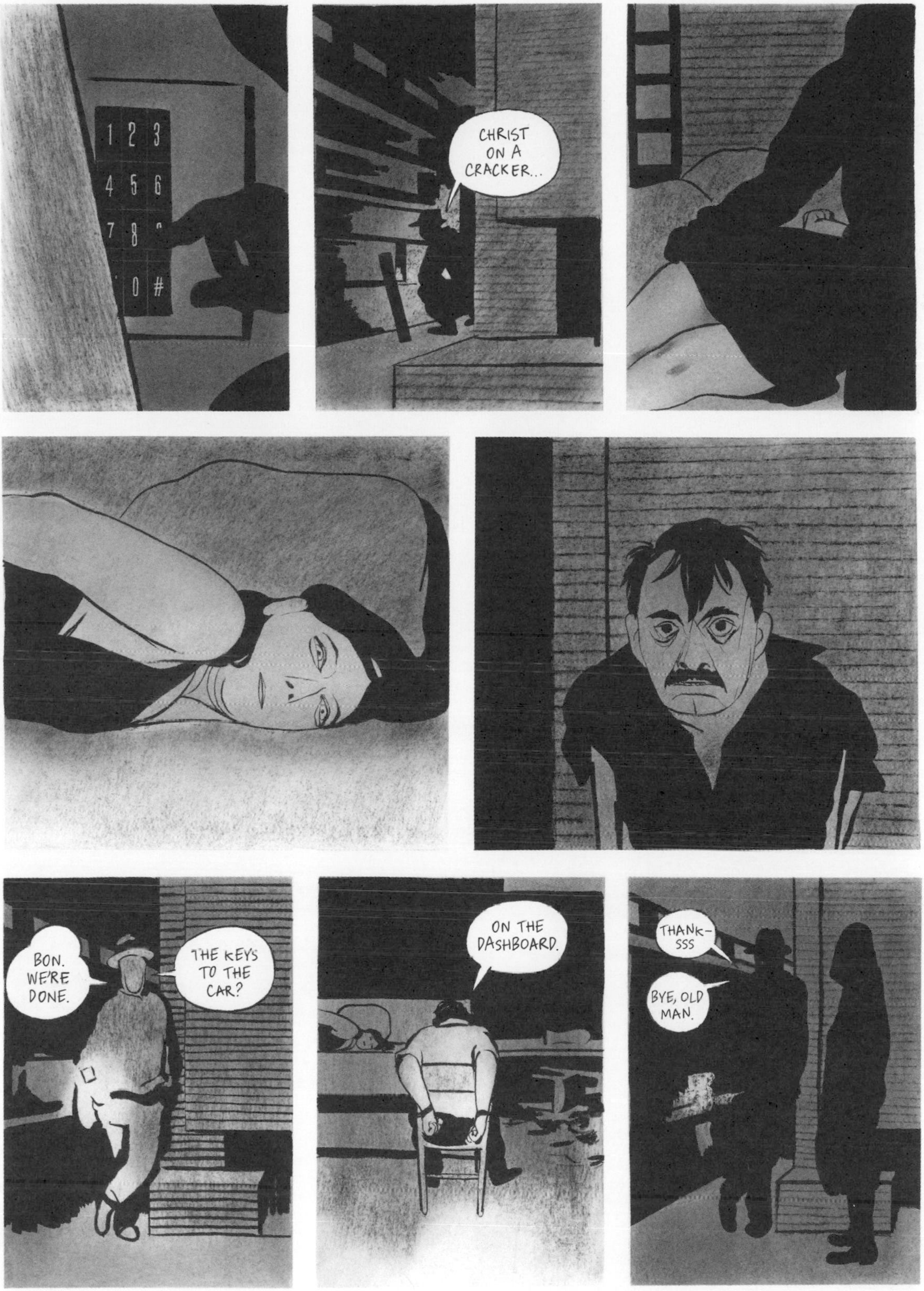
1 2 3
4 5 6
7 8
0 #
CHRIST ON A CRACKER...
BON. WE'RE DONE.
THE KEYS TO THE CAR?
ON THE DASHBOARD.
THANK-SSS
BYE, OLD MAN.

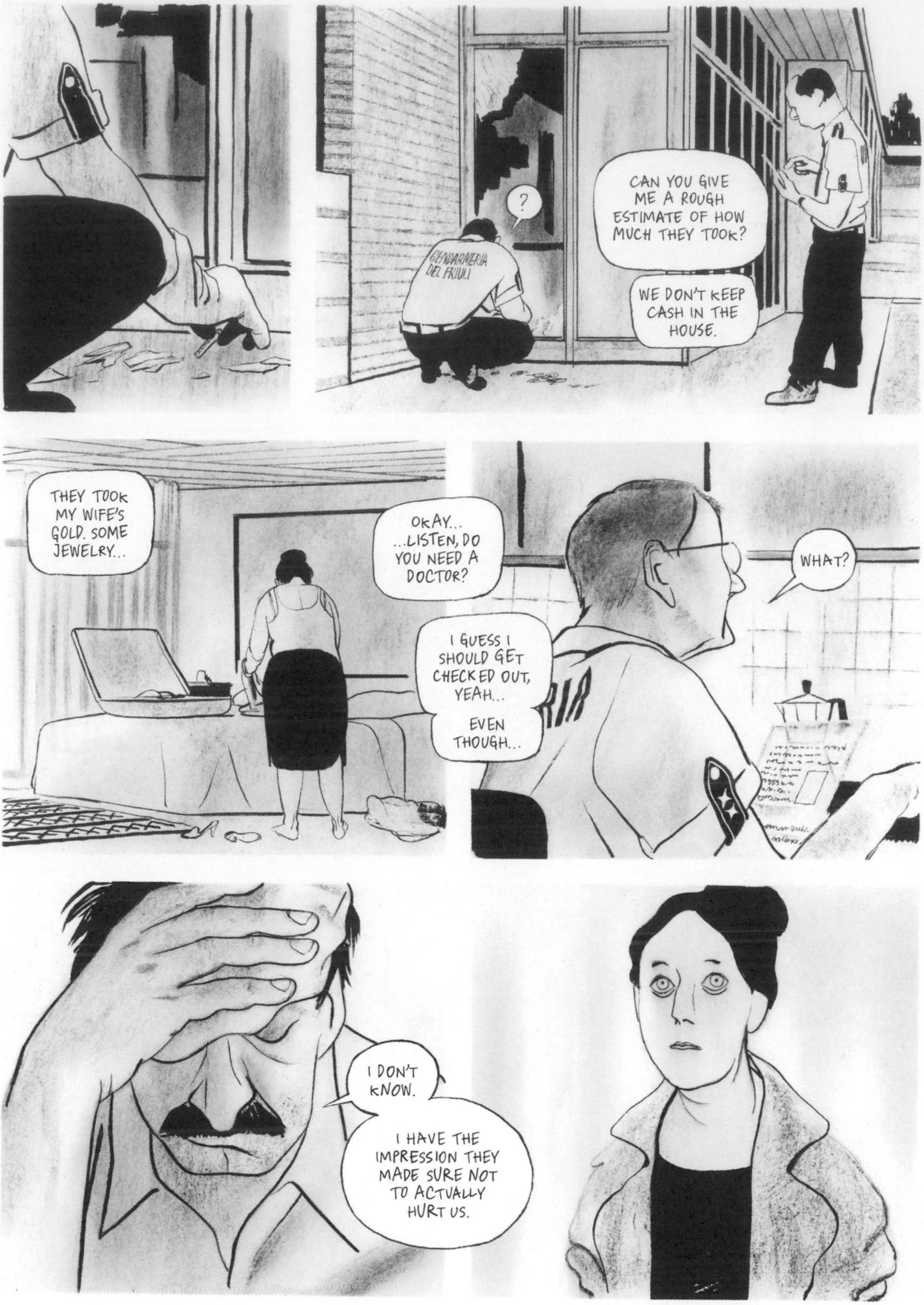
?
CAN YOU GIVE ME A ROUGH ESTIMATE OF HOW MUCH THEY TOOK?
WE DON'T KEEP CASH IN THE HOUSE.
GENDARMERIA DEL FRIULI
THEY TOOK MY WIFE'S GOLD. SOME JEWELRY...
OKAY... ...LISTEN, DO YOU NEED A DOCTOR?
WHAT?
I GUESS I SHOULD GET CHECKED OUT, YEAH...
EVEN THOUGH...
I DON'T KNOW.
I HAVE THE IMPRESSION THEY MADE SURE NOT TO ACTUALLY HURT US.

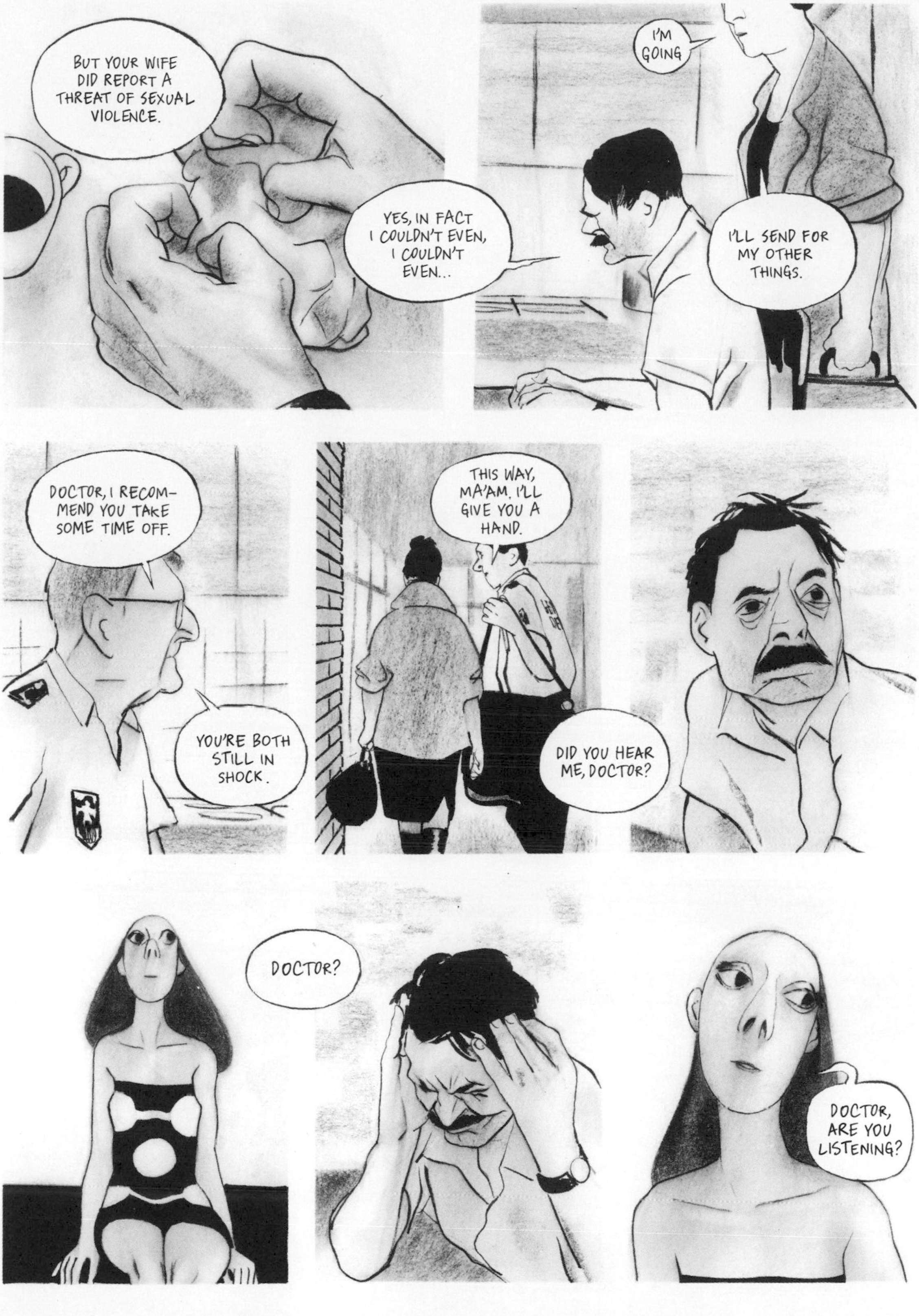
BUT YOUR WIFE DID REPORT A THREAT OF SEXUAL VIOLENCE.
YES, IN FACT I COULDN'T EVEN, I COULDN'T EVEN...
I'M GOING
I'LL SEND FOR MY OTHER THINGS.
DOCTOR, I RECOMMEND YOU TAKE SOME TIME OFF.
YOU'RE BOTH STILL IN SHOCK.
THIS WAY, MA'AM. I'LL GIVE YOU A HAND.
DID YOU HEAR ME, DOCTOR?
DOCTOR?
DOCTOR, ARE YOU LISTENING?

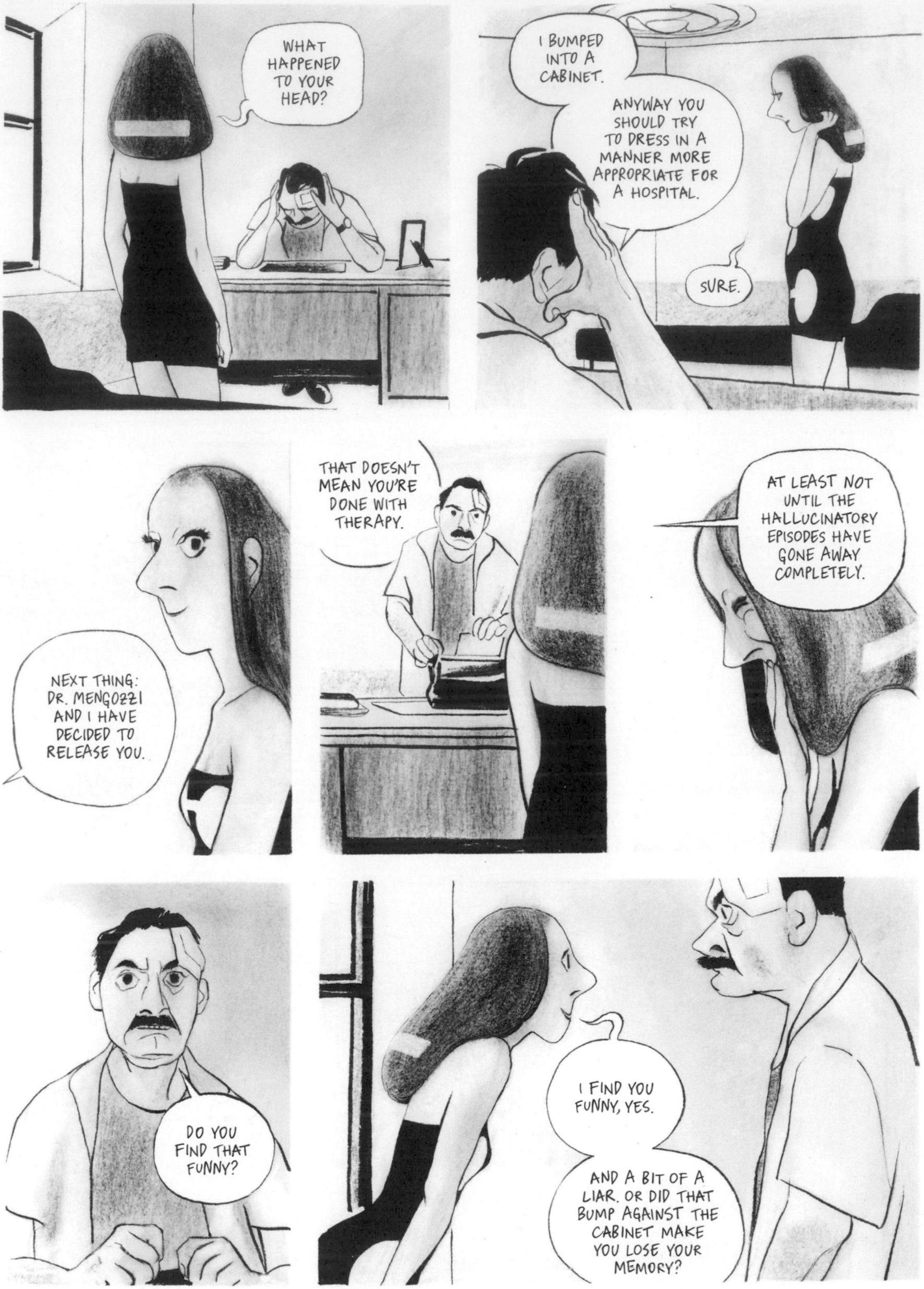
WHAT HAPPENED TO YOUR HEAD?
I BUMPED INTO A CABINET.
ANYWAY YOU SHOULD TRY TO DRESS IN A MANNER MORE APPROPRIATE FOR A HOSPITAL.
SURE.
NEXT THING: DR. MENGOZZI AND I HAVE DECIDED TO RELEASE YOU.
THAT DOESN'T MEAN YOU'RE DONE WITH THERAPY.
AT LEAST NOT UNTIL THE HALLUCINATORY EPISODES HAVE GONE AWAY COMPLETELY.
DO YOU FIND THAT FUNNY?
I FIND YOU FUNNY, YES.
AND A BIT OF A LIAR. OR DID THAT BUMP AGAINST THE CABINET MAKE YOU LOSE YOUR MEMORY?

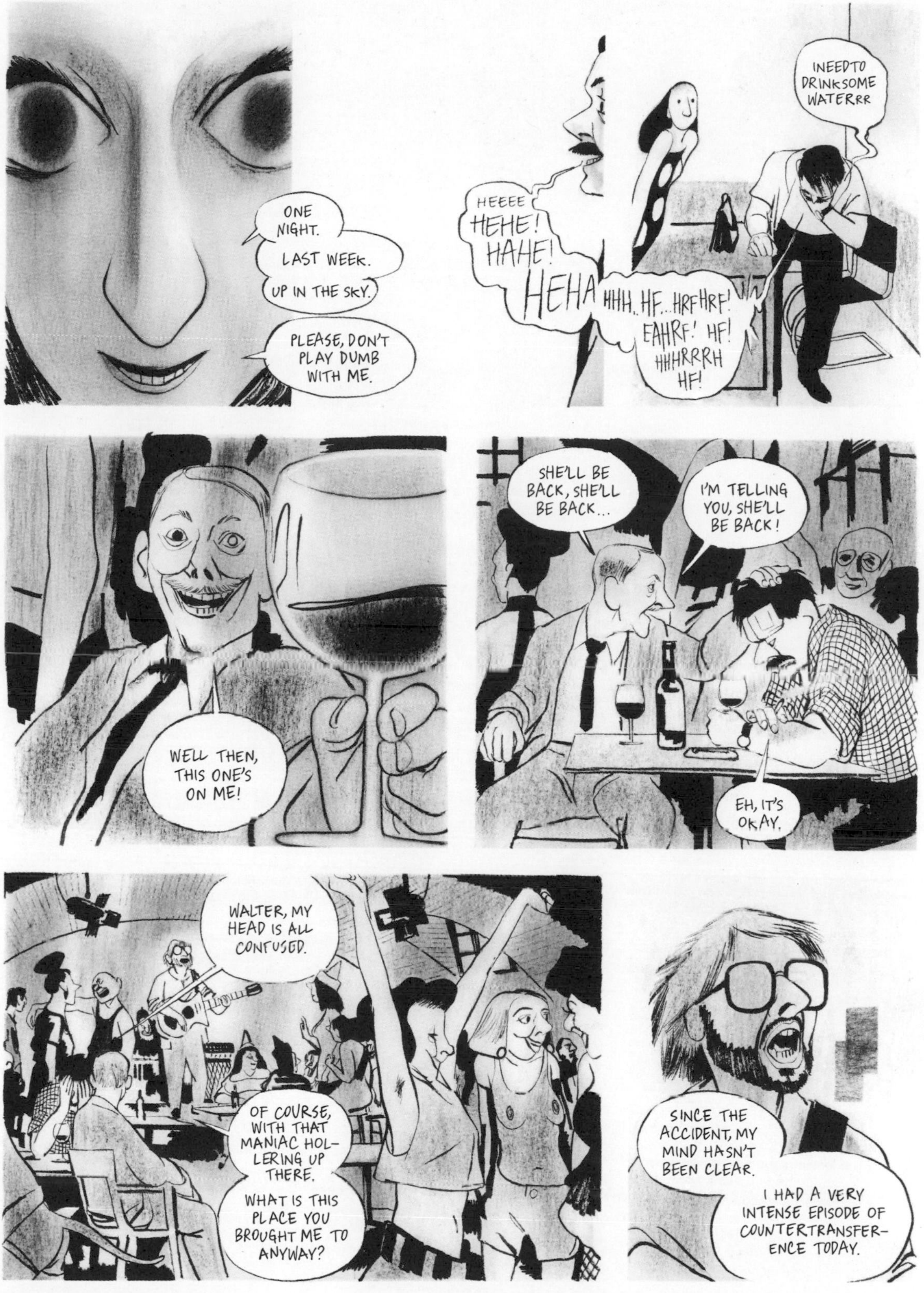
ONE NIGHT.
LAST WEEK.
UP IN THE SKY.
PLEASE, DON'T PLAY DUMB WITH ME.
HEEEE HEHE! HAHE! HEHA
INEEDTO DRINKSOME WATERrr
HHH.. HF...HRFHRF! EAHRF! HF! HHHRRRH HF!
WELL THEN, THIS ONE'S ON ME!
SHE'LL BE BACK, SHE'LL BE BACK...
I'M TELLING YOU, SHE'LL BE BACK!
EH, IT'S OKAY.
WALTER, MY HEAD IS ALL CONFUSED.
OF COURSE, WITH THAT MANIAC HOLLERING UP THERE.
WHAT IS THIS PLACE YOU BROUGHT ME TO ANYWAY?
SINCE THE ACCIDENT, MY MIND HASN'T BEEN CLEAR.
I HAD A VERY INTENSE EPISODE OF COUNTERTRANSFERENCE TODAY.

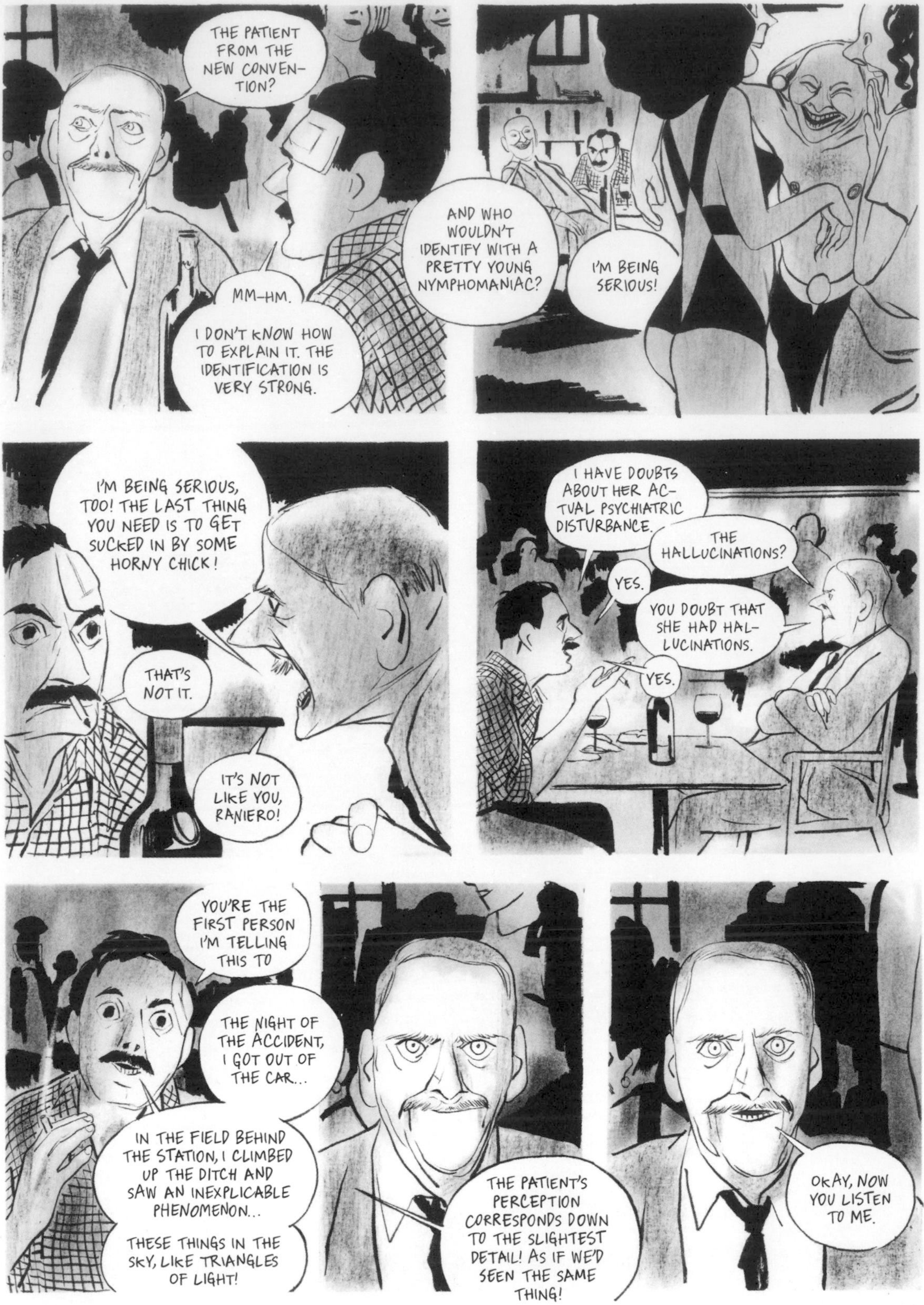

THE PATIENT FROM THE NEW CONVENTION?
MM-HM.
I DON'T KNOW HOW TO EXPLAIN IT. THE IDENTIFICATION IS VERY STRONG.
AND WHO WOULDN'T IDENTIFY WITH A PRETTY YOUNG NYMPHOMANIAC?
I'M BEING SERIOUS!
I'M BEING SERIOUS, TOO! THE LAST THING YOU NEED IS TO GET SUCKED IN BY SOME HORNY CHICK!
THAT'S NOT IT.
IT'S NOT LIKE YOU, RANIERO!
I HAVE DOUBTS ABOUT HER ACTUAL PSYCHIATRIC DISTURBANCE.
THE HALLUCINATIONS?
YES.
YOU DOUBT THAT SHE HAD HALLUCINATIONS.
YES.
YOU'RE THE FIRST PERSON I'M TELLING THIS TO
THE NIGHT OF THE ACCIDENT, I GOT OUT OF THE CAR...
IN THE FIELD BEHIND THE STATION, I CLIMBED UP THE DITCH AND SAW AN INEXPLICABLE PHENOMENON...
THESE THINGS IN THE SKY, LIKE TRIANGLES OF LIGHT!
THE PATIENT'S PERCEPTION CORRESPONDS DOWN TO THE SLIGHTEST DETAIL! AS IF WE'D SEEN THE SAME THING!
OKAY, NOW YOU LISTEN TO ME.

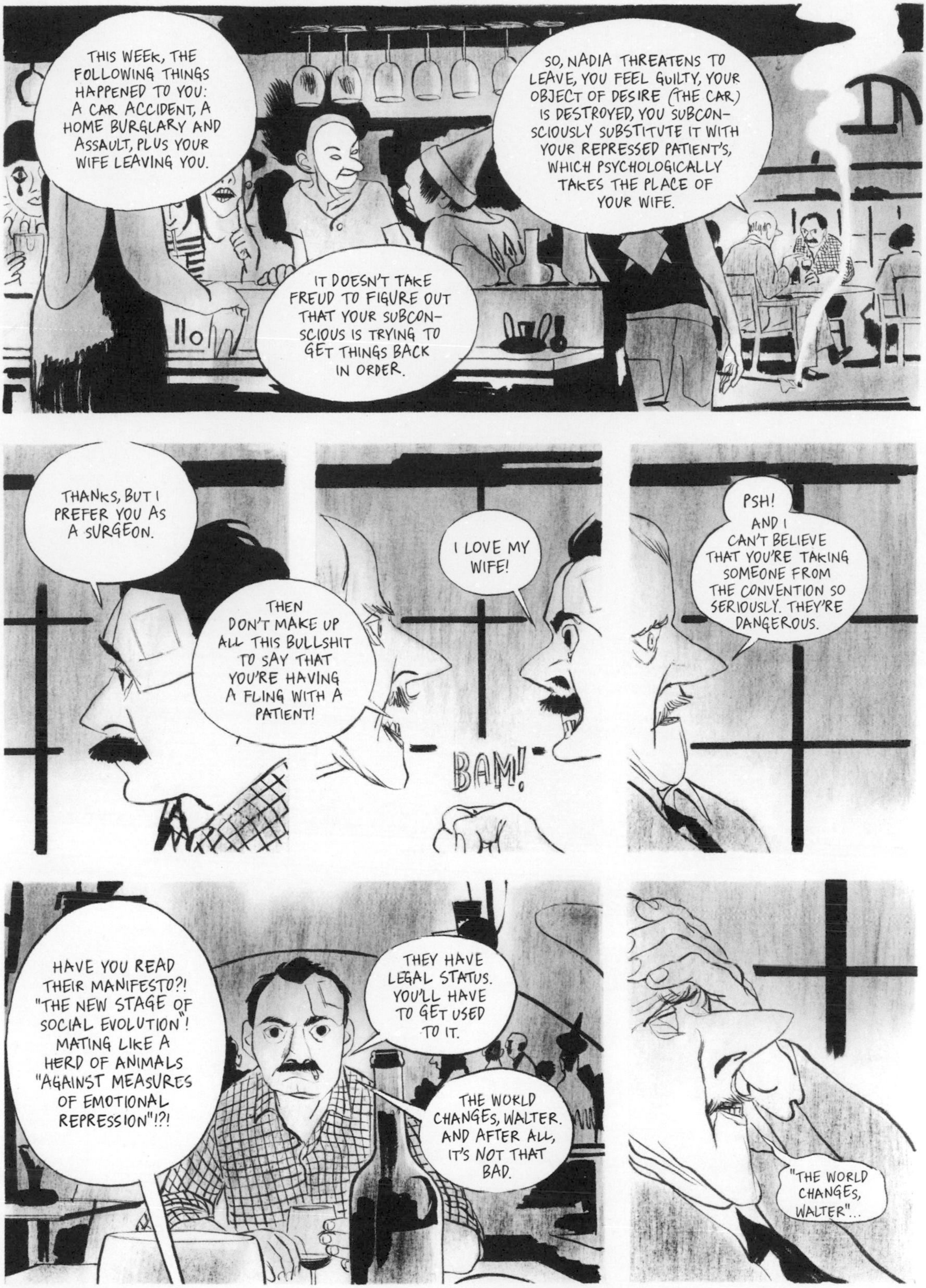

THIS WEEK, THE FOLLOWING THINGS HAPPENED TO YOU: A CAR ACCIDENT, A HOME BURGLARY AND ASSAULT, PLUS YOUR WIFE LEAVING YOU.
SO, NADIA THREATENS TO LEAVE, YOU FEEL GUILTY, YOUR OBJECT OF DESIRE (THE CAR) IS DESTROYED, YOU SUBCONSCIOUSLY SUBSTITUTE IT WITH YOUR REPRESSED PATIENT'S, WHICH PSYCHOLOGICALLY TAKES THE PLACE OF YOUR WIFE.
IT DOESN'T TAKE FREUD TO FIGURE OUT THAT YOUR SUBCONSCIOUS IS TRYING TO GET THINGS BACK IN ORDER.
THANKS, BUT I PREFER YOU AS A SURGEON.
THEN DON'T MAKE UP ALL THIS BULLSHIT TO SAY THAT YOU'RE HAVING A FLING WITH A PATIENT!
I LOVE MY WIFE!
BAM!
PSH! AND I CAN'T BELIEVE THAT YOU'RE TAKING SOMEONE FROM THE CONVENTION SO SERIOUSLY. THEY'RE DANGEROUS.
HAVE YOU READ THEIR MANIFESTO?! "THE NEW STAGE OF SOCIAL EVOLUTION"! MATING LIKE A HERD OF ANIMALS "AGAINST MEASURES OF EMOTIONAL REPRESSION"!?!
THEY HAVE LEGAL STATUS. YOU'LL HAVE TO GET USED TO IT.
THE WORLD CHANGES, WALTER. AND AFTER ALL, IT'S NOT THAT BAD.
"THE WORLD CHANGES, WALTER"...

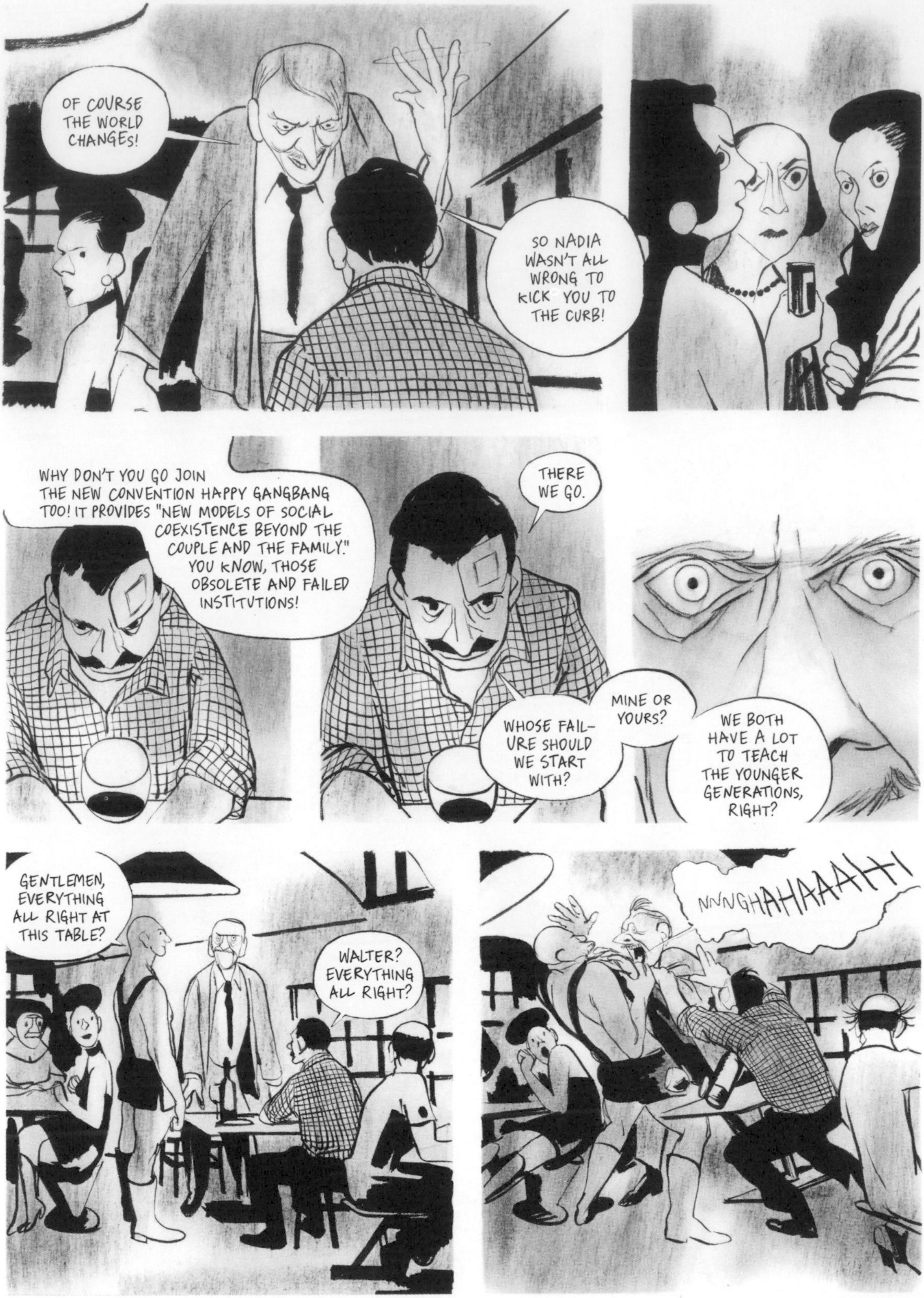
OF COURSE THE WORLD CHANGES!
SO NADIA WASN'T ALL WRONG TO KICK YOU TO THE CURB!
WHY DON'T YOU GO JOIN THE NEW CONVENTION HAPPY GANGBANG TOO! IT PROVIDES "NEW MODELS OF SOCIAL COEXISTENCE BEYOND THE COUPLE AND THE FAMILY." YOU KNOW, THOSE OBSOLETE AND FAILED INSTITUTIONS!
THERE WE GO.
WHOSE FAIL-URE SHOULD WE START WITH?
MINE OR YOURS?
WE BOTH HAVE A LOT TO TEACH THE YOUNGER GENERATIONS, RIGHT?
GENTLEMEN, EVERYTHING ALL RIGHT AT THIS TABLE?
WALTER? EVERYTHING ALL RIGHT?
NNNGHAHAAAAH!

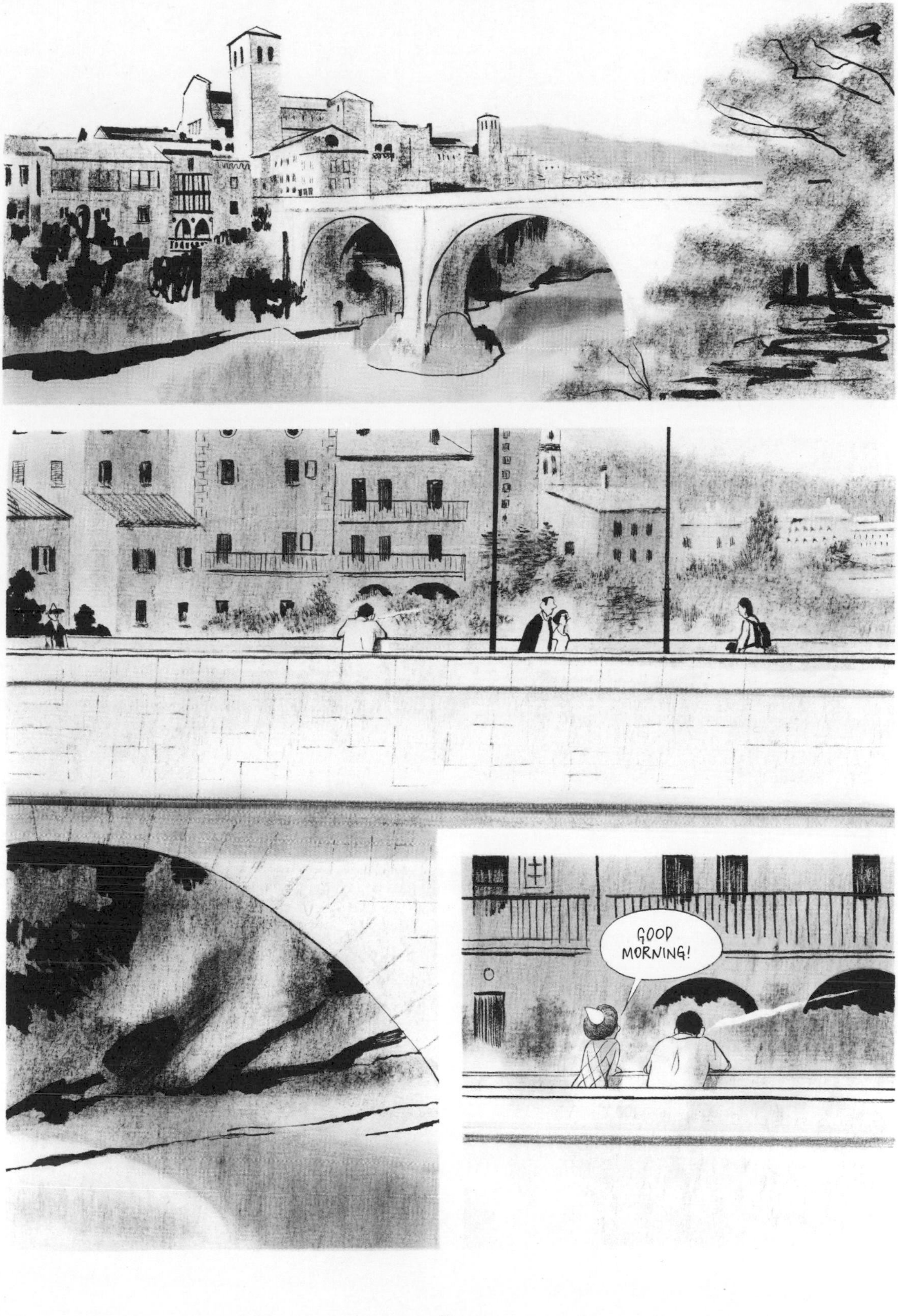
GOOD MORNING!

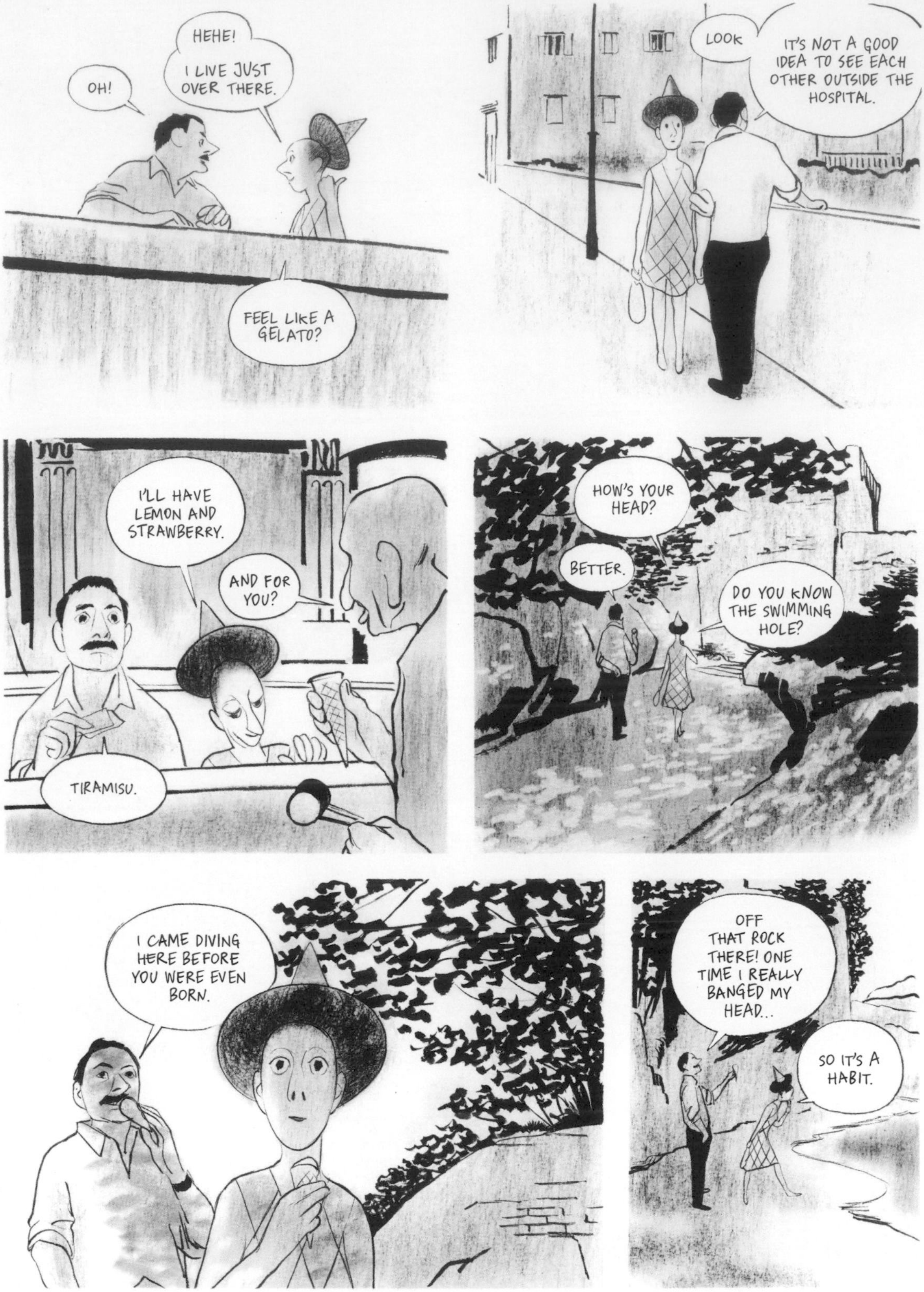
OH!
HEHE!
I LIVE JUST OVER THERE.
FEEL LIKE A GELATO?
LOOK
IT'S NOT A GOOD IDEA TO SEE EACH OTHER OUTSIDE THE HOSPITAL.
I'LL HAVE LEMON AND STRAWBERRY.
AND FOR YOU?
TIRAMISU.
HOW'S YOUR HEAD?
BETTER.
DO YOU KNOW THE SWIMMING HOLE?
I CAME DIVING HERE BEFORE YOU WERE EVEN BORN.
OFF THAT ROCK THERE! ONE TIME I REALLY BANGED MY HEAD...
SO IT'S A HABIT.

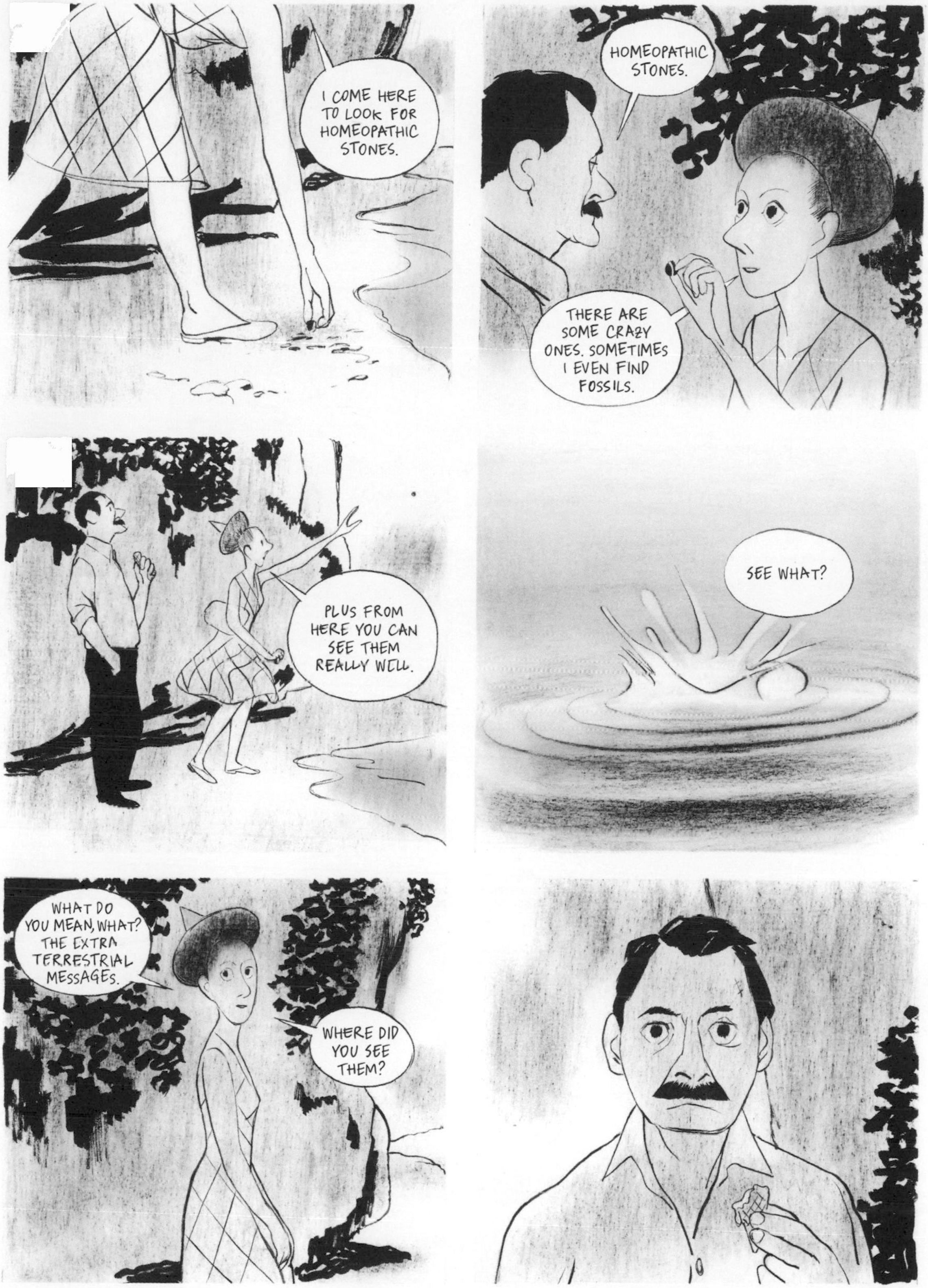
I COME HERE TO LOOK FOR HOMEOPATHIC STONES.
HOMEOPATHIC STONES.
THERE ARE SOME CRAZY ONES. SOMETIMES I EVEN FIND FOSSILS.
PLUS FROM HERE YOU CAN SEE THEM REALLY WELL.
SEE WHAT?
WHAT DO YOU MEAN, WHAT? THE EXTRA TERRESTRIAL MESSAGES.
WHERE DID YOU SEE THEM?

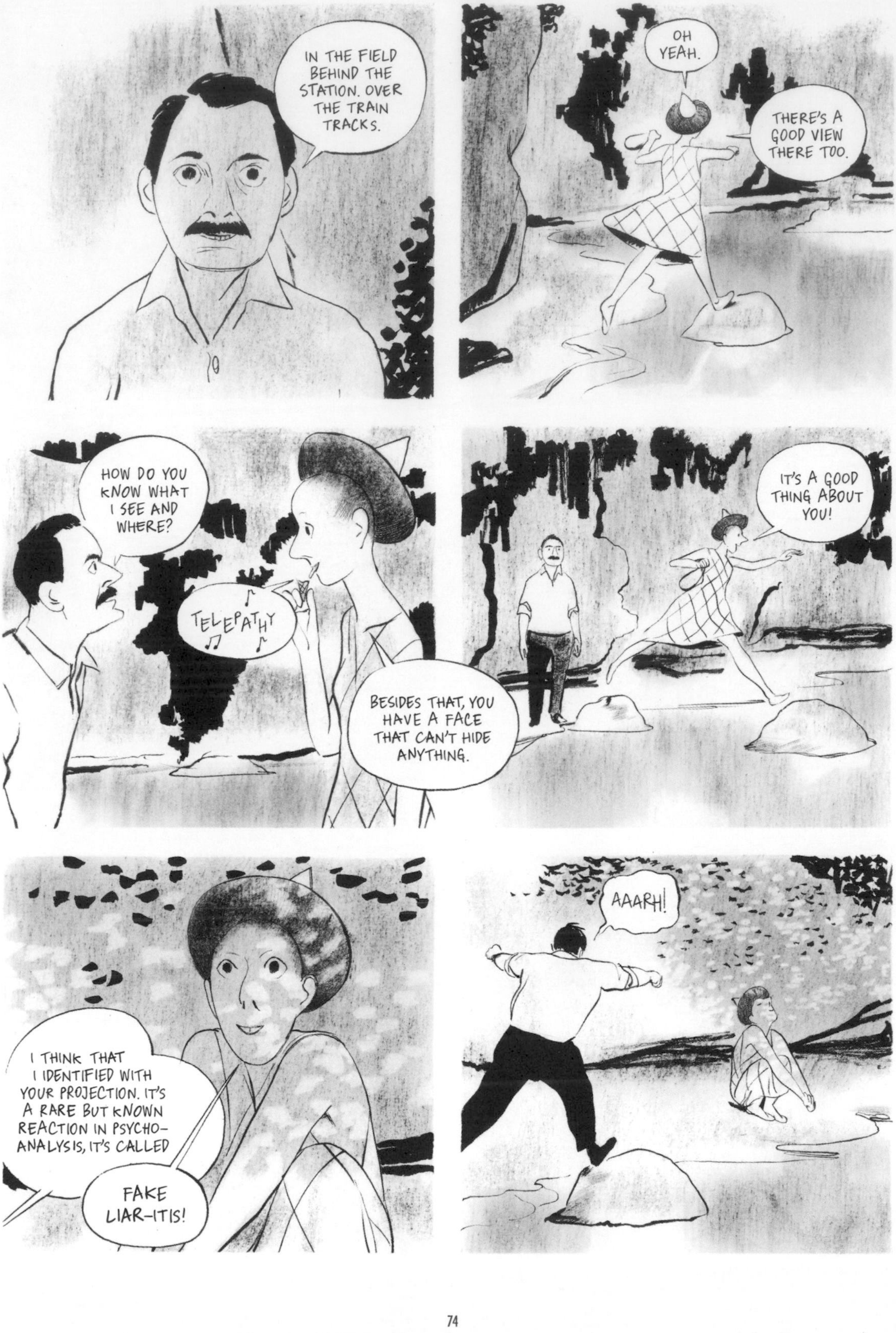
IN THE FIELD BEHIND THE STATION. OVER THE TRAIN TRACKS.
OH YEAH.
THERE'S A GOOD VIEW THERE TOO.
HOW DO YOU KNOW WHAT I SEE AND WHERE?
TELEPATHY
BESIDES THAT, YOU HAVE A FACE THAT CAN'T HIDE ANYTHING.
IT'S A GOOD THING ABOUT YOU!
I THINK THAT I IDENTIFIED WITH YOUR PROJECTION. IT'S A RARE BUT KNOWN REACTION IN PSYCHO-ANALYSIS, IT'S CALLED
FAKE LIAR-ITIS!
AAARH!

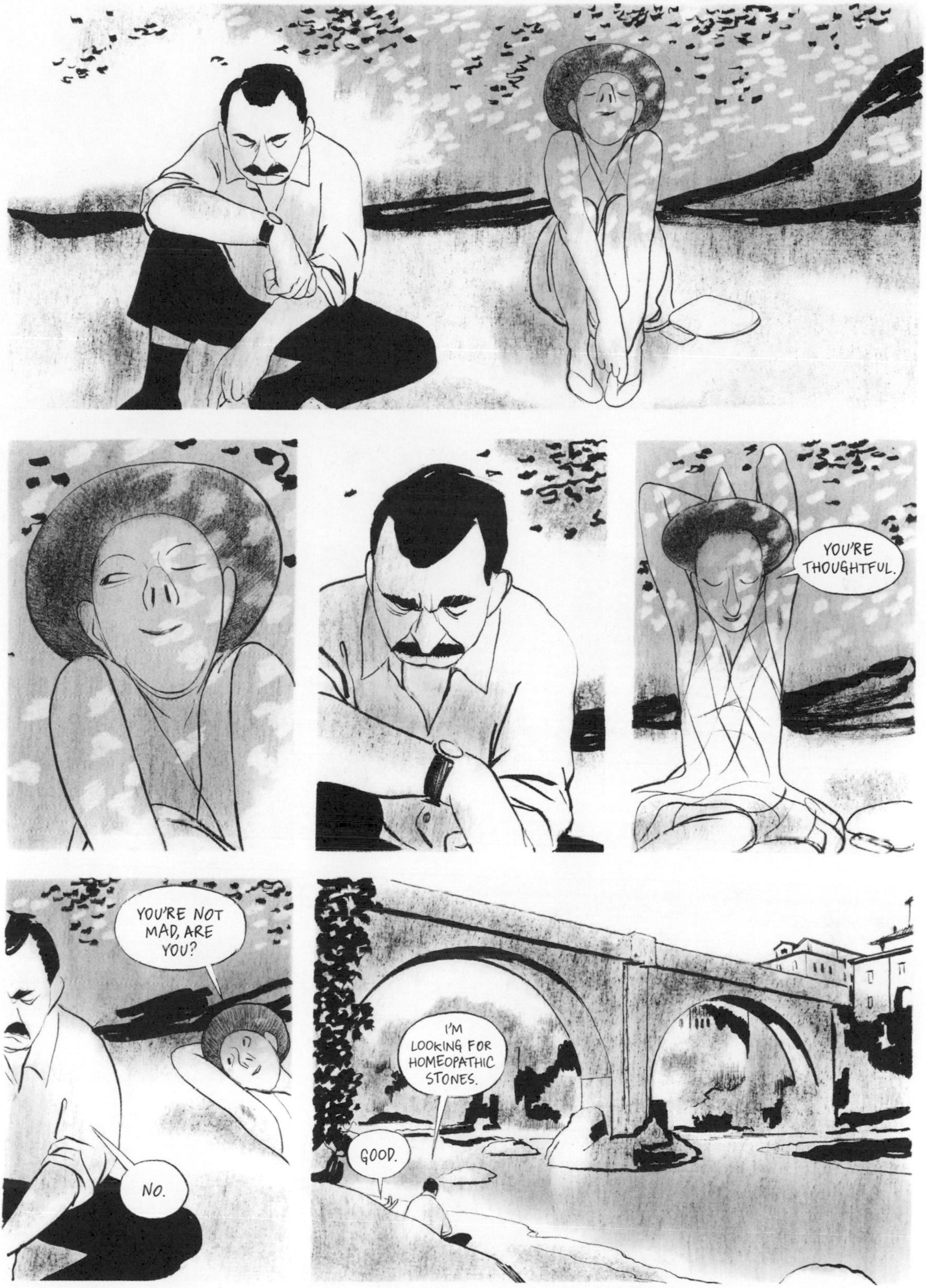
YOU'RE THOUGHTFUL.
YOU'RE NOT MAD, ARE YOU?
NO.
I'M LOOKING FOR HOMEOPATHIC STONES.
GOOD.

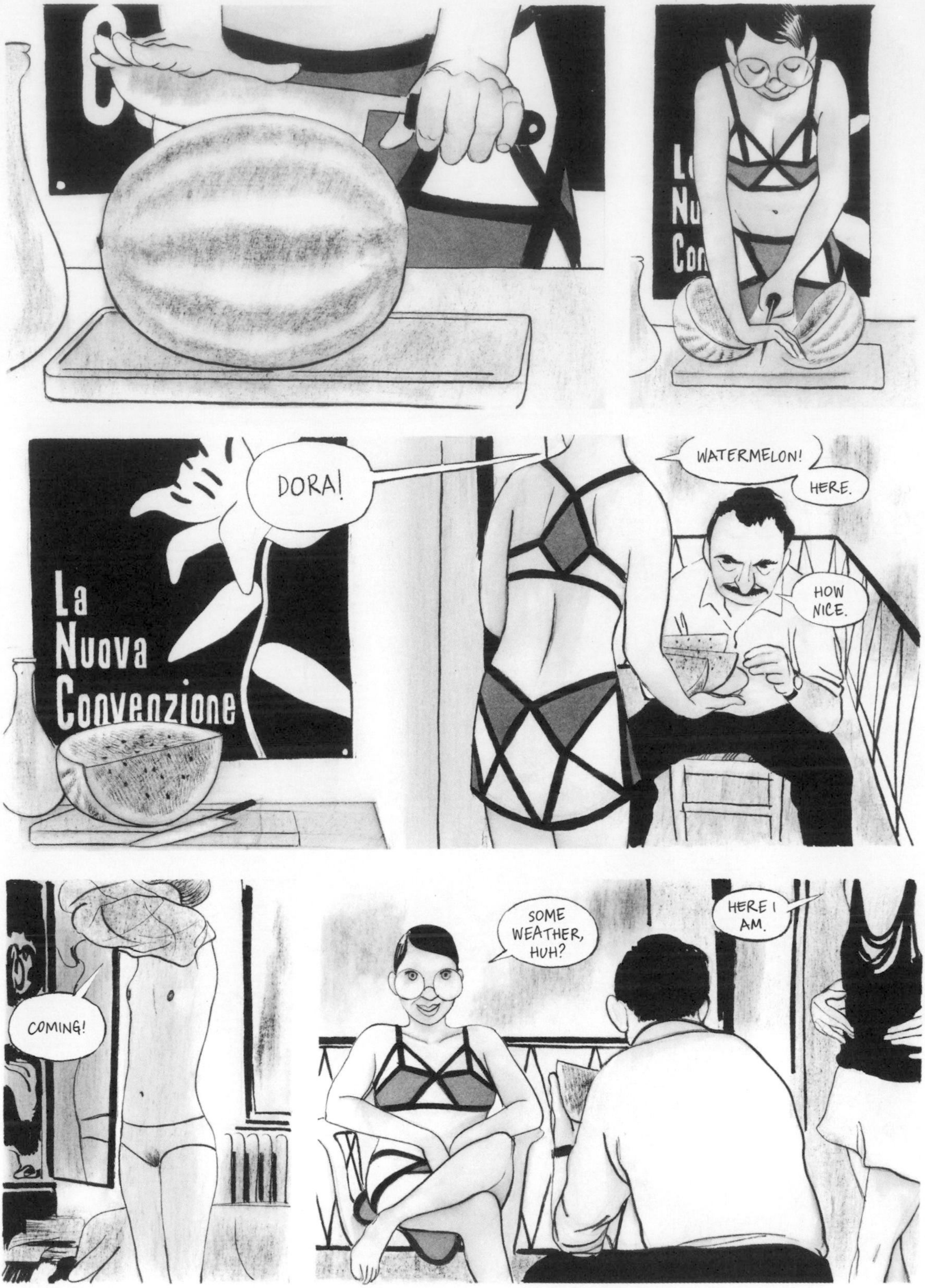
La Nuova Convenzione
La Nuova Convenzione
DORA!
WATERMELON!
HERE.
HOW NICE.
COMING!
SOME WEATHER, HUH?
HERE I AM.

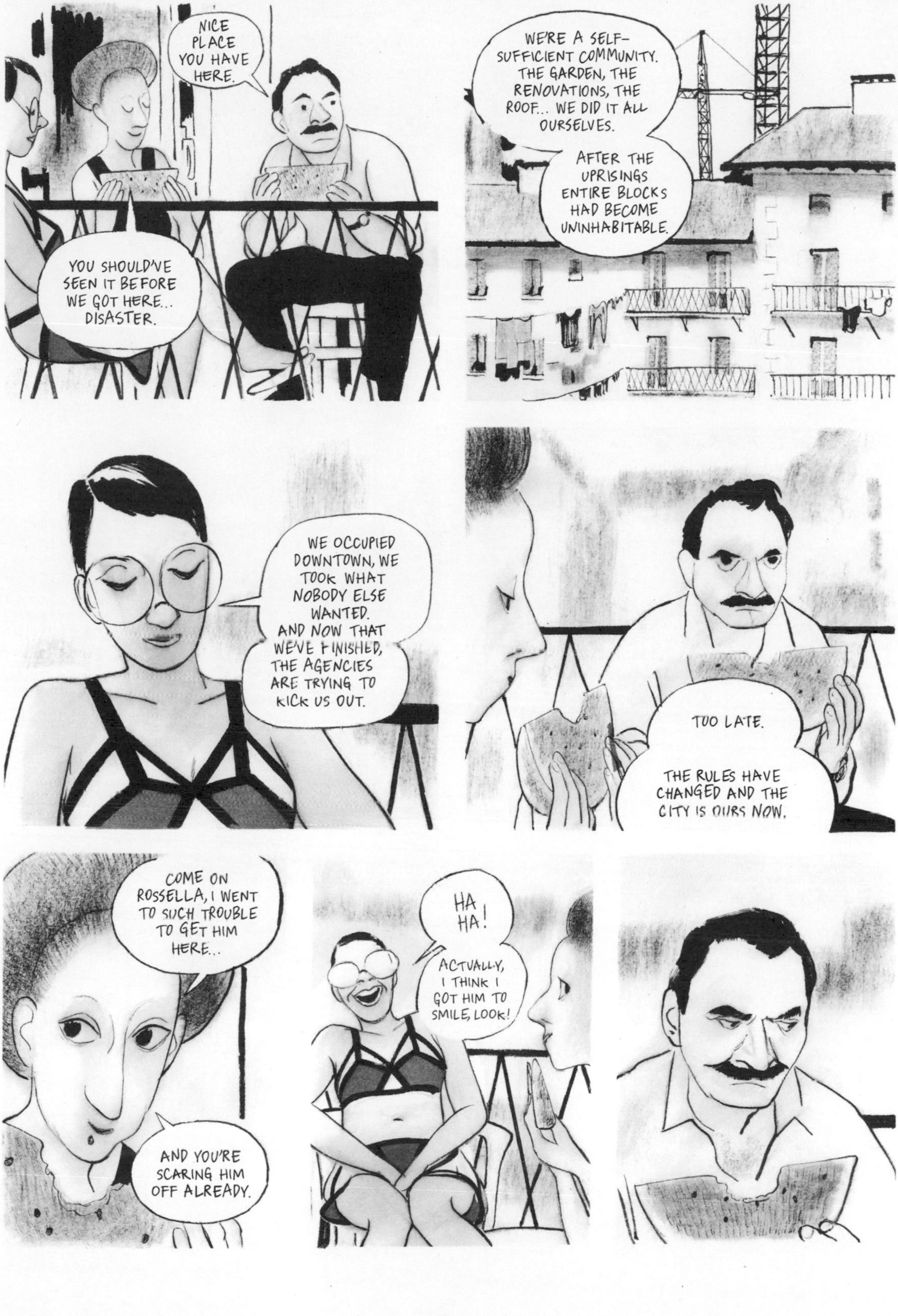
NICE PLACE YOU HAVE HERE.
YOU SHOULD'VE SEEN IT BEFORE WE GOT HERE... DISASTER.
WE'RE A SELF-SUFFICIENT COMMUNITY. THE GARDEN, THE RENOVATIONS, THE ROOF... WE DID IT ALL OURSELVES.
AFTER THE UPRISINGS ENTIRE BLOCKS HAD BECOME UNINHABITABLE.
WE OCCUPIED DOWNTOWN, WE TOOK WHAT NOBODY ELSE WANTED. AND NOW THAT WE'VE FINISHED, THE AGENCIES ARE TRYING TO KICK US OUT.
TOO LATE.
THE RULES HAVE CHANGED AND THE CITY IS OURS NOW.
COME ON ROSSELLA, I WENT TO SUCH TROUBLE TO GET HIM HERE...
AND YOU'RE SCARING HIM OFF ALREADY.
HA HA!
ACTUALLY, I THINK I GOT HIM TO SMILE, LOOK!

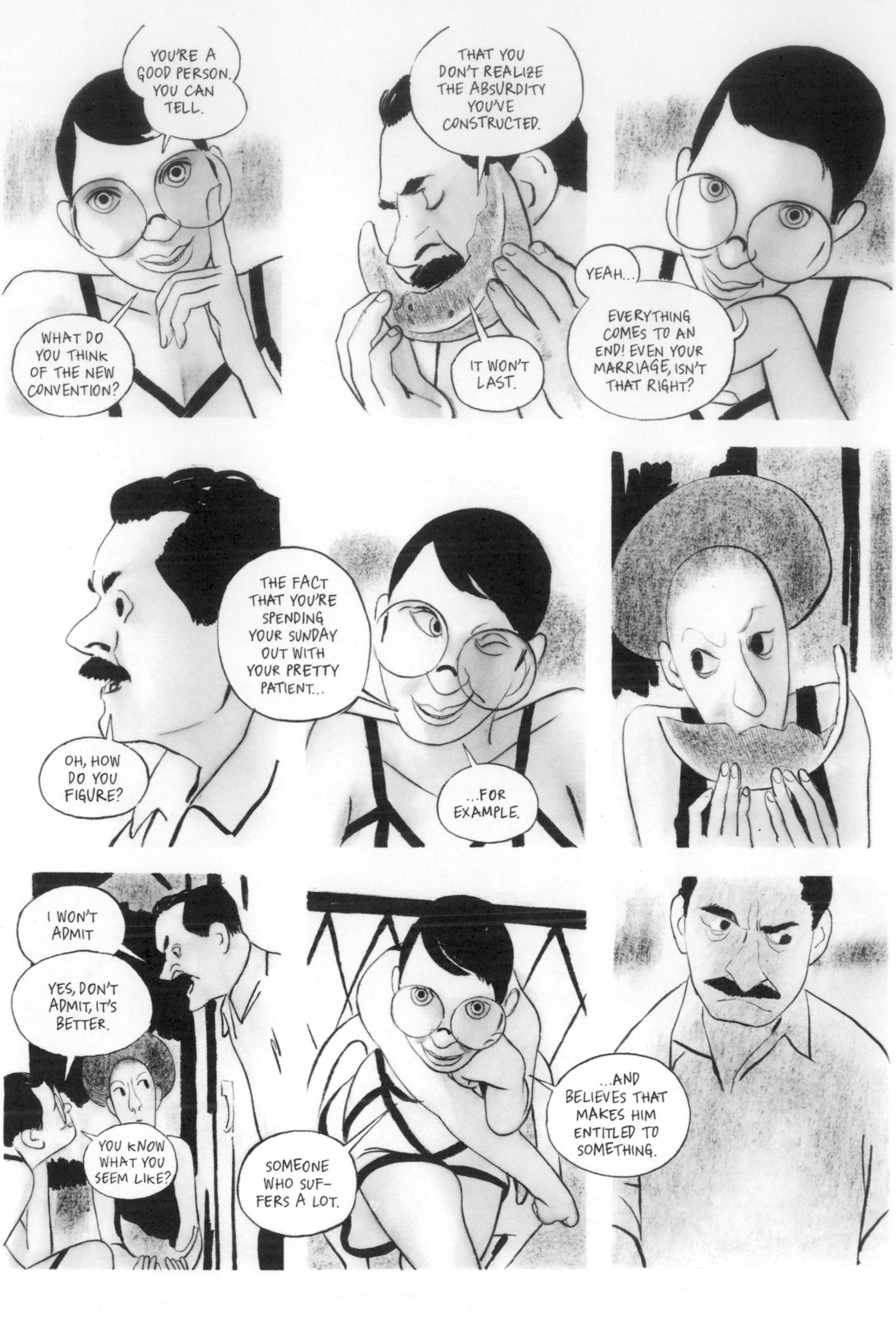
YOU'RE A GOOD PERSON. YOU CAN TELL.
WHAT DO YOU THINK OF THE NEW CONVENTION?
THAT YOU DON'T REALIZE THE ABSURDITY YOU'VE CONSTRUCTED.
IT WON'T LAST.
YEAH...
EVERYTHING COMES TO AN END! EVEN YOUR MARRIAGE, ISN'T THAT RIGHT?
OH, HOW DO YOU FIGURE?
THE FACT THAT YOU'RE SPENDING YOUR SUNDAY OUT WITH YOUR PRETTY PATIENT...
...FOR EXAMPLE.
I WON'T ADMIT
YES, DON'T ADMIT, IT'S BETTER.
YOU KNOW WHAT YOU SEEM LIKE?
SOMEONE WHO SUF-FERS A LOT.
...AND BELIEVES THAT MAKES HIM ENTITLED TO SOMETHING.

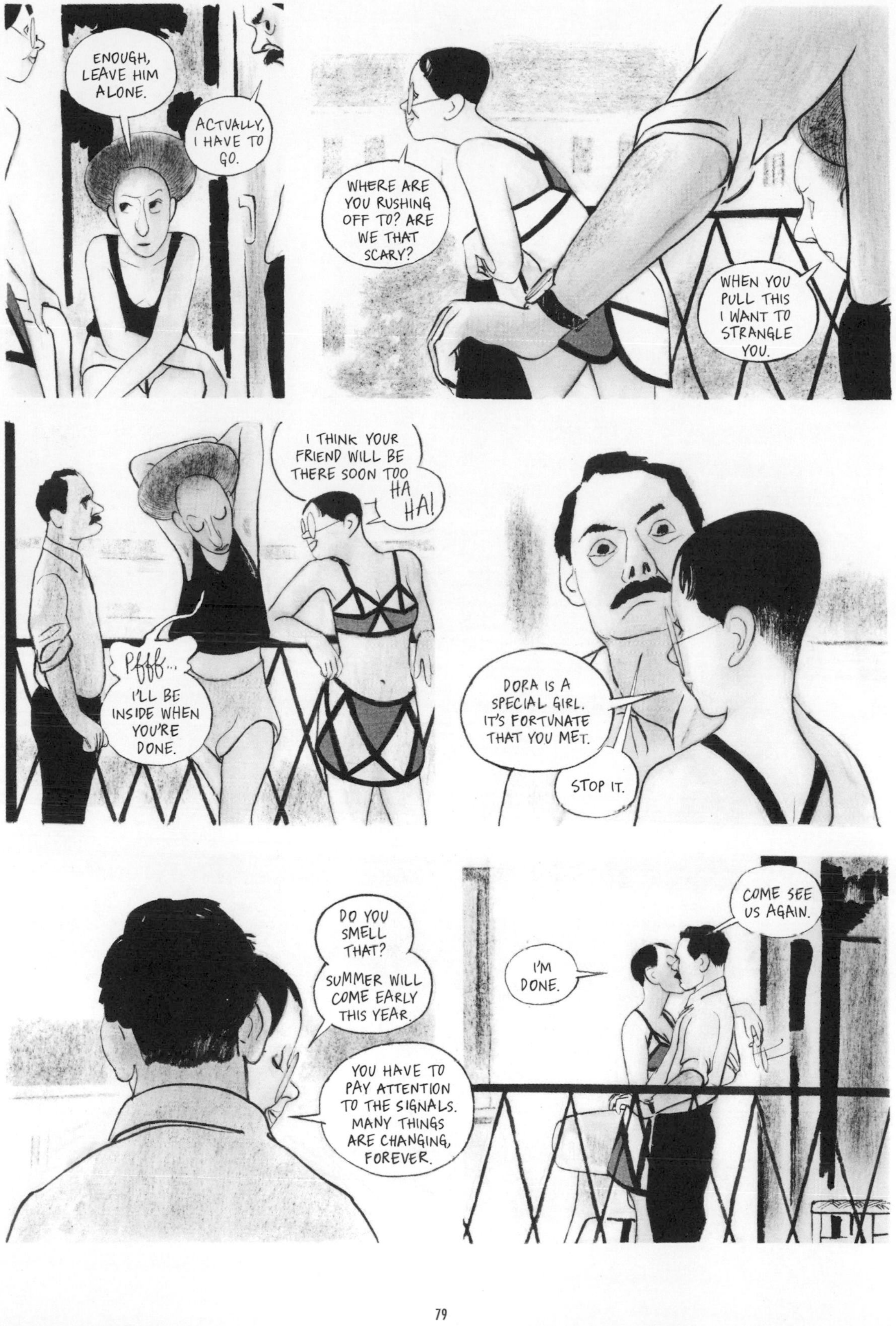
ENOUGH, LEAVE HIM ALONE.
ACTUALLY, I HAVE TO GO.
WHERE ARE YOU RUSHING OFF TO? ARE WE THAT SCARY?
WHEN YOU PULL THIS I WANT TO STRANGLE YOU.
I THINK YOUR FRIEND WILL BE THERE SOON TOO HA HA!
Pfff... I'LL BE INSIDE WHEN YOU'RE DONE.
DORA IS A SPECIAL GIRL. IT'S FORTUNATE THAT YOU MET.
STOP IT.
DO YOU SMELL THAT?
SUMMER WILL COME EARLY THIS YEAR.
YOU HAVE TO PAY ATTENTION TO THE SIGNALS. MANY THINGS ARE CHANGING, FOREVER.
COME SEE US AGAIN.
I'M DONE.

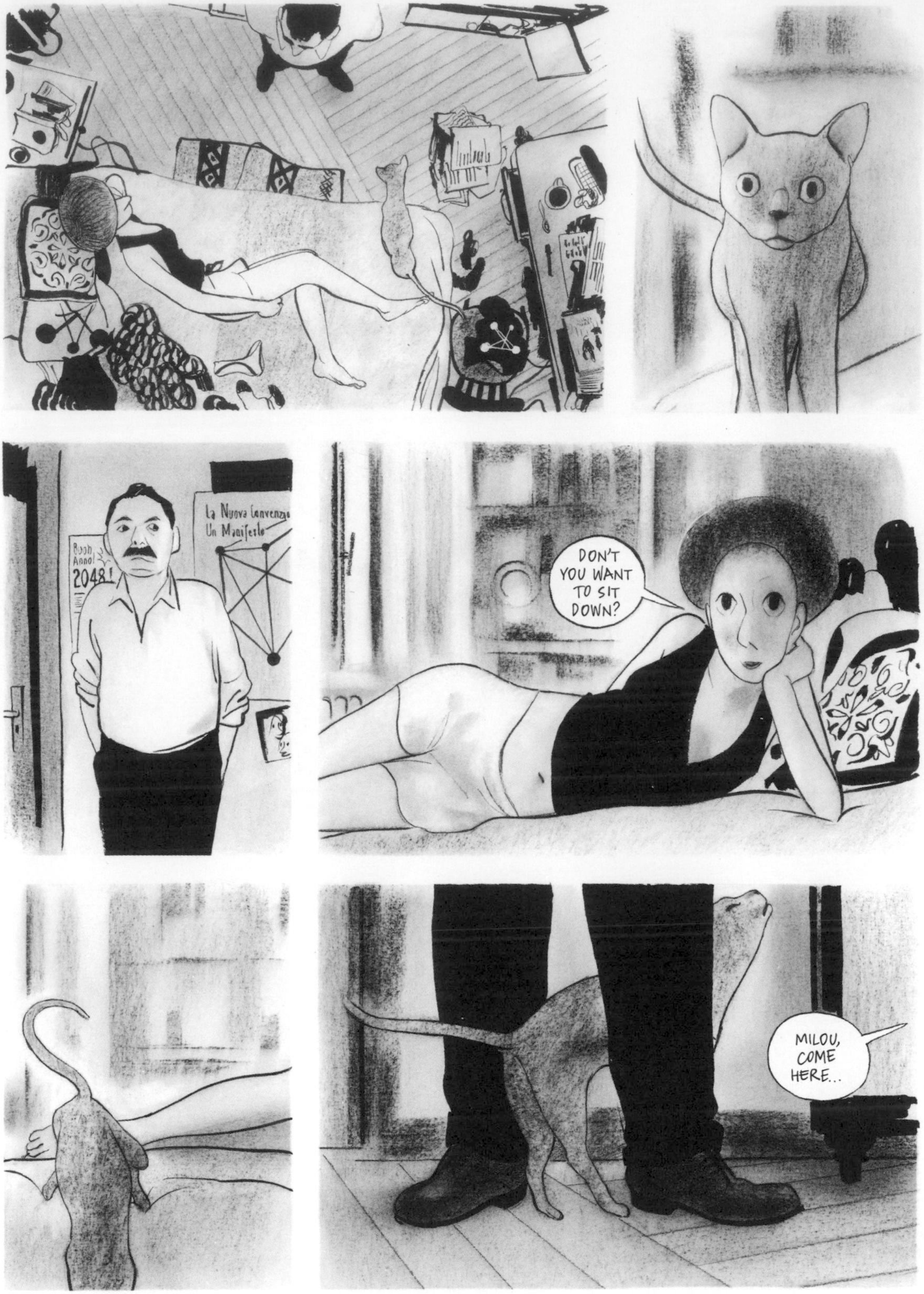
DON'T YOU WANT TO SIT DOWN?
MILOU, COME HERE...

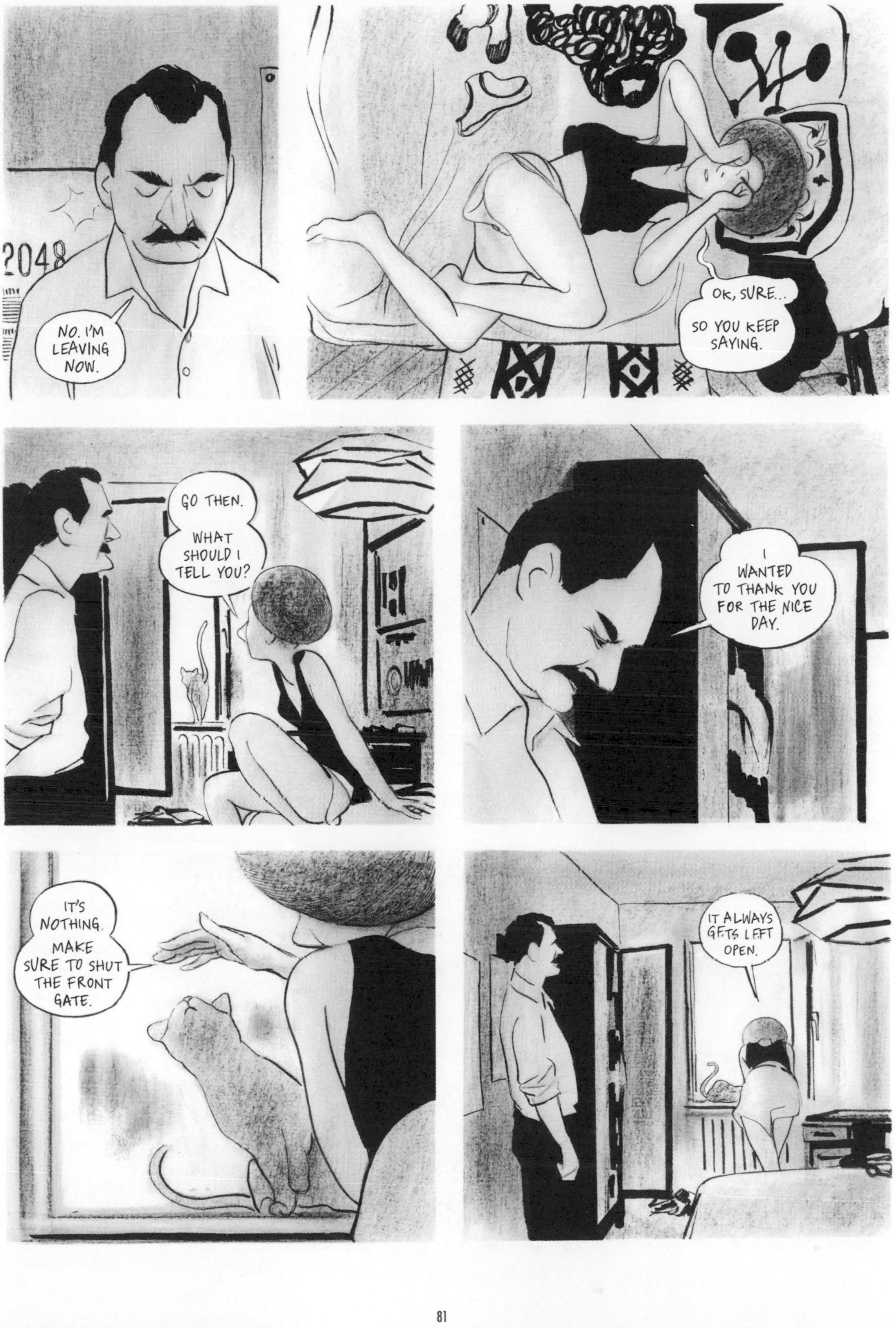
2048
NO. I'M LEAVING NOW.
OK, SURE... SO YOU KEEP SAYING.
GO THEN. WHAT SHOULD I TELL YOU?
I WANTED TO THANK YOU FOR THE NICE DAY.
IT'S NOTHING. MAKE SURE TO SHUT THE FRONT GATE.
IT ALWAYS GETS LEFT OPEN.

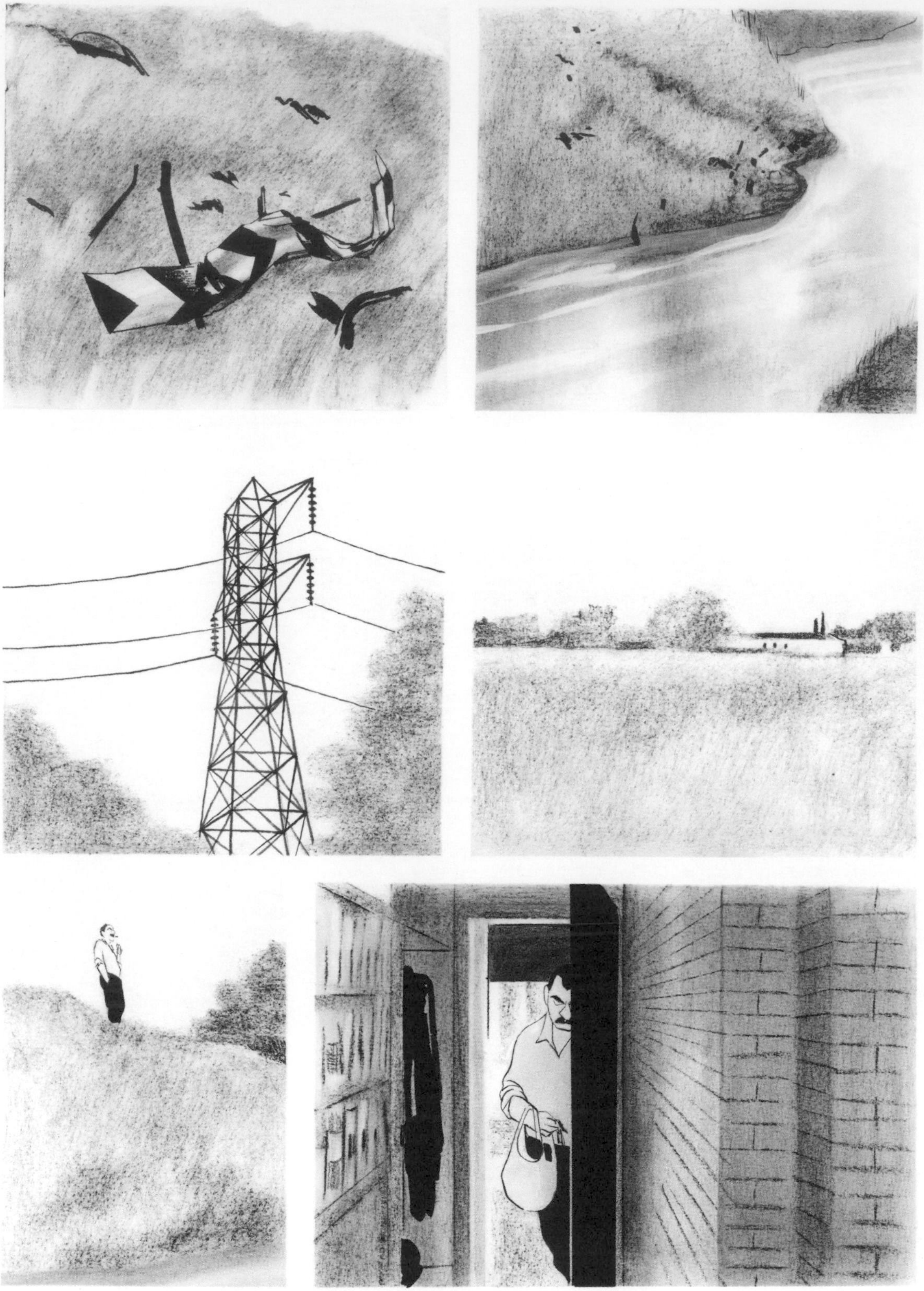

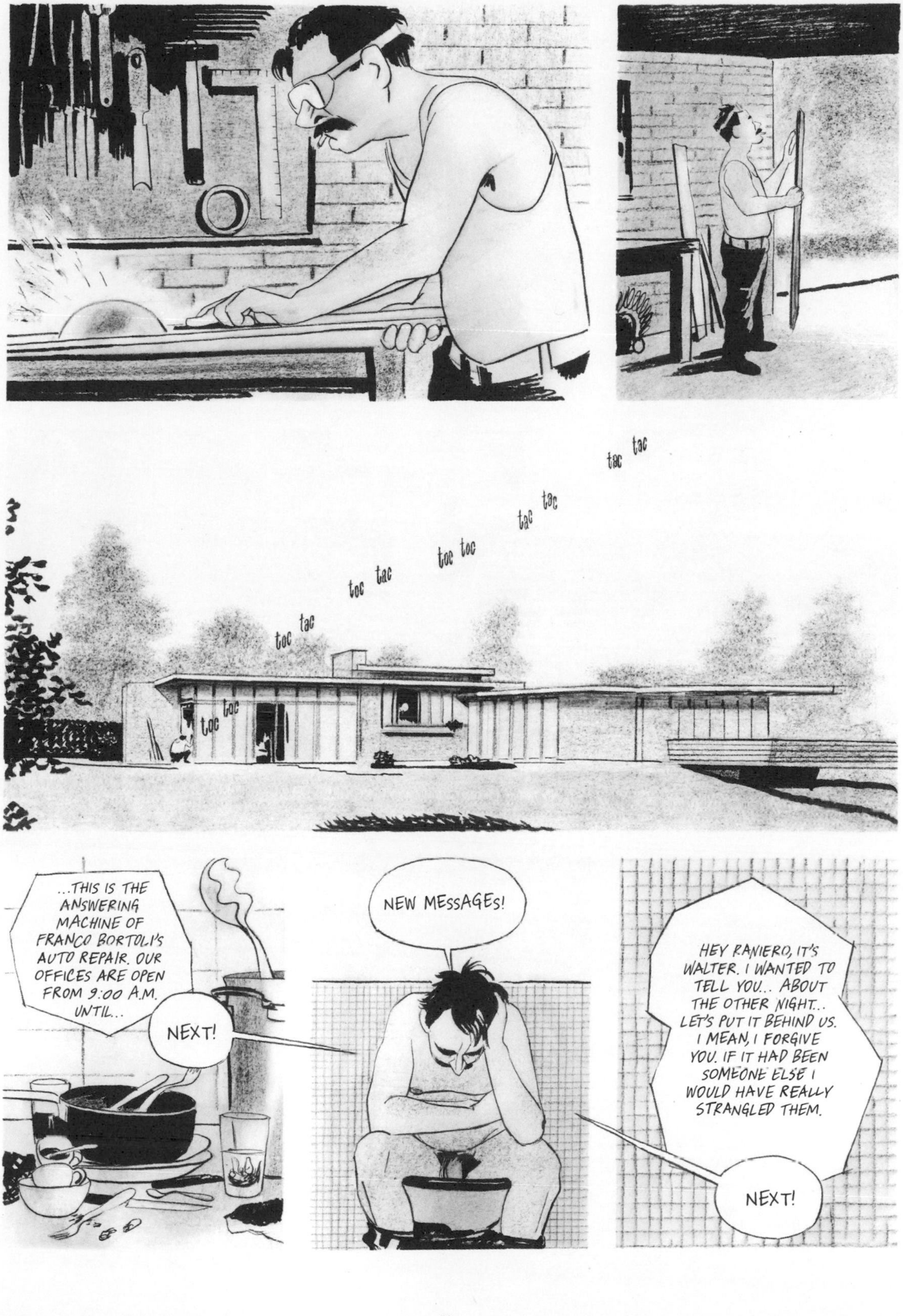
toc toc
toc tac
toc tac
toc toc
tac tac
tac tac
...THIS IS THE ANSWERING MACHINE OF FRANCO BORTOLI'S AUTO REPAIR. OUR OFFICES ARE OPEN FROM 9:00 A.M. UNTIL...
NEXT!
NEW MESSAGES!
HEY RANIERO, IT'S WALTER. I WANTED TO TELL YOU... ABOUT THE OTHER NIGHT... LET'S PUT IT BEHIND US. I MEAN, I FORGIVE YOU. IF IT HAD BEEN SOMEONE ELSE I WOULD HAVE REALLY STRANGLED THEM.
NEXT!

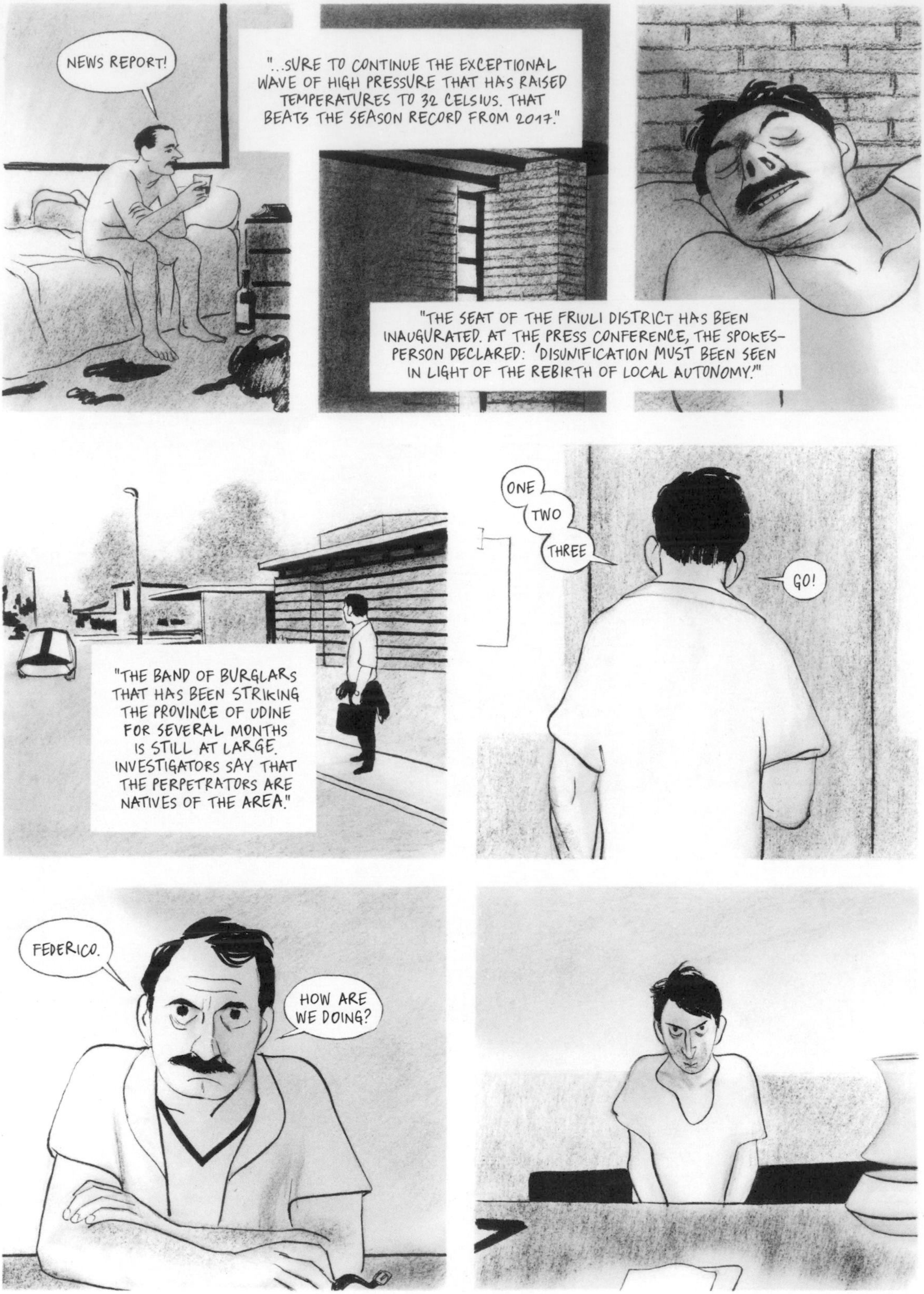
NEWS REPORT!
"...SURE TO CONTINUE THE EXCEPTIONAL WAVE OF HIGH PRESSURE THAT HAS RAISED TEMPERATURES TO 32 CELSIUS. THAT BEATS THE SEASON RECORD FROM 2017."
"THE SEAT OF THE FRIULI DISTRICT HAS BEEN INAUGURATED. AT THE PRESS CONFERENCE, THE SPOKESPERSON DECLARED: 'DISUNIFICATION MUST BEEN SEEN IN LIGHT OF THE REBIRTH OF LOCAL AUTONOMY.'"
"THE BAND OF BURGLARS THAT HAS BEEN STRIKING THE PROVINCE OF UDINE FOR SEVERAL MONTHS IS STILL AT LARGE. INVESTIGATORS SAY THAT THE PERPETRATORS ARE NATIVES OF THE AREA."
ONE
TWO
THREE
GO!
FEDERICO.
HOW ARE WE DOING?

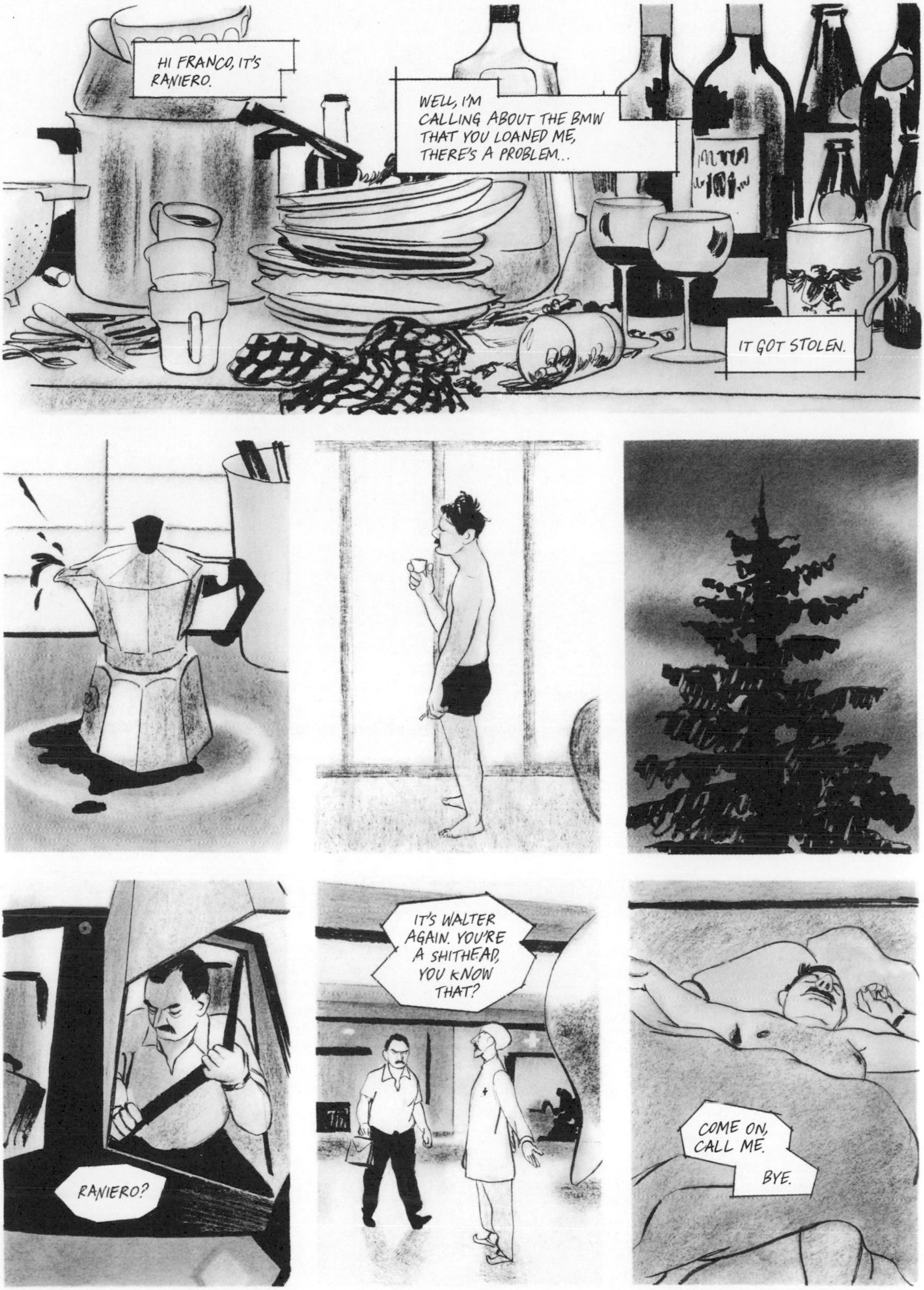
HI FRANCO, IT'S RANIERO.
WELL, I'M CALLING ABOUT THE BMW THAT YOU LOANED ME, THERE'S A PROBLEM...
IT GOT STOLEN.
RANIERO?
IT'S WALTER AGAIN. YOU'RE A SHITHEAD, YOU KNOW THAT?
COME ON, CALL ME.
BYE.

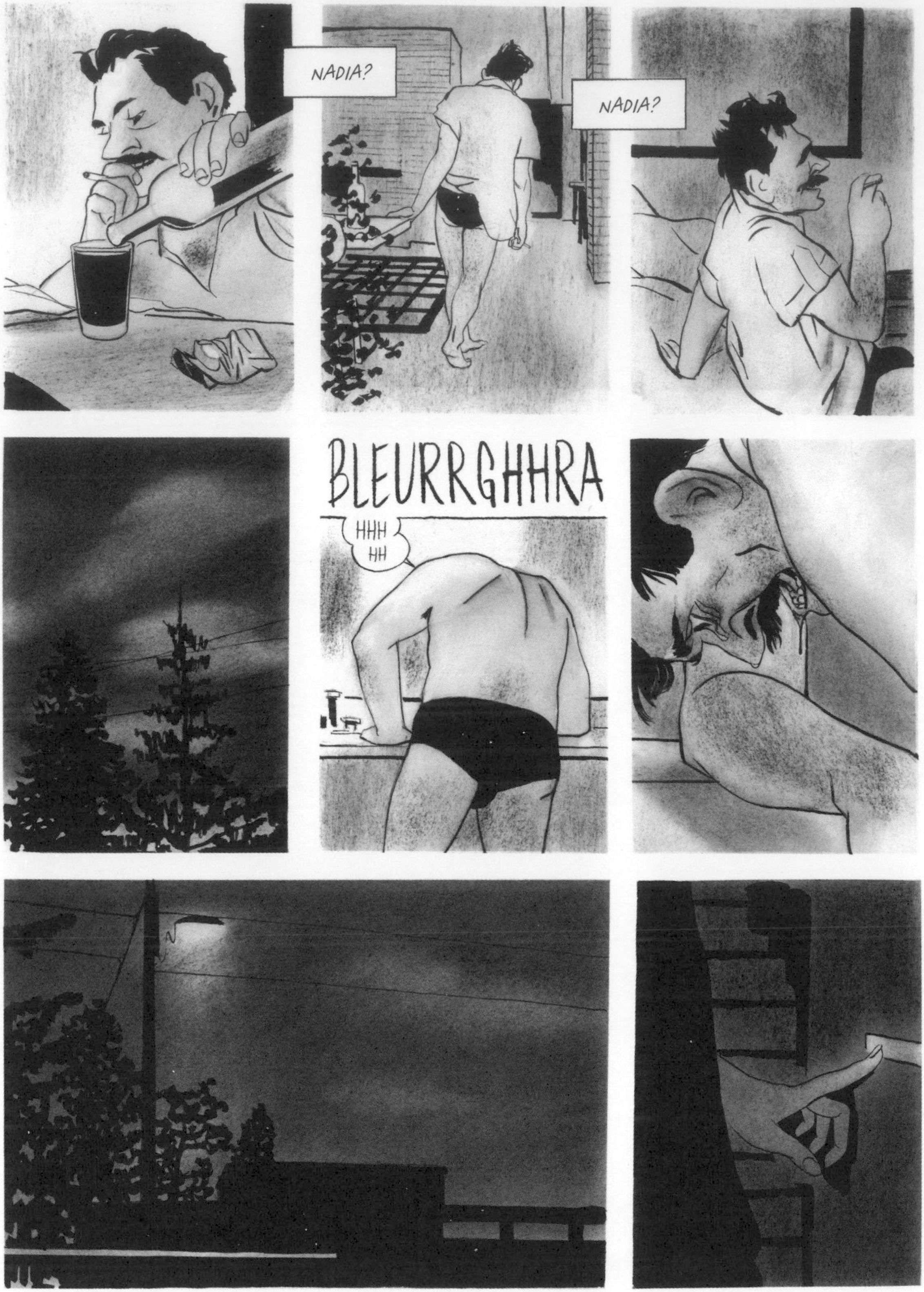
NADIA?
NADIA?
BLEURRGHHRA
HHH HH

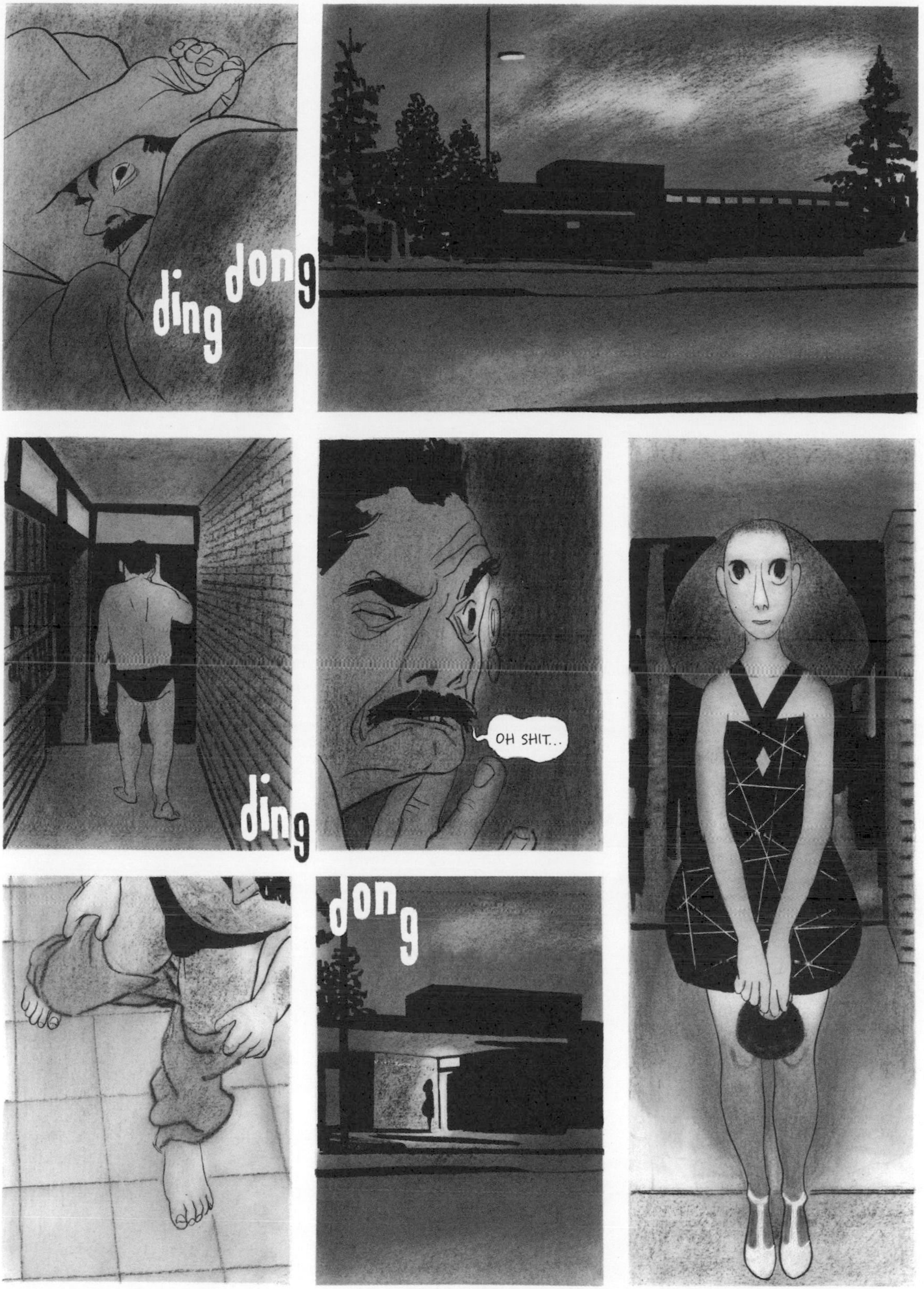
ding dong
ding
OH SHIT...
dong

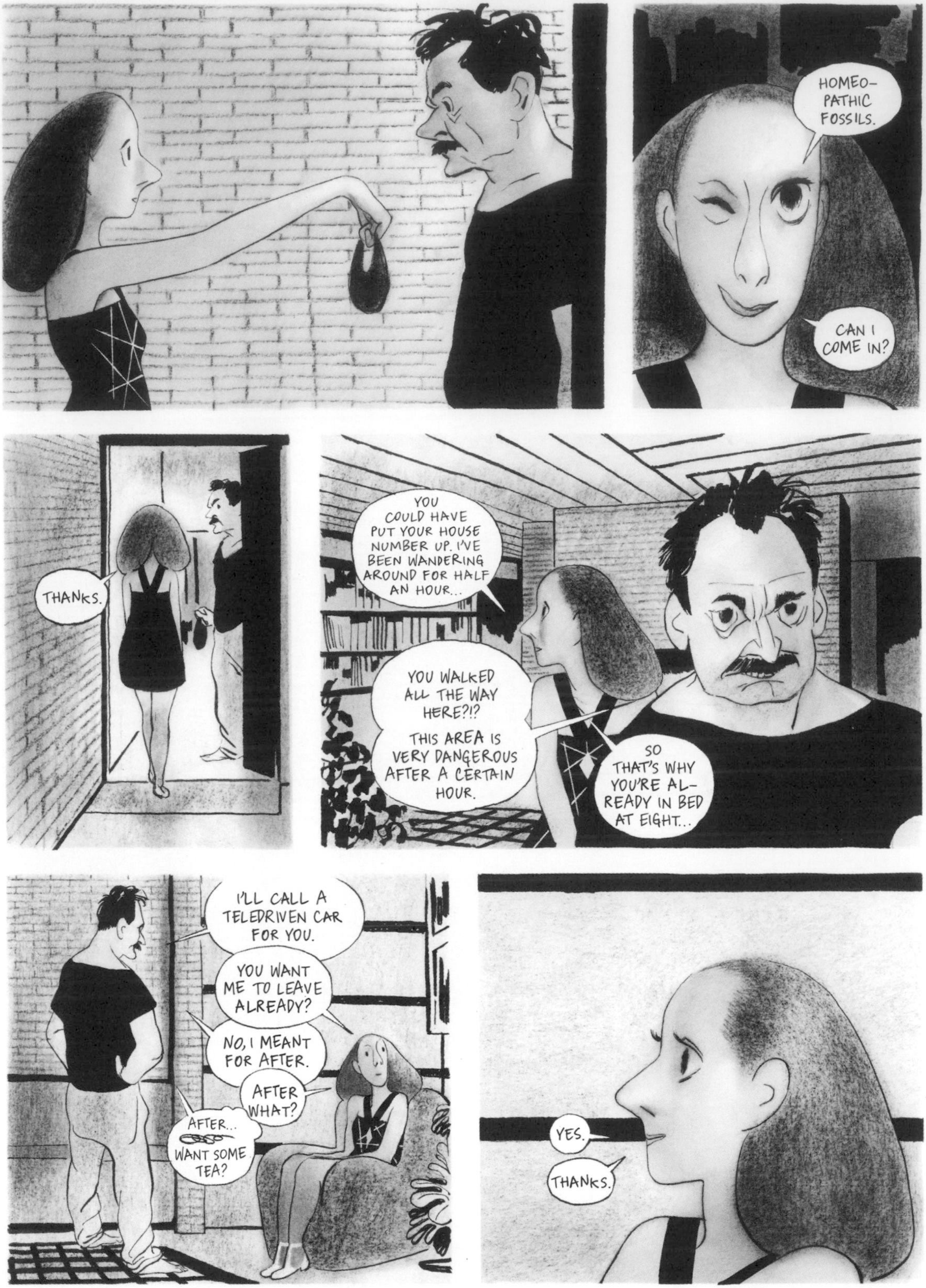
HOMEO-PATHIC FOSSILS.
CAN I COME IN?
THANKS.
YOU COULD HAVE PUT YOUR HOUSE NUMBER UP. I'VE BEEN WANDERING AROUND FOR HALF AN HOUR...
YOU WALKED ALL THE WAY HERE?!?
THIS AREA IS VERY DANGEROUS AFTER A CERTAIN HOUR.
SO THAT'S WHY YOU'RE AL-READY IN BED AT EIGHT...
I'LL CALL A TELEDRIVEN CAR FOR YOU.
YOU WANT ME TO LEAVE ALREADY?
NO, I MEANT FOR AFTER.
AFTER WHAT?
AFTER...
WANT SOME TEA?
YES.
THANKS.

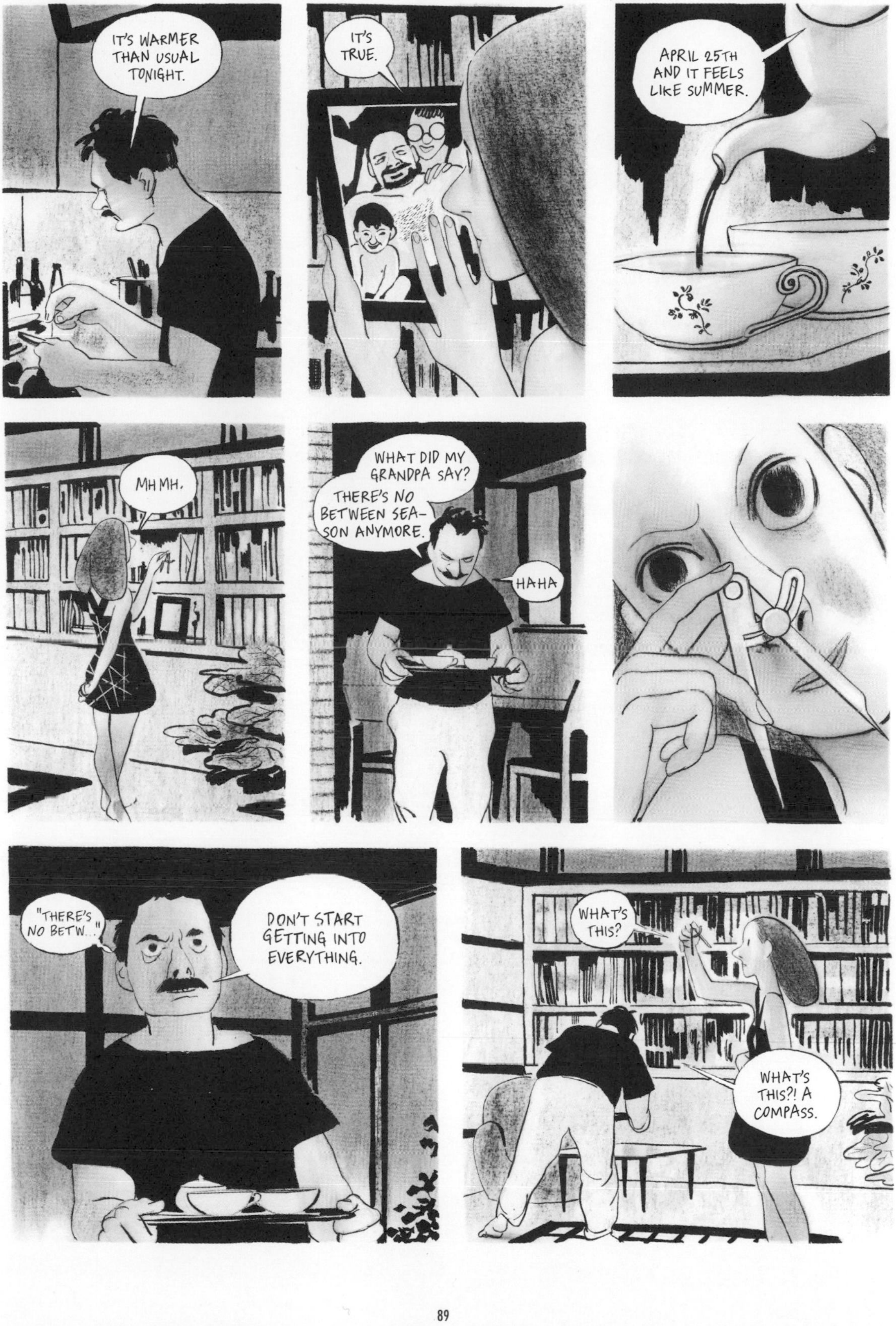
IT'S WARMER THAN USUAL TONIGHT.
IT'S TRUE.
APRIL 25TH AND IT FEELS LIKE SUMMER.
MHMH.
WHAT DID MY GRANDPA SAY?
THERE'S NO BETWEEN SEA-SON ANYMORE.
HAHA
"THERE'S NO BETW..."
DON'T START GETTING INTO EVERYTHING.
WHAT'S THIS?
WHAT'S THIS?! A COMPASS.

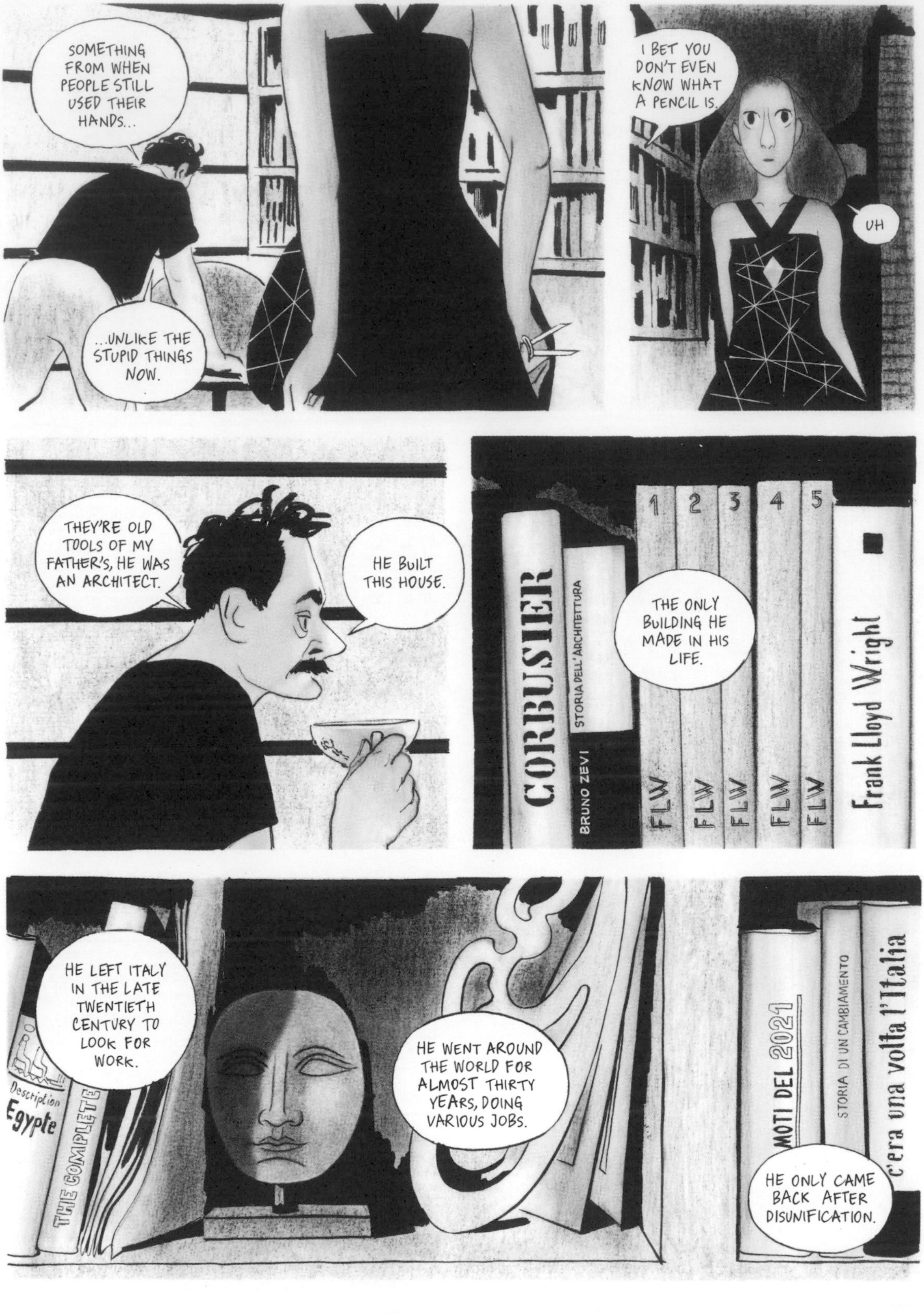
SOMETHING FROM WHEN PEOPLE STILL USED THEIR HANDS...
...UNLIKE THE STUPID THINGS NOW.
I BET YOU DON'T EVEN KNOW WHAT A PENCIL IS.
UH
THEY'RE OLD TOOLS OF MY FATHER'S, HE WAS AN ARCHITECT.
HE BUILT THIS HOUSE.
CORBUSIER
STORIA DELL'ARCHITETTURA
BRUNO ZEVI
1 2 3 4 5
FLW FLW FLW FLW FLW
Frank Lloyd Wright
THE ONLY BUILDING HE MADE IN HIS LIFE.
HE LEFT ITALY IN THE LATE TWENTIETH CENTURY TO LOOK FOR WORK.
Description Egypte
THE COMPLETE
HE WENT AROUND THE WORLD FOR ALMOST THIRTY YEARS, DOING VARIOUS JOBS.
MOTI DEL 2021
STORIA DI UN CAMBIAMENTO
c'era una volta l'Italia
HE ONLY CAME BACK AFTER DISUNIFICATION.

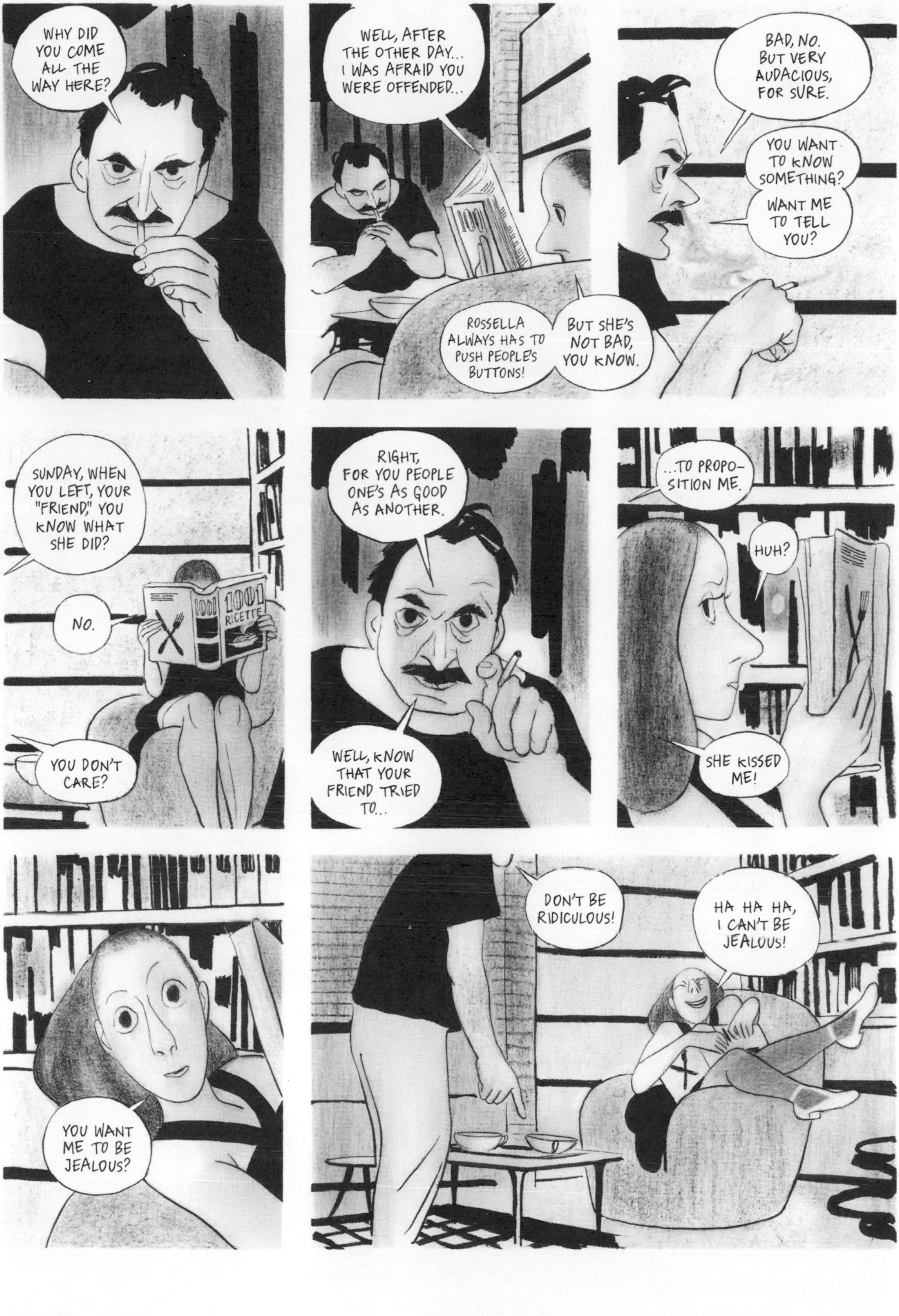
WHY DID YOU COME ALL THE WAY HERE?
WELL, AFTER THE OTHER DAY... I WAS AFRAID YOU WERE OFFENDED...
ROSSELLA ALWAYS HAS TO PUSH PEOPLE'S BUTTONS!
BUT SHE'S NOT BAD, YOU KNOW.
BAD, NO. BUT VERY AUDACIOUS, FOR SURE.
YOU WANT TO KNOW SOMETHING?
WANT ME TO TELL YOU?
SUNDAY, WHEN YOU LEFT, YOUR "FRIEND," YOU KNOW WHAT SHE DID?
NO.
YOU DON'T CARE?
RIGHT, FOR YOU PEOPLE ONE'S AS GOOD AS ANOTHER.
WELL, KNOW THAT YOUR FRIEND TRIED TO...
...TO PROPOSITION ME.
HUH?
SHE KISSED ME!
YOU WANT ME TO BE JEALOUS?
DON'T BE RIDICULOUS!
HA HA HA, I CAN'T BE JEALOUS!

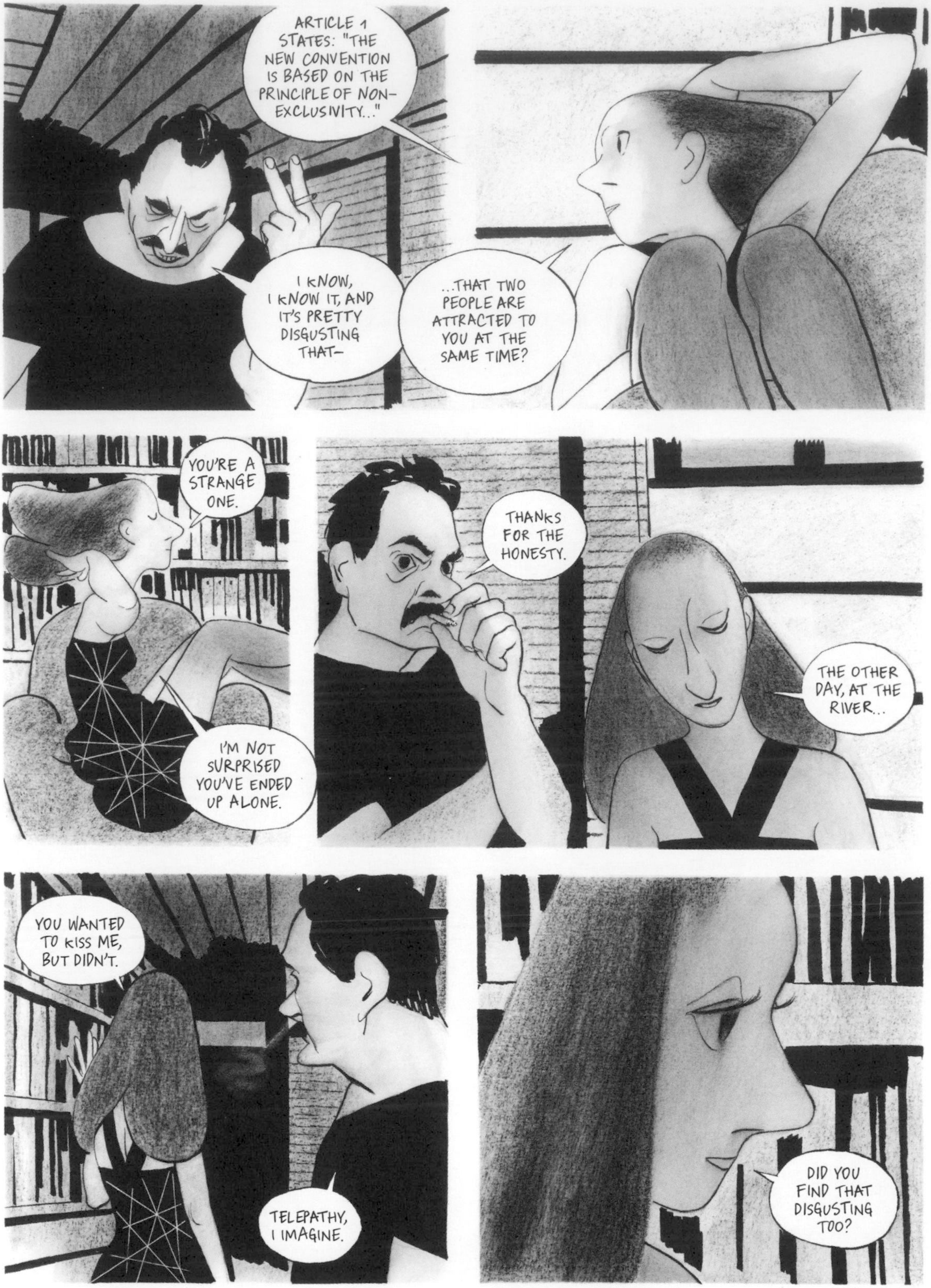
ARTICLE 1 STATES: "THE NEW CONVENTION IS BASED ON THE PRINCIPLE OF NON-EXCLUSIVITY..."
I KNOW, I KNOW IT, AND IT'S PRETTY DISGUSTING THAT—
...THAT TWO PEOPLE ARE ATTRACTED TO YOU AT THE SAME TIME?
YOU'RE A STRANGE ONE.
I'M NOT SURPRISED YOU'VE ENDED UP ALONE.
THANKS FOR THE HONESTY.
THE OTHER DAY, AT THE RIVER...
YOU WANTED TO KISS ME, BUT DIDN'T.
TELEPATHY, I IMAGINE.
DID YOU FIND THAT DISGUSTING TOO?

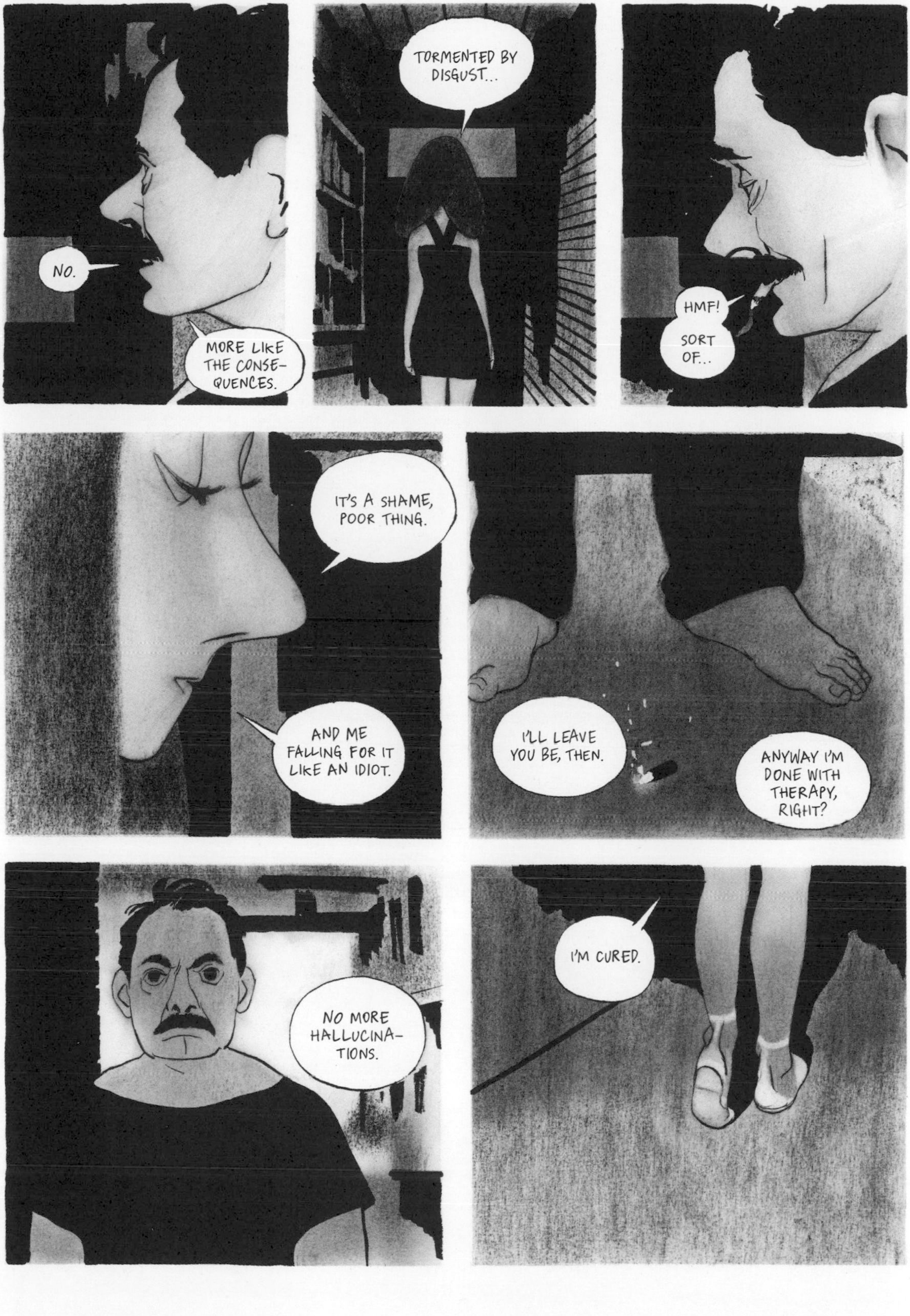
NO.
MORE LIKE THE CONSE-QUENCES.
TORMENTED BY DISGUST...
HMF!
SORT OF...
IT'S A SHAME, POOR THING.
AND ME FALLING FOR IT LIKE AN IDIOT.
I'LL LEAVE YOU BE, THEN.
ANYWAY I'M DONE WITH THERAPY, RIGHT?
NO MORE HALLUCINA-TIONS.
I'M CURED.

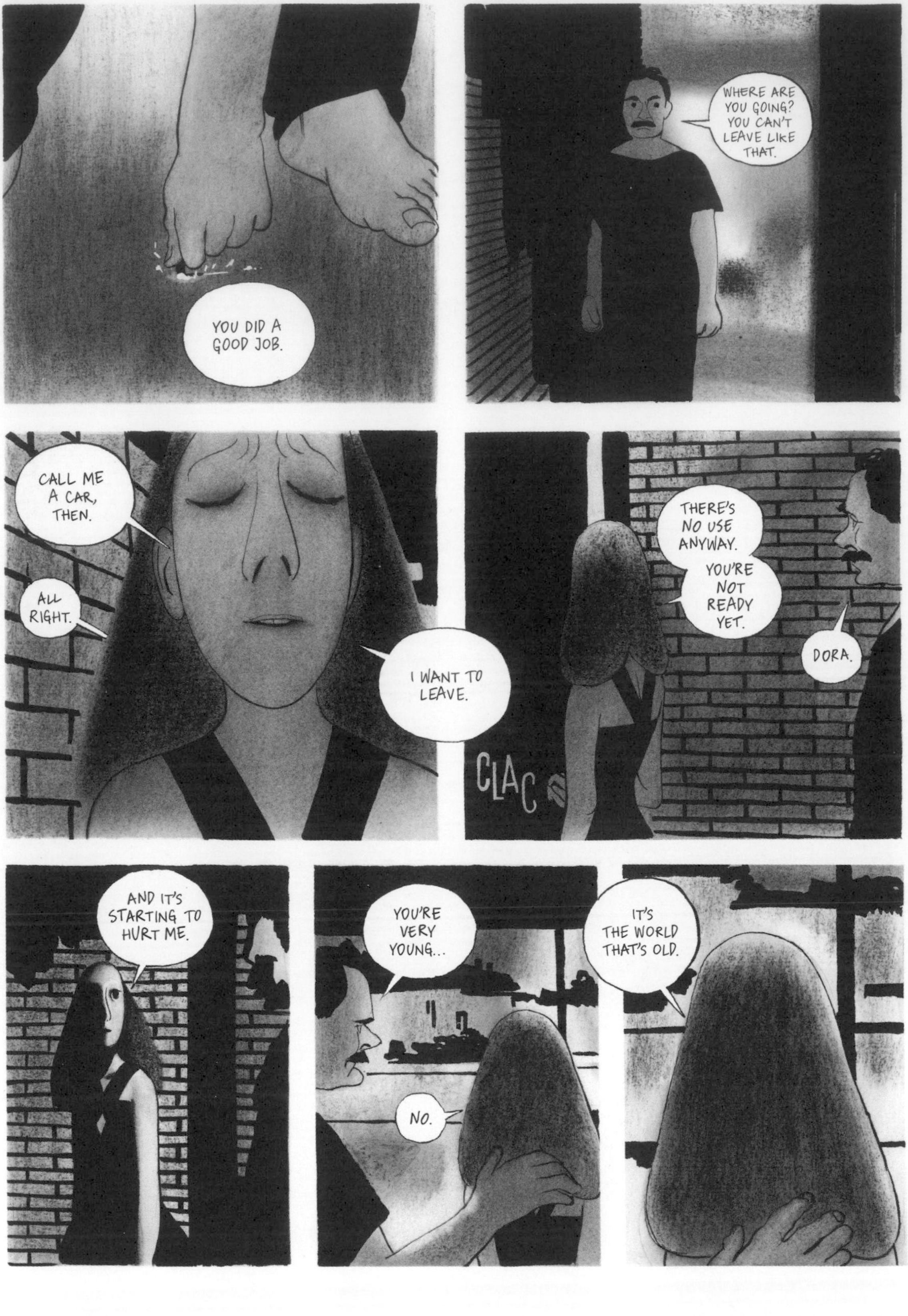
YOU DID A GOOD JOB.
WHERE ARE YOU GOING? YOU CAN'T LEAVE LIKE THAT.
CALL ME A CAR, THEN.
ALL RIGHT.
I WANT TO LEAVE.
THERE'S NO USE ANYWAY.
YOU'RE NOT READY YET.
DORA.
CLAC
AND IT'S STARTING TO HURT ME.
YOU'RE VERY YOUNG...
NO.
IT'S THE WORLD THAT'S OLD.

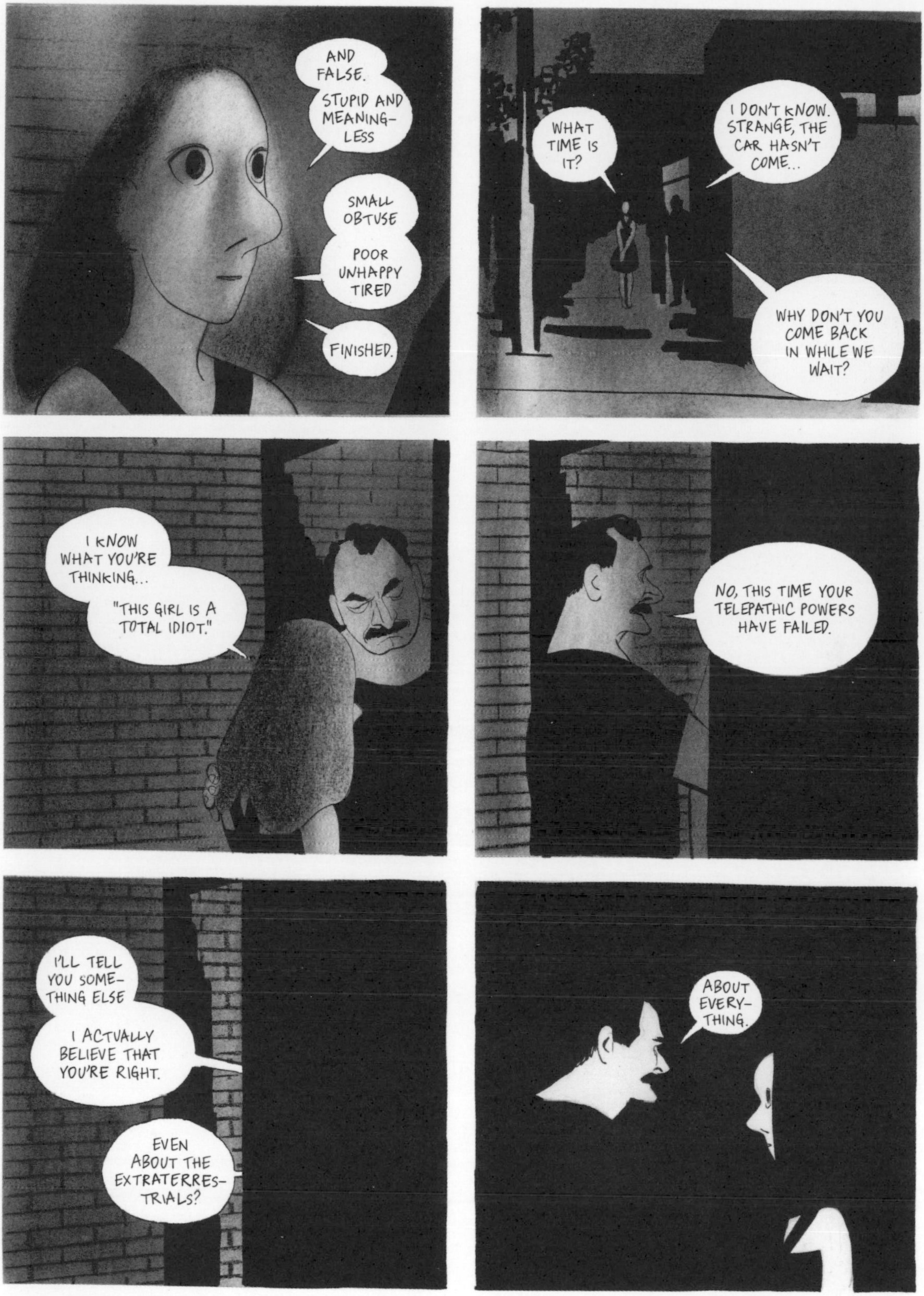
AND FALSE.
STUPID AND MEANING-LESS
SMALL OBTUSE
POOR UNHAPPY TIRED
FINISHED.
WHAT TIME IS IT?
I DON'T KNOW. STRANGE, THE CAR HASN'T COME...
WHY DON'T YOU COME BACK IN WHILE WE WAIT?
I KNOW WHAT YOU'RE THINKING...
"THIS GIRL IS A TOTAL IDIOT."
NO, THIS TIME YOUR TELEPATHIC POWERS HAVE FAILED.
I'LL TELL YOU SOME-THING ELSE
I ACTUALLY BELIEVE THAT YOU'RE RIGHT.
EVEN ABOUT THE EXTRATERRES-TRIALS?
ABOUT EVERY-THING.

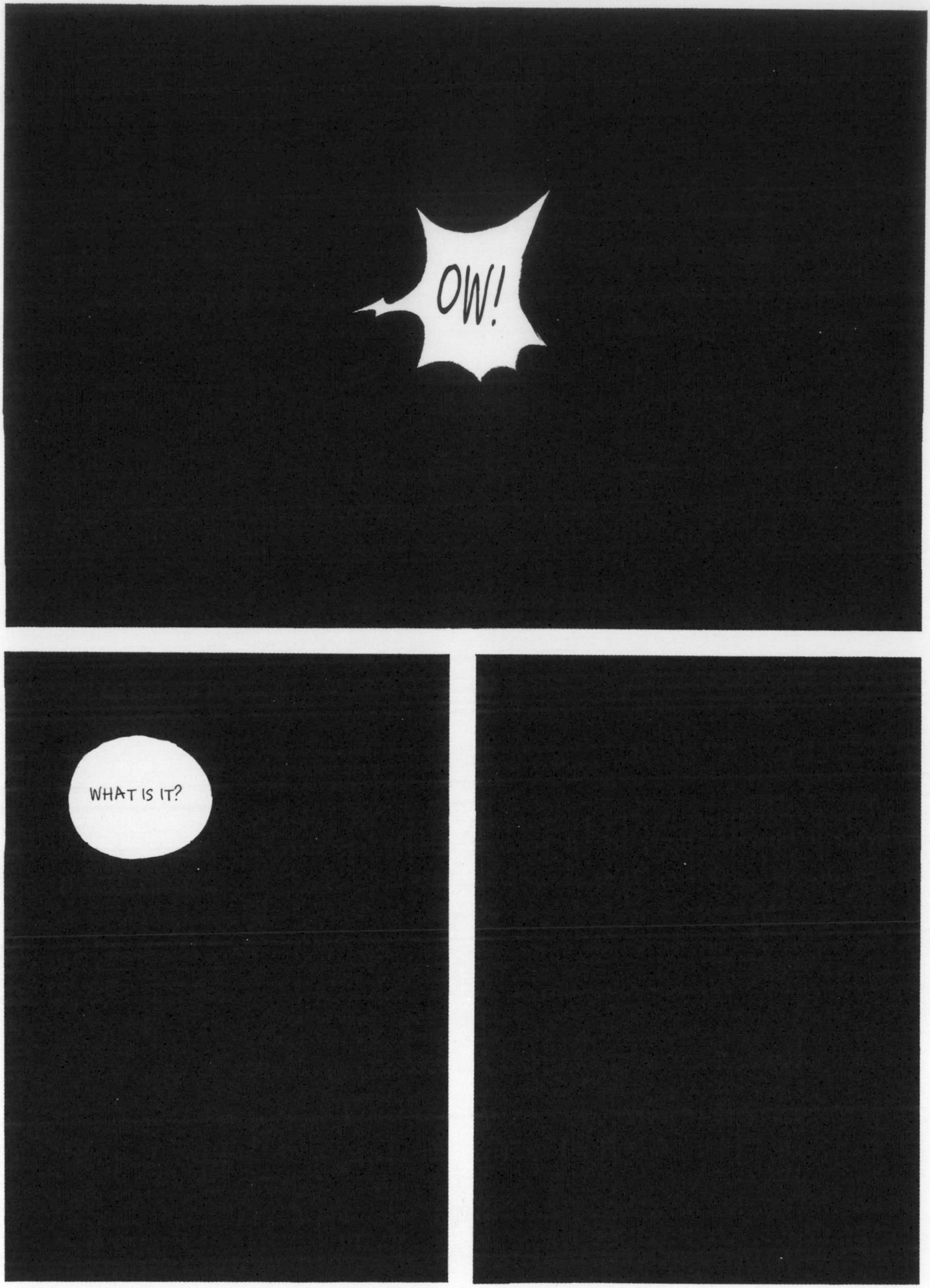
OW!
WHAT IS IT?

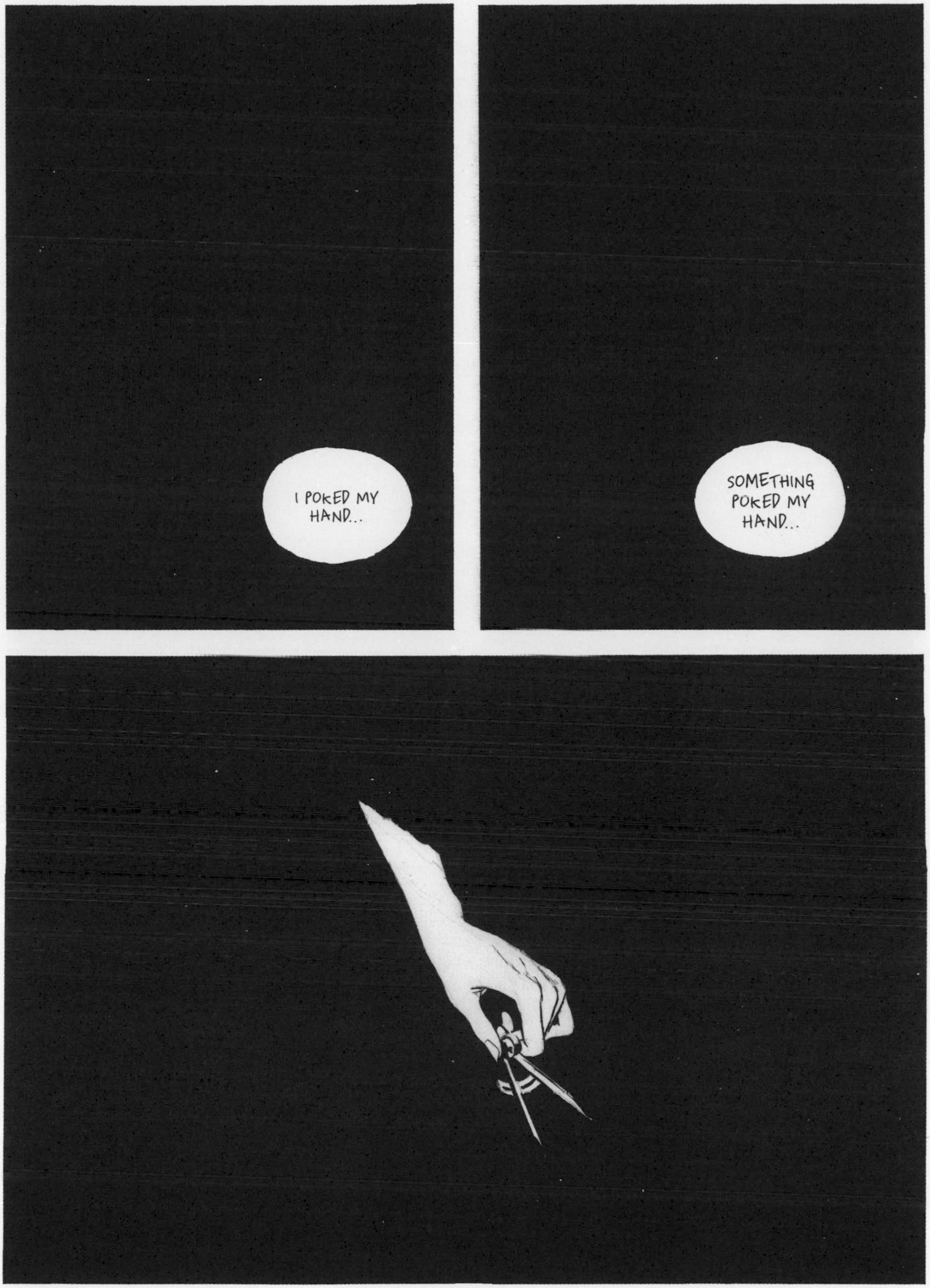
I POKED MY HAND...
SOMETHING POKED MY HAND...

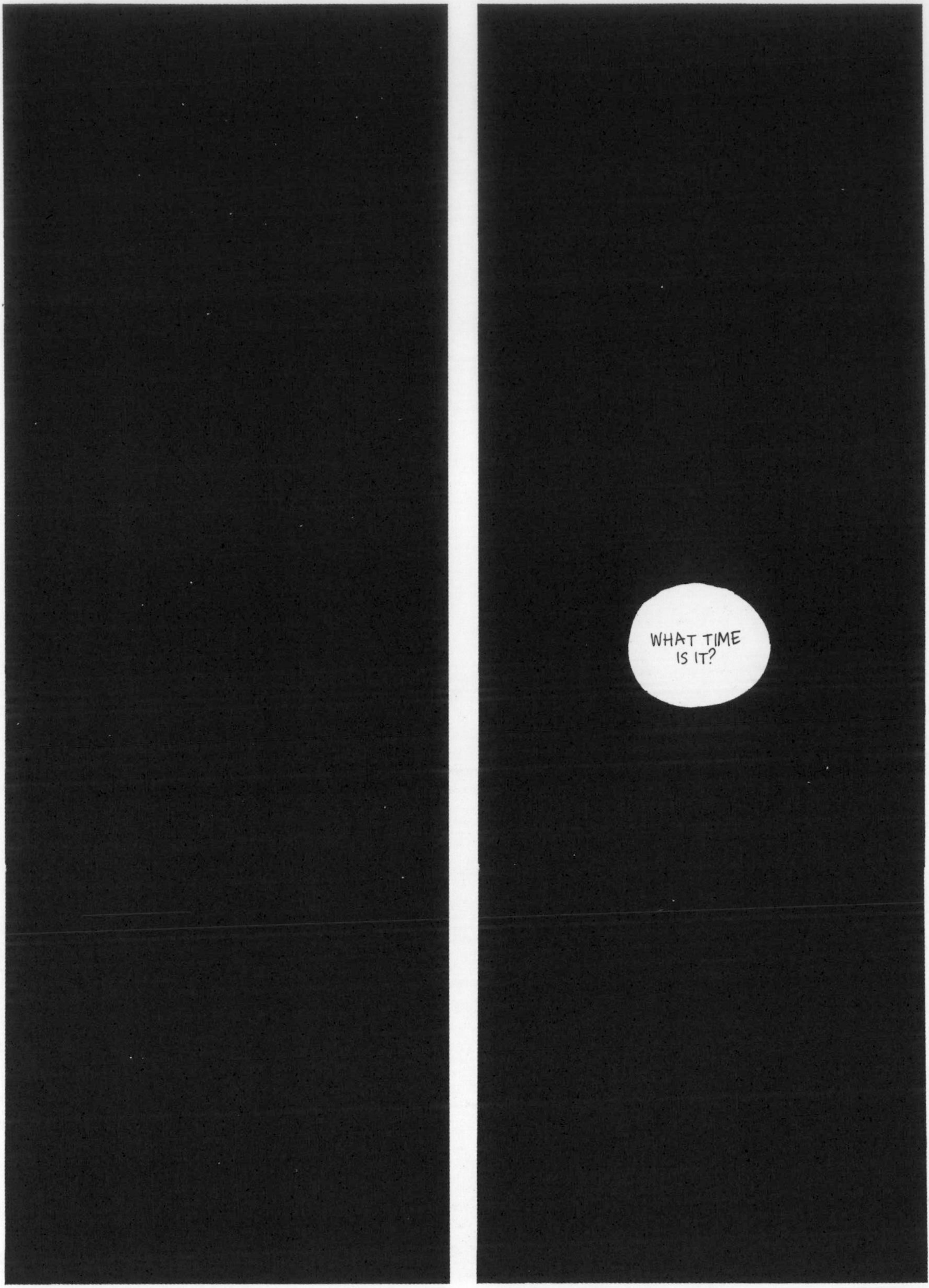
WHAT TIME IS IT?

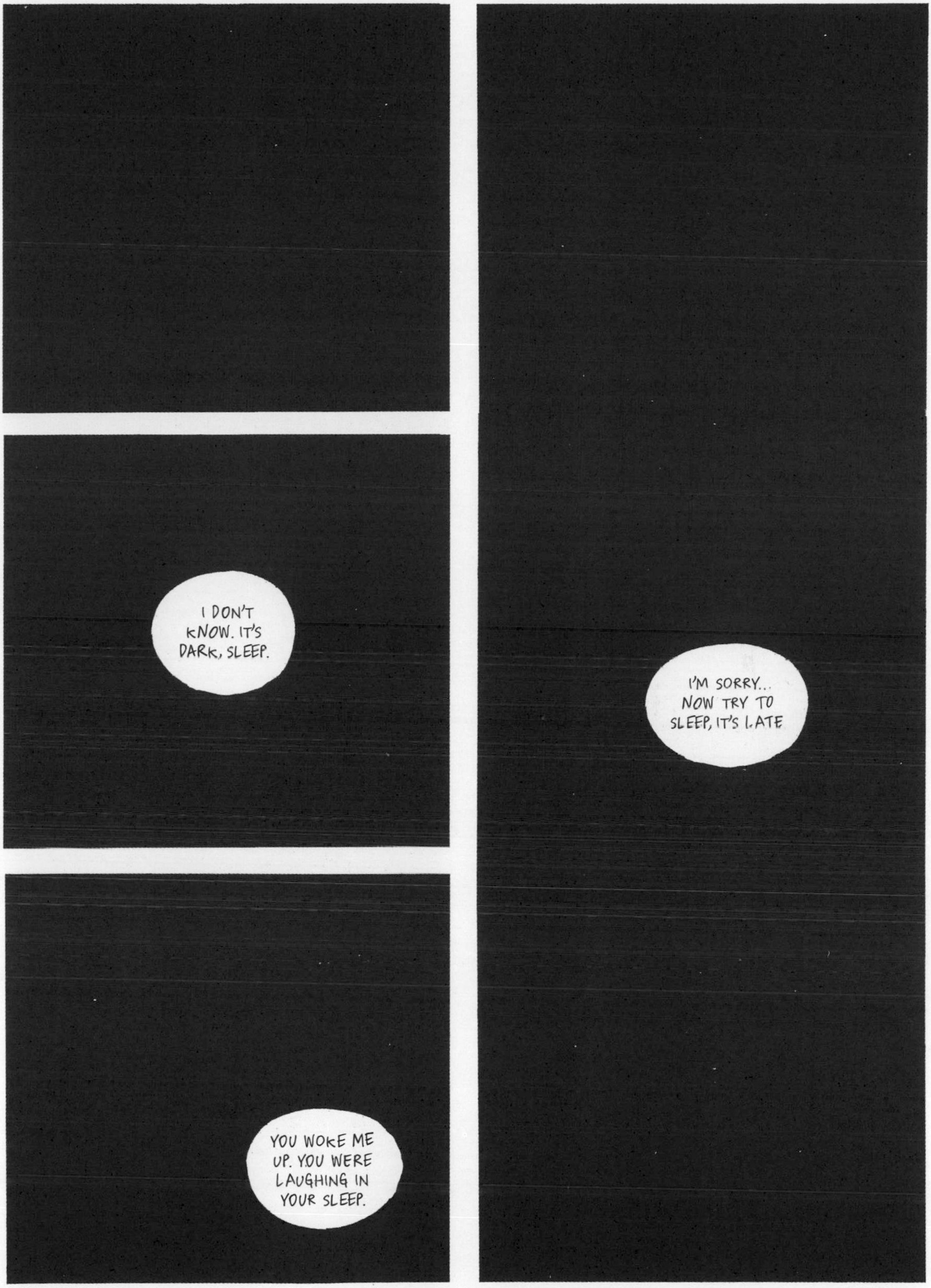
I DON'T KNOW. IT'S DARK, SLEEP.
YOU WOKE ME UP. YOU WERE LAUGHING IN YOUR SLEEP.
I'M SORRY... NOW TRY TO SLEEP, IT'S LATE

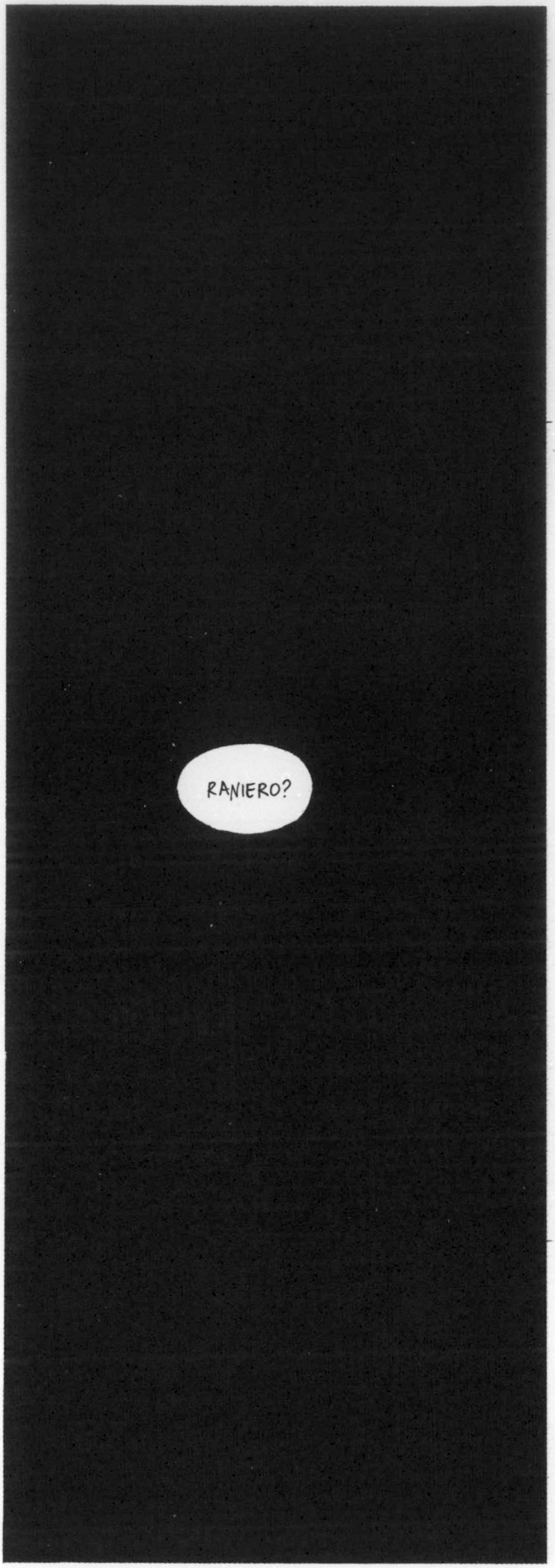
RANIERO?

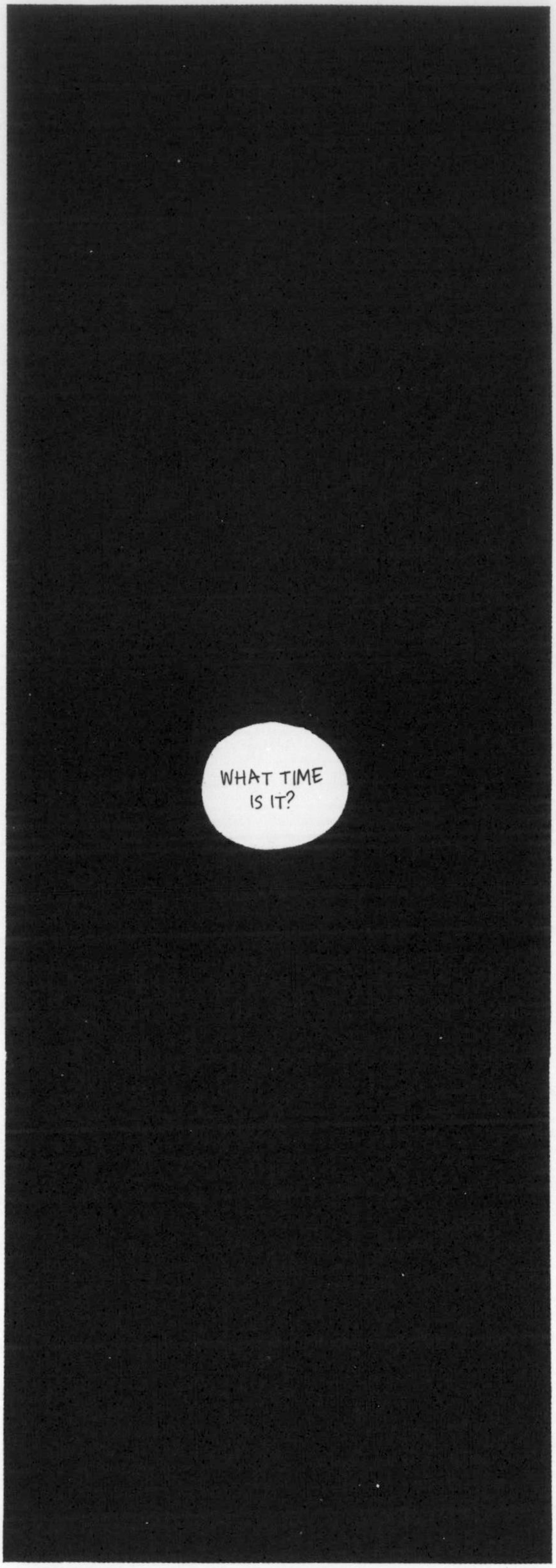
WHAT TIME IS IT?

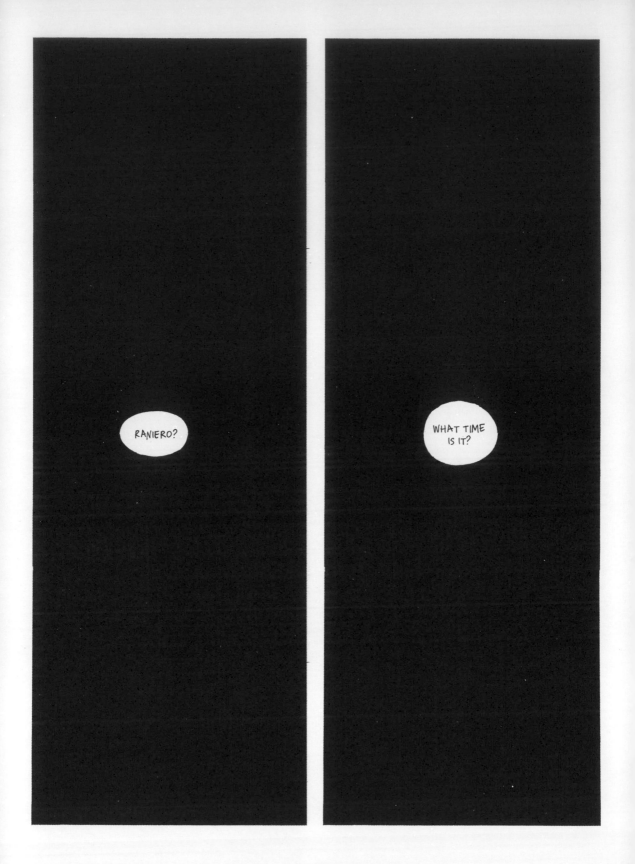

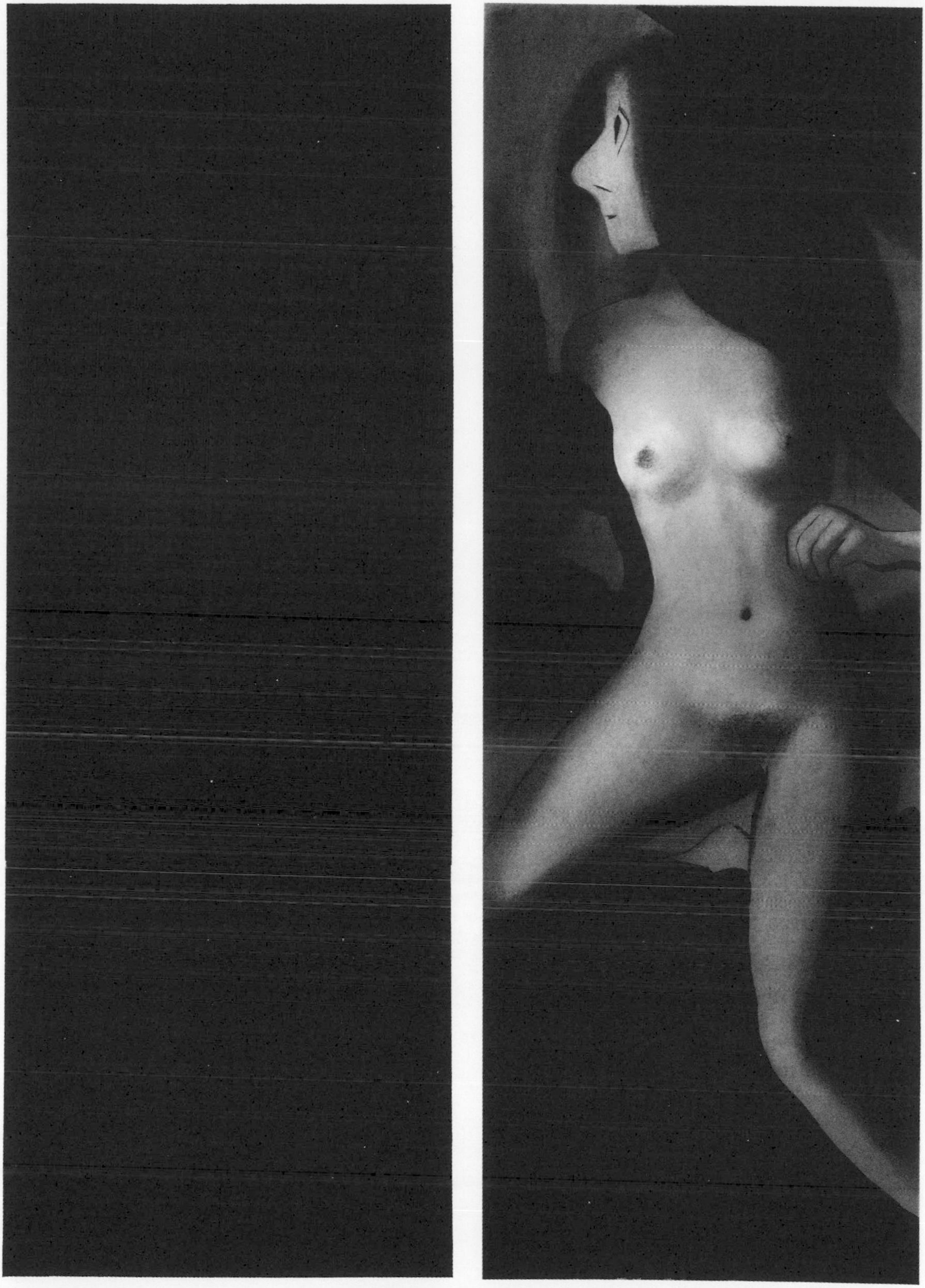

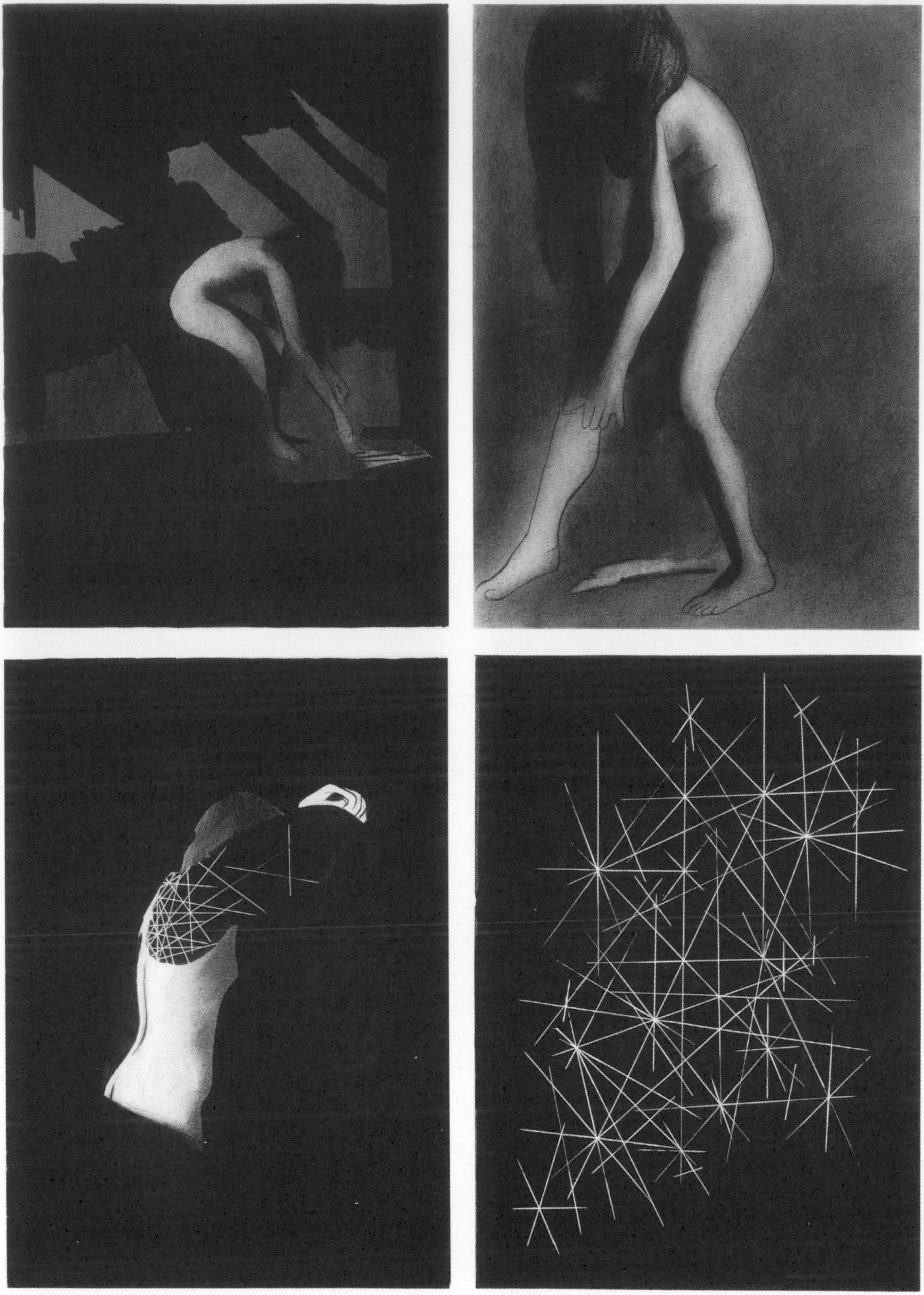

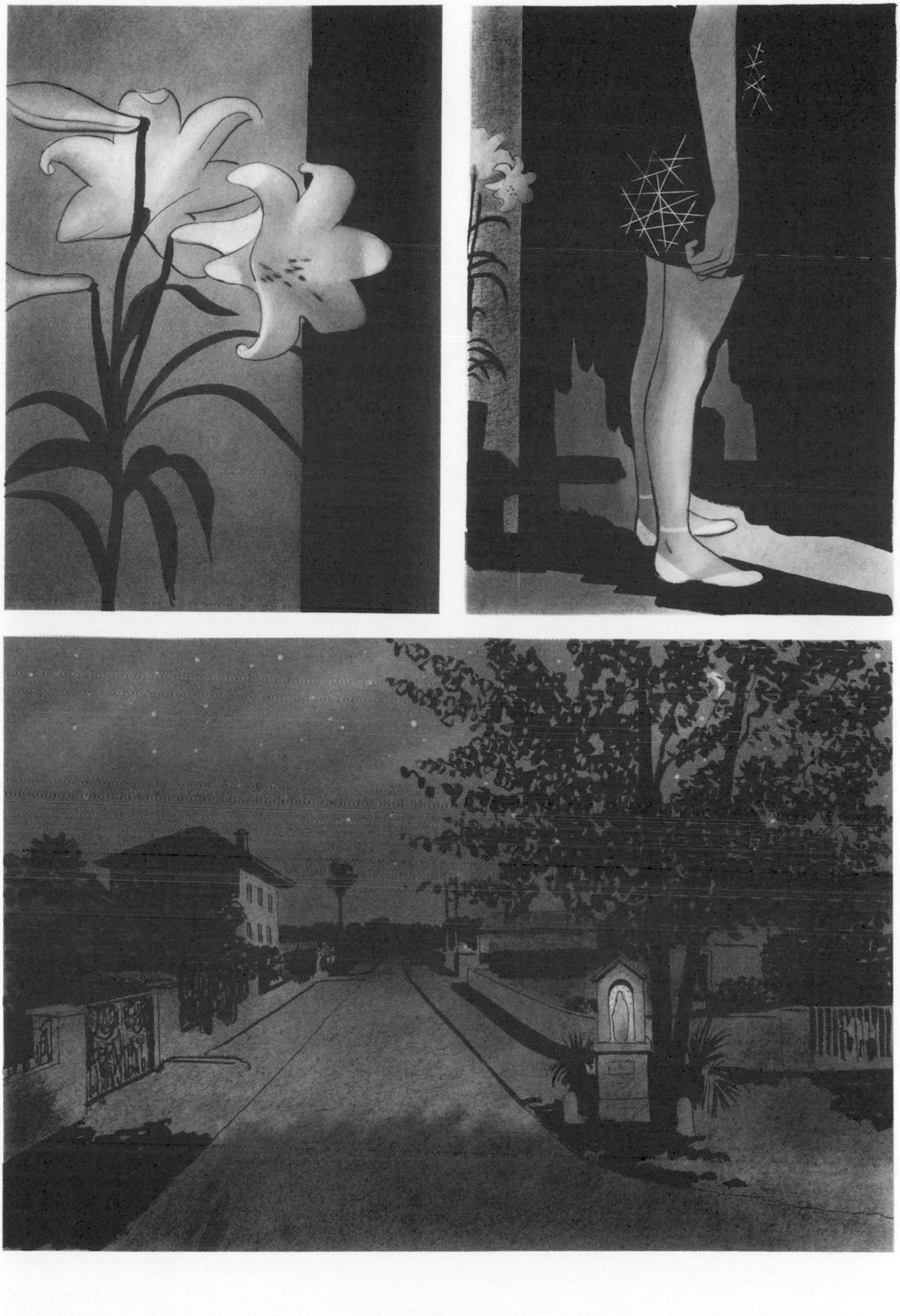

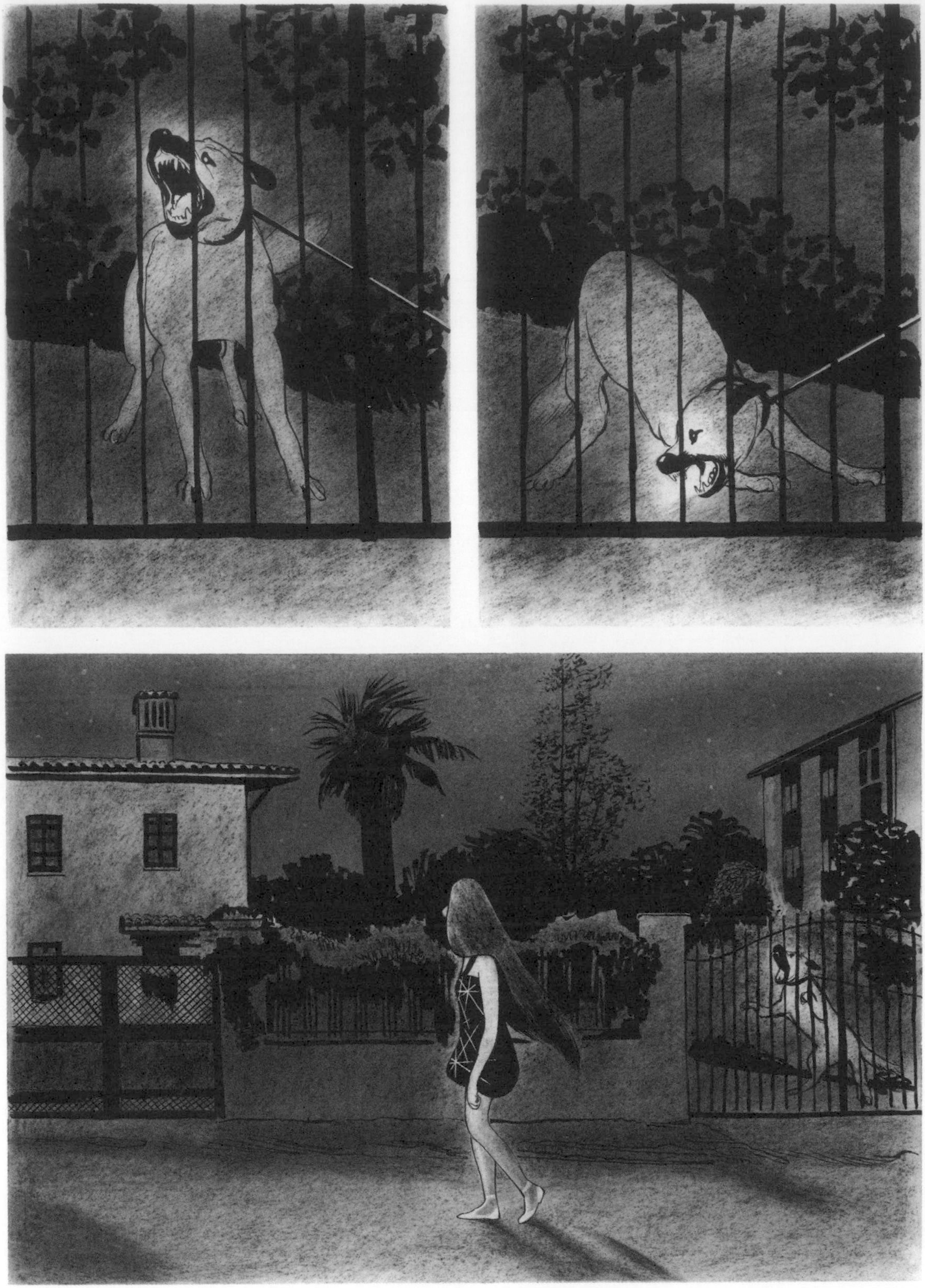

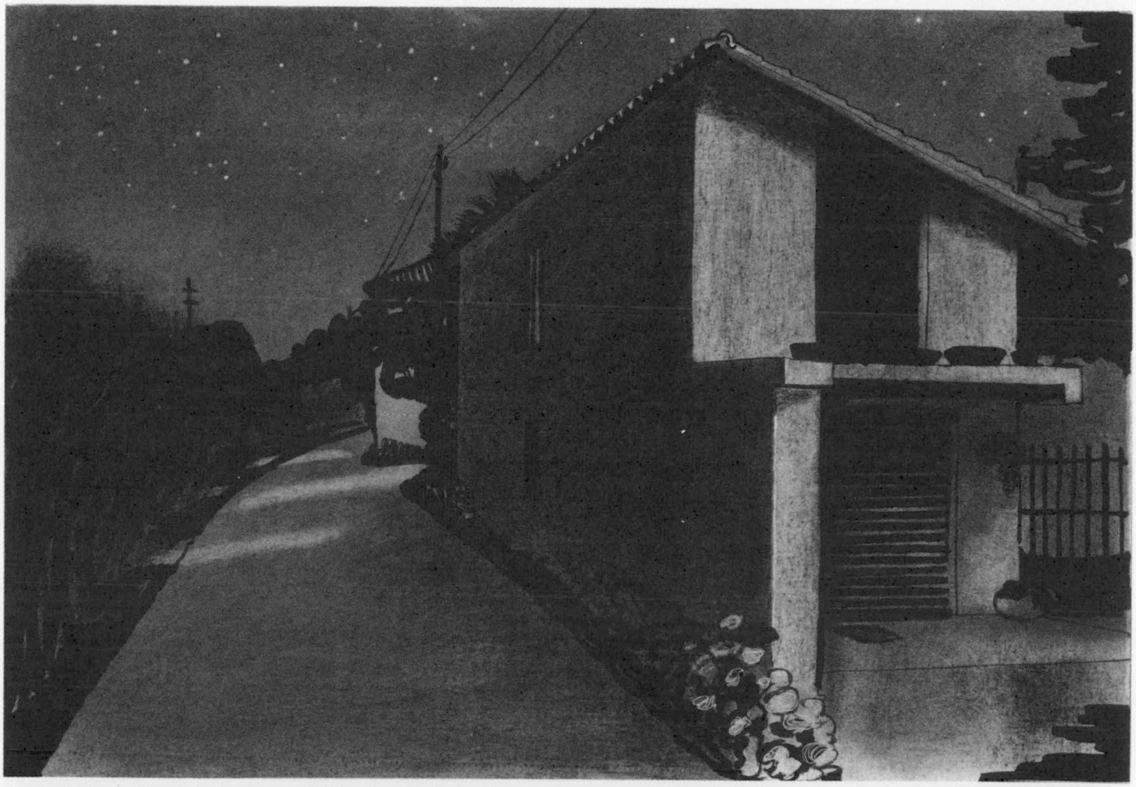

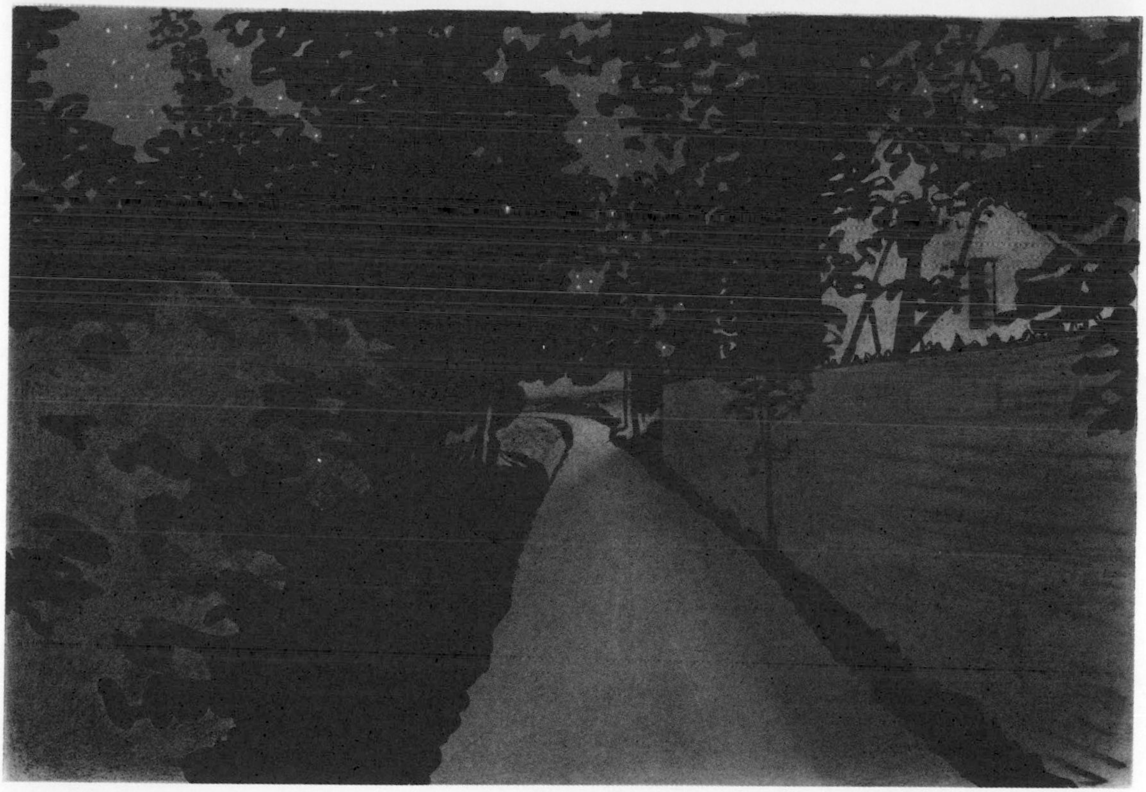

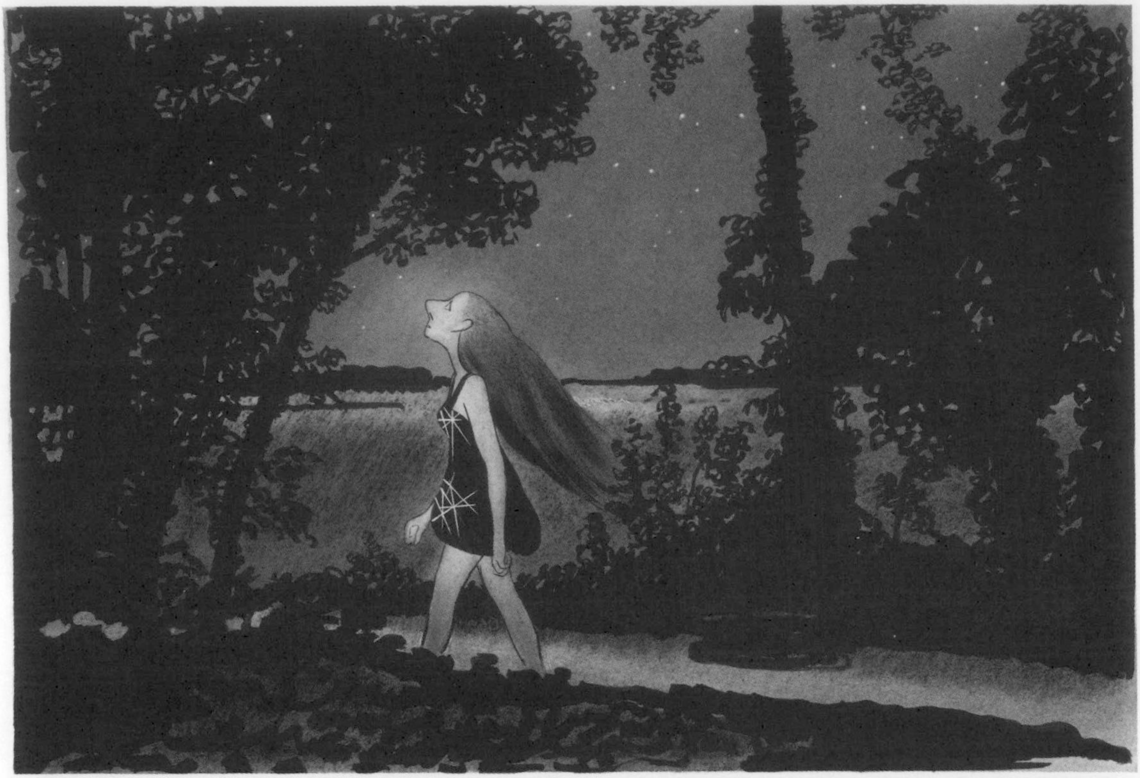

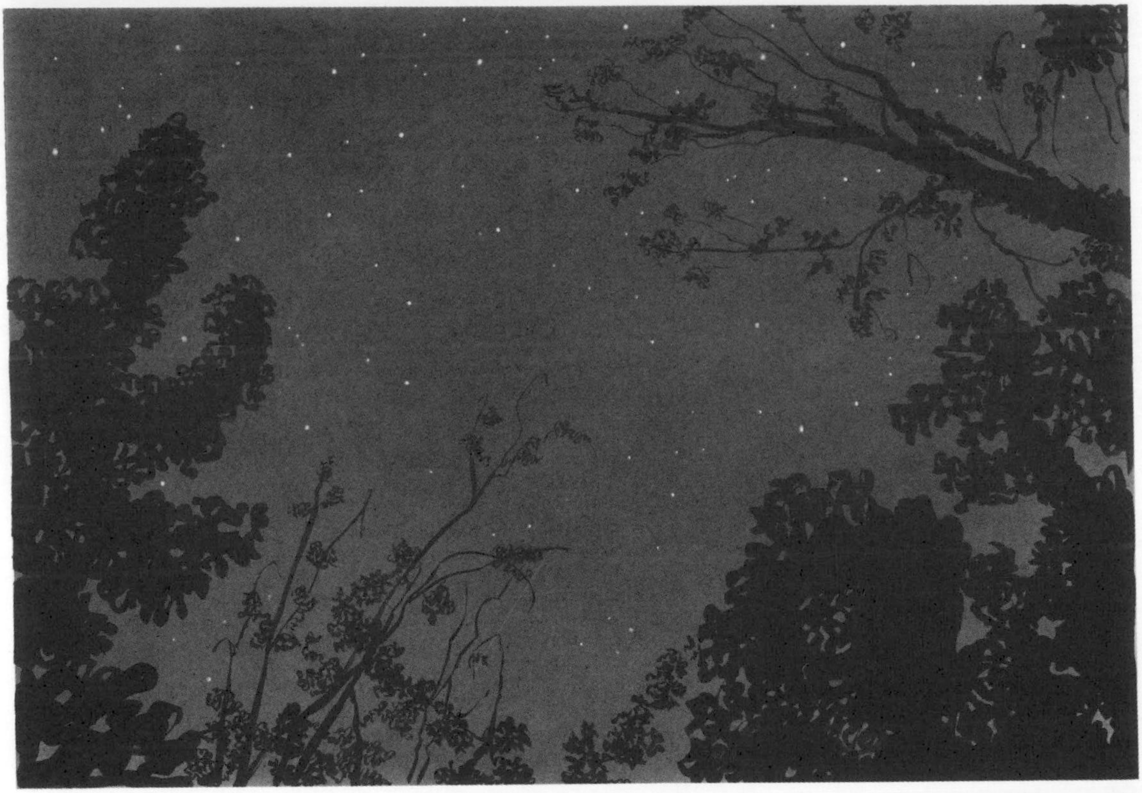

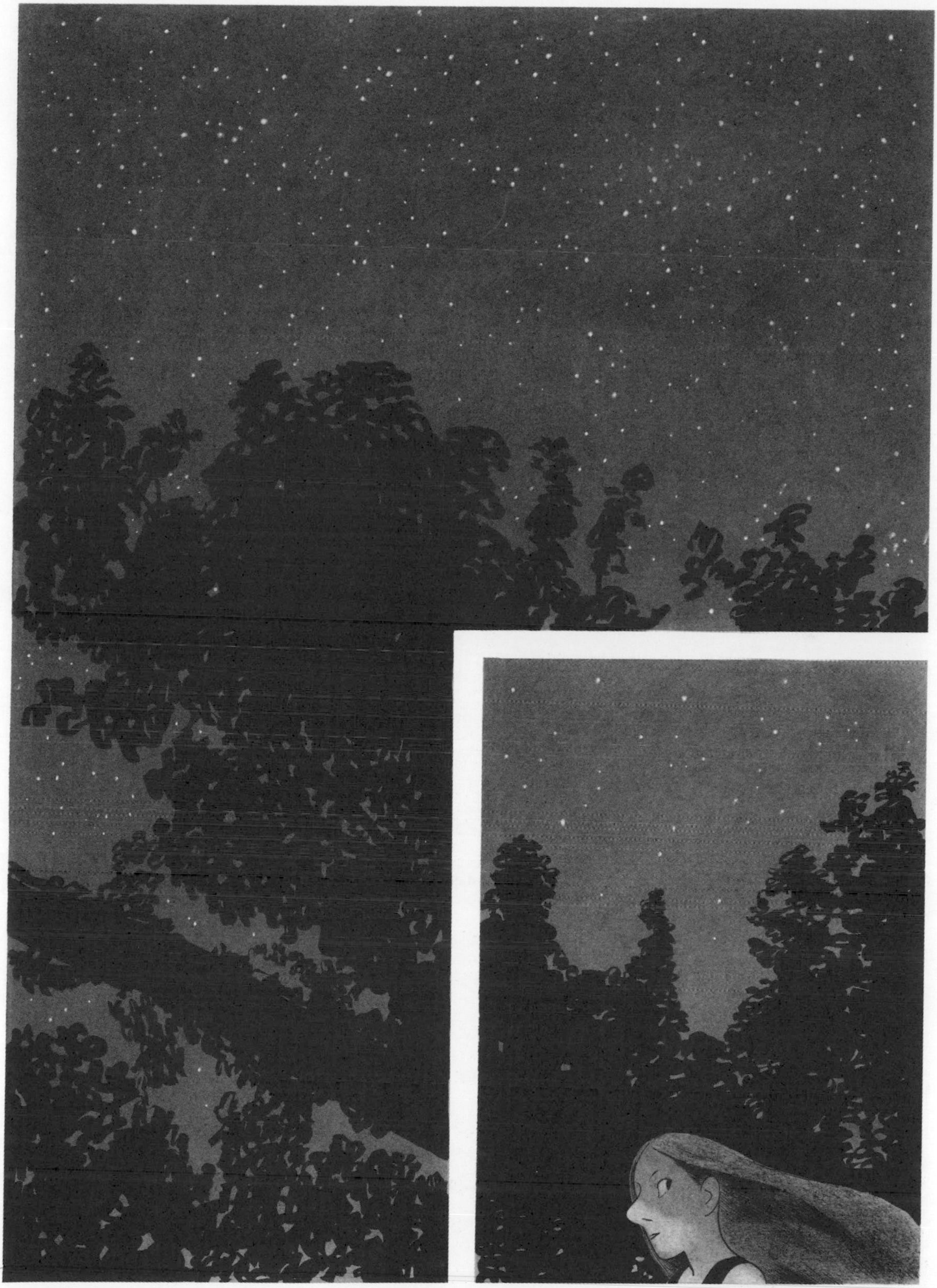

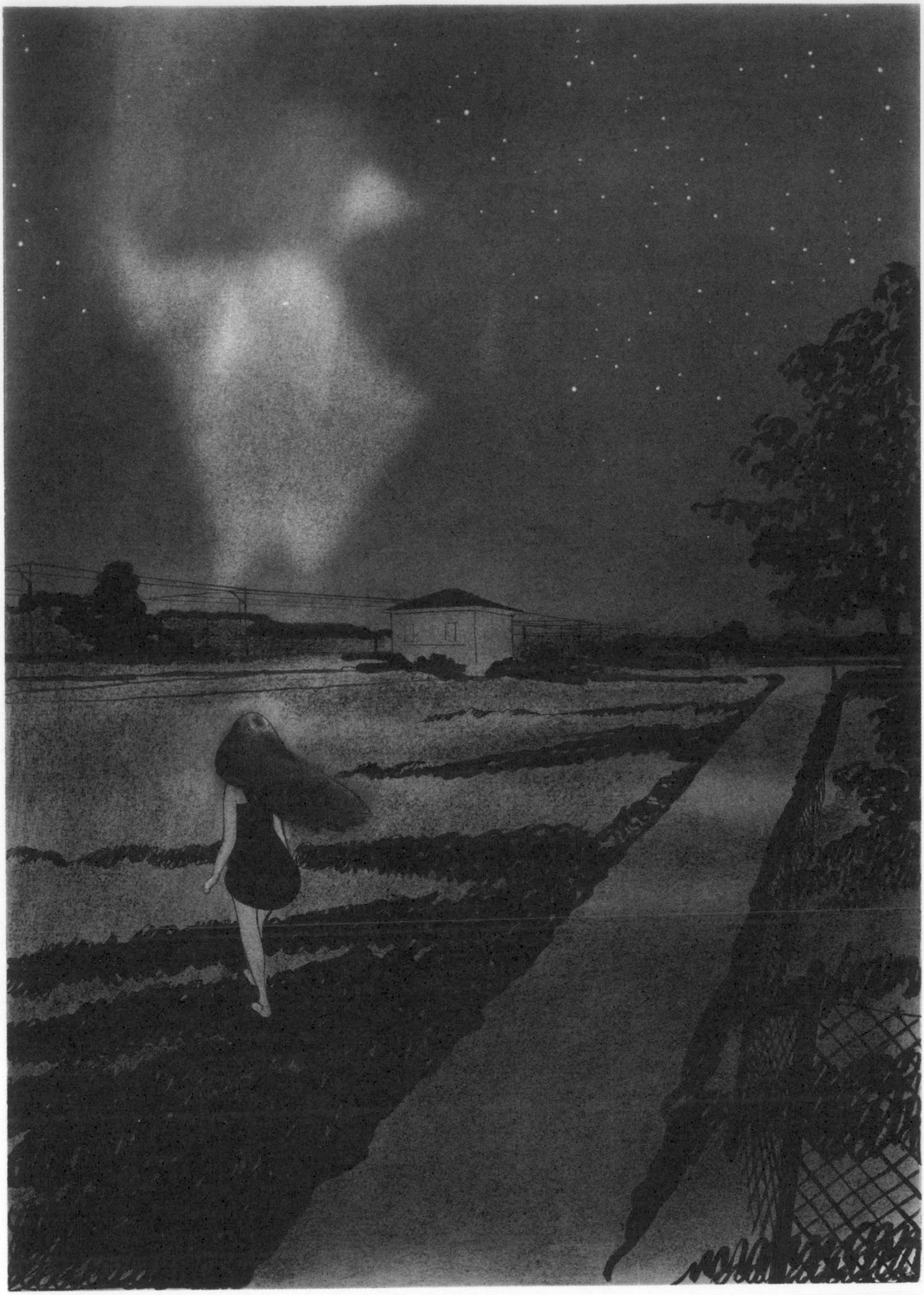

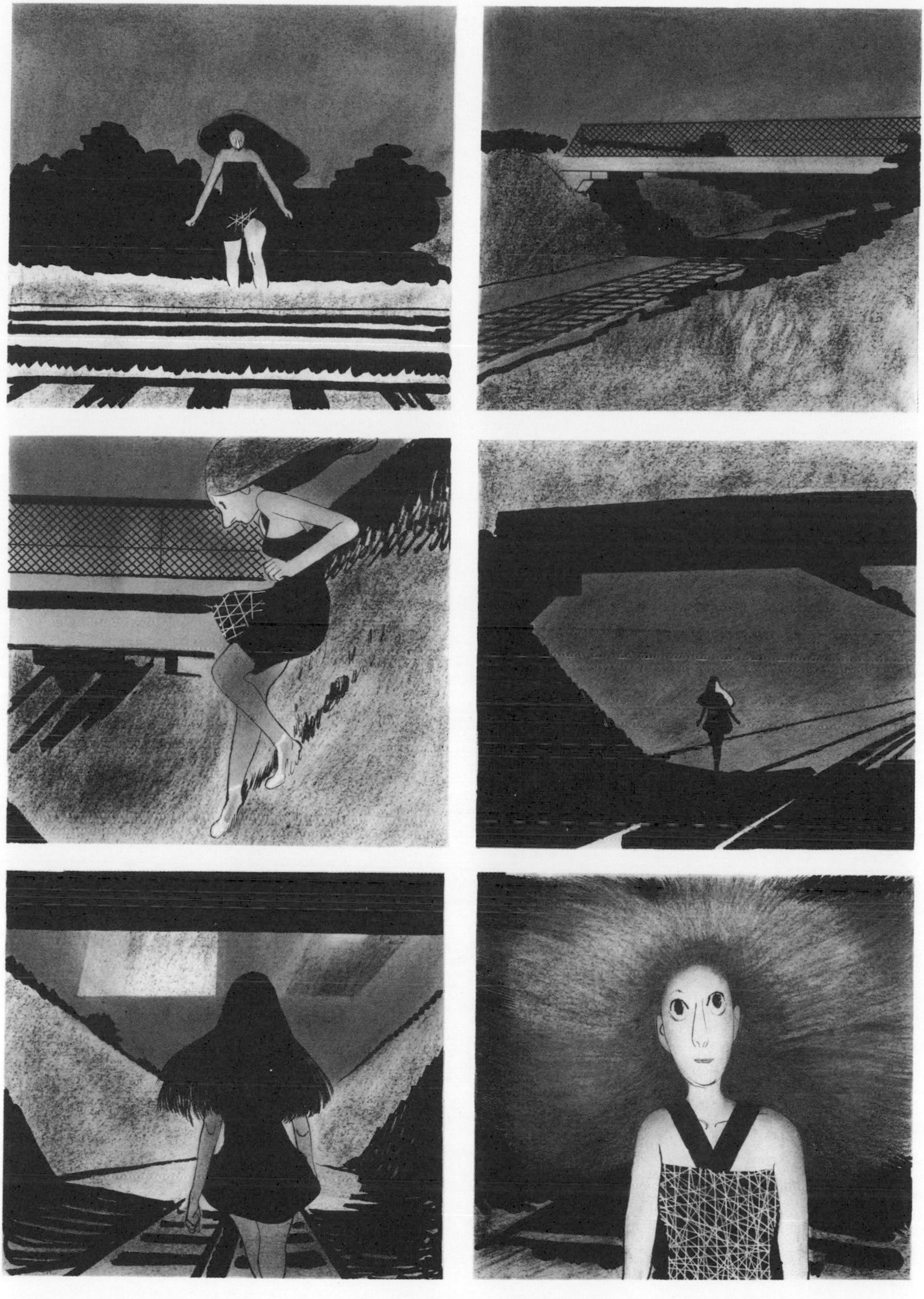

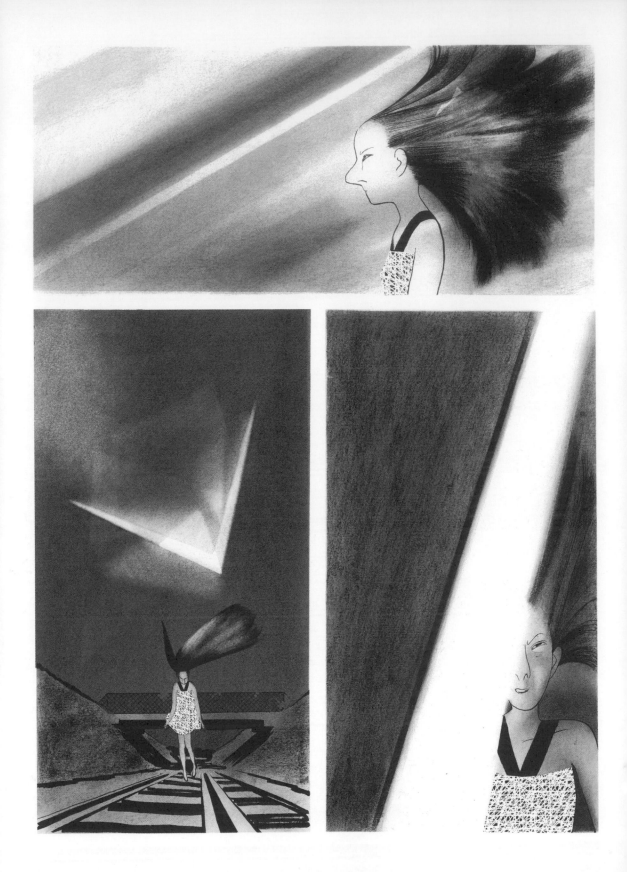

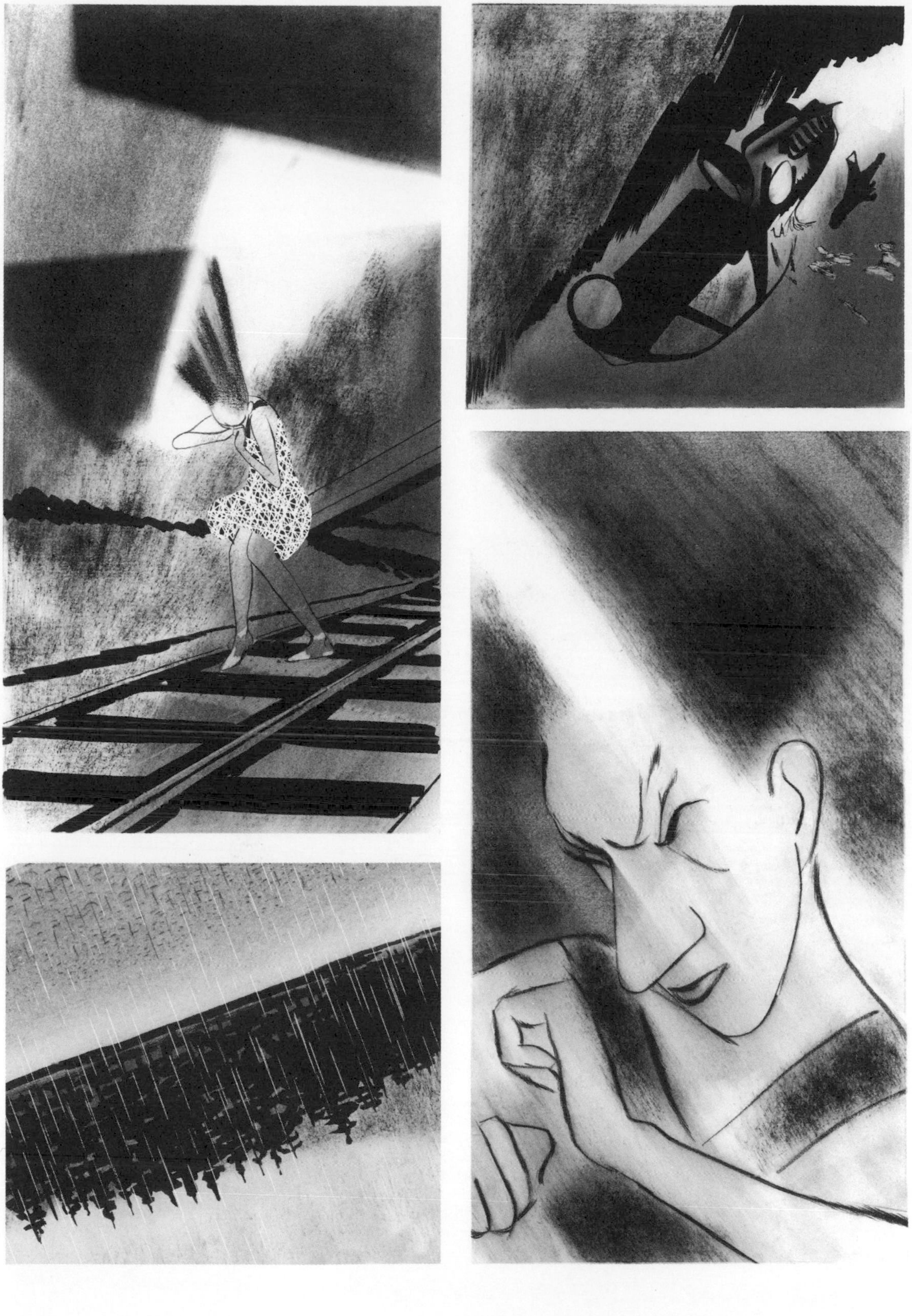

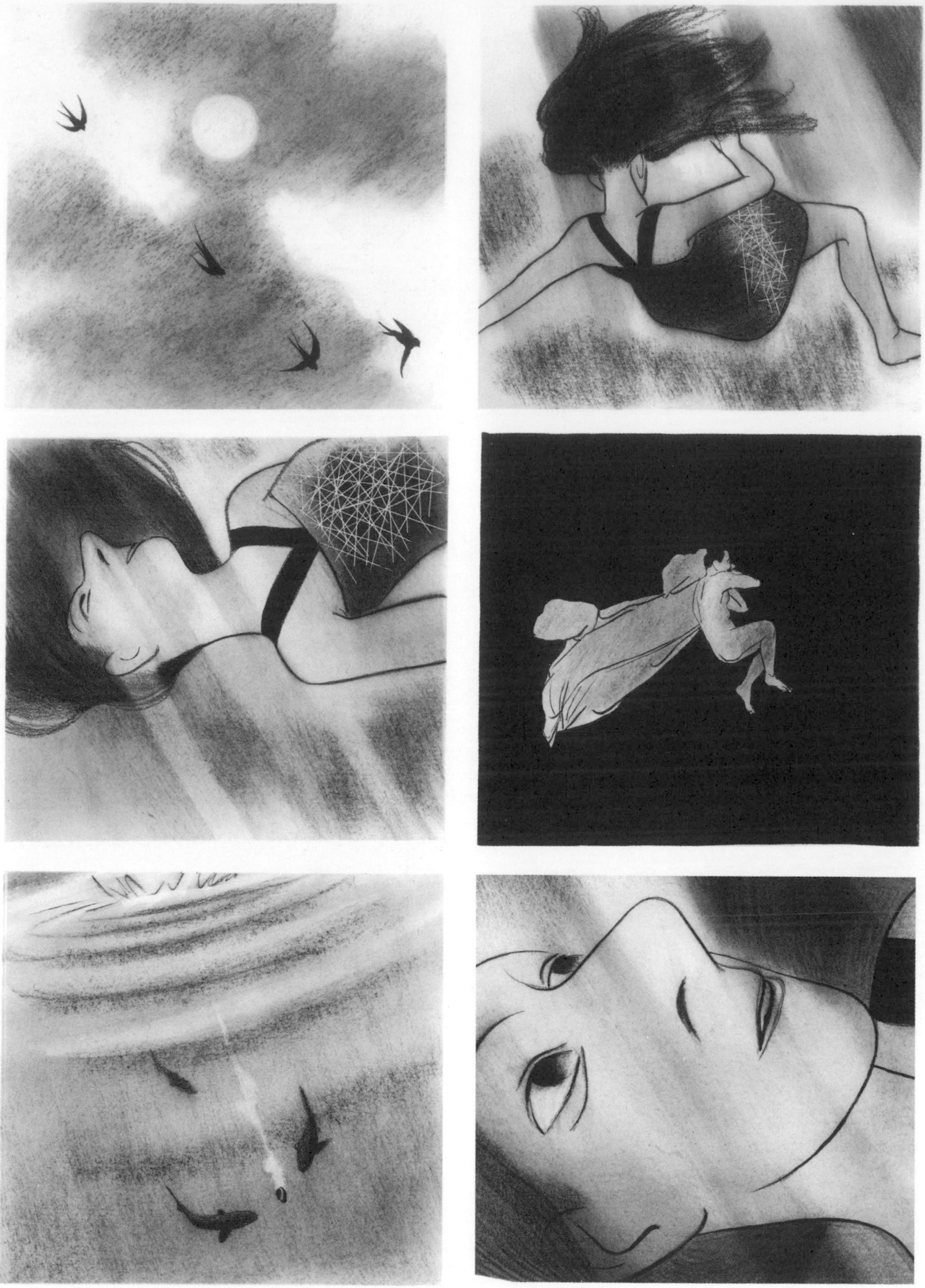

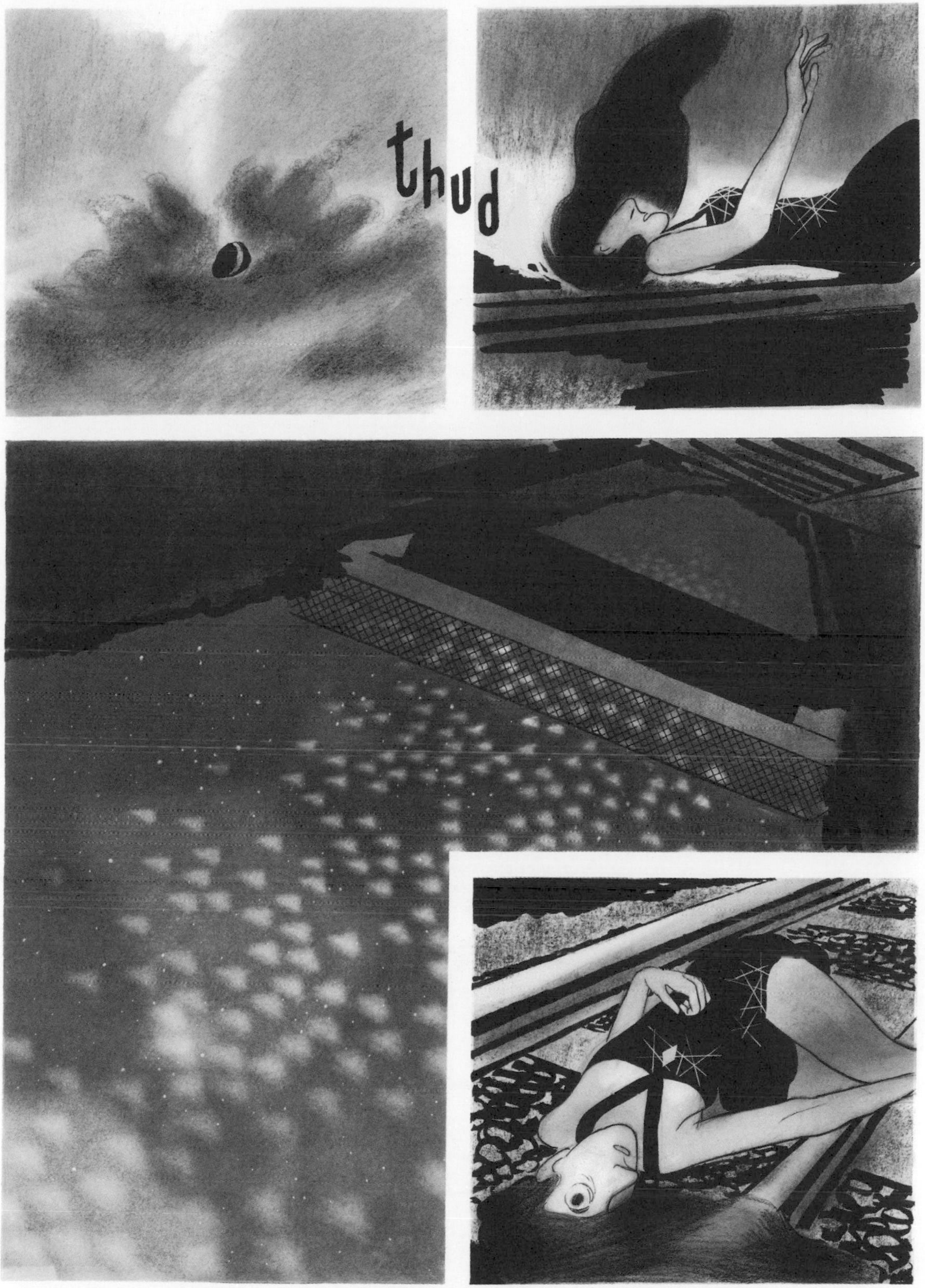
thud

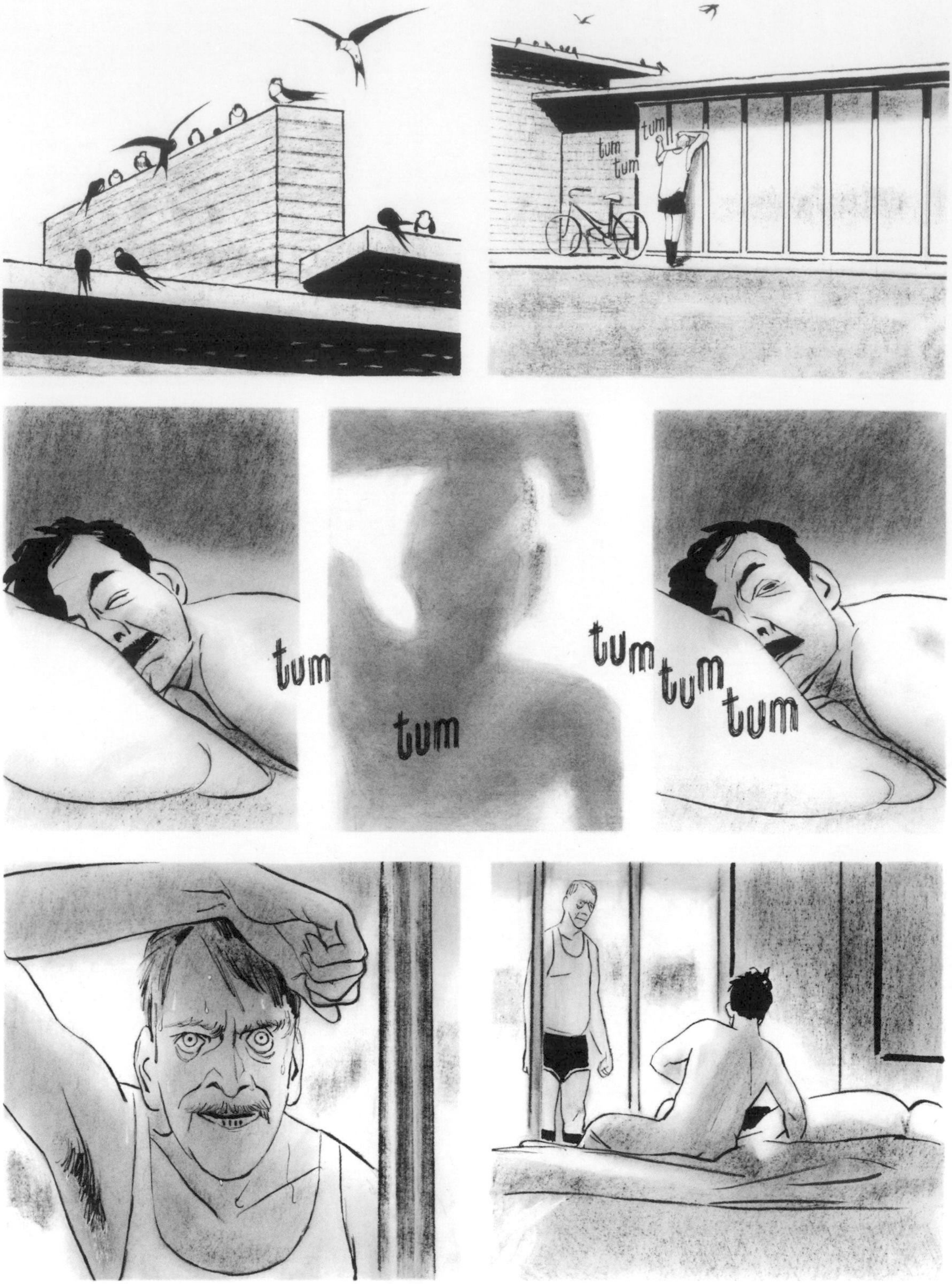
tum
tum
tum
tum
tum
tum
tum
tum
tum

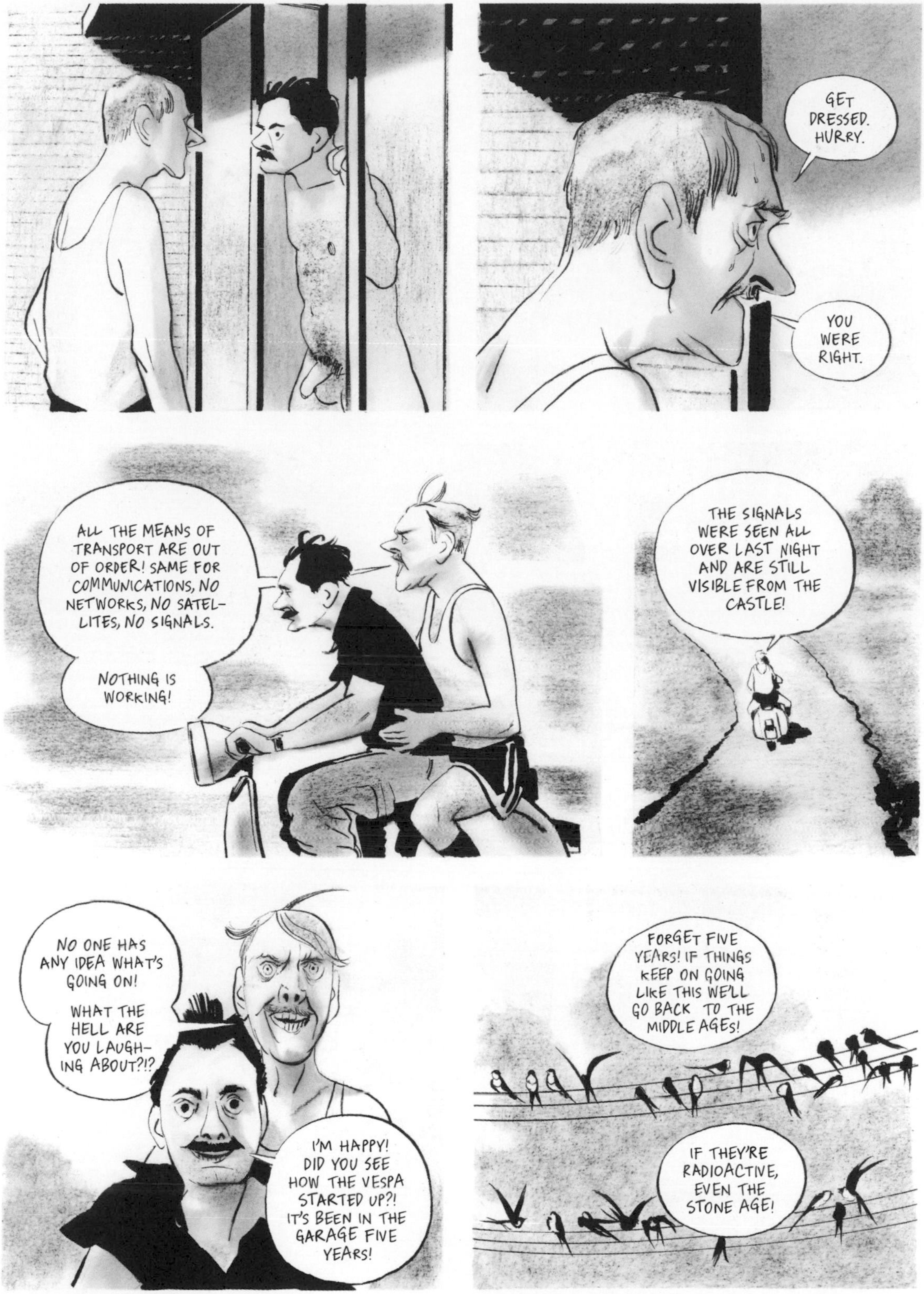
GET DRESSED. HURRY.
YOU WERE RIGHT.
ALL THE MEANS OF TRANSPORT ARE OUT OF ORDER! SAME FOR COMMUNICATIONS, NO NETWORKS, NO SATEL-LITES, NO SIGNALS.
NOTHING IS WORKING!
THE SIGNALS WERE SEEN ALL OVER LAST NIGHT AND ARE STILL VISIBLE FROM THE CASTLE!
NO ONE HAS ANY IDEA WHAT'S GOING ON!
WHAT THE HELL ARE YOU LAUGH-ING ABOUT?!?
I'M HAPPY! DID YOU SEE HOW THE VESPA STARTED UP?! IT'S BEEN IN THE GARAGE FIVE YEARS!
FORGET FIVE YEARS! IF THINGS KEEP ON GOING LIKE THIS WE'LL GO BACK TO THE MIDDLE AGES!
IF THEY'RE RADIOACTIVE, EVEN THE STONE AGE!

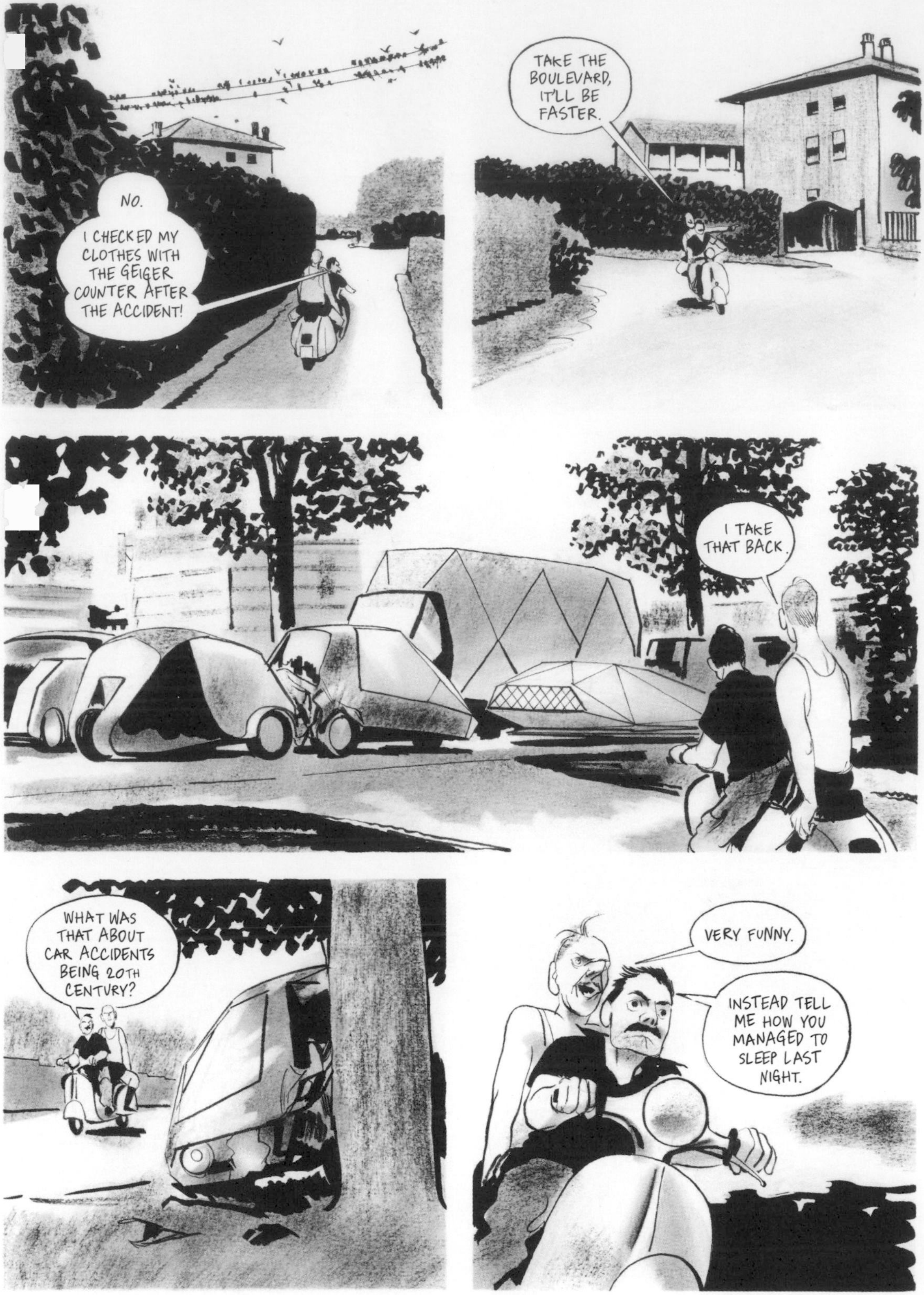
NO.
I CHECKED MY CLOTHES WITH THE GEIGER COUNTER AFTER THE ACCIDENT!
TAKE THE BOULEVARD, IT'LL BE FASTER.
I TAKE THAT BACK.
WHAT WAS THAT ABOUT CAR ACCIDENTS BEING 20TH CENTURY?
VERY FUNNY.
INSTEAD TELL ME HOW YOU MANAGED TO SLEEP LAST NIGHT.

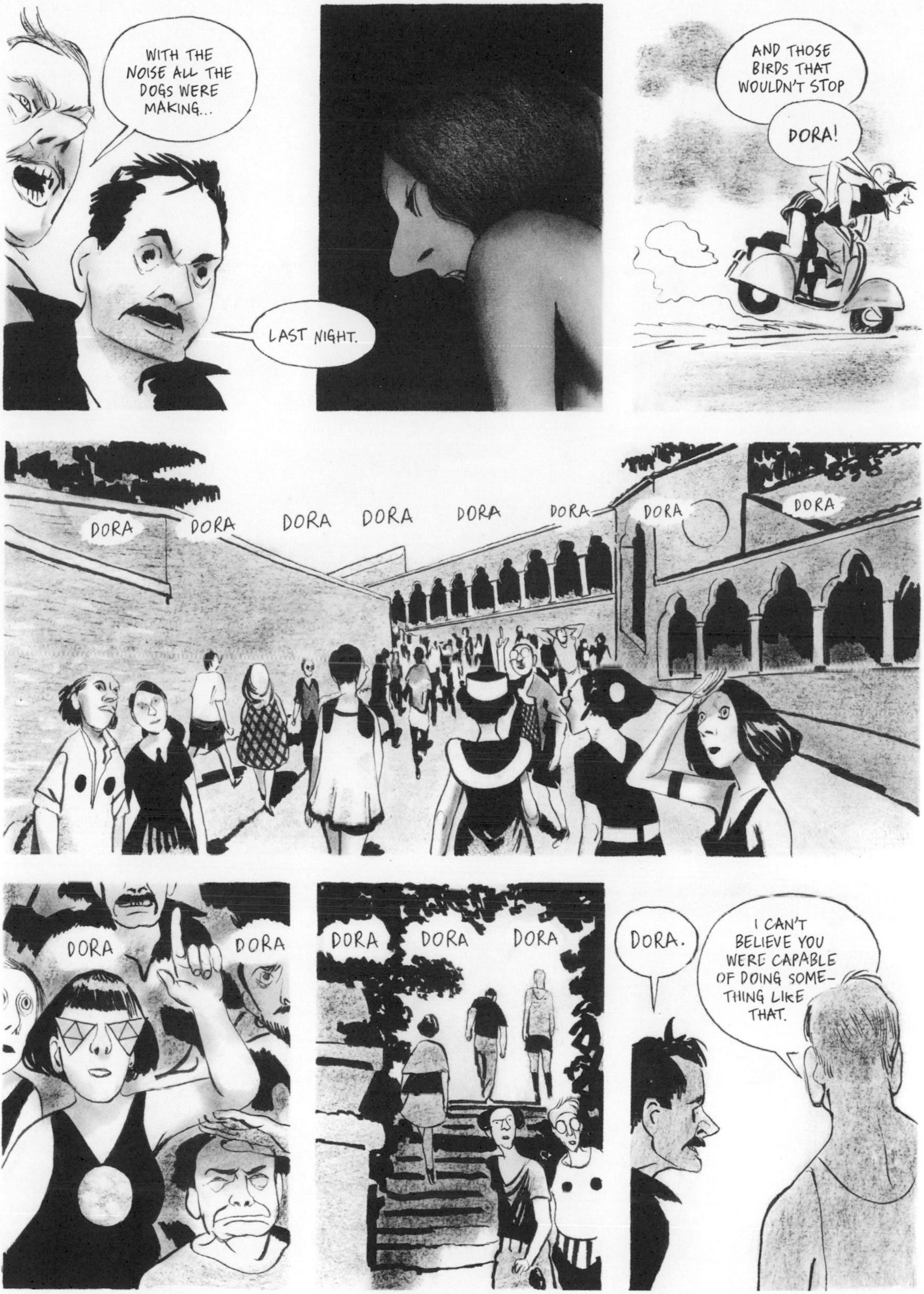
WITH THE NOISE ALL THE DOGS WERE MAKING...
LAST NIGHT.
AND THOSE BIRDS THAT WOULDN'T STOP
DORA!
DORA
DORA
DORA
DORA
DORA
DORA
DORA
DORA
DORA
DORA
DORA
DORA
DORA
DORA.
I CAN'T BELIEVE YOU WERE CAPABLE OF DOING SOMETHING LIKE THAT.

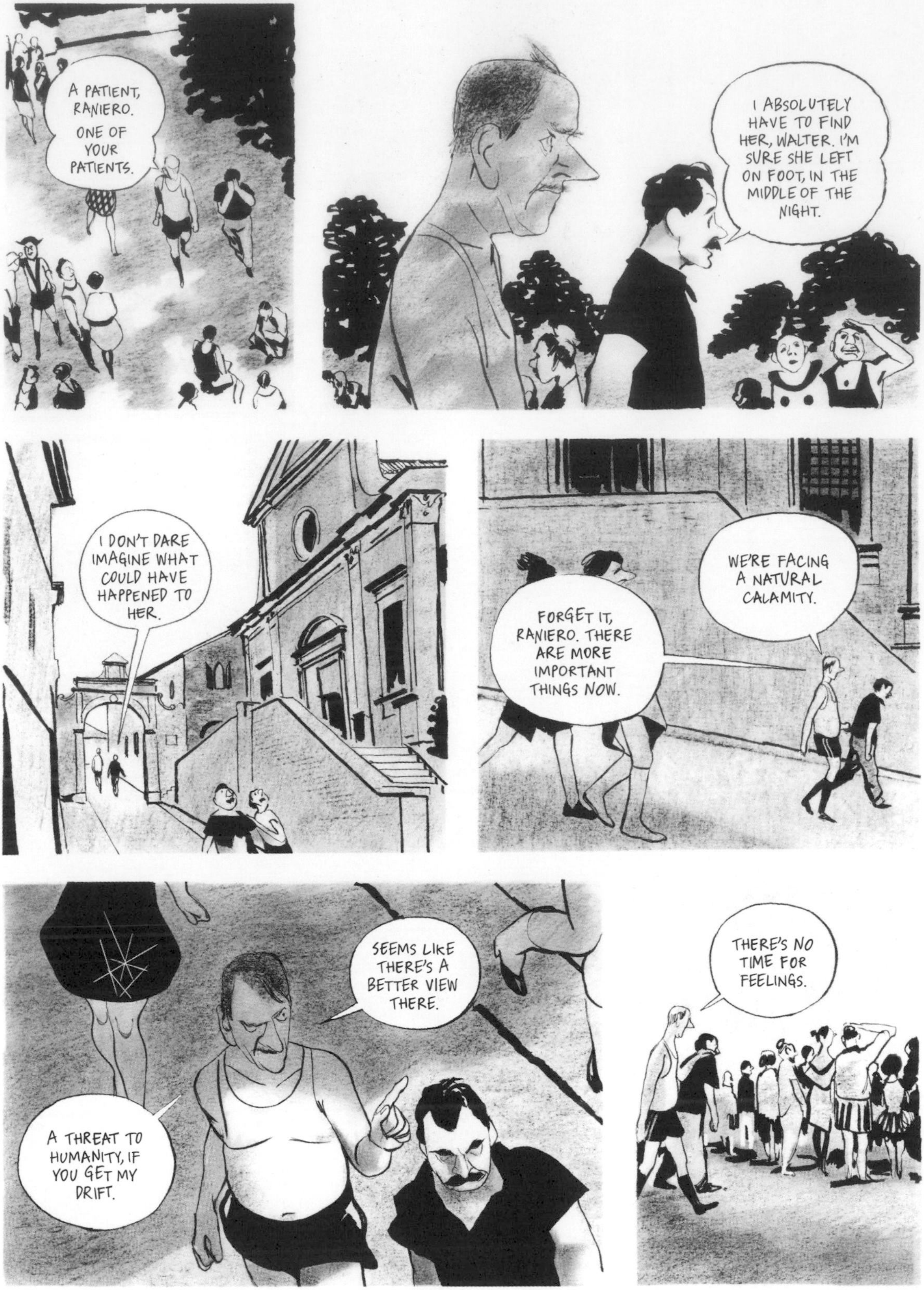
A PATIENT, RANIERO.
ONE OF YOUR PATIENTS.
I ABSOLUTELY HAVE TO FIND HER, WALTER. I'M SURE SHE LEFT ON FOOT, IN THE MIDDLE OF THE NIGHT.
I DON'T DARE IMAGINE WHAT COULD HAVE HAPPENED TO HER.
WE'RE FACING A NATURAL CALAMITY.
FORGET IT, RANIERO. THERE ARE MORE IMPORTANT THINGS NOW.
SEEMS LIKE THERE'S A BETTER VIEW THERE.
A THREAT TO HUMANITY, IF YOU GET MY DRIFT.
THERE'S NO TIME FOR FEELINGS.

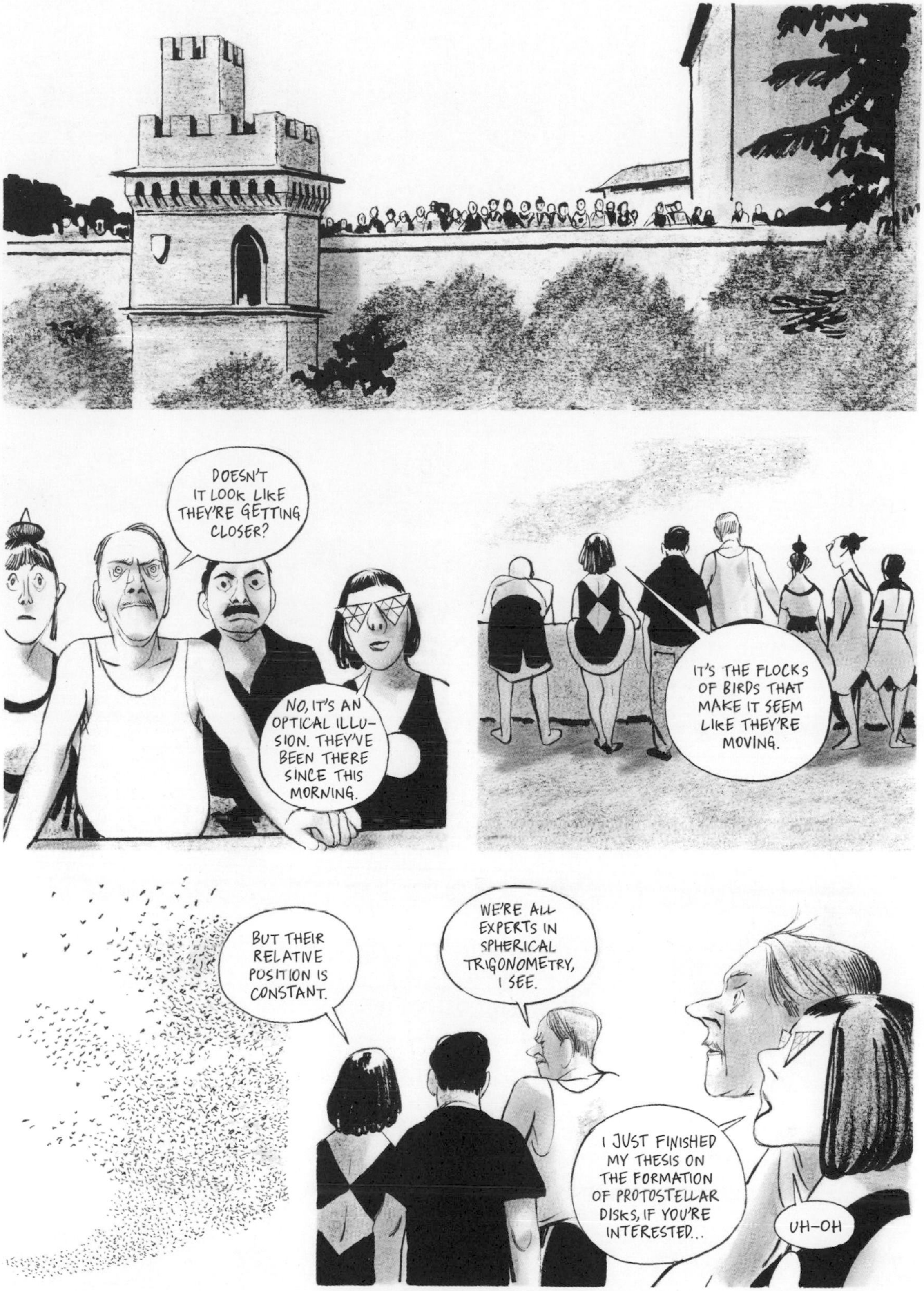
DOESN'T IT LOOK LIKE THEY'RE GETTING CLOSER?
NO, IT'S AN OPTICAL ILLUSION. THEY'VE BEEN THERE SINCE THIS MORNING.
IT'S THE FLOCKS OF BIRDS THAT MAKE IT SEEM LIKE THEY'RE MOVING.
BUT THEIR RELATIVE POSITION IS CONSTANT.
WE'RE ALL EXPERTS IN SPHERICAL TRIGONOMETRY, I SEE.
I JUST FINISHED MY THESIS ON THE FORMATION OF PROTOSTELLAR DISKS, IF YOU'RE INTERESTED...
UH-OH

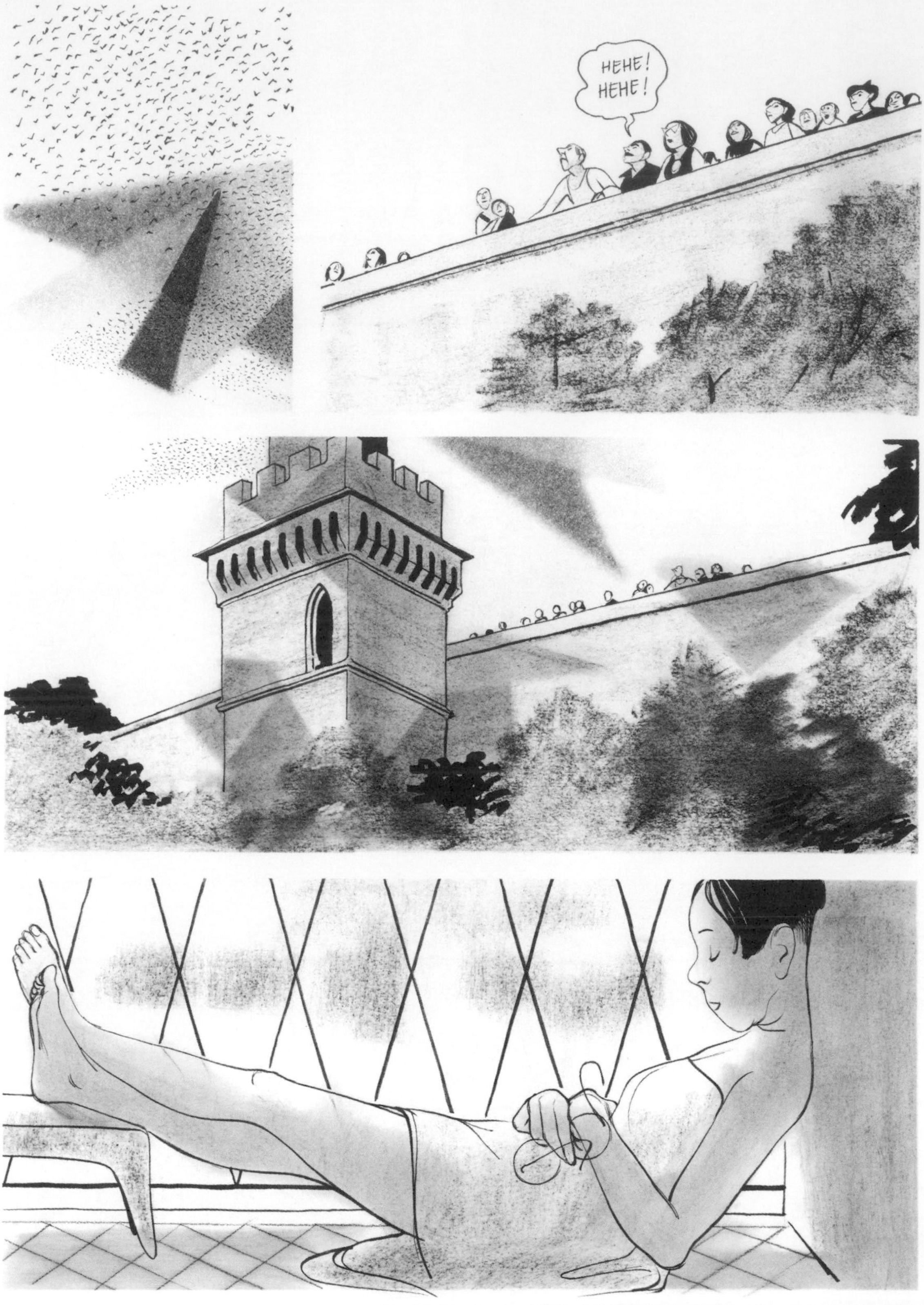
HEHE!
HEHE!

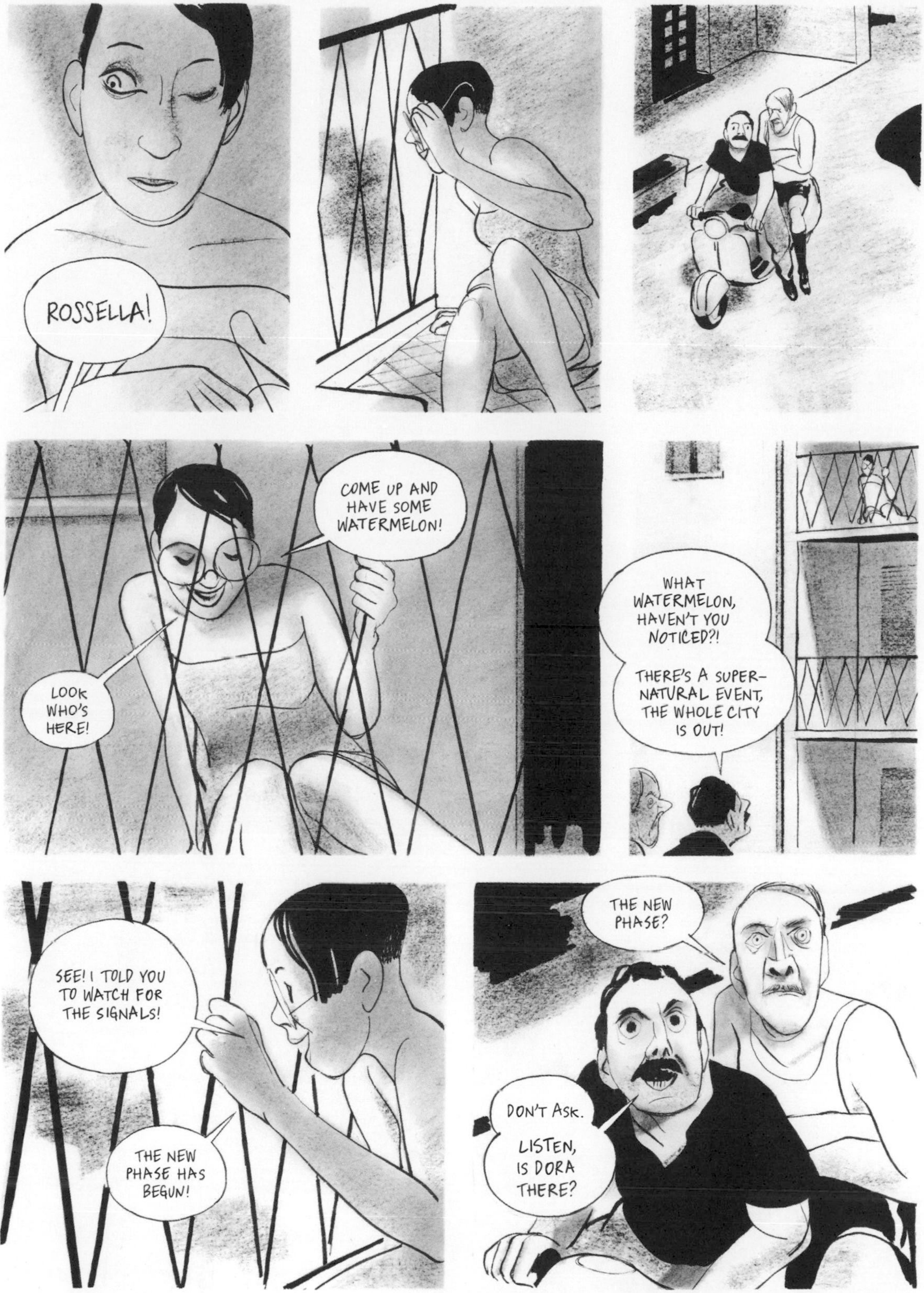
ROSSELLA!
COME UP AND HAVE SOME WATERMELON!
LOOK WHO'S HERE!
WHAT WATERMELON, HAVEN'T YOU NOTICED?!
THERE'S A SUPER-NATURAL EVENT, THE WHOLE CITY IS OUT!
SEE! I TOLD YOU TO WATCH FOR THE SIGNALS!
THE NEW PHASE HAS BEGUN!
THE NEW PHASE?
DON'T ASK.
LISTEN, IS DORA THERE?

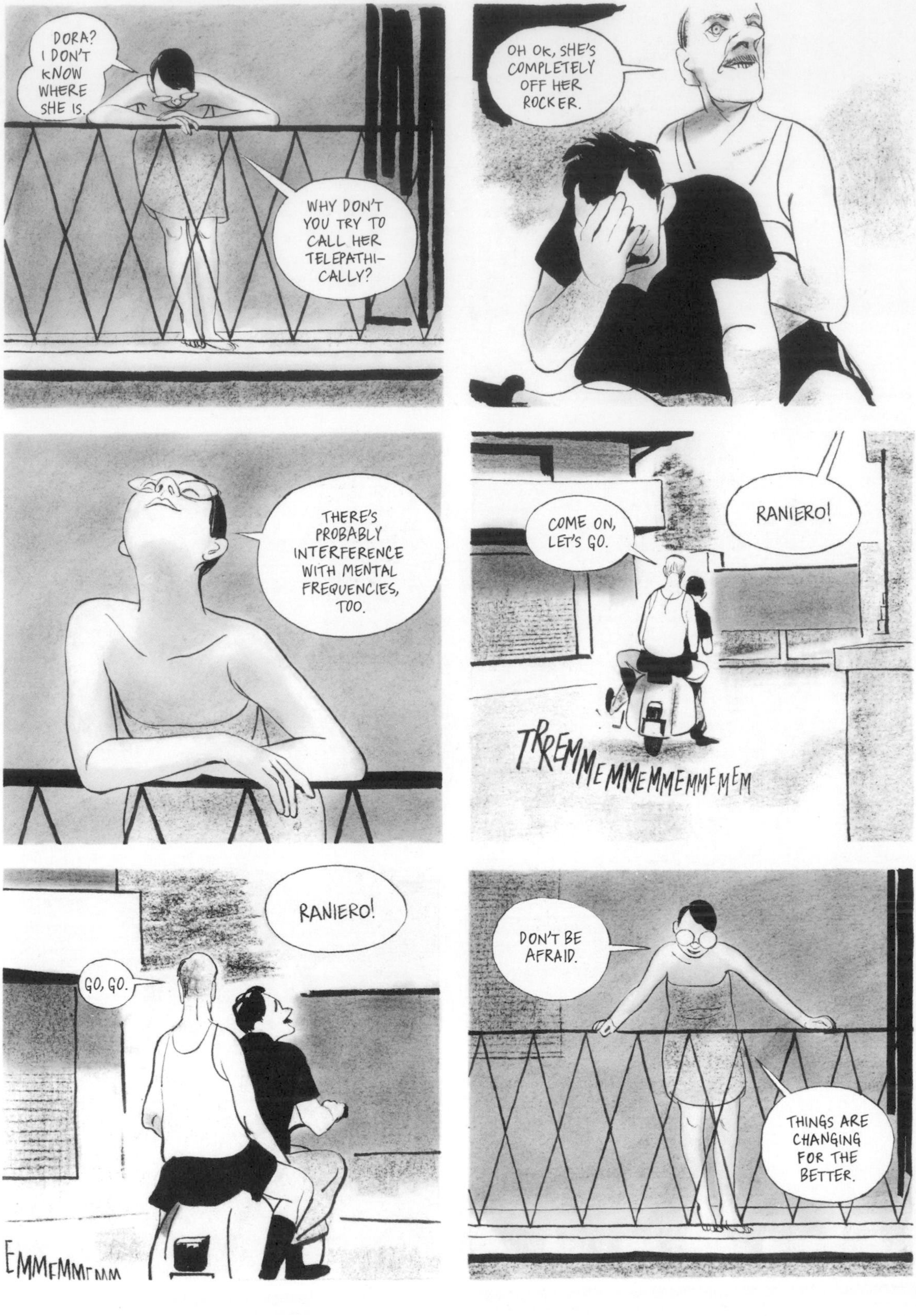
DORA? I DON'T KNOW WHERE SHE IS.
WHY DON'T YOU TRY TO CALL HER TELEPATHI-CALLY?
OH OK, SHE'S COMPLETELY OFF HER ROCKER.
THERE'S PROBABLY INTERFERENCE WITH MENTAL FREQUENCIES, TOO.
RANIERO!
COME ON, LET'S GO.
TRREMMMEMMMEMMEMMEMEM
RANIERO!
GO, GO.
EMMEMMEMM
DON'T BE AFRAID.
THINGS ARE CHANGING FOR THE BETTER.

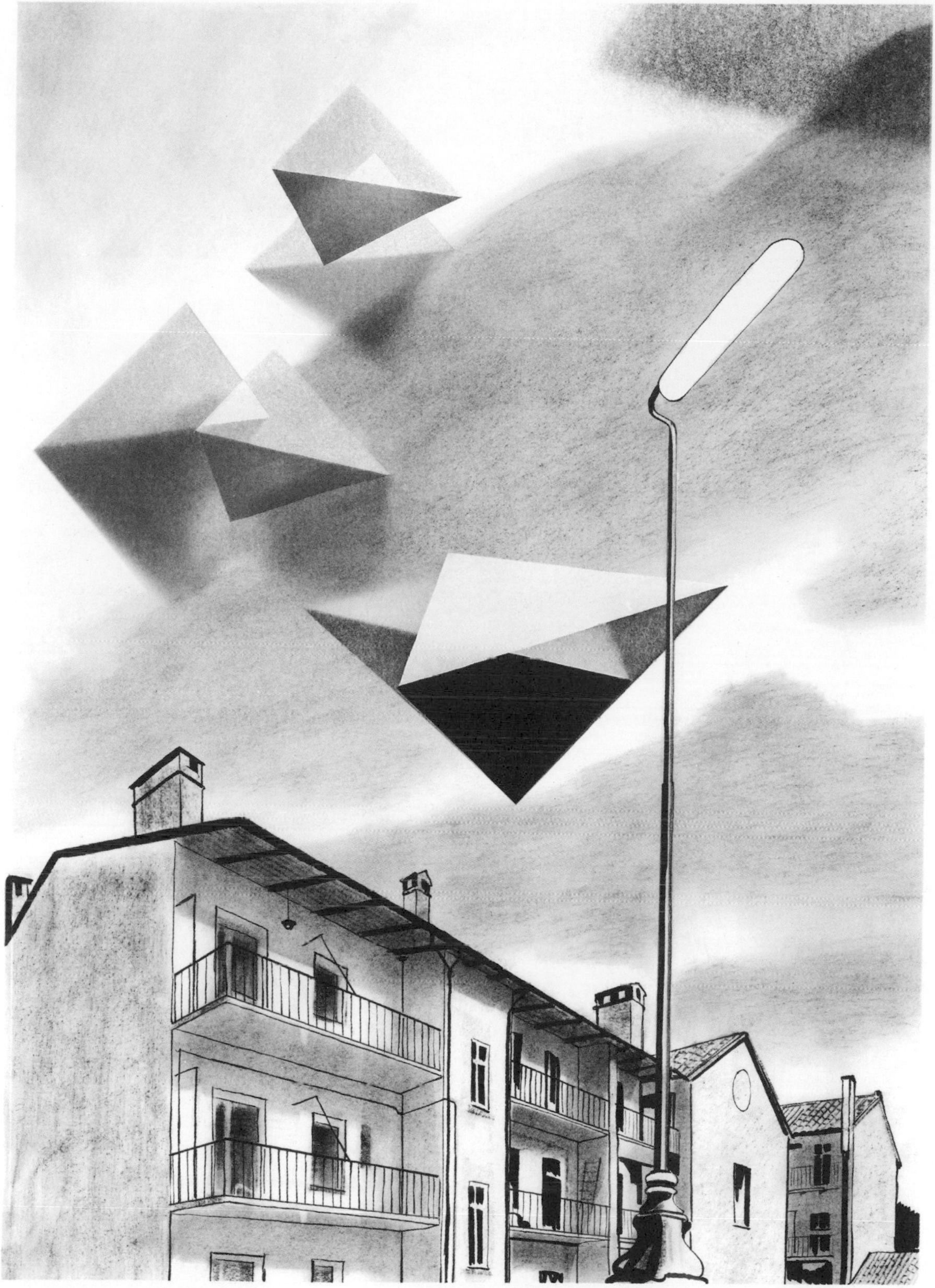

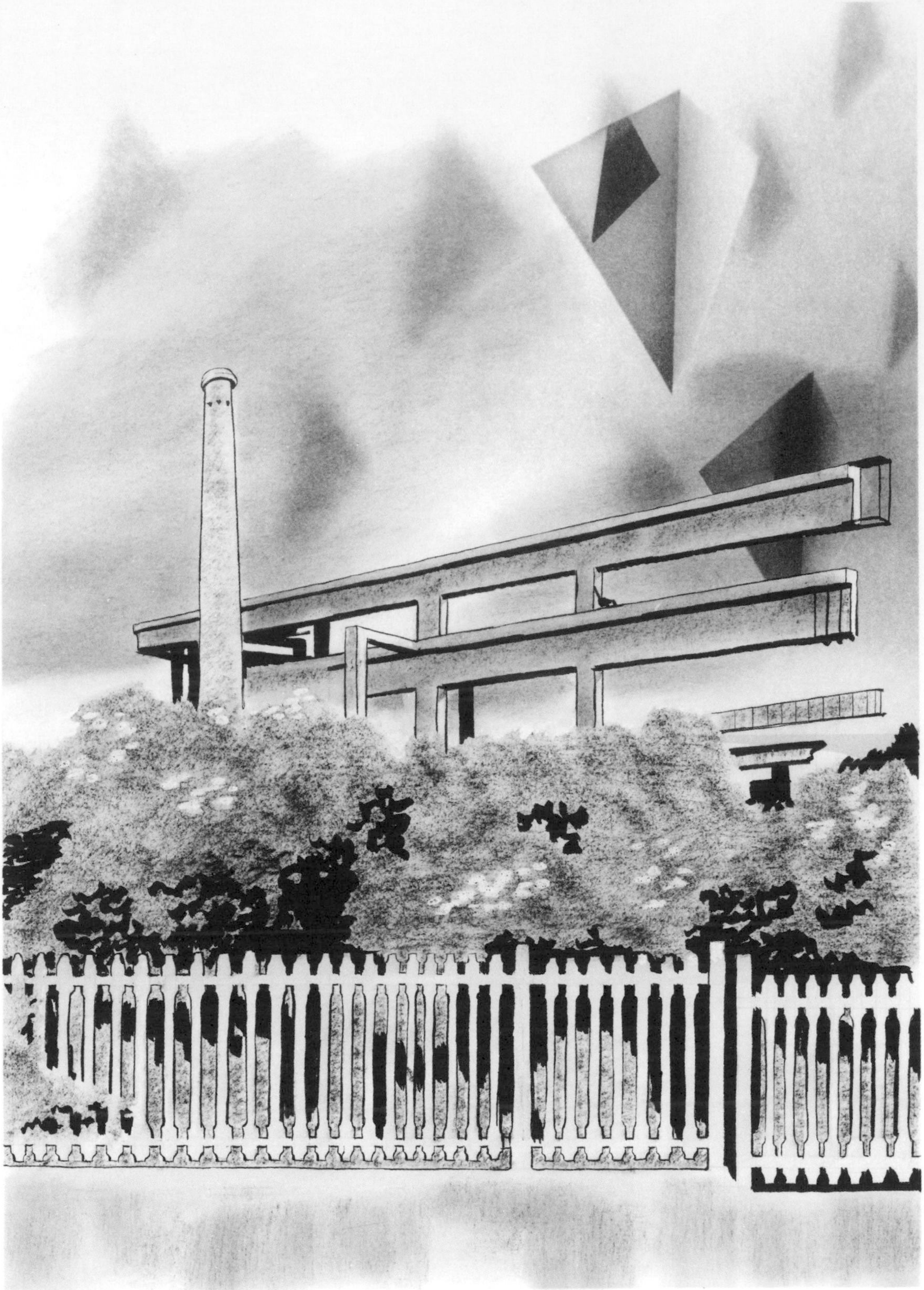

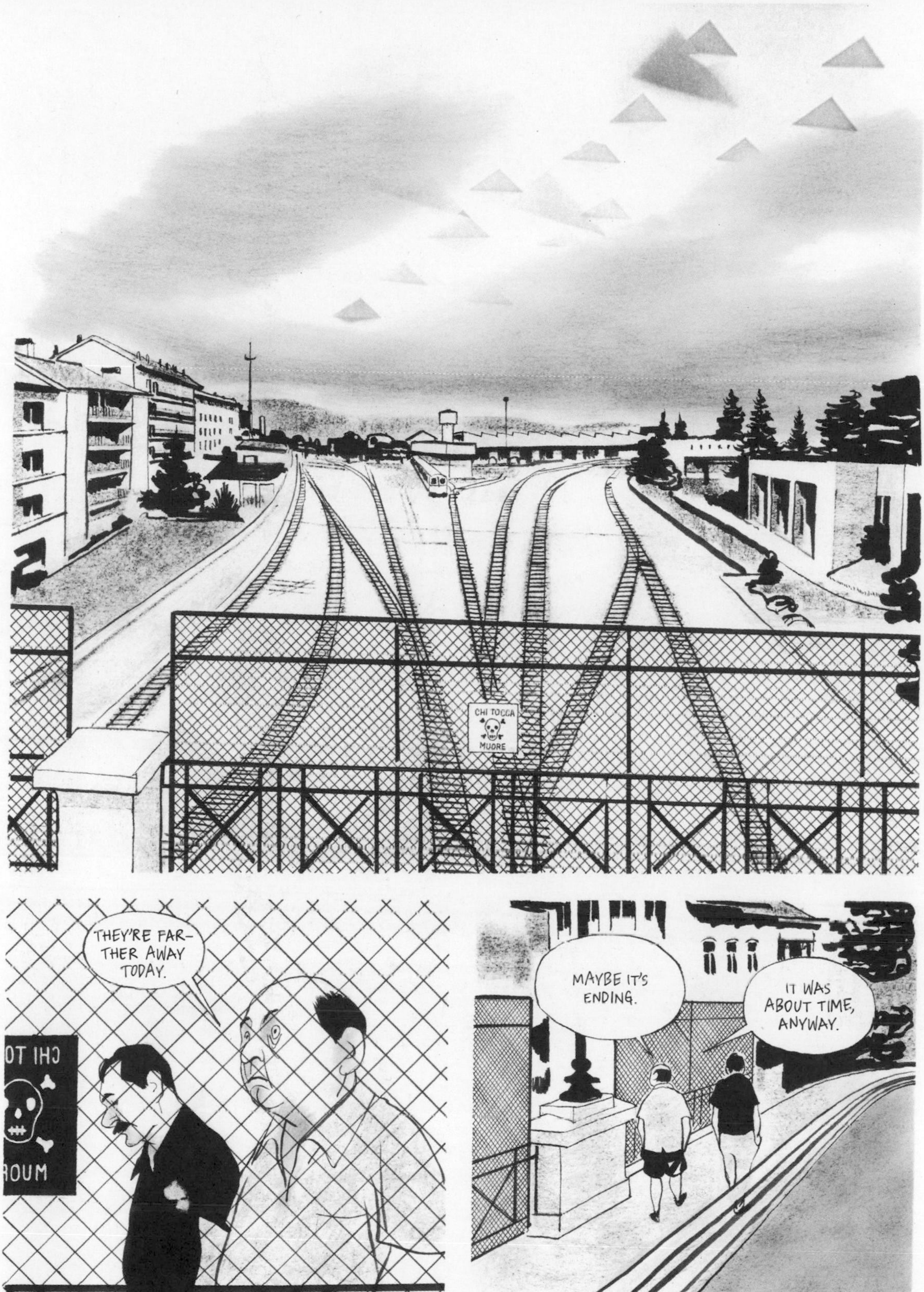
CHI TOCCA
MUORE
THEY'RE FAR-THER AWAY TODAY.
MAYBE IT'S ENDING.
IT WAS ABOUT TIME, ANYWAY.

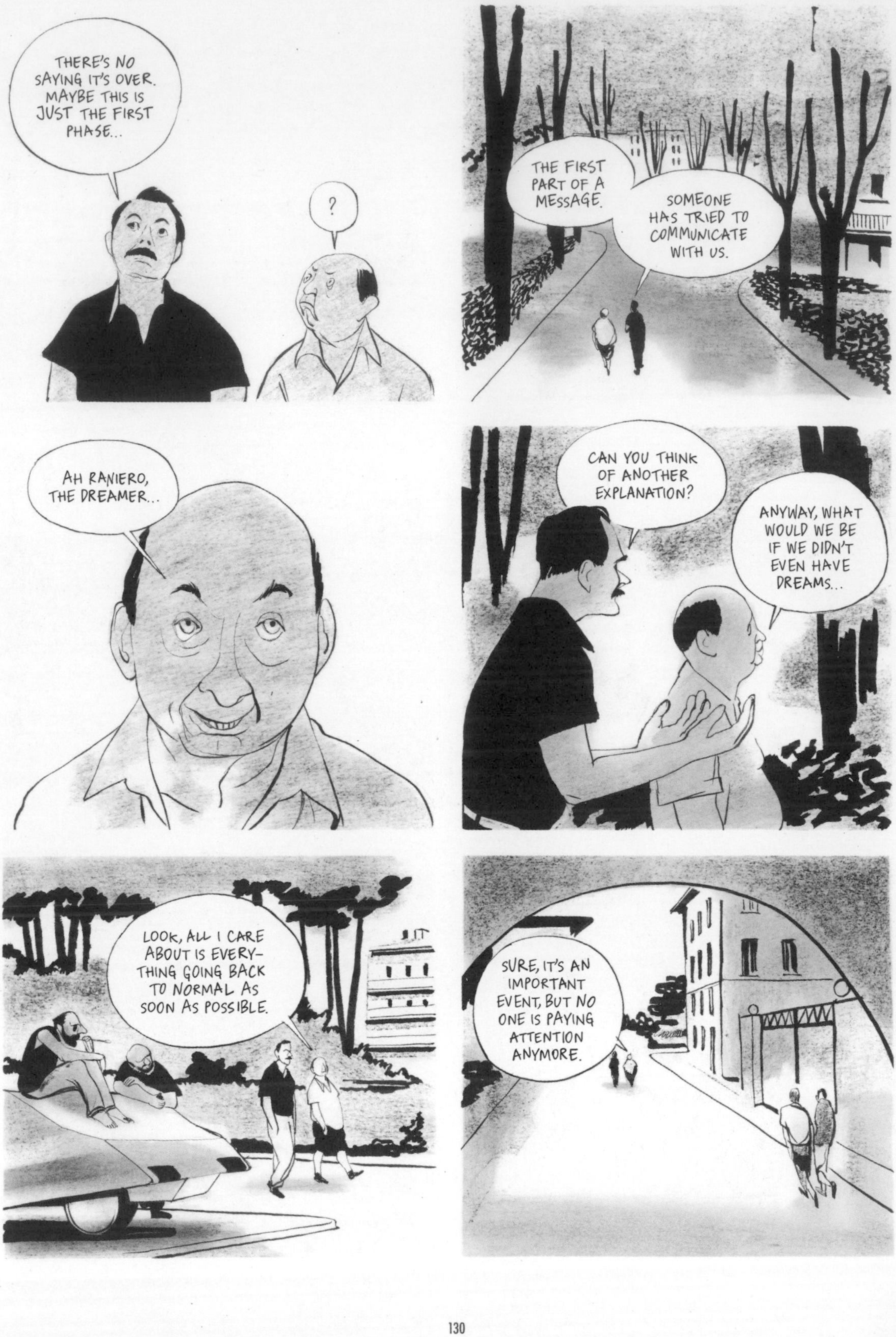
THERE'S NO SAYING IT'S OVER. MAYBE THIS IS JUST THE FIRST PHASE...
?
THE FIRST PART OF A MESSAGE.
SOMEONE HAS TRIED TO COMMUNICATE WITH US.
AH RANIERO, THE DREAMER...
CAN YOU THINK OF ANOTHER EXPLANATION?
ANYWAY, WHAT WOULD WE BE IF WE DIDN'T EVEN HAVE DREAMS...
LOOK, ALL I CARE ABOUT IS EVERY-THING GOING BACK TO NORMAL AS SOON AS POSSIBLE.
SURE, IT'S AN IMPORTANT EVENT, BUT NO ONE IS PAYING ATTENTION ANYMORE.

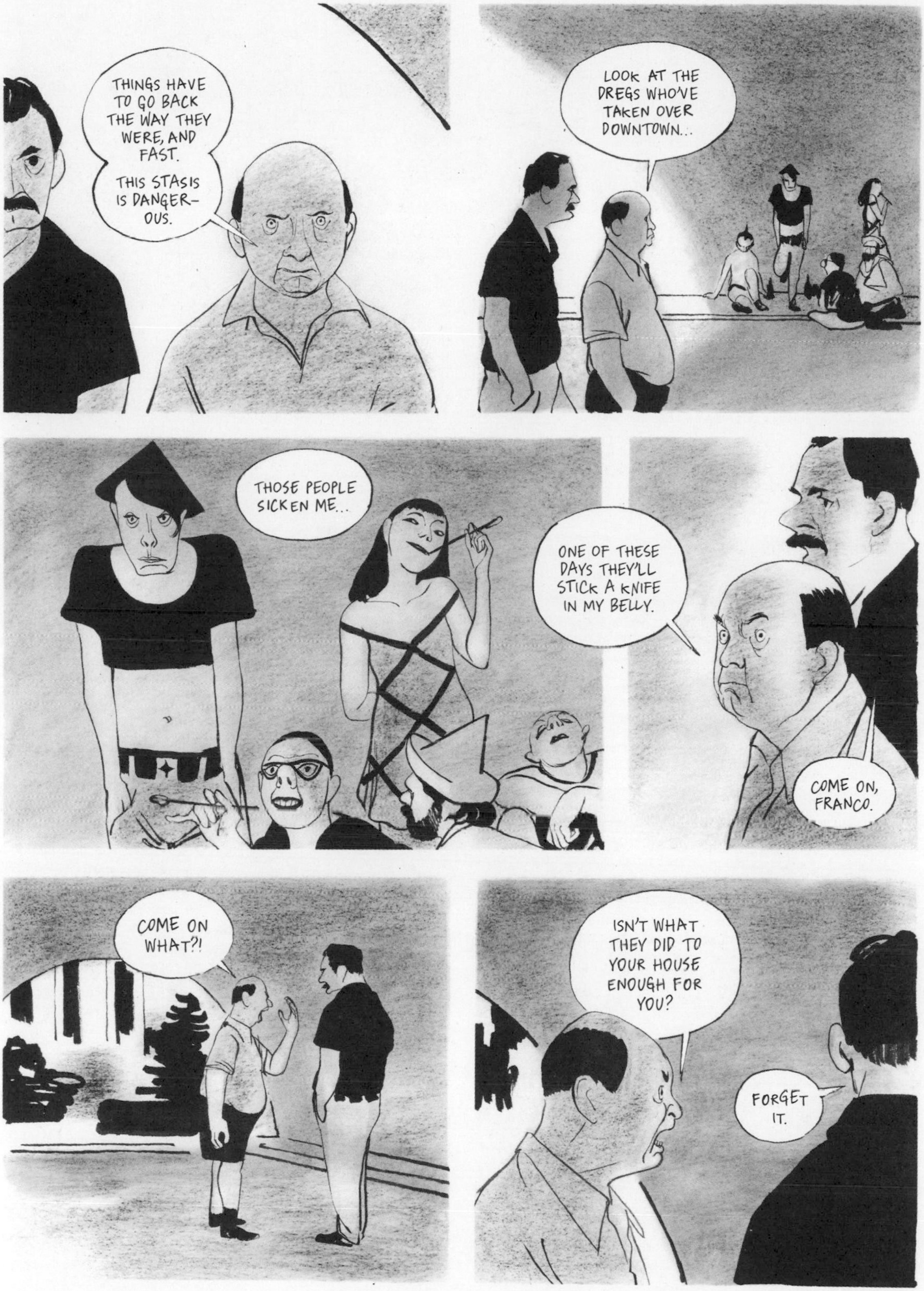
THINGS HAVE TO GO BACK THE WAY THEY WERE, AND FAST.
THIS STASIS IS DANGER-OUS.
LOOK AT THE DREGS WHO'VE TAKEN OVER DOWNTOWN...
THOSE PEOPLE SICKEN ME...
ONE OF THESE DAYS THEY'LL STICK A KNIFE IN MY BELLY.
COME ON, FRANCO.
COME ON WHAT?!
ISN'T WHAT THEY DID TO YOUR HOUSE ENOUGH FOR YOU?
FORGET IT.

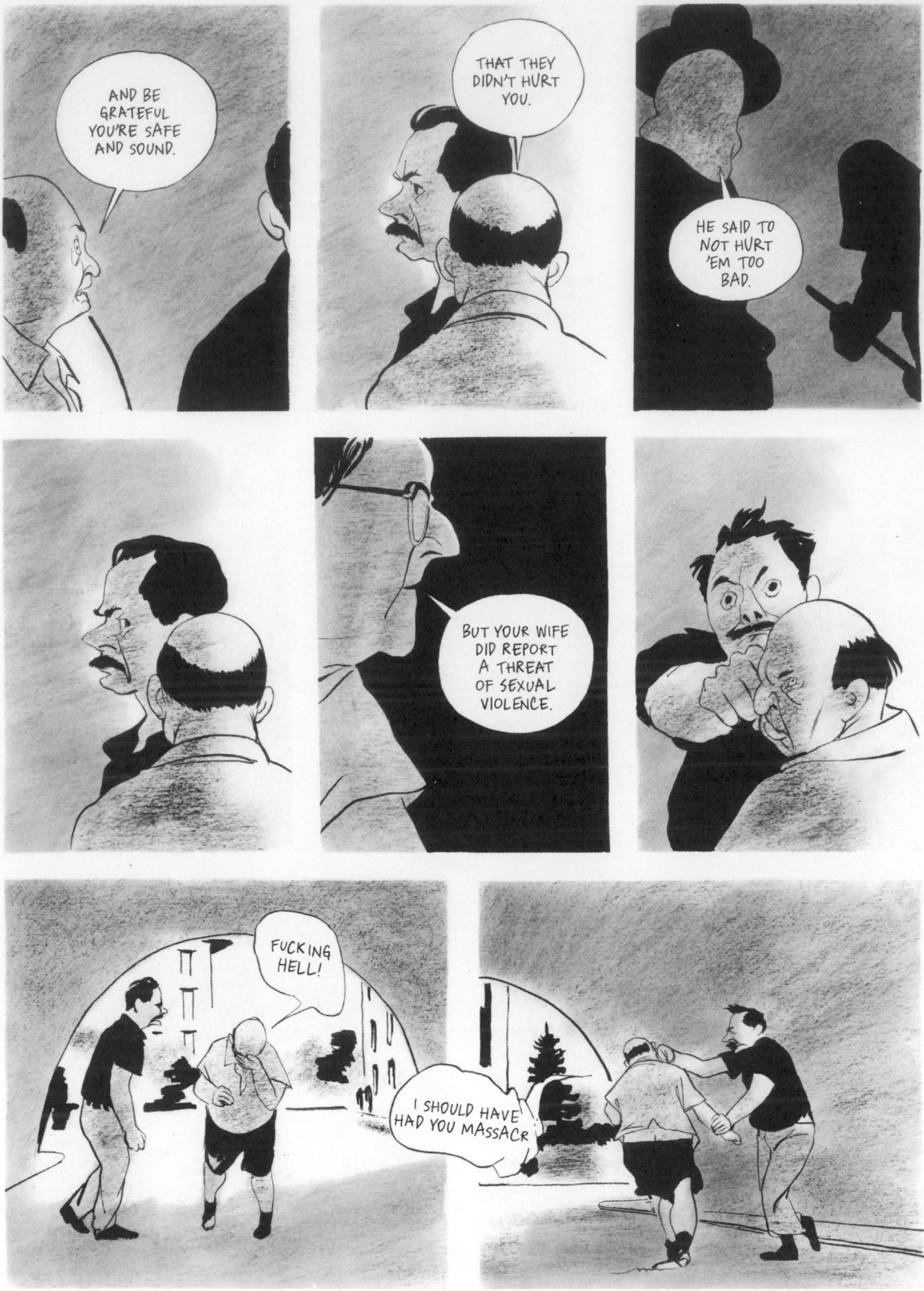
AND BE GRATEFUL YOU'RE SAFE AND SOUND.
THAT THEY DIDN'T HURT YOU.
HE SAID TO NOT HURT 'EM TOO BAD.
BUT YOUR WIFE DID REPORT A THREAT OF SEXUAL VIOLENCE.
FUCKING HELL!
I SHOULD HAVE HAD YOU MASSACR

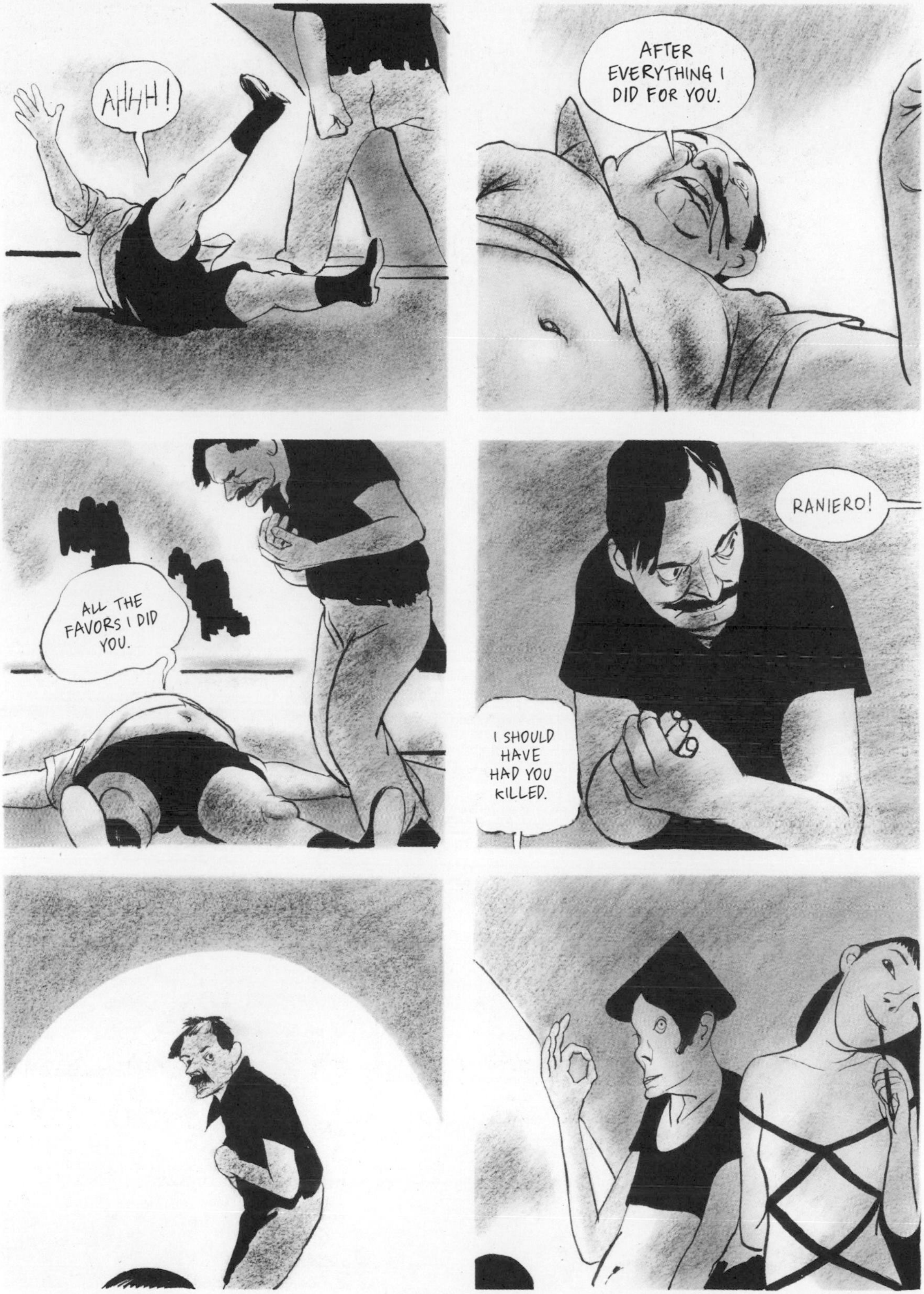
AHHH!
AFTER EVERYTHING I DID FOR YOU.
ALL THE FAVORS I DID YOU.
RANIERO!
I SHOULD HAVE HAD YOU KILLED.

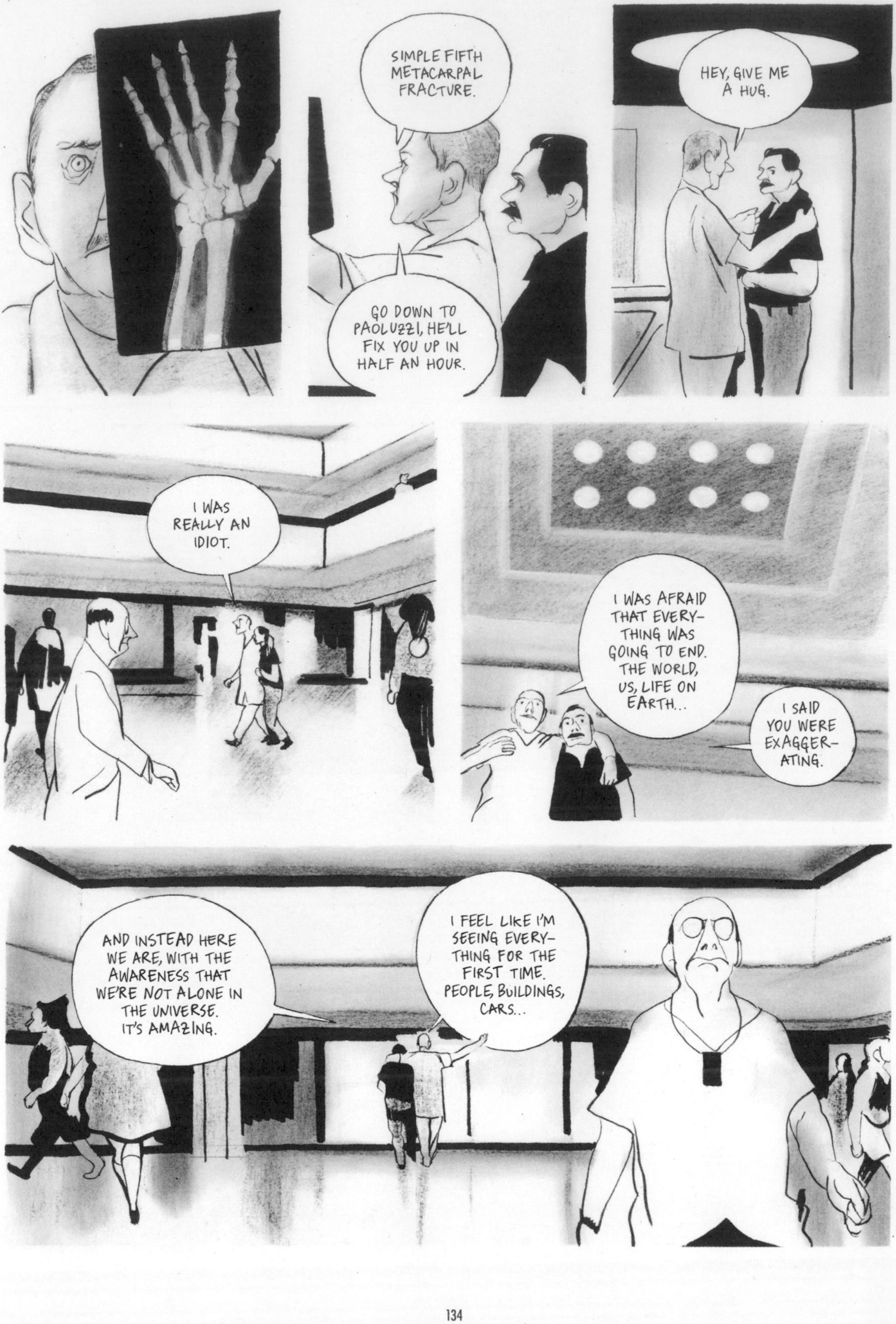
SIMPLE FIFTH METACARPAL FRACTURE.
GO DOWN TO PAOLUZZI, HE'LL FIX YOU UP IN HALF AN HOUR.
HEY, GIVE ME A HUG.
I WAS REALLY AN IDIOT.
I WAS AFRAID THAT EVERY-THING WAS GOING TO END. THE WORLD, US, LIFE ON EARTH...
I SAID YOU WERE EXAGGER-ATING.
AND INSTEAD HERE WE ARE, WITH THE AWARENESS THAT WE'RE NOT ALONE IN THE UNIVERSE. IT'S AMAZING.
I FEEL LIKE I'M SEEING EVERY-THING FOR THE FIRST TIME. PEOPLE, BUILDINGS, CARS...

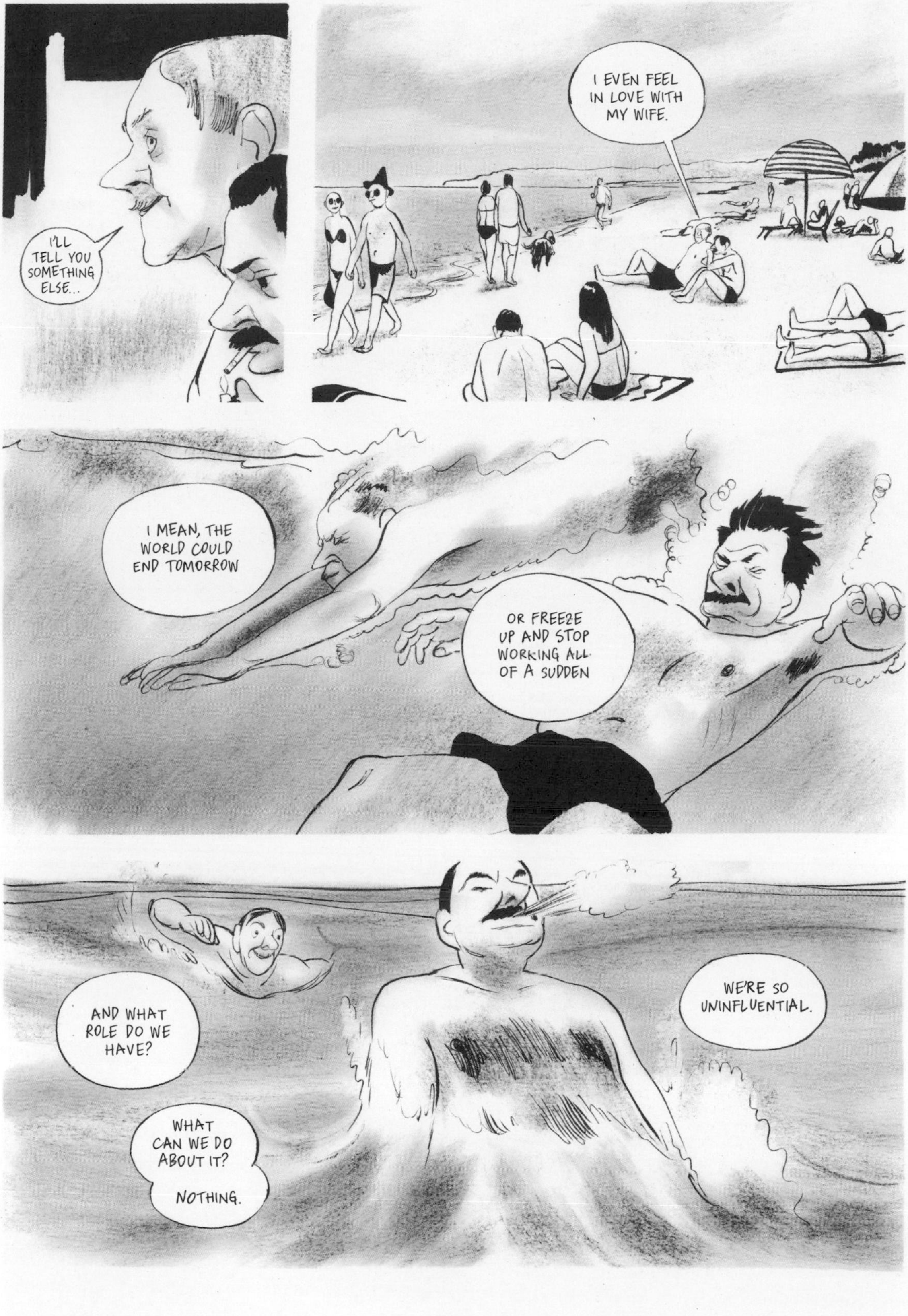

I'LL TELL YOU SOMETHING ELSE...
I EVEN FEEL IN LOVE WITH MY WIFE.
I MEAN, THE WORLD COULD END TOMORROW
OR FREEZE UP AND STOP WORKING ALL OF A SUDDEN
AND WHAT ROLE DO WE HAVE?
WHAT CAN WE DO ABOUT IT?
NOTHING.
WE'RE SO UNINFLUENTIAL.

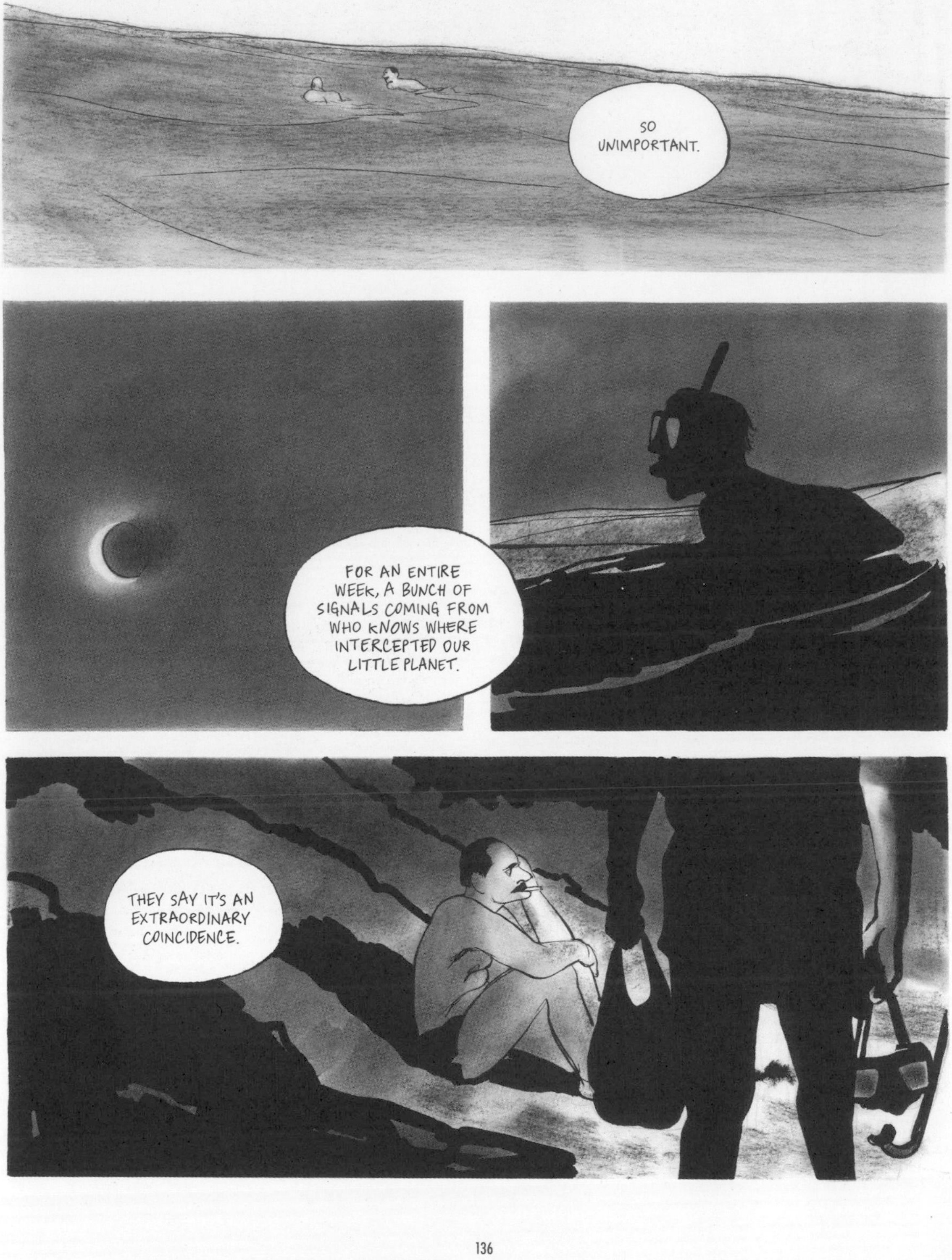
SO UNIMPORTANT.
FOR AN ENTIRE WEEK, A BUNCH OF SIGNALS COMING FROM WHO KNOWS WHERE INTERCEPTED OUR LITTLE PLANET.
THEY SAY IT'S AN EXTRAORDINARY COINCIDENCE.

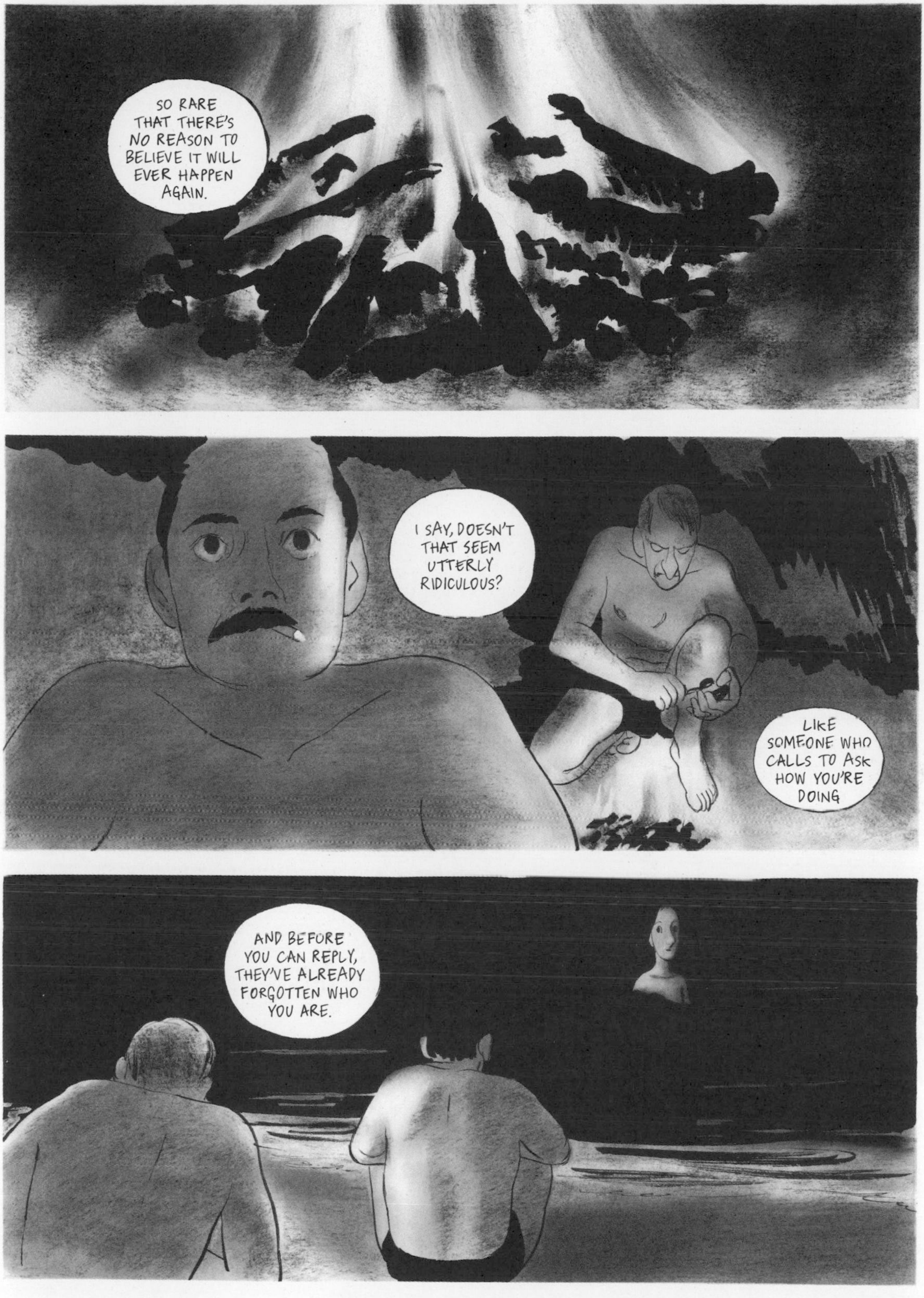
SO RARE THAT THERE'S NO REASON TO BELIEVE IT WILL EVER HAPPEN AGAIN.
I SAY, DOESN'T THAT SEEM UTTERLY RIDICULOUS?
LIKE SOMEONE WHO CALLS TO ASK HOW YOU'RE DOING
AND BEFORE YOU CAN REPLY, THEY'VE ALREADY FORGOTTEN WHO YOU ARE.

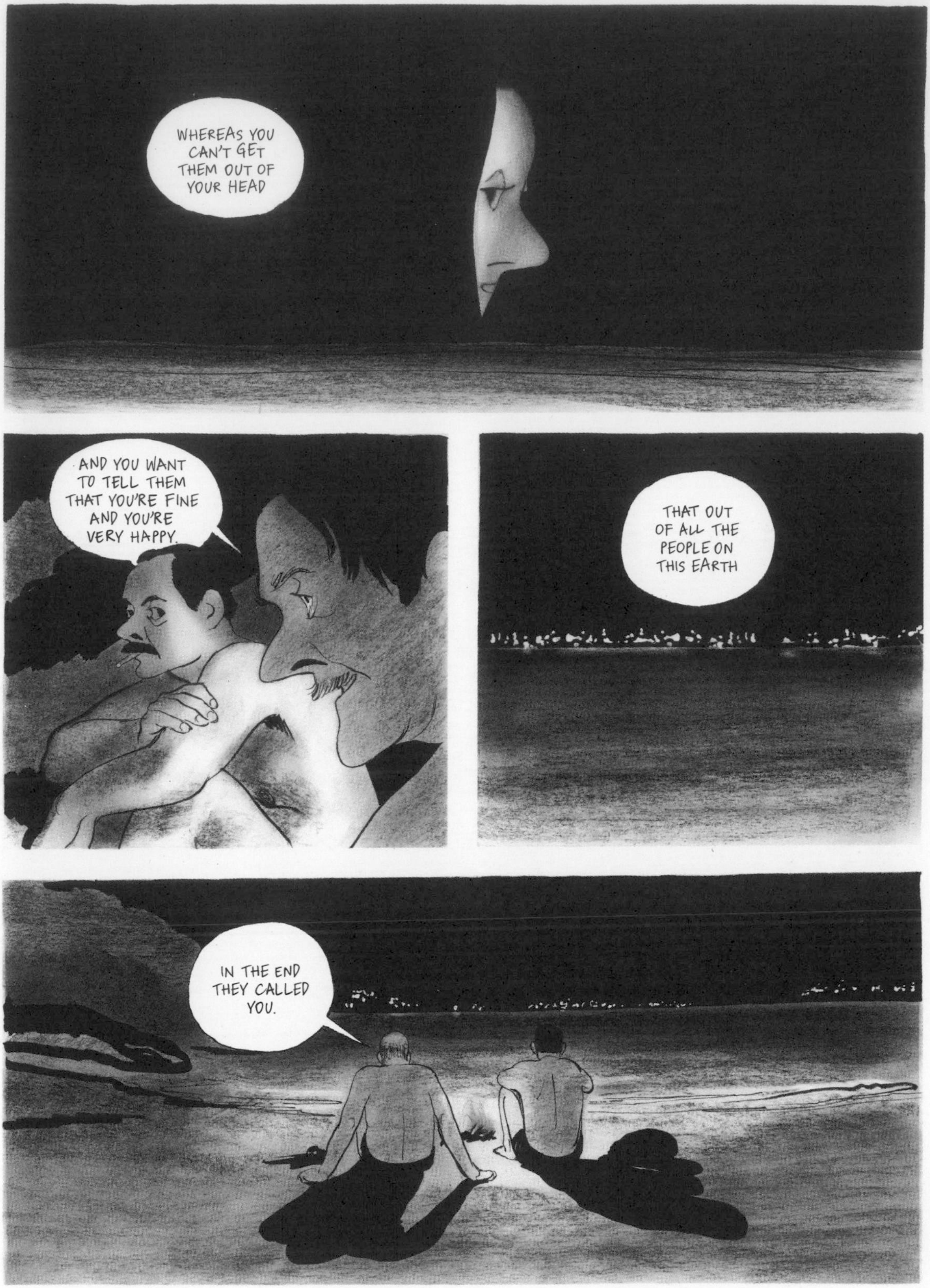
WHEREAS YOU CAN'T GET THEM OUT OF YOUR HEAD
AND YOU WANT TO TELL THEM THAT YOU'RE FINE AND YOU'RE VERY HAPPY.
THAT OUT OF ALL THE PEOPLE ON THIS EARTH
IN THE END THEY CALLED YOU.

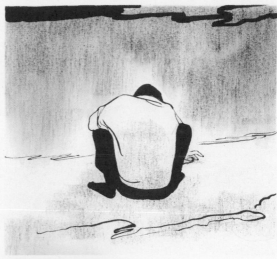

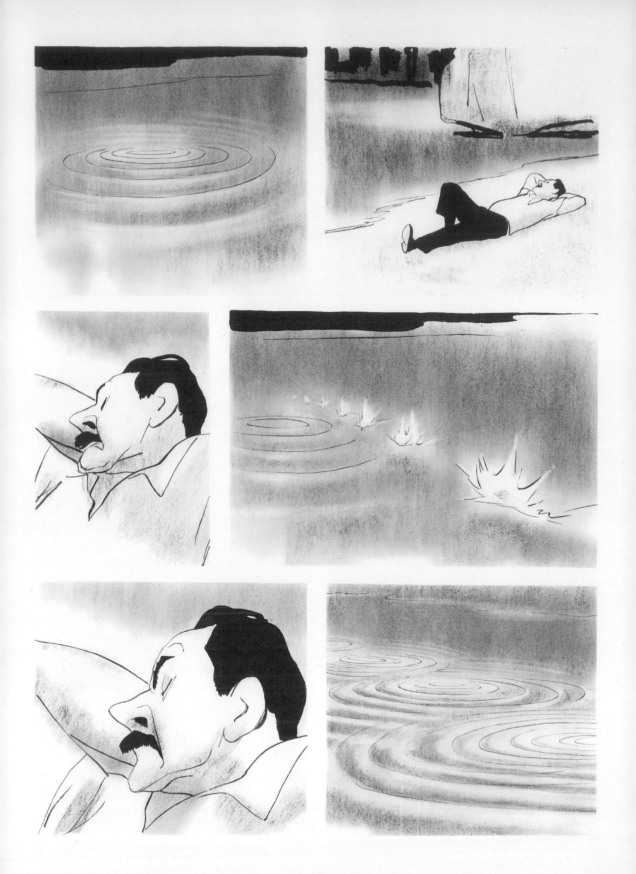

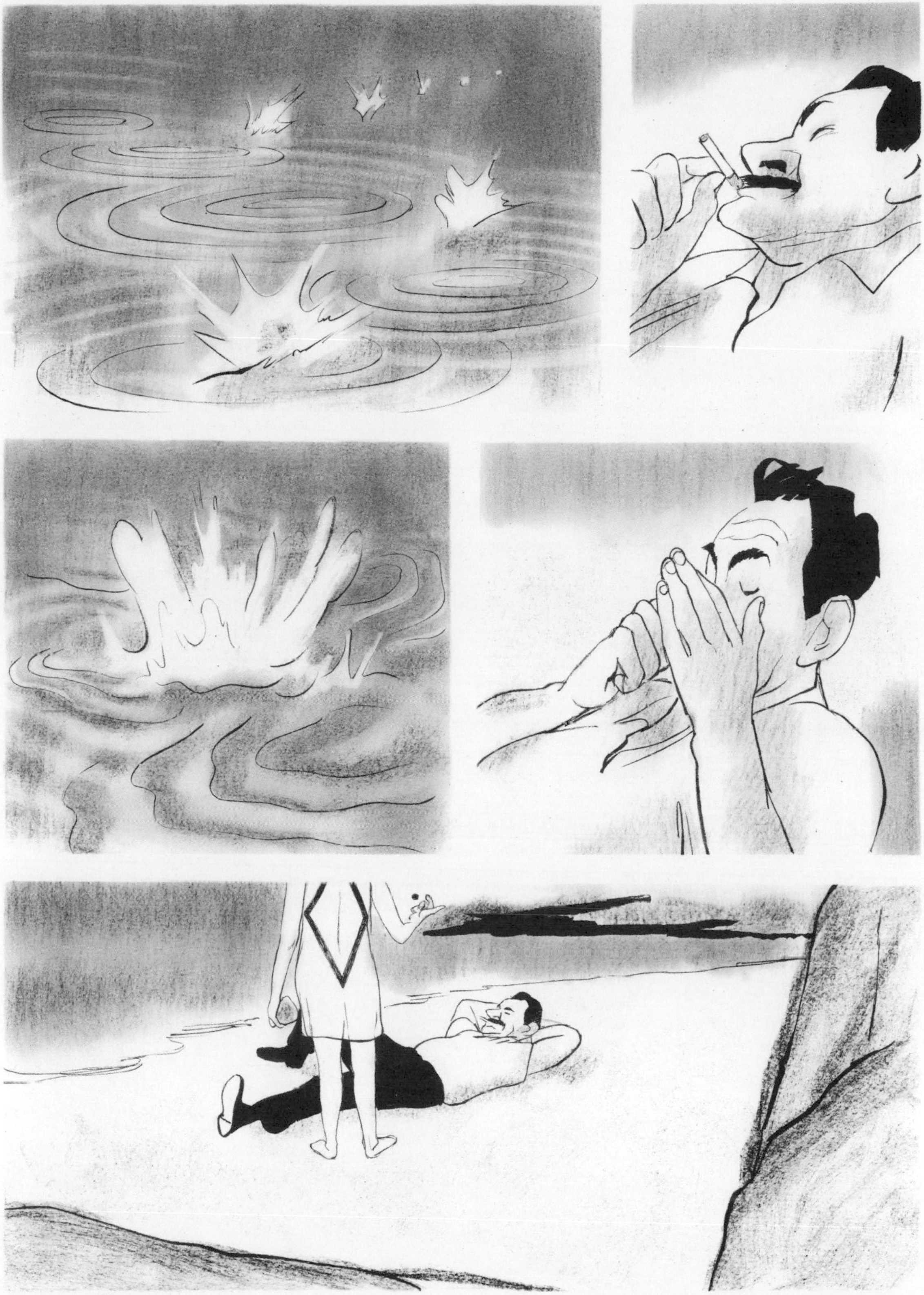

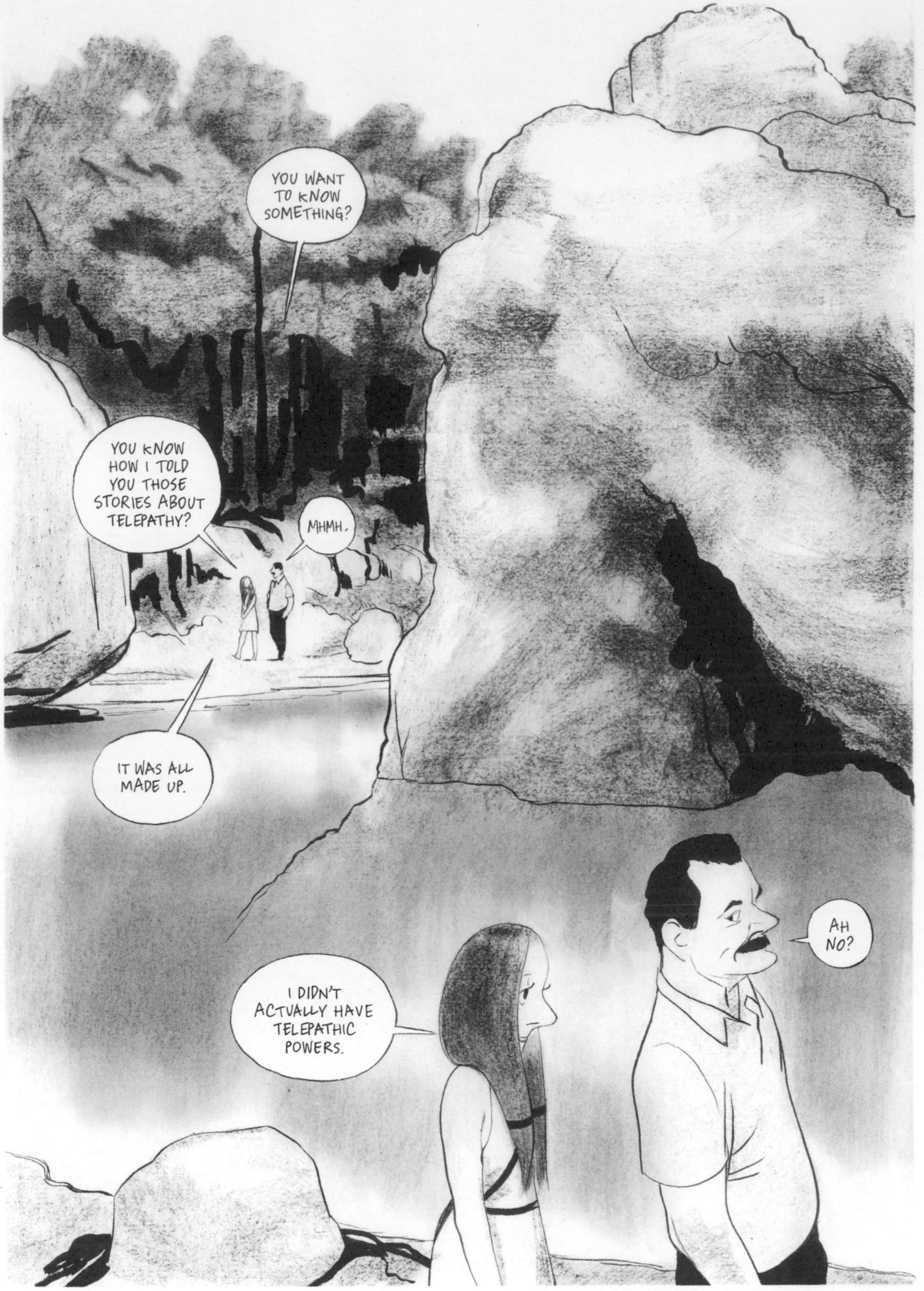
YOU WANT TO KNOW SOMETHING?
YOU KNOW HOW I TOLD YOU THOSE STORIES ABOUT TELEPATHY?
MHMH.
IT WAS ALL MADE UP.
I DIDN'T ACTUALLY HAVE TELEPATHIC POWERS.
AH NO?

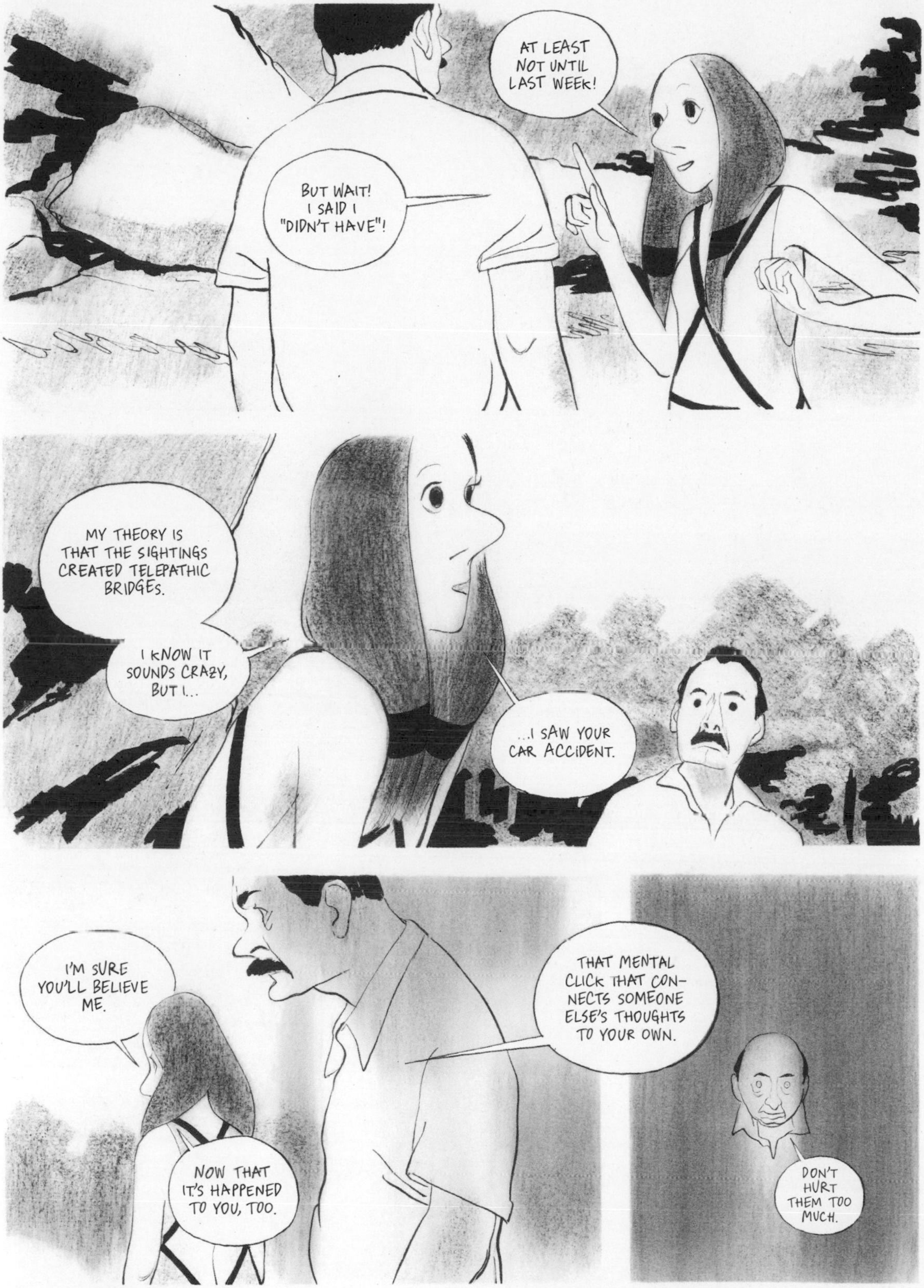
AT LEAST NOT UNTIL LAST WEEK!
BUT WAIT! I SAID I "DIDN'T HAVE"!
MY THEORY IS THAT THE SIGHTINGS CREATED TELEPATHIC BRIDGES.
I KNOW IT SOUNDS CRAZY, BUT I...
...I SAW YOUR CAR ACCIDENT.
I'M SURE YOU'LL BELIEVE ME.
NOW THAT IT'S HAPPENED TO YOU, TOO.
THAT MENTAL CLICK THAT CON-NECTS SOMEONE ELSE'S THOUGHTS TO YOUR OWN.
DON'T HURT THEM TOO MUCH.

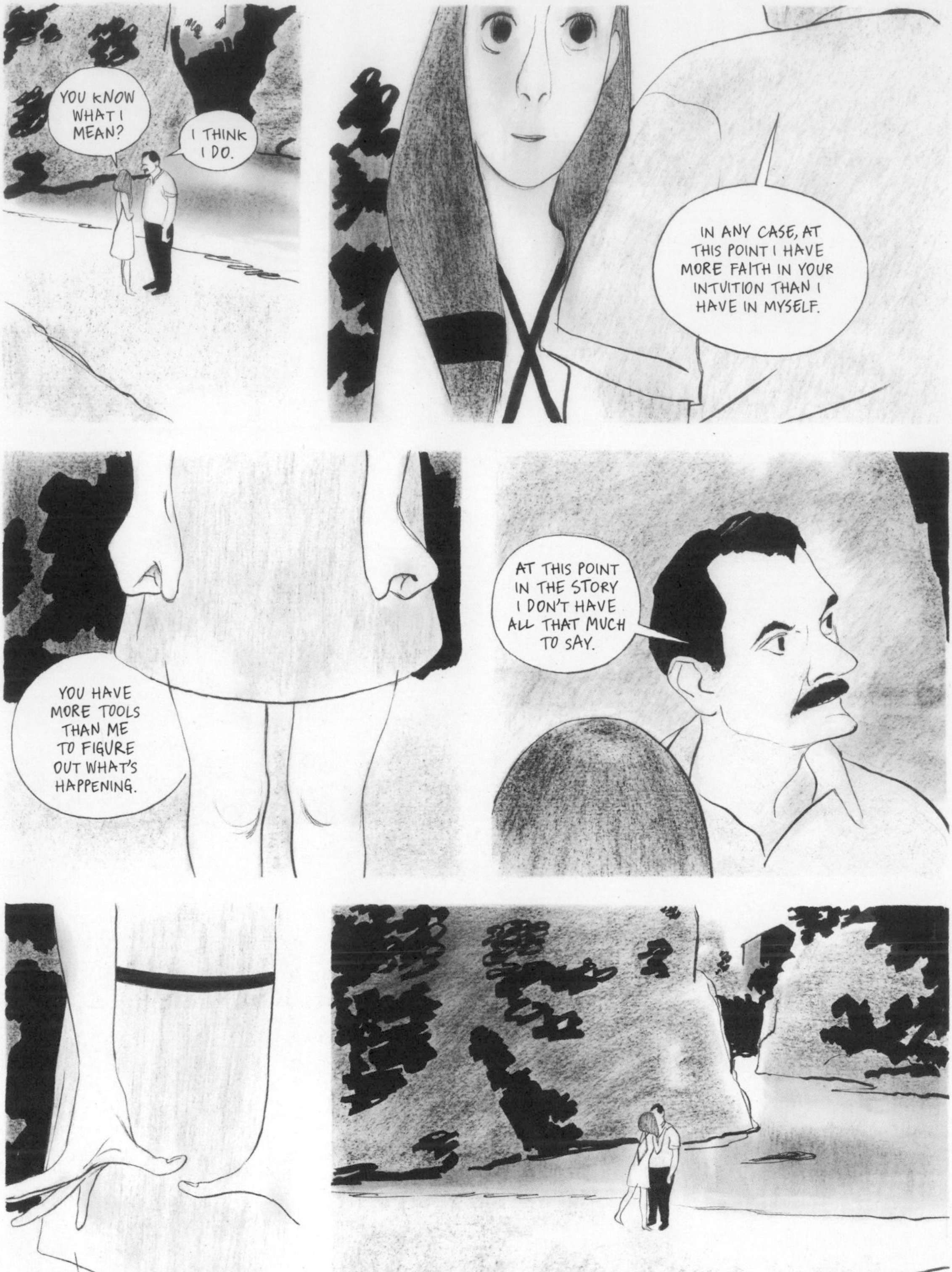
YOU KNOW WHAT I MEAN?
I THINK I DO.
IN ANY CASE, AT THIS POINT I HAVE MORE FAITH IN YOUR INTUITION THAN I HAVE IN MYSELF.
YOU HAVE MORE TOOLS THAN ME TO FIGURE OUT WHAT'S HAPPENING.
AT THIS POINT IN THE STORY I DON'T HAVE ALL THAT MUCH TO SAY.

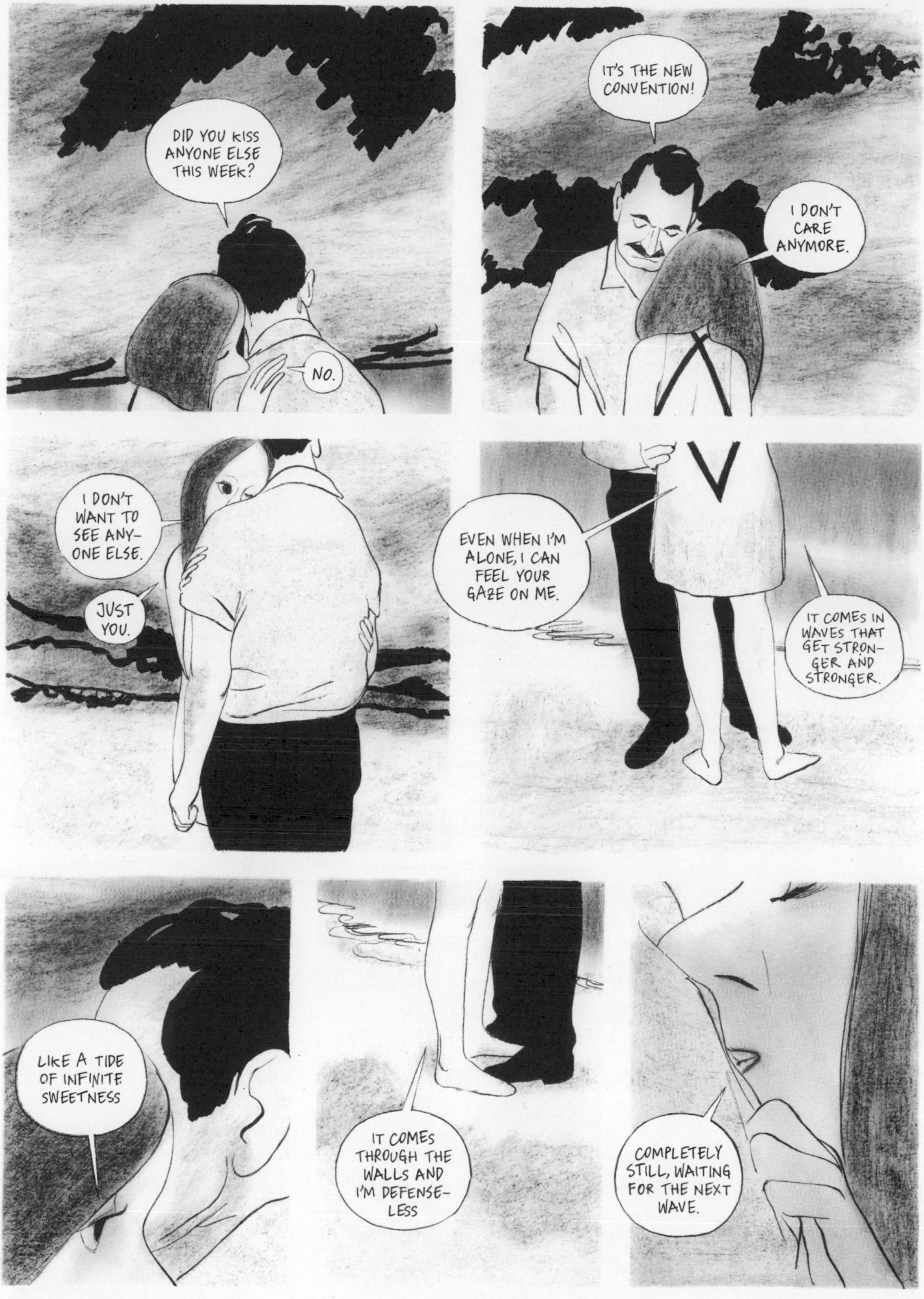
DID YOU KISS ANYONE ELSE THIS WEEK?
NO.
IT'S THE NEW CONVENTION!
I DON'T CARE ANYMORE.
I DON'T WANT TO SEE ANY-ONE ELSE.
JUST YOU.
EVEN WHEN I'M ALONE, I CAN FEEL YOUR GAZE ON ME.
IT COMES IN WAVES THAT GET STRON-GER AND STRONGER.
LIKE A TIDE OF INFINITE SWEETNESS
IT COMES THROUGH THE WALLS AND I'M DEFENSE-LESS
COMPLETELY STILL, WAITING FOR THE NEXT WAVE.

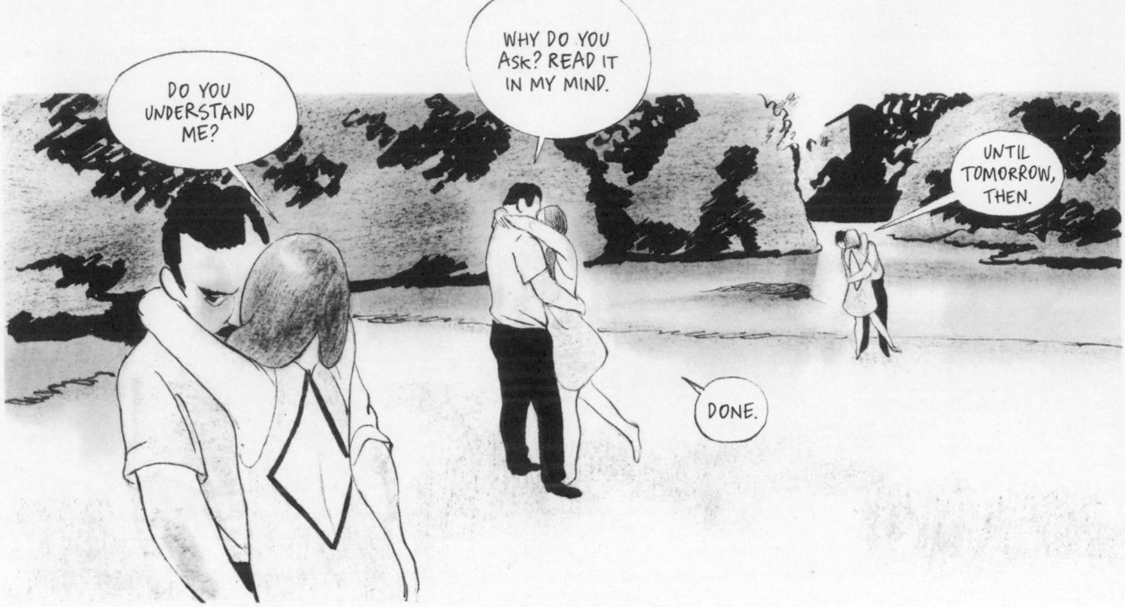
DO YOU UNDERSTAND ME?
WHY DO YOU ASK? READ IT IN MY MIND.
DONE.
UNTIL TOMORROW, THEN.

THE INTERVIEW

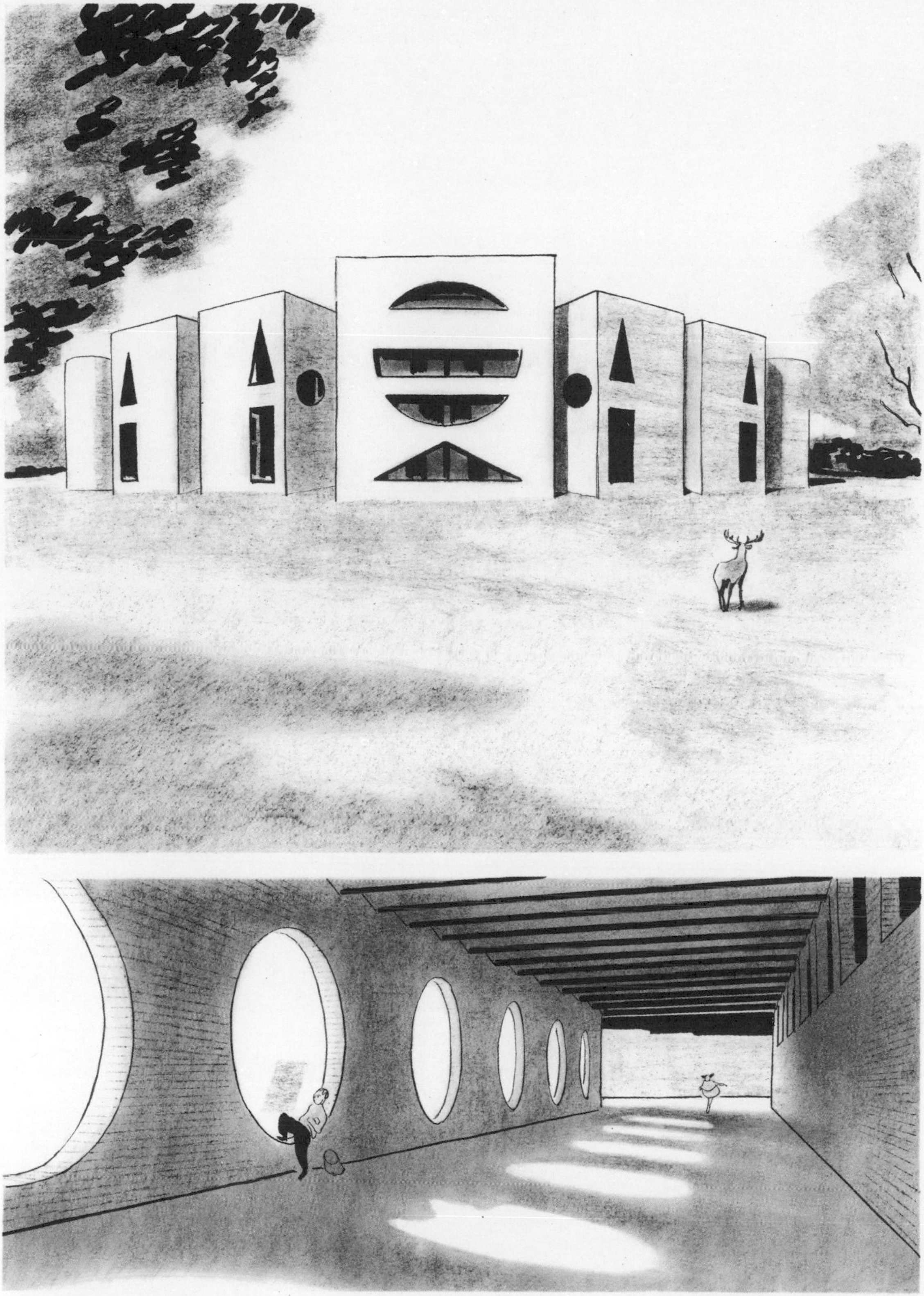

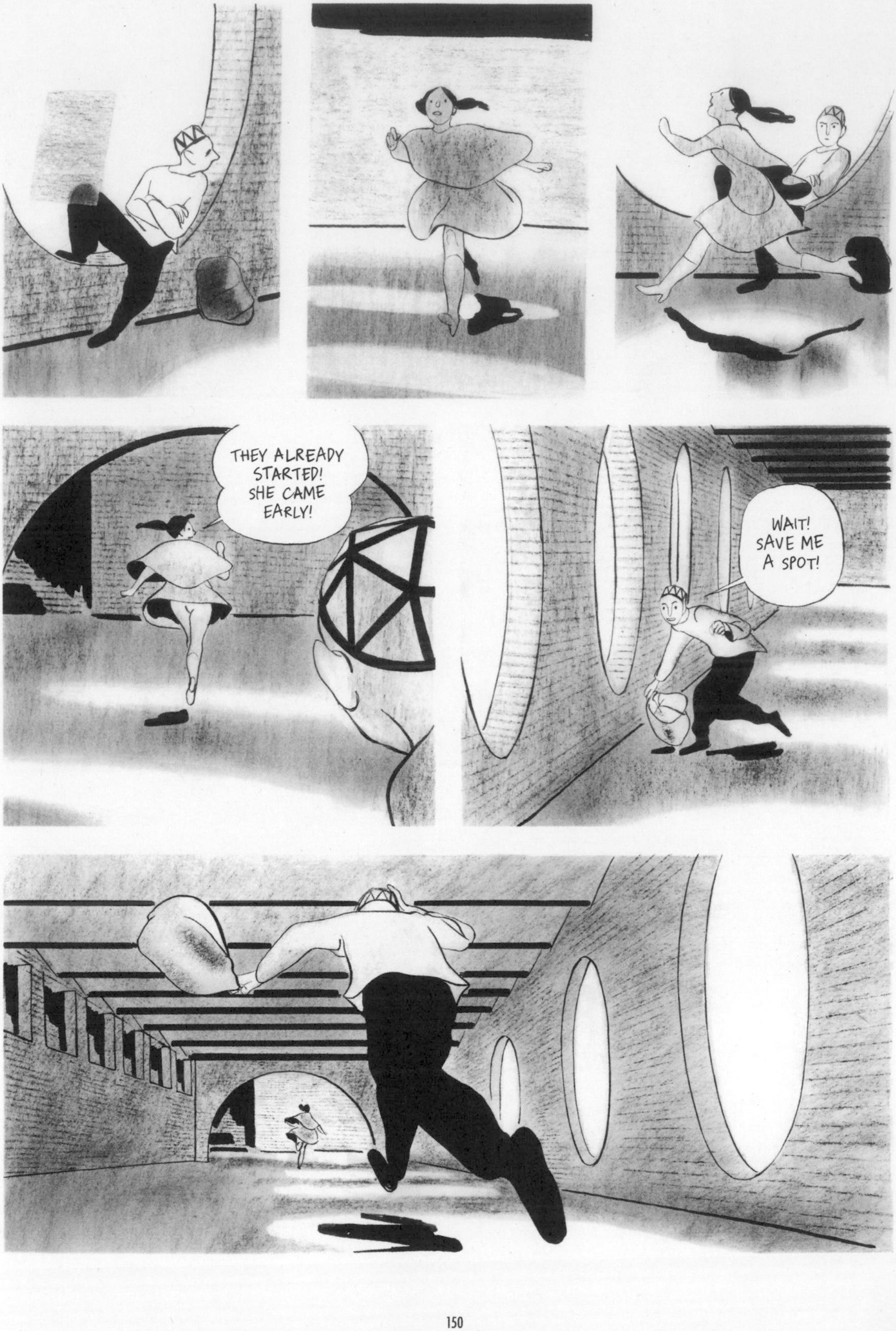
THEY ALREADY STARTED! SHE CAME EARLY!
WAIT! SAVE ME A SPOT!

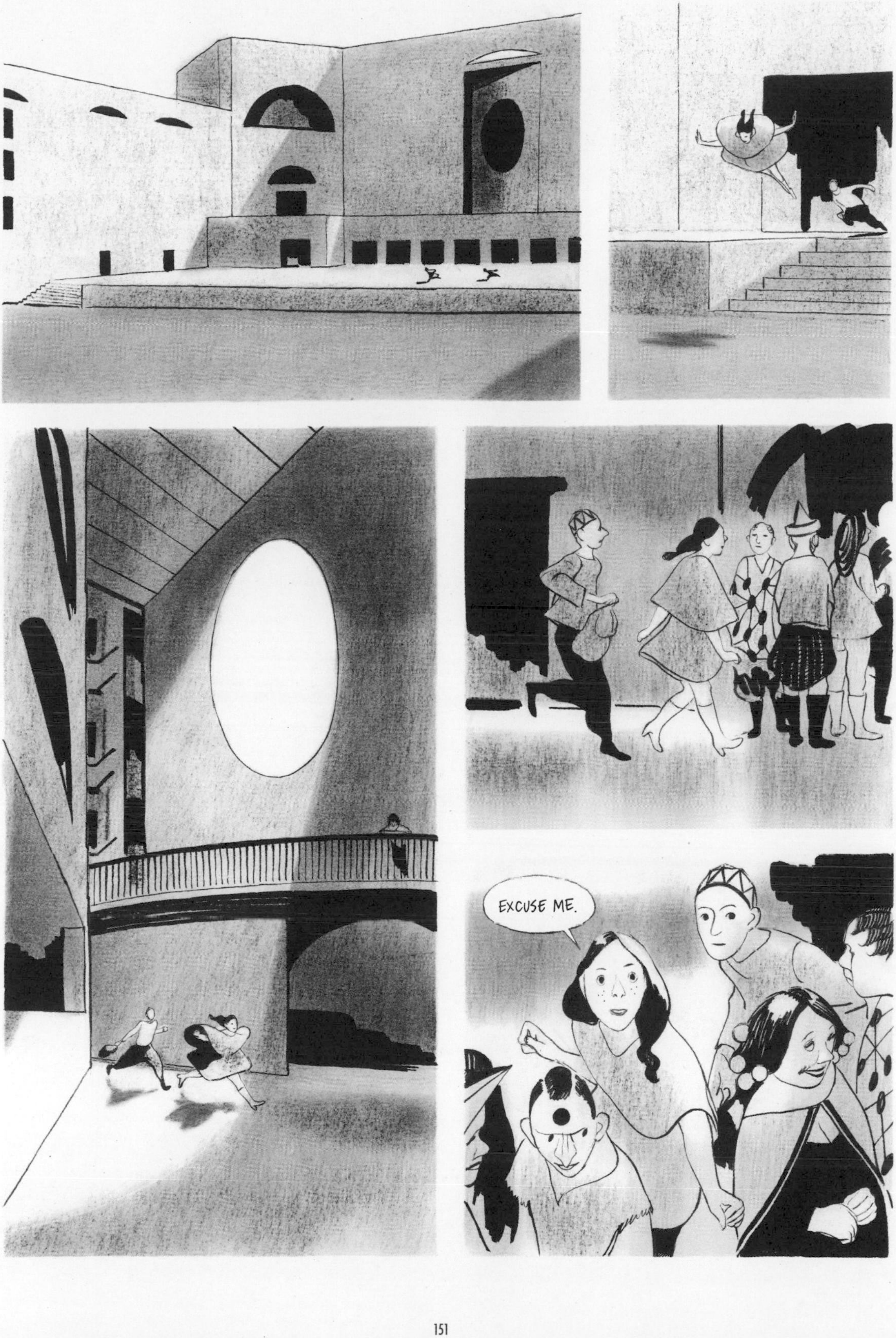
EXCUSE ME.

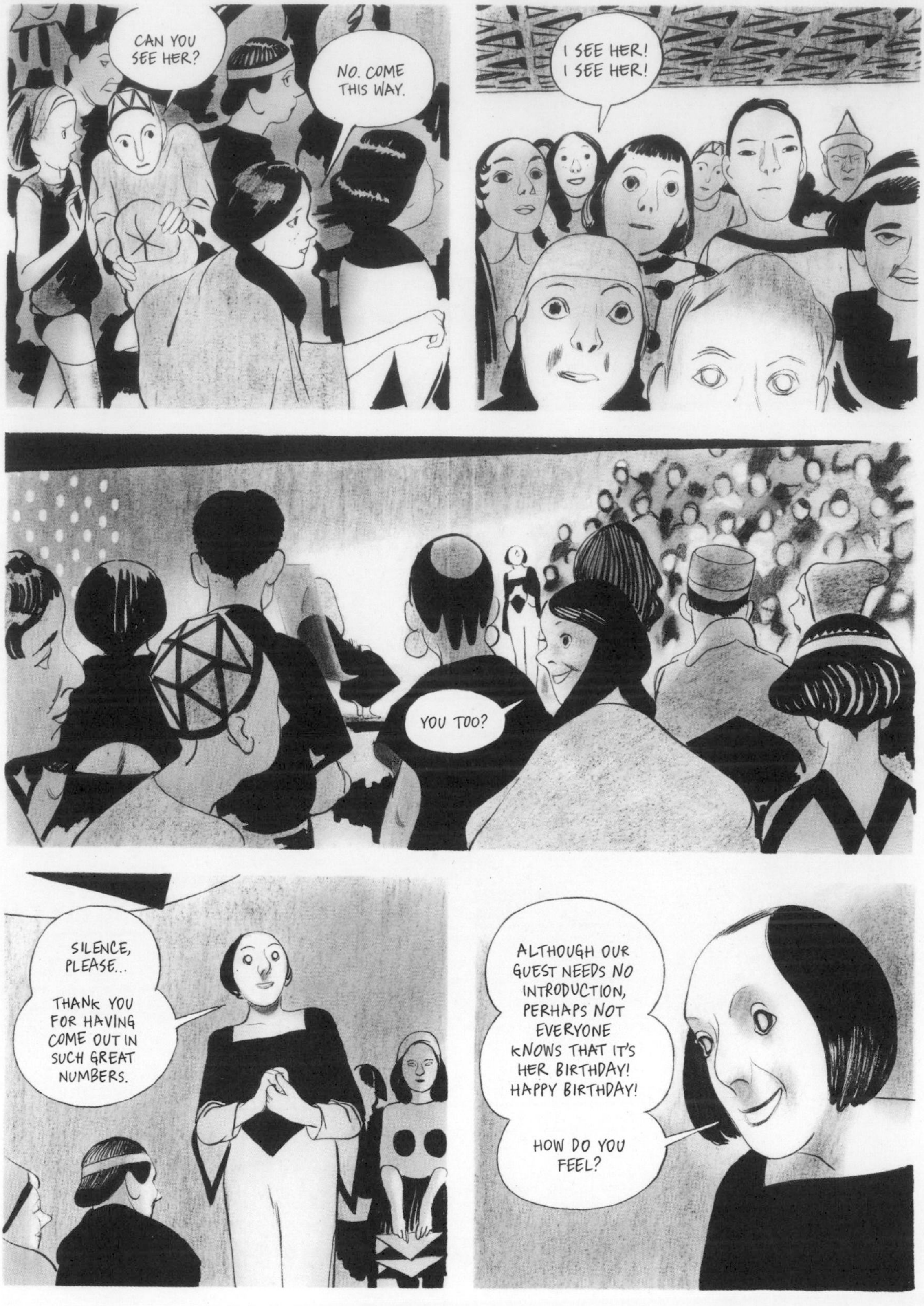
CAN YOU SEE HER?
NO. COME THIS WAY.
I SEE HER! I SEE HER!
YOU TOO?
SILENCE, PLEASE...
THANK YOU FOR HAVING COME OUT IN SUCH GREAT NUMBERS.
ALTHOUGH OUR GUEST NEEDS NO INTRODUCTION, PERHAPS NOT EVERYONE KNOWS THAT IT'S HER BIRTHDAY! HAPPY BIRTHDAY!
HOW DO YOU FEEL?

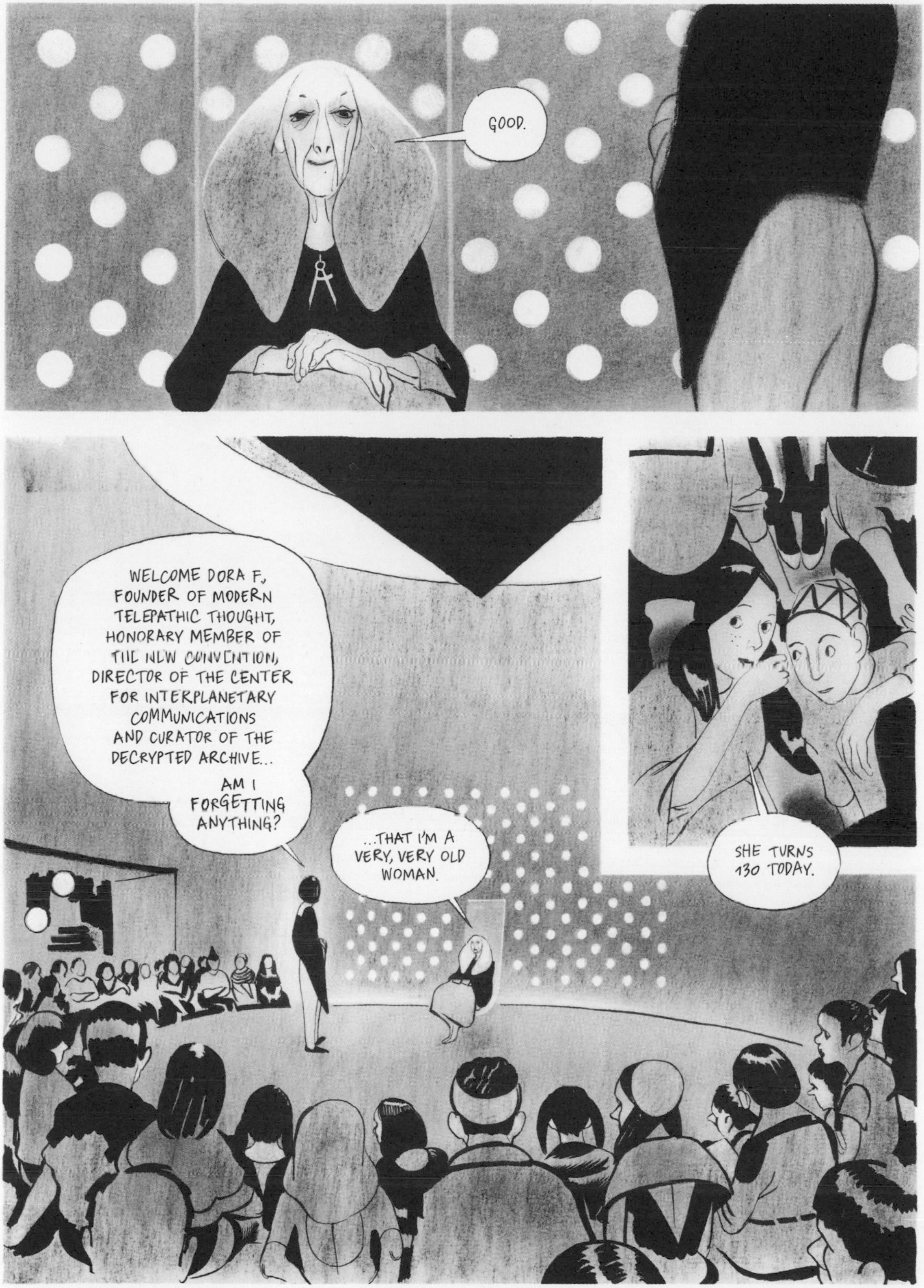
GOOD.
WELCOME DORA F., FOUNDER OF MODERN TELEPATHIC THOUGHT, HONORARY MEMBER OF THE NEW CONVENTION, DIRECTOR OF THE CENTER FOR INTERPLANETARY COMMUNICATIONS AND CURATOR OF THE DECRYPTED ARCHIVE...
AM I FORGETTING ANYTHING?
...THAT I'M A VERY, VERY OLD WOMAN.
SHE TURNS 130 TODAY.

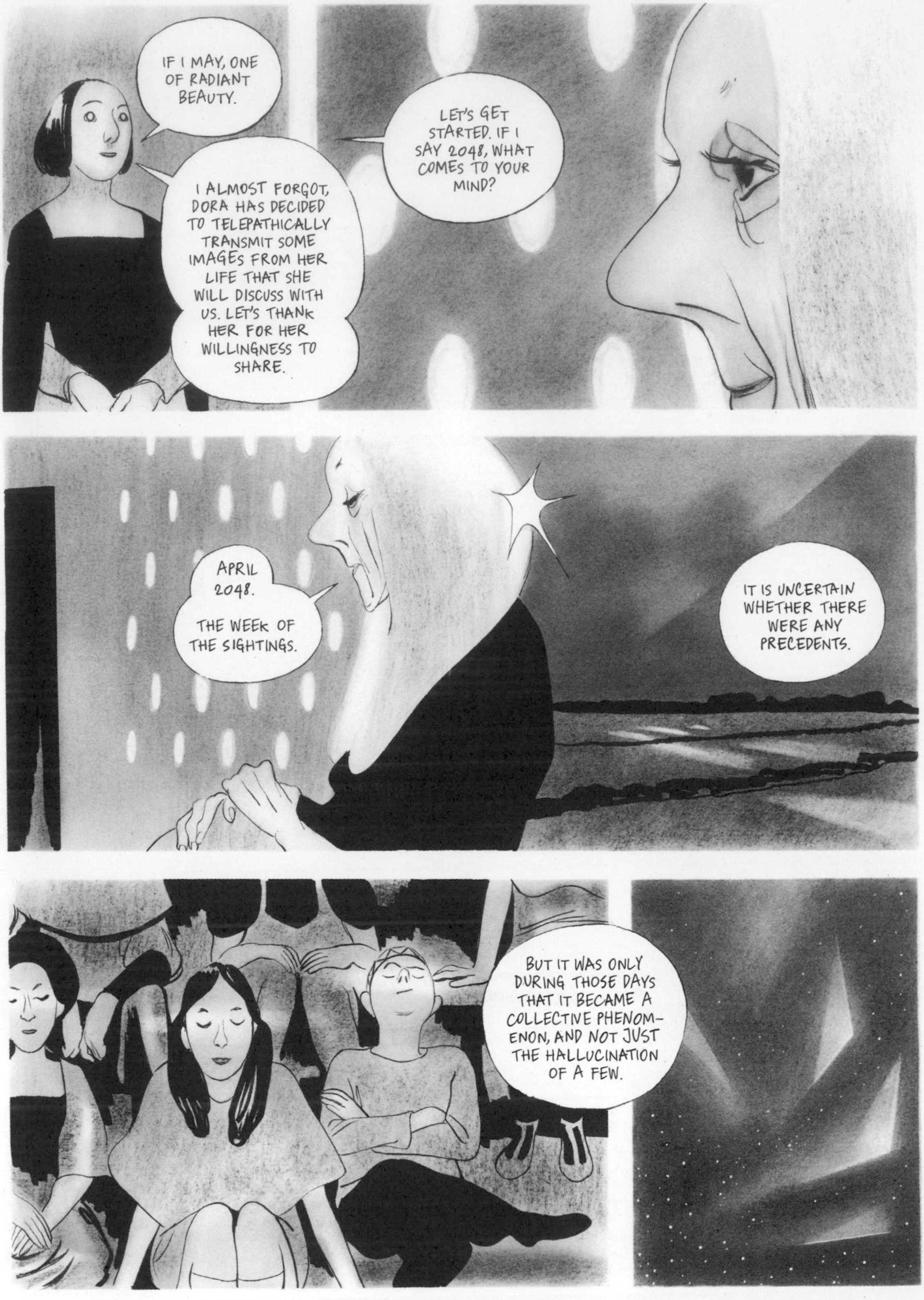
IF I MAY, ONE OF RADIANT BEAUTY.
I ALMOST FORGOT, DORA HAS DECIDED TO TELEPATHICALLY TRANSMIT SOME IMAGES FROM HER LIFE THAT SHE WILL DISCUSS WITH US. LET'S THANK HER FOR HER WILLINGNESS TO SHARE.
LET'S GET STARTED. IF I SAY 2048, WHAT COMES TO YOUR MIND?
APRIL 2048.
THE WEEK OF THE SIGHTINGS.
IT IS UNCERTAIN WHETHER THERE WERE ANY PRECEDENTS.
BUT IT WAS ONLY DURING THOSE DAYS THAT IT BECAME A COLLECTIVE PHENOM-ENON, AND NOT JUST THE HALLUCINATION OF A FEW.

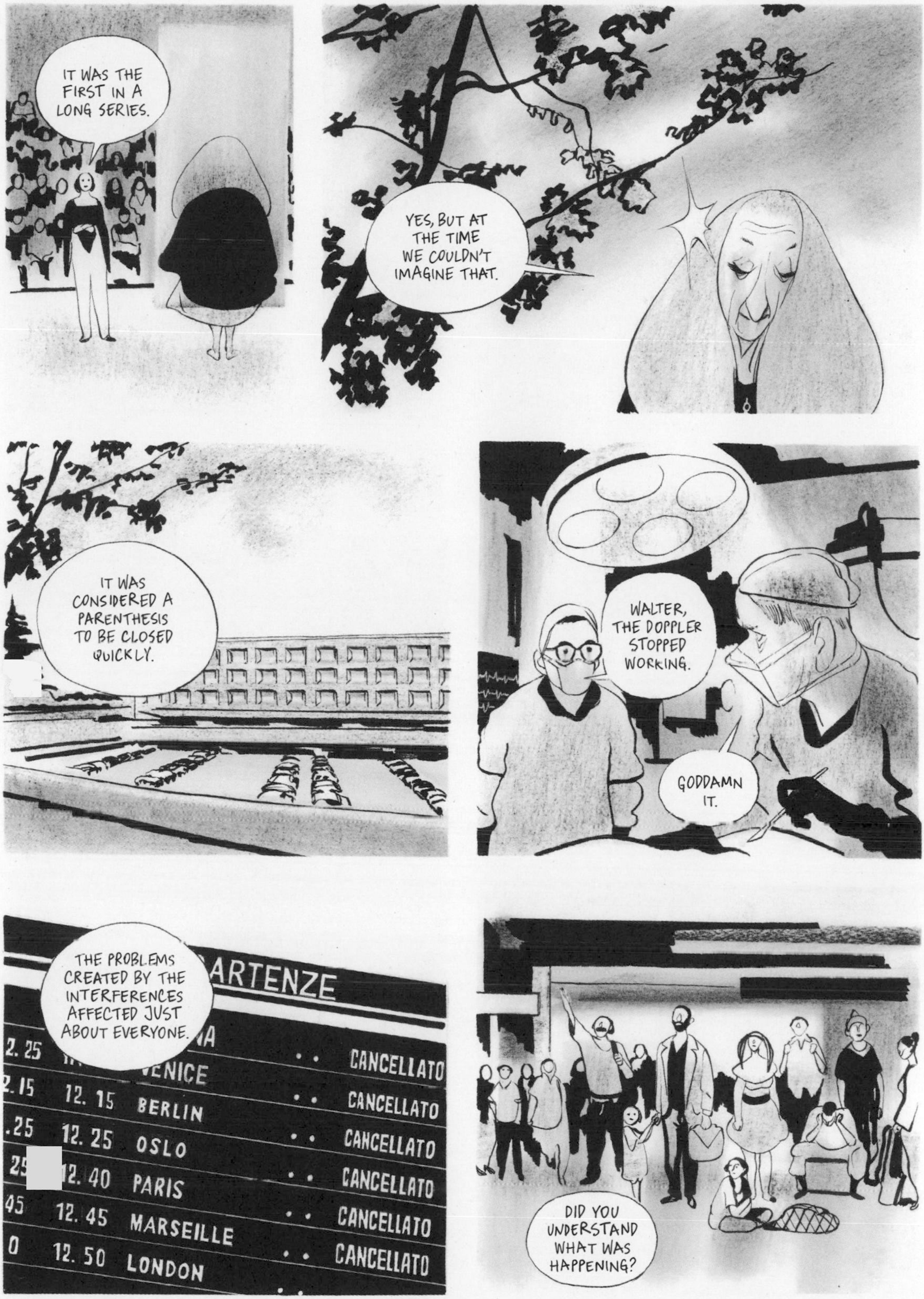
IT WAS THE FIRST IN A LONG SERIES.
YES, BUT AT THE TIME WE COULDN'T IMAGINE THAT.
IT WAS CONSIDERED A PARENTHESIS TO BE CLOSED QUICKLY.
WALTER, THE DOPPLER STOPPED WORKING.
GODDAMN IT.
THE PROBLEMS CREATED BY THE INTERFERENCES AFFECTED JUST ABOUT EVERYONE.
ARTENZE
2. 25 NA CANCELLATO
VENICE CANCELLATO
12. 15 BERLIN CANCELLATO
12. 25 OSLO CANCELLATO
12. 40 PARIS CANCELLATO
12. 45 MARSEILLE CANCELLATO
12. 50 LONDON CANCELLATO
DID YOU UNDERSTAND WHAT WAS HAPPENING?

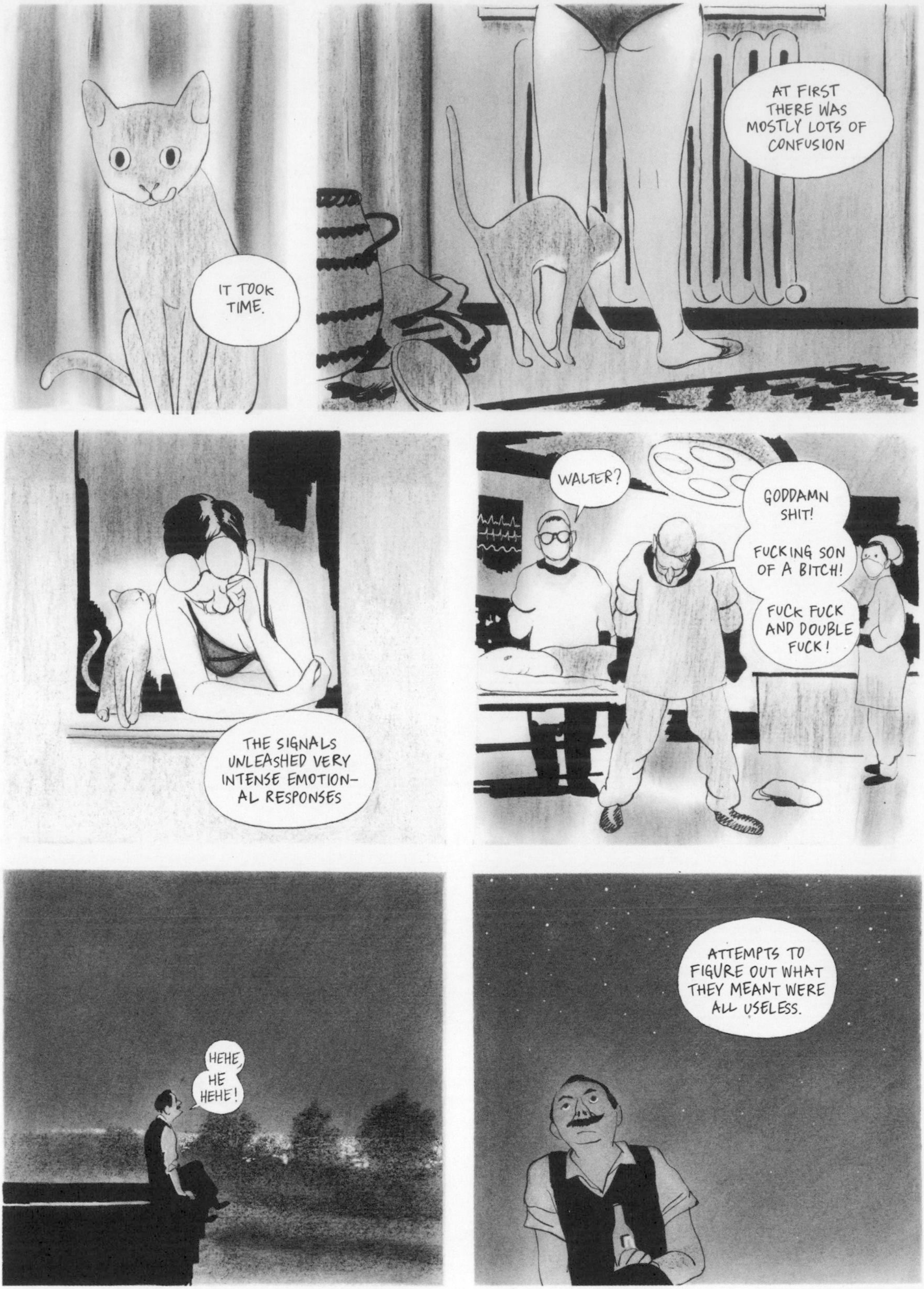
IT TOOK TIME.
AT FIRST THERE WAS MOSTLY LOTS OF CONFUSION
THE SIGNALS UNLEASHED VERY INTENSE EMOTION-AL RESPONSES
WALTER?
GODDAMN SHIT!
FUCKING SON OF A BITCH!
FUCK FUCK AND DOUBLE FUCK!
HEHE, HE HEHE!
ATTEMPTS TO FIGURE OUT WHAT THEY MEANT WERE ALL USELESS.

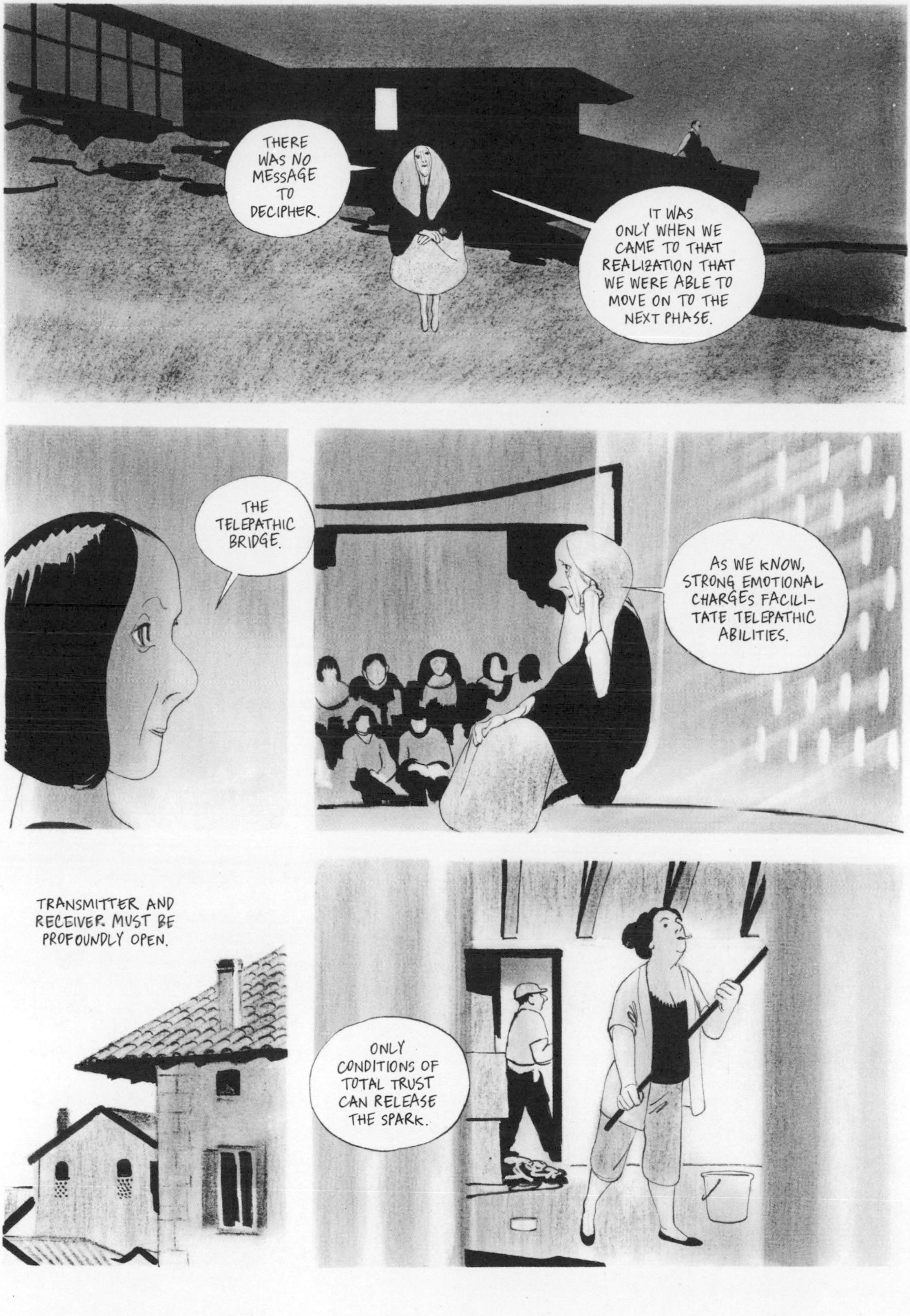
THERE WAS NO MESSAGE TO DECIPHER.
IT WAS ONLY WHEN WE CAME TO THAT REALIZATION THAT WE WERE ABLE TO MOVE ON TO THE NEXT PHASE.
THE TELEPATHIC BRIDGE.
AS WE KNOW, STRONG EMOTIONAL CHARGES FACILI-TATE TELEPATHIC ABILITIES.
TRANSMITTER AND RECEIVER MUST BE PROFOUNDLY OPEN.
ONLY CONDITIONS OF TOTAL TRUST CAN RELEASE THE SPARK.

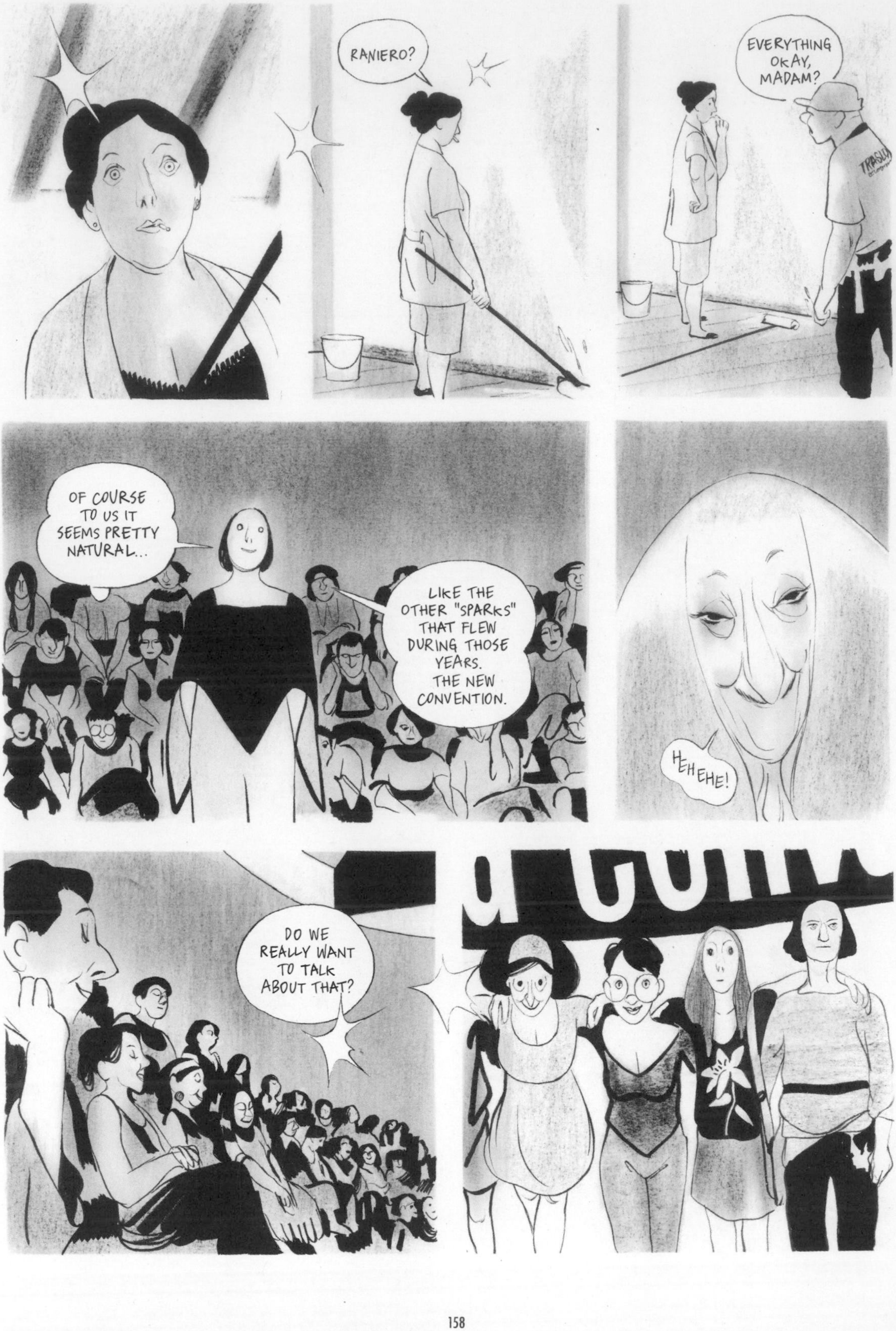
RANIERO?
EVERYTHING OKAY, MADAM?
OF COURSE TO US IT SEEMS PRETTY NATURAL...
LIKE THE OTHER "SPARKS" THAT FLEW DURING THOSE YEARS. THE NEW CONVENTION.
HEHEHE!
DO WE REALLY WANT TO TALK ABOUT THAT?

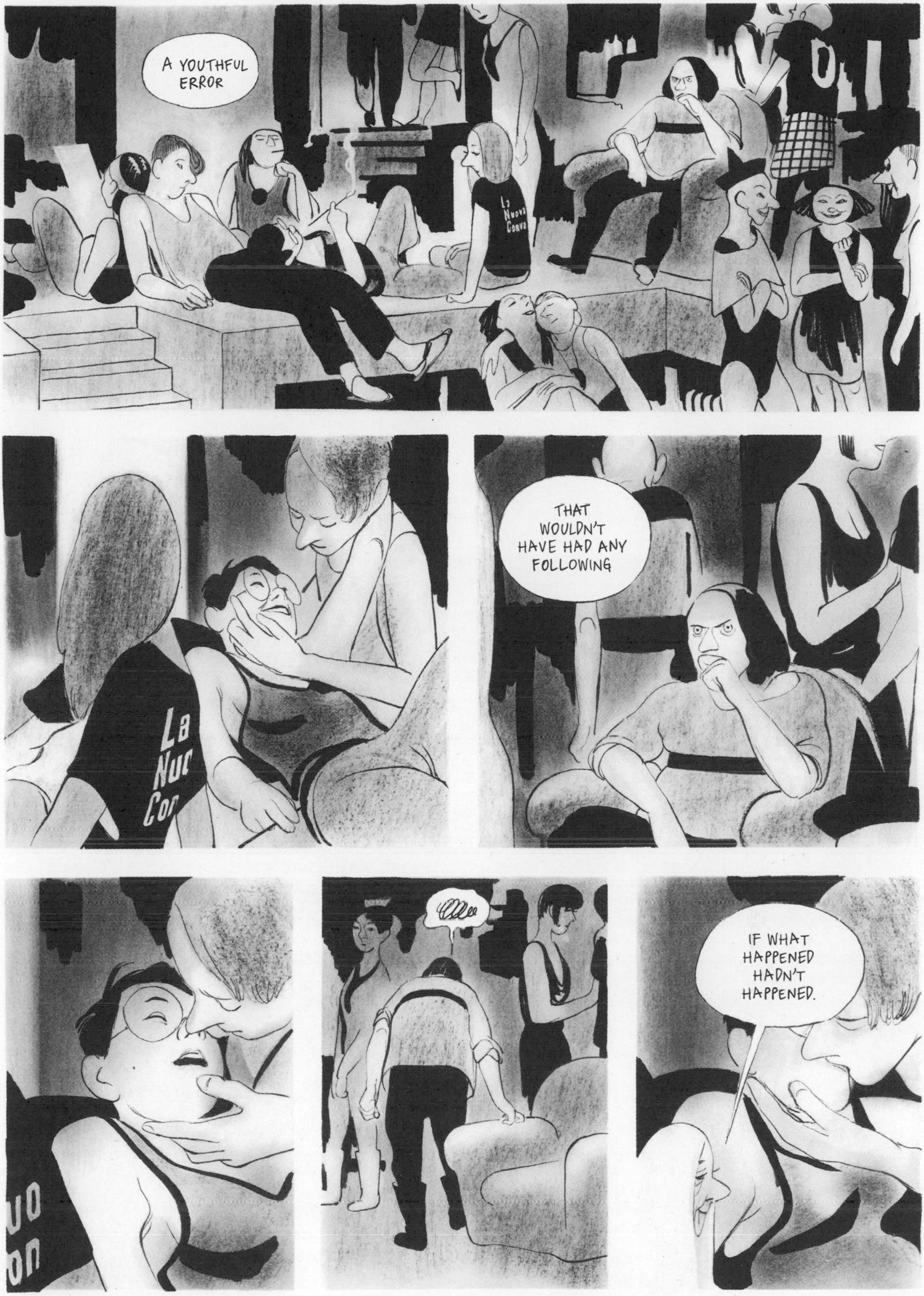
A YOUTHFUL ERROR
THAT WOULDN'T HAVE HAD ANY FOLLOWING
IF WHAT HAPPENED HADN'T HAPPENED.

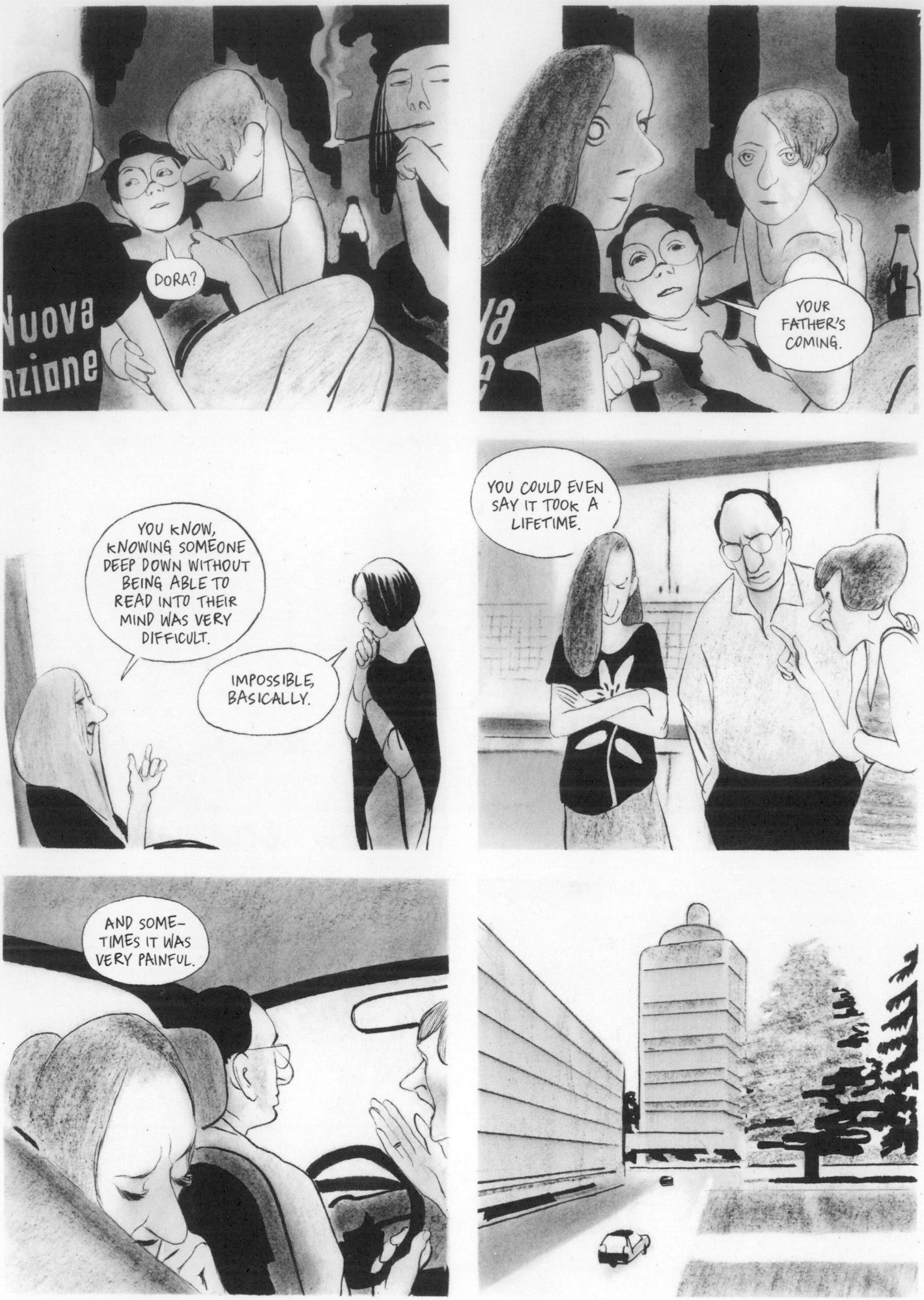
Nuova
nzione
DORA?
YOUR FATHER'S COMING.
YOU KNOW, KNOWING SOMEONE DEEP DOWN WITHOUT BEING ABLE TO READ INTO THEIR MIND WAS VERY DIFFICULT.
IMPOSSIBLE, BASICALLY.
YOU COULD EVEN SAY IT TOOK A LIFETIME.
AND SOME-TIMES IT WAS VERY PAINFUL.

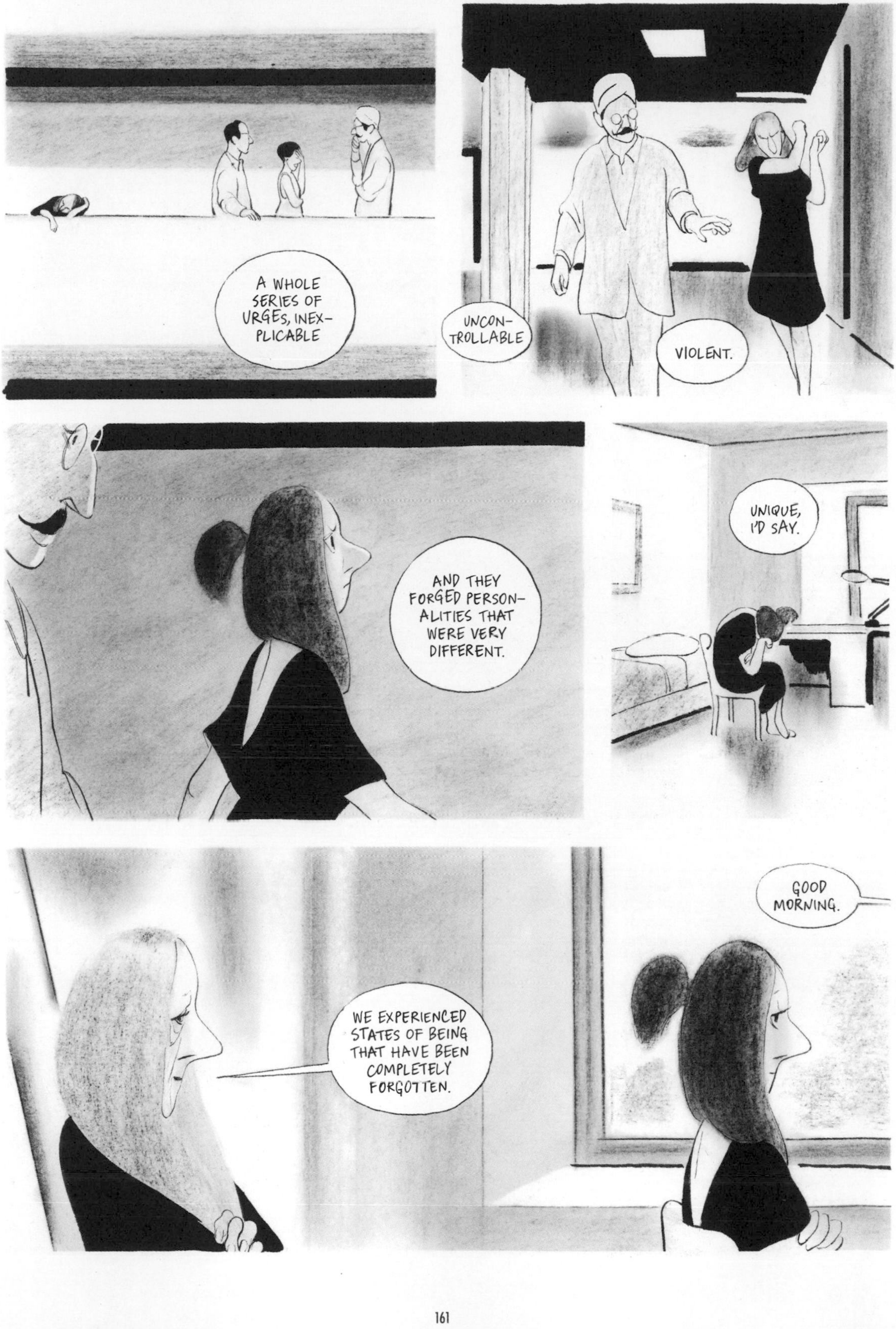
A WHOLE SERIES OF URGES, INEXPLICABLE
UNCONTROLLABLE
VIOLENT.
AND THEY FORGED PERSONALITIES THAT WERE VERY DIFFERENT.
UNIQUE, I'D SAY.
WE EXPERIENCED STATES OF BEING THAT HAVE BEEN COMPLETELY FORGOTTEN.
GOOD MORNING.

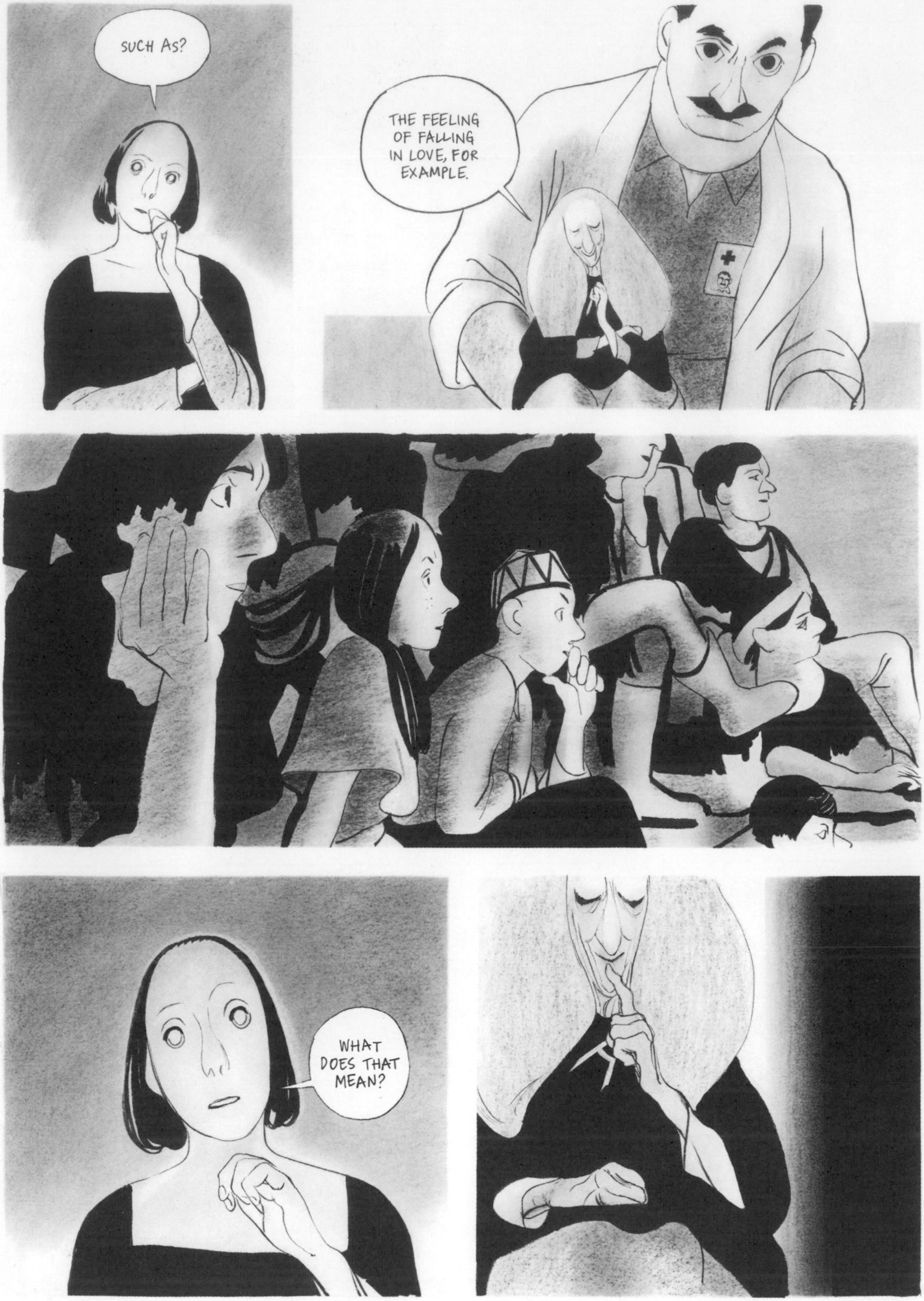
SUCH AS?
THE FEELING OF FALLING IN LOVE, FOR EXAMPLE.
WHAT DOES THAT MEAN?

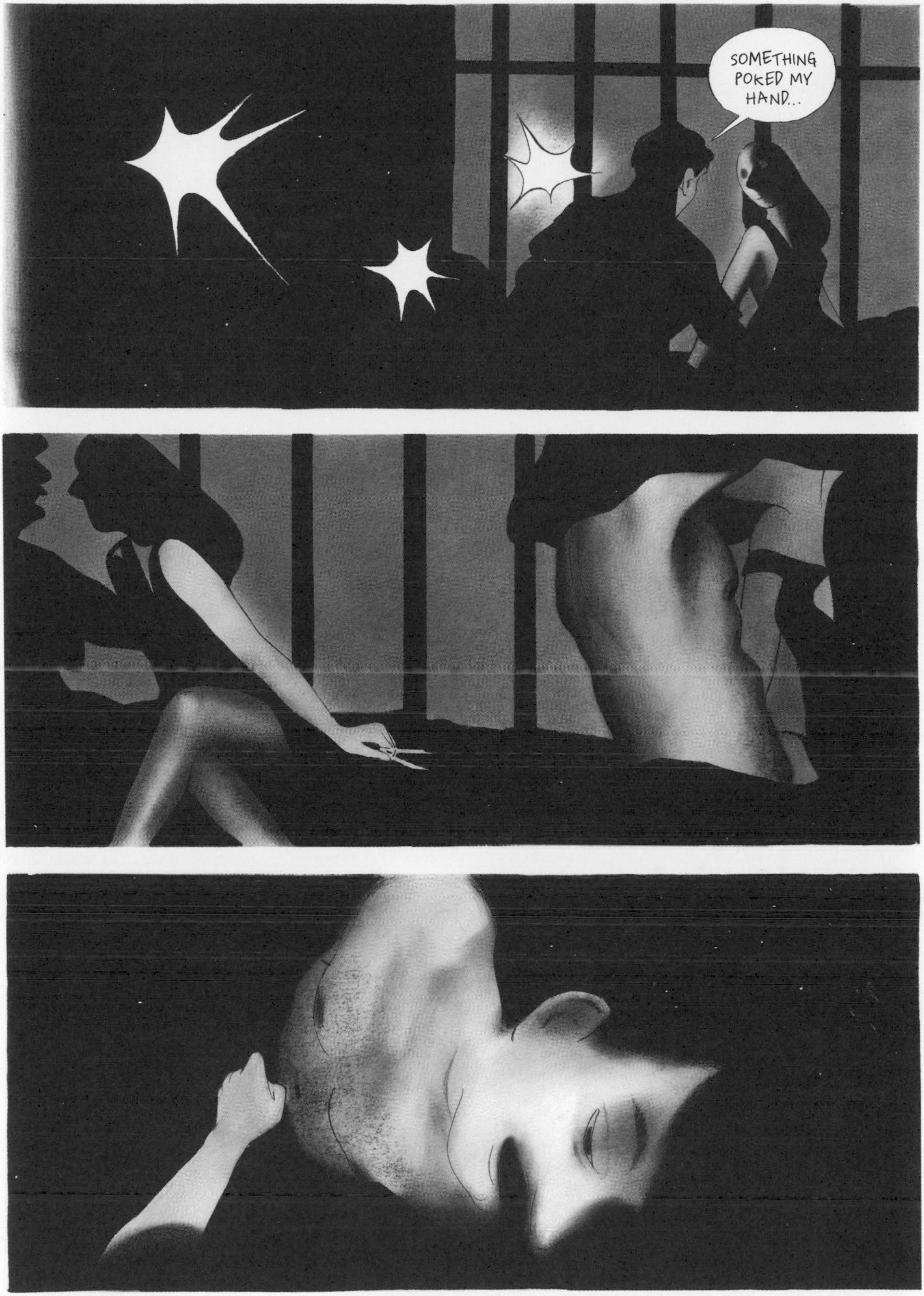
SOMETHING POKED MY HAND...

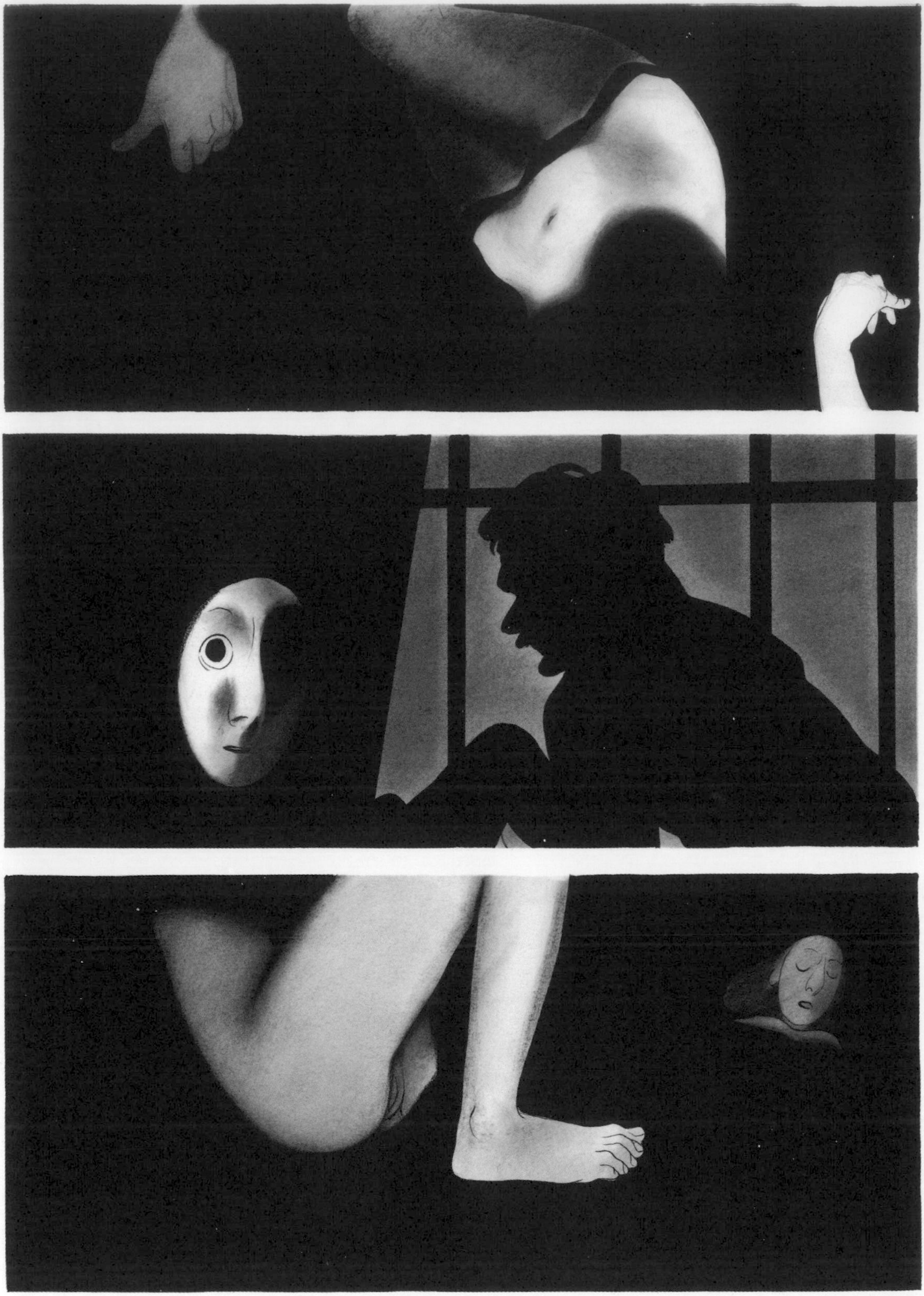

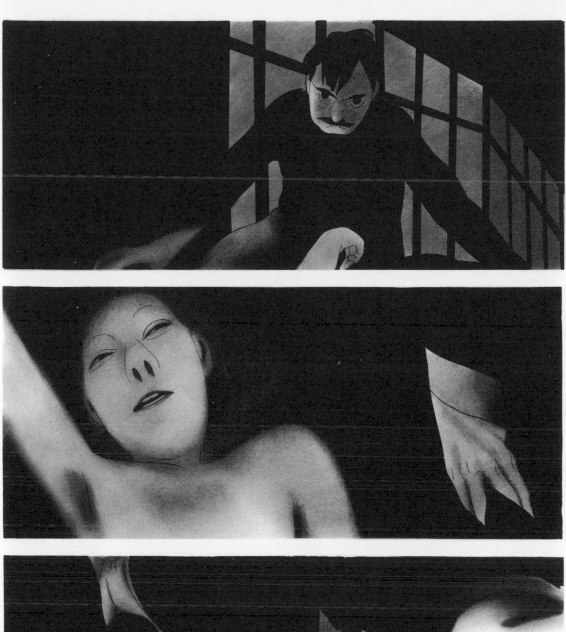

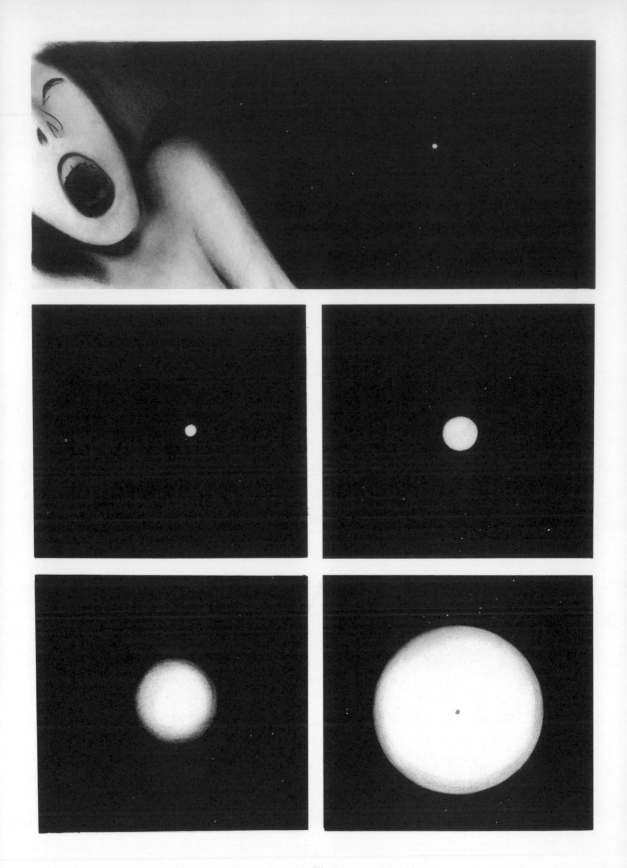

nfh!

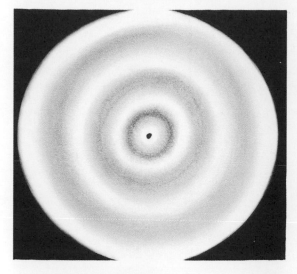

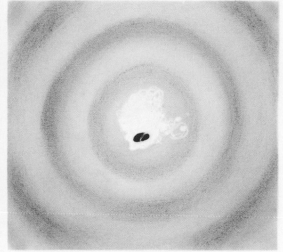

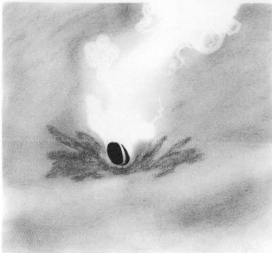

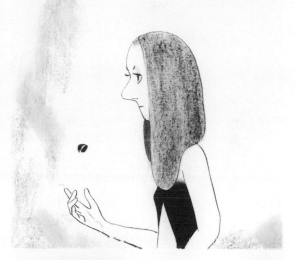

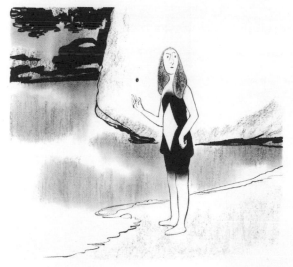

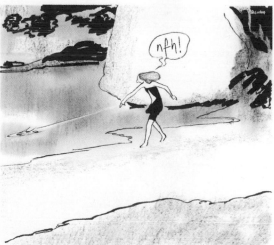

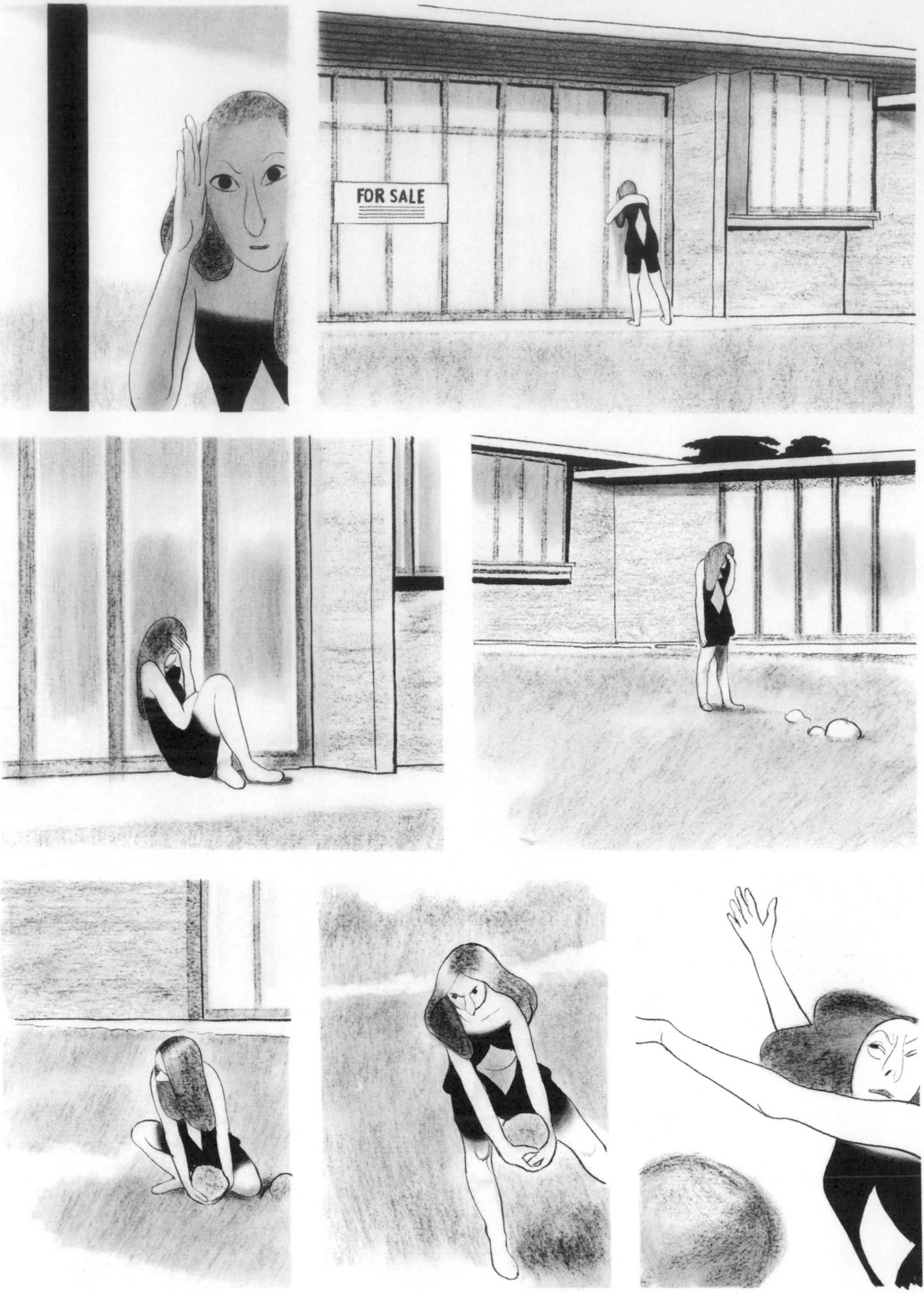
FOR SALE

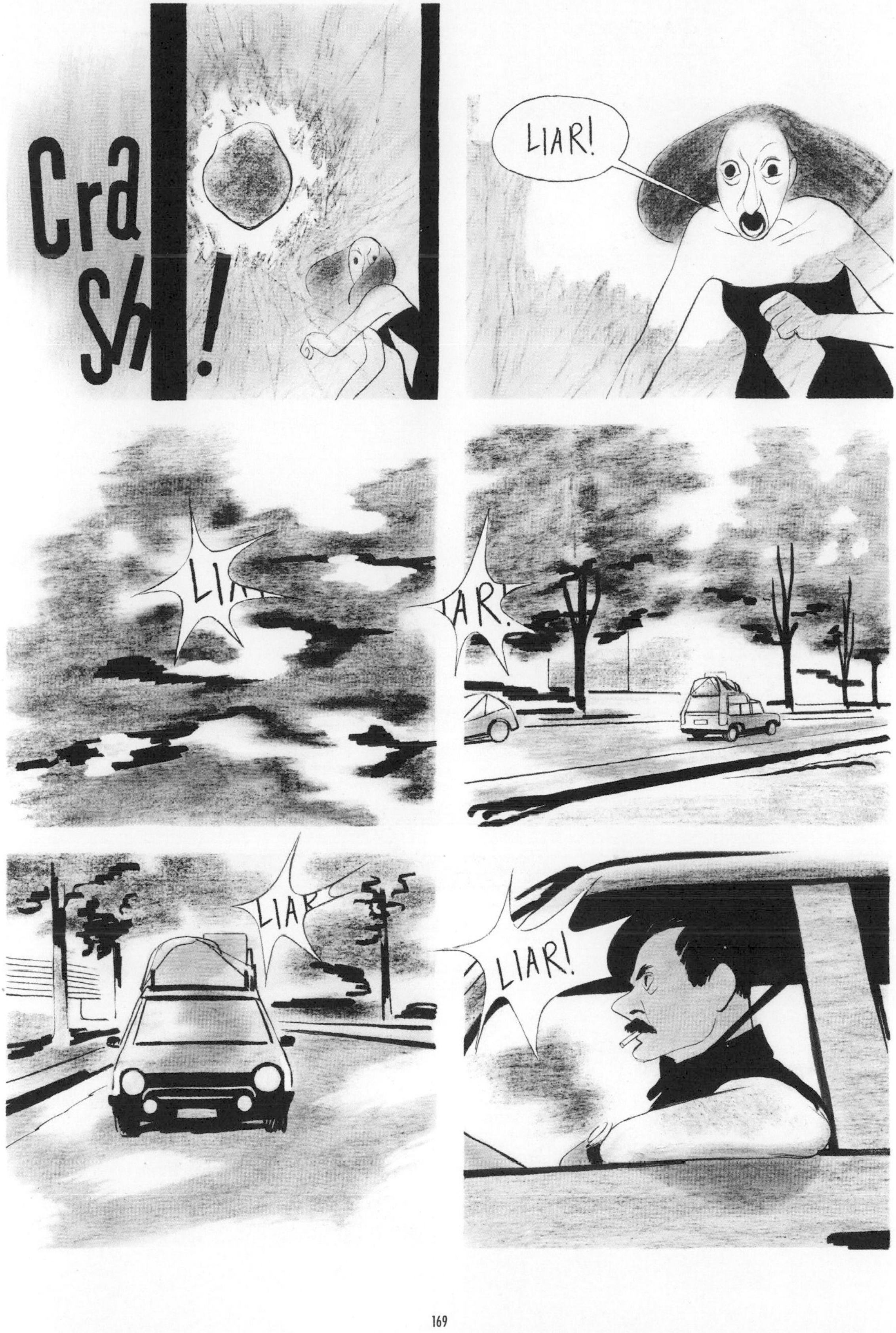
Crash!
LIAR!
LI
AR!
LIA
LIAR!

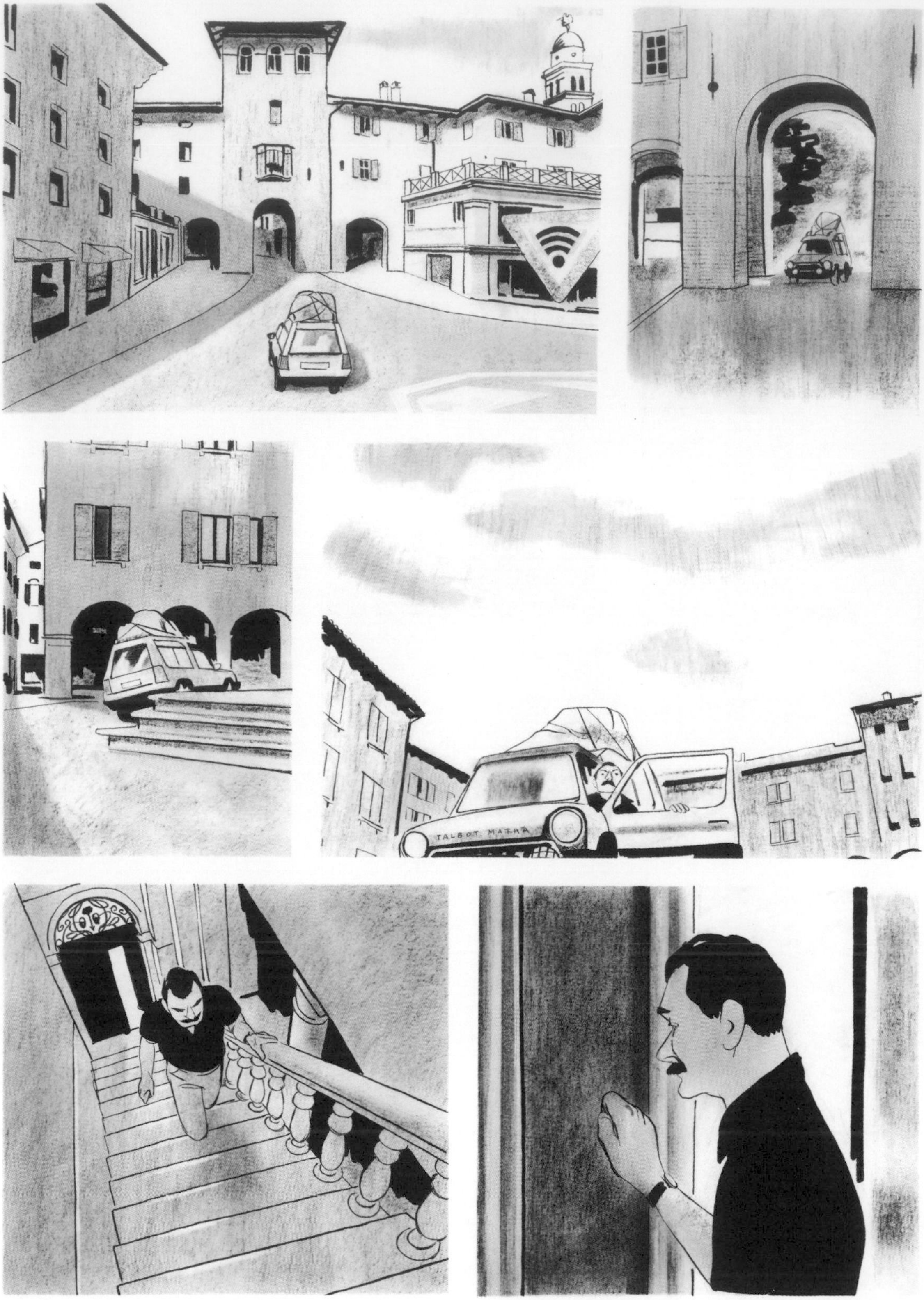
TALBOT MATRA

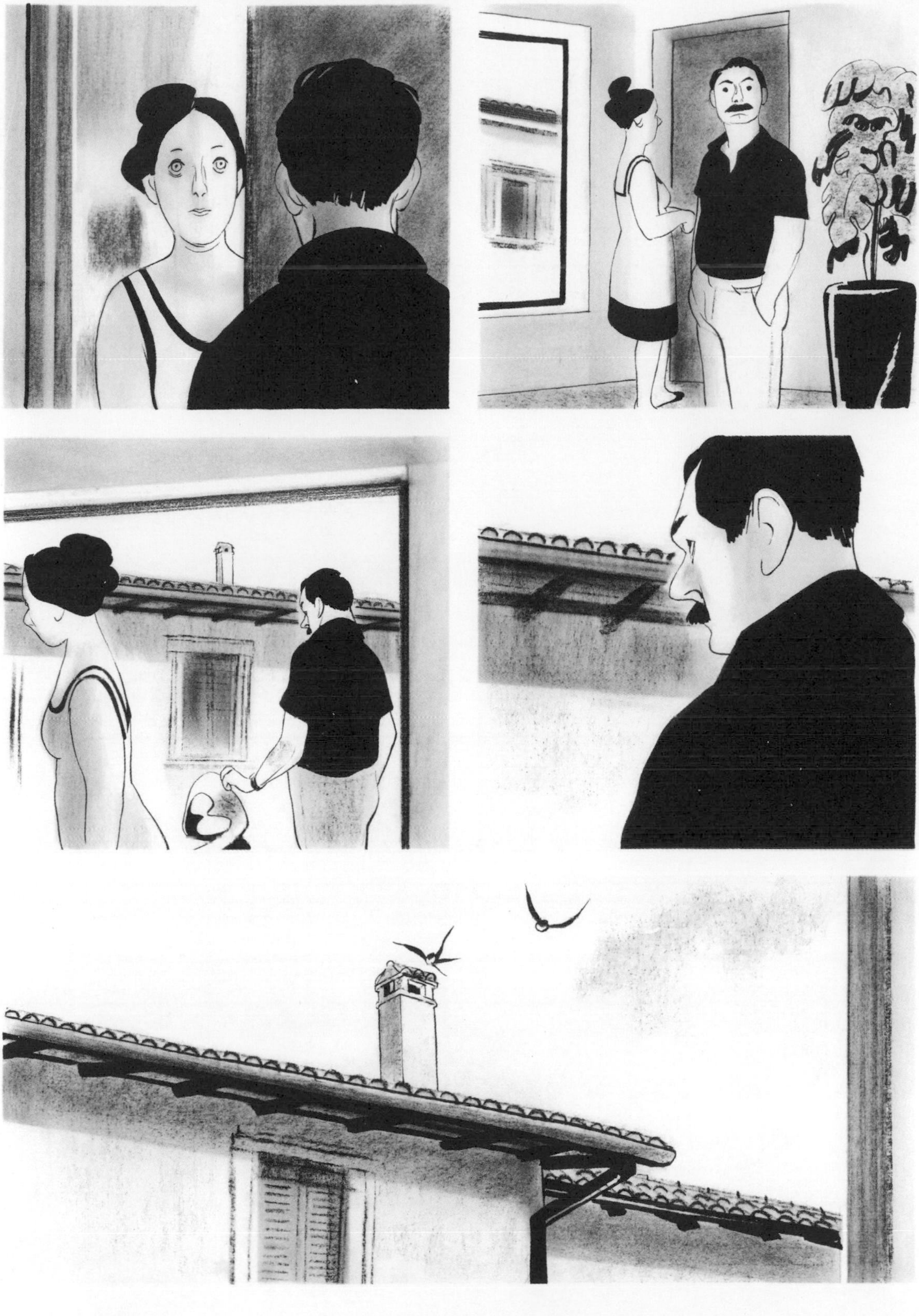

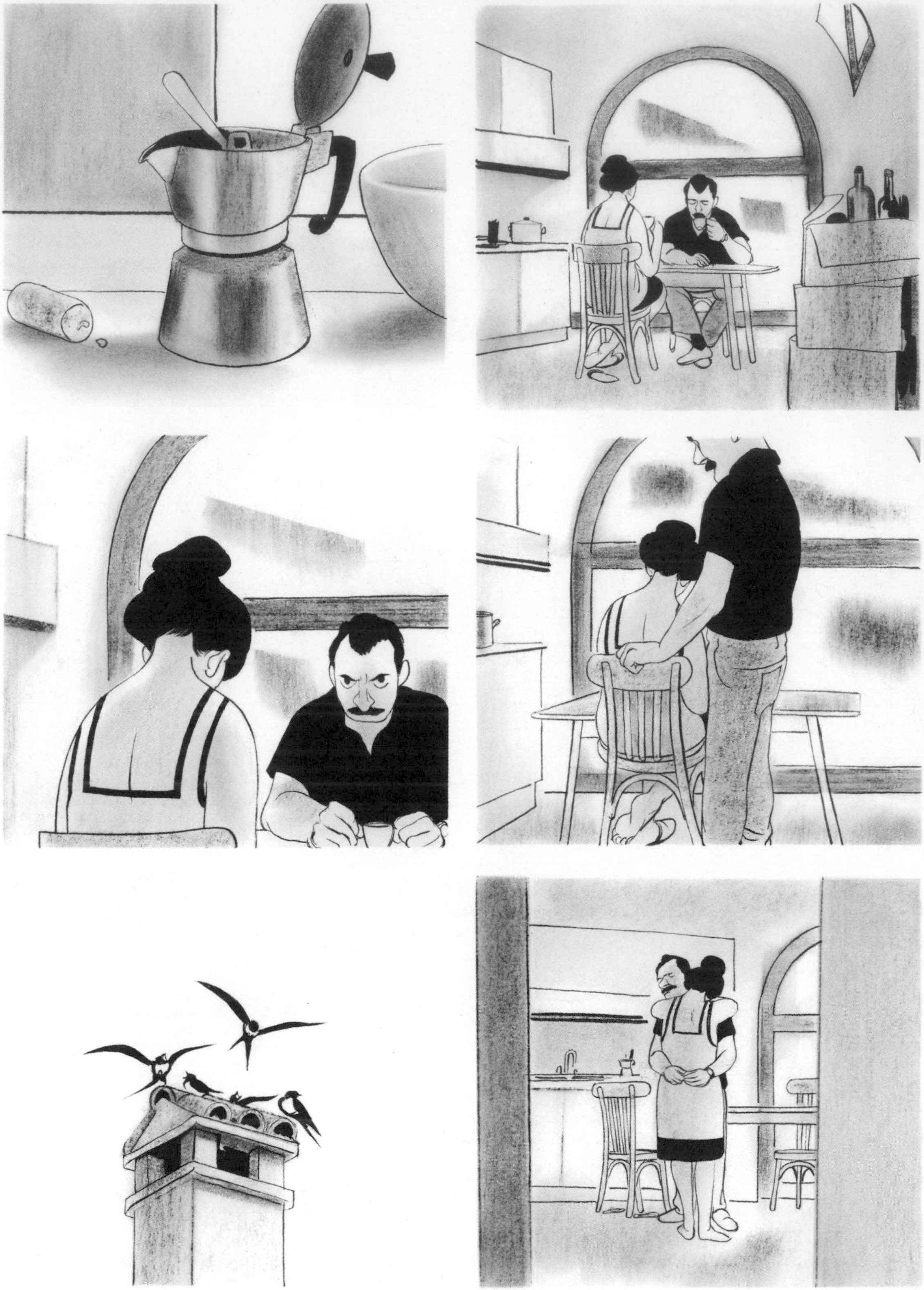

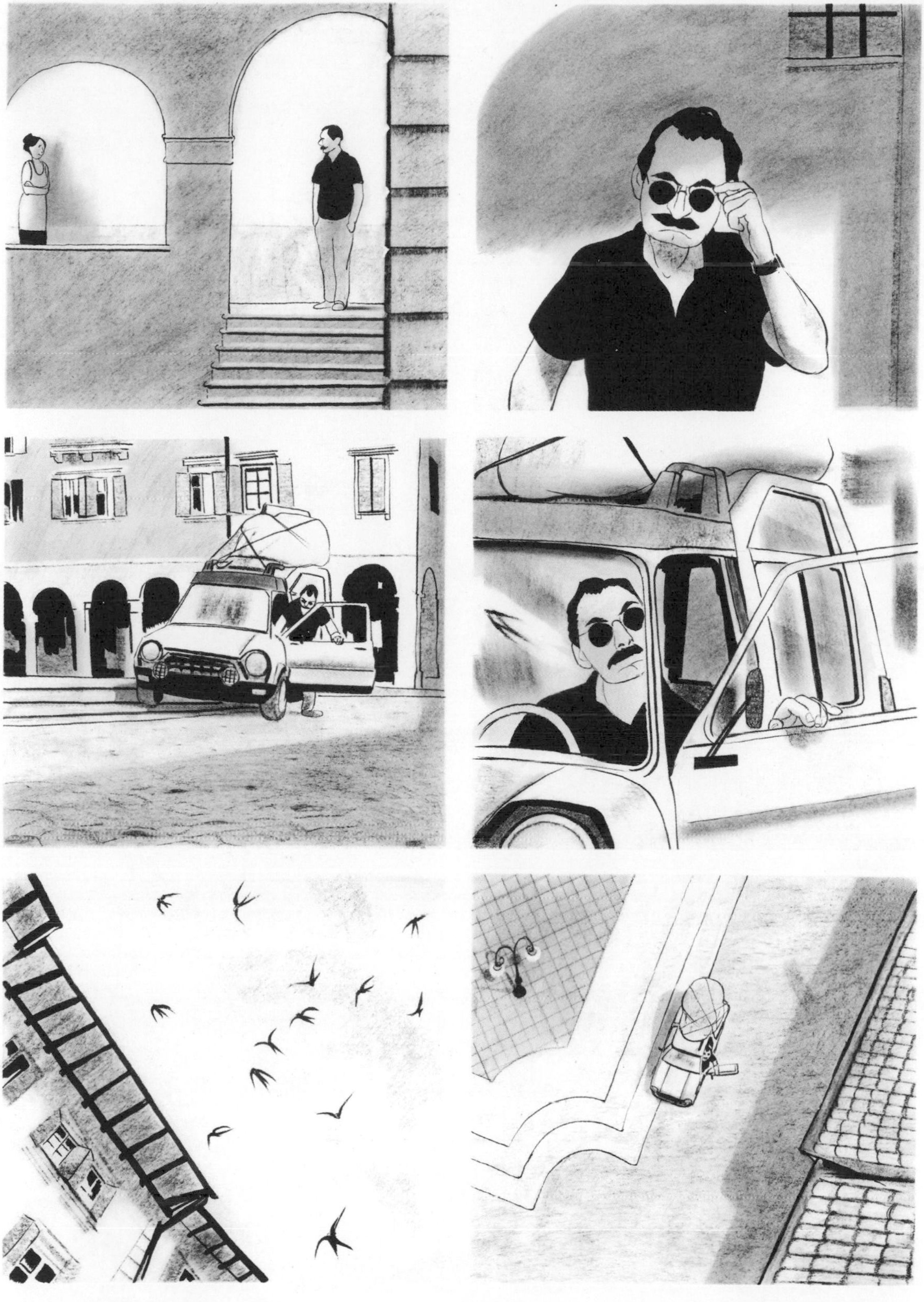

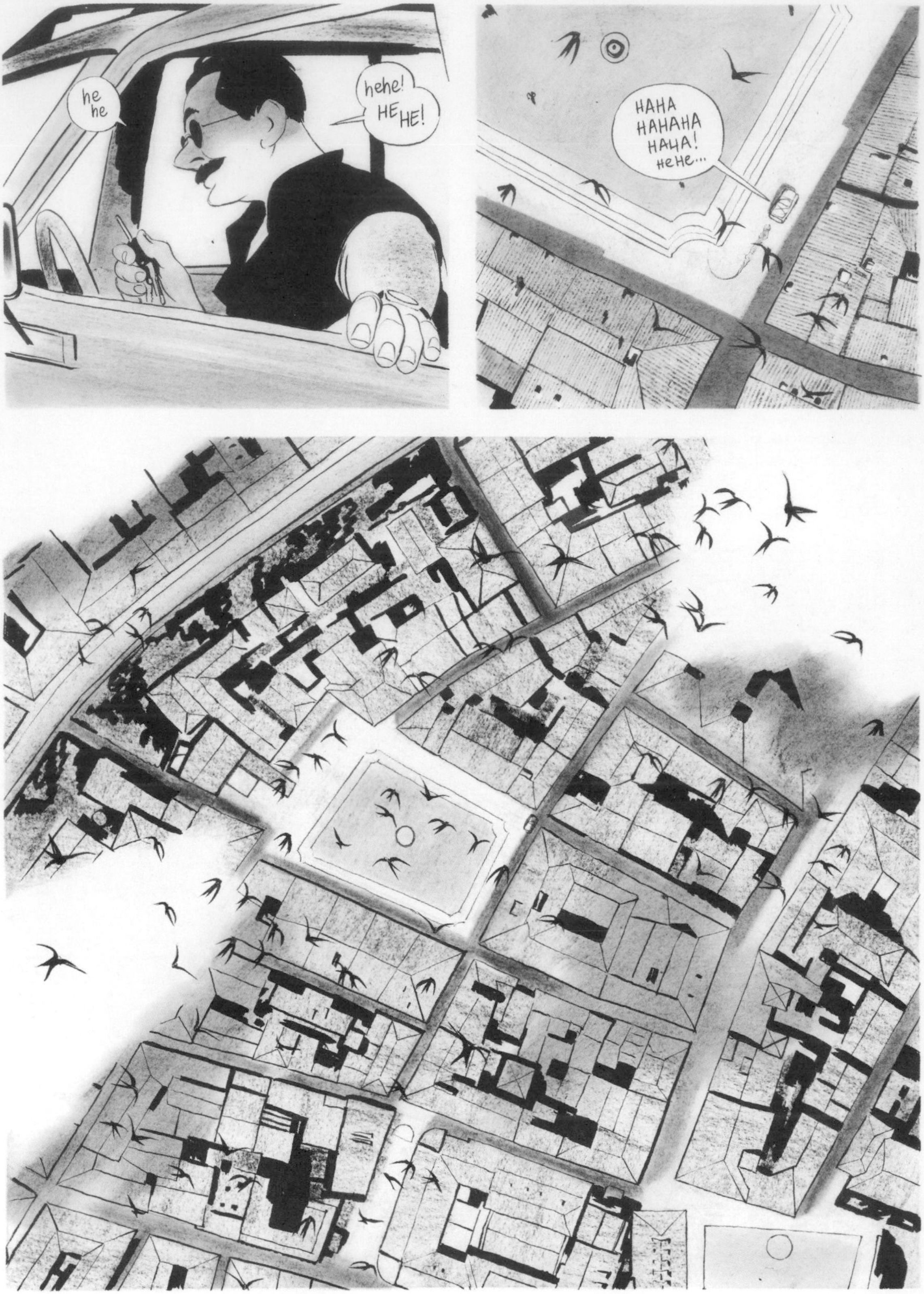
he he
hehe! HE HE!
HAHA HAHAHA HAHA! heHe...

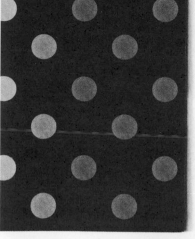

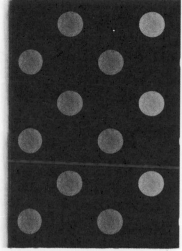

THANKS.

WOULD YOU LIKE TO TAKE A BREAK?

SURE.

WE'LL RESUME IN HALF AN HOUR.

FIN

The "special effects" in this book were conceived of and created by Anne-Lise Vernejoul (www.annelisevernejoul.com). Without her help this comic would not have been so beautiful. My greatest thanks go to her.

I'd also like to thank: Patrick von Massow, Volker Zimmermann, Massimo Colella, Laurent Lombard, Alessandro Tota, Luigi Critone, Julien Brugeas, Andrea Ciardi, Delicut, and Dani.

This book is dedicated to my parents.

M.F.